THE
LATER SWING ERA,
1942 TO 1955

THE LATER SWING ERA, 1942 TO 1955

Lawrence McClellan Jr.

GREENWOOD PRESS
Westport, Connecticut • London

Library of Congress Cataloging-in-Publication Data

McClellan, Lawrence, Jr.
    The later swing era, 1942 to 1955 / Lawrence McClellan, Jr.
      p. cm.
    Includes bibliographical references and index.
    ISBN 0-313-30157-3 (alk. paper)
    1. Swing (Music)—History and criticism.   2. Jazz musicians—United States.
    3. Singers—United States. I. Title.
    ML3518.M33 2004
    781.65'4—dc22   2004044864

British Library Cataloguing in Publication Data is available.

Library of Congress Catalog Card Number: 2004044864
ISBN: 0-313-30157-3

First published in 2004

Greenwood Press, 88 Post Road West, Westport, CT 06881
An imprint of Greenwood Publishing Group, Inc.
www.greenwood.com

Printed in the United States of America

The paper used in this book complies with the
Permanent Paper Standard issued by the National
Information Standards Organization (Z39.48-1984).

10 9 8 7 6 5 4 3 2 1

For My Mother,
Mrs. Loette McClellan

Contents

A photographic essay follows page 152.

♪

Acknowledgments

A number of persons have made contributions toward my work on this book and deserve my sincere gratitude. They are: Warrick Carter, President of Columbia College–Chicago, for recommending me to Greenwood Press; the late Norbert Carnovale who served as the initial project advisor; Vincent Pelote, Esther Smith, and the staff at the Institute of Jazz Studies–Rutgers University for their assistance; Beatrice Greene, Metro Vololshin, Diane Ota, and the music reference staff at the Boston Public Library for their assistance; members of the library staff at Berklee College of Music for their assistance; Mary Deane for the enormous task of typing and retyping more versions of this manuscript than either of us cares to remember; Dave Oliphant for his guidance with the format of this manuscript; the McClellan family (Peggy, Smiley, Ronnie, Jimmy, and Paul); and friends Larry Ridley, Walter Beasley, and Ron Taplin for their encouragement.

I am indeed grateful to Berklee College of Music and Provost Harry Chalmiers for granting me a sabbatical leave to lay much of the groundwork for the project. A special note of gratitude goes to Eric Levy, Acquisitions Editor, and Rob Kirkpatrick, Senior Editor, at Greenwood Press for their patience and support during the preparation of this manuscript. I am also grateful to my girlfriend, Nancy Sposato, who encouraged me and lovingly tolerated my preoccupation with the project. My mother, Mrs. Loette McClellan, encouraged me to pursue an education, and to her I give my greatest gratitude: the dedication of this book.

Lawrence McClellan, Jr.

♪

Introduction

The Later Swing Era began shortly after the United States entered World War II. During the war, America's way of life underwent drastic changes both socially and economically. More women entered the work force as war industries dramatically increased production to help meet the demands brought on by the country's war effort. Similarly, many African-Americans migrated from the South to the Midwest and North to work in military production plants and improve their lives. At the same time, the stress and upward mobility resulting from the war increased Americans' need to seek outlets from these pressures through entertainment. Such entertainment included ballroom dancing and socializing in nightclubs where live music was performed regularly by big bands, vocalists, and small groups. As a result, the country's music industry underwent major changes. Numerous musicians were drafted into the military, where many of them were fortunate enough to perform in service bands around the country and overseas. Other servicemen were not so lucky. With large numbers of male musicians involved in military service, a number of all-female or "all-girl" bands were formed; they toured throughout the country and overseas to entertain the troops. Likewise, all-male civilian bands toured domestically to meet heavy performance schedules and traveled overseas to support the war effort.

The high demand for musical entertainment during the war by both GIs and civilians made the Later Swing Era one of the most creative periods in the history of American popular music. Although big bands dominated the music scene at the time of World War II, the role of band vocalists began to change. Vocalists who were central to connecting big bands with their audiences held a rather low status in these large organizations. In many cases, the bands' sidemen held a higher status than vocalists. That situation started to change during the war, however, as more singers gained popularity and embarked on solo careers, while others actually went on to become movie stars. As the war proceeded and vocalists gained a foothold in the music industry, big bands started on a downward trend because of the financial burden involved in leading large musical organizations. A number of big bands dissolved, some disbanded temporarily and formed small groups, and others switched to a danceable or "sweet" music style that appealed to the masses. At that point, small groups began to evolve as vocal soloists chose to sing mostly with piano trios or quartets that included a guitar or one wind instrument. In some cases, small-group leaders could sing and play an instrument, which added variety to the group's overall performance and presentation. Other small-group instrumental combinations varied depending on the music styles played. For example, bassist John Kirby's sextet consisted of trumpet, clarinet-alto saxophone, tenor saxophone, piano, bass, and drums. The group's arrangements were written to give it a large sound to emulate the big band as closely as possible. Another example was pianist-vocalist Nat "King" Cole's trio, which included bass and drums. This particular trio format was widely imitated during the era by such artists as Art Tatum and Oscar Peterson. Yet another example was saxophonist-vocalist Louis Jordan's Tympani Five, which included a trumpet and rhythm section. Jordan expanded his group to a sextet or septet at various times but retained its original name.

In addition to the aforementioned swing groups, other small groups emerged along with different musical styles that coexisted during the era. The Dixieland Revival Movement—a return to traditional jazz—paved the way for many small groups to perform their brand of music around the country. With their emphasis on group improvisation or "contrapuntal" playing, Dixieland bands were basically small swing-style groups that added immensely to the rich musical diversity that existed between 1942 and 1955. Other small groups such as the ones led by Charlie Parker and Dizzy Gillespie that played the new bebop style emerged, in many ways, as a reaction to swing and traditional jazz. Many jazz writers considered this new musical style radical at the time, and some criticism resulted from the press. In any event, the music continued to develop and, by the mid-fifties, reached a level of maturity and acceptance consistent with its fresh creativity. Yet another style emerged that became known as the "cool school." This new style included elements of swing, European symphonic music, and bop. Although the style had part of its beginnings in Gil Evans' arrangements for Claude Thornhill's big band in the late 1940s, it emerged fully in the early fifties and featured trumpeter Miles Davis with Evans' arrangements for a nine-piece band. The originators of this style basically wanted to get a full orchestral sound with the smallest number of instruments.[1] Although not fully recognized as a "legitimate" Swing Era style in many jazz histories, the "jump blues" pioneered by musicians such as Louis Jordan is, in fact, a major musical genre that developed during the forties and early fifties.[2]

While the popularity of vocalists and small groups increased after the war, the status of big bands continued in a downward spiral. As already pointed out, many big bands disbanded, and others continued on the road to success by performing in a danceable music style. Some leaders played hard-swinging Kansas City blues–styled jazz for both dancers and listeners, while others adopted a style that included European "classical" music elements and promoted it as concert jazz. Another small cadre of big-band leaders such as Billy Eckstine and Dizzy Gillespie played bebop. Numerous big bands struggled financially or disbanded, while many others succeeded. In any event, the extremely large number of big bands that existed at the beginning of World War II had decreased substantially by the early fifties. This unfortunate fact, however, opened the door for vocalists and smaller bands to increase the level of creativity and innovation in jazz during the Later Swing Era.

Most Swing Era histories have focused on the music, musicians, and socioeconomic conditions in the United States between 1930 and the end of World War II in 1945. Few such histories have looked at swing music, its characteristics, and its accompanying social conditions beyond 1945. The present history, therefore, has extended the boundaries of the era and will look at swing music, the musicians, the country's changing socioeconomic conditions, the different musical styles that emerged and/or coexisted with swing, and some of the sweeping changes that took place in the nation's music industry from the beginning of World War II to 1955. A major goal of the present history thus includes the identification of vocalists, instrumentalists, arrangers/composers, bandleaders, and performance organizations that made notable contributions to music in the Later Swing Era. Realization of this goal entailed a review of the performances of individual musicians as well as ensembles via recordings, analysis of different arranging and compositional styles, and identification of important performance venues that made an impact on the era. Another goal consisted of looking at gender and race issues during and after World War II, the effects of the war on the country's socioeconomic climate, and ways in which these factors interfaced with the music and/or swing industry.

Most Swing Era histories have also hailed big-band leaders as the era's most significant musical figures. Few, however, have considered vocalists, arrangers/composers, and instrumentalists who were not full-time big-band directors as real leaders in the swing industry. Here, four highly respected musicians are presented as a diverse group of leading musical figures who brought innovative music to the lives of many people during the era. This presentation includes discussions of the music these artists recorded along with their different approaches to jazz performance. The present study also investigates a variety of big bands, their leaders, performance characteristics, personnel, and some venues at which they appeared. In addition, a number of vocalists are discussed with regard to their success in the music industry, important recordings, musical styles, and contributions to the era. This study also explores the important role small groups played in fostering different musical styles that contributed to greater individual and group creativity as opposed to the structured big-band arrangements that dominated jazz performance during the 1930s and early 1940s. Finally, the second half of this book (A to Z) presents brief profiles of musicians, performance organizations, entrepreneurs and/or producers, venues (such as nightclubs, ballrooms, and festivals), record labels, and various organizations that either began or flourished during the era. These profiles highlight the contributions made by numerous individuals and organizations not always covered in the book's five chapters.

The importance of this unique era in American history is evidenced by the fact that jazz actually became a part of the music curriculum in higher education at that time, and much of it is based on big-band swing music. For example, Boston's Berklee College of Music was founded as the Schillinger House in 1945, and its curriculum consisted mainly of theory/ arranging/composition and big-band performance. North Texas State University (now the University of North Texas) also offered a jazz program in the 1940s, and it officially appointed a director in 1947. More colleges and universities later established jazz programs based on the big-band performance and writing model. Subsequently, secondary schools adapted the same model to their curricula as college graduates with jazz training entered the public-school music teaching profession. Although recent years have witnessed the rise of more small groups in the music industry and on television, the big-band model still exists in secondary and postsecondary school music programs. Most of these school bands, furthermore, currently perform swing music as part of their repertoire.

In addition to education, the big-band swing model is still alive and well in other institutions such as Carnegie Hall, Lincoln Center, and The Smithsonian. Each one of these institutions has a jazz orchestra that performs a variety of big-band music, including that from the Swing Era. There are also examples of community-based bands that perform swing music similar to what arranger-composer Mike Crotty's Sunday Morning Jazz Band did in Maryland in April 1979. Basically, Crotty's rehearsal band performed the music of Boyd Raeburn's mid-1940s band for a concert at Frankie Condon's Supper Club in Rockville. In preparing for the performance, Crotty re-created Raeburn's original instrumentation, with the addition of two French horns, a harp, and a bass saxophone to the normal lineup of five reeds, four trumpets, three trombones, and rhythm section. Columnist Allen Scott reviewed the concert and concluded that "it was a fine sampler of an amazing repertoire that deserves to be heard again and again."[3] This story is just one of many in which big bands around the country have tried to re-create Swing Era music and present it to modern-day audiences. Other community-based music organizations such as the

Boston Jazz Repertory Orchestra continue to perform big-band literature from yesteryear that includes swing music. Just as present-day big bands recognize the enduring quality of swing through performance, jazz histories are still trying to recapture the legacy of swing. Hopefully, this book will help pinpoint the essence of some great music that was created and performed between 1942 and 1955.

NOTES

1. Ian Carr et al., eds. *Jazz: The Rough Guide* (London: Penguin Books, 1995), p. 200.

2. Degen Pener, *The Swing Book* (Boston: Back Bay Books, 1999), p. 102.

3. Allen Scott, "Rediscovering Boyd Raeburn," *Radio Free Jazz* (July 1979): 13–14.

Chapter 1

♪

Music and Socioeconomic Characteristics

Shortly after the United States entered World War II, the Later Swing Era commenced as big bands were practically dominating the popular music industry. During the war, the country found itself in chaos, and bands came to a standstill when their one-nighters were cancelled and news bulletins interrupted remote broadcasts. As the shock of the sudden attack subsided, the country mobilized with a large number of bandleaders and sidemen volunteering for active duty. Meanwhile, other musicians waited for the draft and participated in morale building by performing in USO shows.[1] In fact, numerous musicians played a major role in boosting the morale of American GIs. As Erenberg states, "To boost morale, the music industry worked with the government and the army to bring popular music to the troops."[2] Instrumentalists, vocalists, radio and recording executives, the American Federation of Musicians (AFM), and army personnel worked together to record and distribute popular music on Victory Discs (V-Discs). Union musicians were, in fact, allowed to record for the troops in spite of an AFM strike against the recording industry. The development of V-Discs provided GIs the opportunity to hear American swing overseas on military bases with the installation of service centers as well as radios and phonographs in army barracks. Because there was a lack of popular or swing music on British radio before D-Day, General Dwight Eisenhower ordered the Armed Forces Network to duplicate American broadcasting at home as much as possible. The Armed Forces Radio Service also produced such shows as *Command Performance*, *Mail Call*, and *Jubilee* to entertain the troops. To compete for GI loyalty, enemy radio stations also broadcast swing music as part of their propaganda campaign.[3]

Some of the nation's top bandleaders enlisted in the military to help boost morale by leading service bands overseas. For example, Glenn Miller led his famed Army Air Force (AAF) Orchestra at home and in Europe. His AAF Orchestra contained a forty-two-piece marching band, a nineteen-piece dance ensemble, a radio show, a string ensemble, and a small jazz combo that performed at bond rallies, recorded Victory Discs, and entertained troops. Likewise, Artie Shaw led a navy swing band in the South Pacific, Bob Crosby led a marine swing unit, and Sam Donahue toured Europe with his navy swing band. Claude Thornhill also interrupted his civilian bandleading career for active duty and led military swing units. On the other hand, many African-American musicians found themselves in regular military units instead of service bands because of segregation. As a result, many minority musicians tried to evade the draft by doing such things as filling their stomachs with soapsuds or trying to act gay, but nothing worked. In any event, most of them served honorably. A number of musicians from the bands of Cab Calloway, John Kirby, and Count Basie actually fought in the war, while others like Buck Clayton, Sy Oliver, Mercer Ellington, and Jimmy Crawford were lucky enough to play in one of the few black military bands.[4]

In the United States, the music business looked bleak at the beginning of the war; most people were not in the mood for dancing and going out to nightclubs. However, as the country's mobilization effort increased, the largest spending spree in our nation's history was stimulated. Large amounts of money went into circulation from the defense industry's high production rate. This money, in turn, went to the people who were in a spending mood and wanted entertainment. Army and navy bases were established in numerous locations, and military personnel wanted entertainment while on leave. This high demand for amusement revived the music industry to a point that nightclubs, hotels, and ballrooms overflowed with customers. The bands returned to their busy touring schedules, and one-nighters brought in financial returns never envisioned in the past. In spite of this boom in the entertainment industry, wartime restrictions affected all amusements with a midnight curfew that terminated all dancing and liquor service at that hour. Musicians had to start working an hour earlier, and all performances and radio broadcasts were concluded with the national anthem as an acknowledgment of the musicians' patriotism. Big band musicians also had difficulty traveling between jobs when gasoline and tire rationing became a reality in the fall of 1942. Although these bands spent a great deal of time performing for morale-boosting events, most ration boards did not deem their contributions essential to the war effort. The bands therefore received only basic gasoline rations and had to travel in old chartered buses that left a high degree of uncertainty to scheduled arrivals. To top it all, the draft started to deplete the bands' personnel, and leaders competed fiercely with each other for competent musicians, which resulted in some strained relationships.

The demand for musical entertainment continued during the war, and lucrative one-nighters increased to a point where nightclubs and hotels had to book reservations well in advance of such engagements. Food shortages exacerbated the problem of overcrowding, but people went to the ballrooms anyway. Many bandleaders took advantage of this high demand for entertainment by signing "for the duration" or long-term contracts in advance, and only some of them could be honored. Leaders preferred these kinds of contracts because they were concerned with difficult traveling conditions, as a number of musicians were injured and some even lost their lives in transportation crashes.

As the draft created a shortage of male musicians and the size of some civilian bands grew larger, females became able replacements. For example, trumpeter Elizabeth Rogers joined Woody Herman's brass section, and some bands added string sections containing women because many were proficient on the violin. In fact, Tommy Dorsey's orchestra featured an all-female, nineteen-piece string section at one time during the war. Throughout the war there were a large number of all-female bands that performed for civilians and military personnel. In addition, there were several wives of bandleaders serving in the military who replaced their husbands as leaders until they returned to civilian life.[5] Needless to say, the war opened up greater opportunities for women in several different walks of life. Many became workers in defense plants and USO troupes, which gave them more control over money, leisure time, and geographic mobility. Along with increased independence and the loosening of patriarchal and familial authority came increased demands on women for fidelity. Many females frequented USO shows and dances to meet servicemen and felt that they were helping the war effort by dancing, singing, and talking with servicemen. However, some women were perceived as consumed by "war fever," which brought out their boldness and turned them into hunters who encouraged men. In fact, women's new freedoms created a patriarchal fear that their roles were changing and replacing those normally held by men as the natural hunter. However, all men did not hold that view. For example, one serviceman was pleased that, with many men away at war, there were plenty of women to dance with in the nation's cities and towns.[6] The war also thrust a number of industries (including the swing industry) into a supply-and-demand mode that created an extreme reconfiguration of workers and consumers. While many industries came up with new products, such as automobile plants competing for jeep manufacturing contracts, the swing industry remained static. Without any changes in style, dance music was primarily a patriotic product that supported the war effort. In reality, there was little need for a style conversion in swing. Millions of Americans who were away from home and isolated from their loved ones created a very high demand for the product because they needed comfort, diversion, and social contact through music and dance.

The high demand for dance music and a shortage of men made it possible for female musicians to fill the "dance band shortage" by playing one-nighters to entertain troops, traveling on USO camp shows, and playing swing shift

dances for defense workers. It is important to mention here that the term
"swing shift" implied an extra shift temporarily added to aid wartime
production. Along with the term came propaganda that portrayed female
workers as attractive, patriotic, competent, and temporary. In any event,
conscription played a major role in the rise of "all-girl" bands during the
war. Many of the women in these bands had gained experience a decade earlier
performing in dance halls, ballrooms, carnivals, theaters, and vaudeville
shows in all-girl bands. Some of the better-known all-female bands in
the forties were the International Sweethearts of Rhythm, Eddie Durham's
Darlings of Rhythm, and Ada Leonard's All-American Girl Orchestra.

Though all-female bands made major inroads during the forties, they had
to struggle for recognition as competent and patriotic professionals in the
music industry. Regardless of whether the band members were paid or not,
all-female bands were perceived by the public as amateur organizations.
Furthermore, the public's opinion that female musicians were morale-
boosters and temporary patriotic substitutes made their professional posi-
tions in the music industry barely tolerable. Extra pressure was placed on
women for union loyalty when the AFM and the government reached
an agreement that military bands could not work in venues that might
employ civilian dance orchestras. Most male AFM members wanted recognition as indispensable professionals who deserved first choice for all union
work.[7] Sexual tensions also increased because male musicians viewed jazz
as a masculine phenomenon and concluded that women lacked the power
and aggression needed to play the music. For example, *Downbeat* was
quoted as stating, "Good jazz is a hard, masculine music with a whip to it.
Women like violins, and jazz deals with drums and trumpets."[8] Since men
saw women as "temporary wartime annoyances," they could either "play
like men" or just be "good girls." The first perception caused some women
to downplay or devalue their sexuality, which, in turn, created accusations
that they were homosexual. The latter forced others to emphasize beauty
rather than musical skill. In both cases, women faced close scrutiny and ridicule
while striving to gain respect as professional musicians in the male-dominated
world of swing. Obviously, most men preferred women in traditional roles
as the girl next door or as a wife and mother who supported her man.[9]

As sexual tensions continued beneath the surface in the music industry,
racial tensions reached an all-time high. According to Scanlan, "Racial
problems, inspired by racial prejudices and hatreds, have bedeviled America
from the beginning. And during the Swing Era, Jim Crow played a major,
demeaning role."[10] In pointing out some of the problems African-American
musicians experienced, Scanlan states,

> Working in a black band was enormously different from working in a white
> band. The pay was always lower, "the road" was often a humiliating, gut-
> wrenching place to make a living, and it could be perilous to your health

as well. Covert racism was present as well as the blatant, in-your-face, officially sanctioned kind. Problems extended beyond "whites only" restrictions involving hotels, rooming houses, restaurants, drinking fountains, and toilets.[11]

Prior to World War II, for example, Duke Ellington's band often lived on the train when touring the country. The band's "movable hotel" usually consisted of two Pullman cars and one baggage car. Cab Calloway's band also traveled in a Pullman car and a baggage car. Because location jobs were not available to many black bands, they had to spend as many as eight months on the road each year. Most hotels and ballrooms did not hire black bands at the time, and suitable accommodations were a problem. As a result, those bands needed a reference book that listed small black hotels and rooming houses in various parts of the country to help them avoid embarrassing situations.[12] Some situations simply could not be avoided, however. For example, Cab Calloway once recalled, "in some places like Winston-Salem and Atlanta they had a rope down the middle of the dance hall with the Negroes dancing on one side and the whites on the other."[13] This same kind of discrimination was also prevalent in the North. In the late thirties when Count Basie's band played engagements in New York's Roseland Ballroom and the Famous Door on 52nd Street, African-Americans were not permitted. Consequently, John Hammond, a staunch proponent of desegregation and promoter of the Basie band, struck a deal with the Famous Door's management to purchase an air conditioner for the club if it would change its segregation policy. It agreed reluctantly, and Basie (who especially needed the air-conditioning) packed the club every night for an entire summer.[14]

During the war, racial tensions increased, while the music industry portrayed swing as a national symbol with ideological stories such as "Music Can Destroy Our Racial Bigotry" published by *Downbeat*. In fact, "black and white radicals—and many swing players and fans—believed that swing carried a vision of democratic community rooted in ethnic and racial pluralism—the concepts that defined the war's purpose at home and abroad," according to Erenberg.[15] For example, Frank Bolden, a columnist for the *Pittsburgh Courier*, elevated the interracial quality of swing by declaring that Count Basie, Benny Goodman, Cab Calloway, Tommy Dorsey, and Johnny Hodges "are all brothers of the downbeat, and that's what makes America—America."[16] However, USO and government policy that established separate but equal facilities to avoid racial conflicts undermined the idealistic philosophy of both the black and liberal press. The liberal press, which contained such Jewish columnists and editors as *Downbeat*'s Mike Lewin and *Metronome*'s Barry Ulanov and Leonard Feather, launched an attack against Jim Crow. John Hammond also joined by attacking the AFM's policy of separatism and pressured NBC and CBS radio to desegregate their studio orchestras. As a result, *Downbeat* awarded Duke Ellington's band its first number-one ranking, which was the first time an African-American orchestra ever won a national poll in a white publication. *Metronome* also recognized the achievements of African-American musicians. Nevertheless, the black press and African-Americans launched a stronger attack against the establishment for perpetuating discrimination at home and in the military. For example, the *Pittsburgh Courier*, the Brotherhood of Sleeping Car Porters, and the NAACP focused on the treatment of entertainers and black soldiers and initiated the Double V Campaign for victory abroad and at home. Furthermore, the *Courier* combined its efforts with African-American musicians and both black and white activists such as Paul Robeson, Willie Bryant, W. C. Handy, Lucky Millinder, and Eleanor Roosevelt and strongly rebuked "discrimination, prejudice and bigotry in a land that fosters democracy."[17]

World War II stimulated the economy in many ways by expanding geographical movement for military personnel and civilians throughout the country. Such movement opened up more economic opportunities for blacks, which made a major impact on the traditional racial attitudes in this country. For example, African-American musicians such as Nat "King" Cole, Louis Jordan, Duke Ellington, Art Tatum, Benny Carter, and Coleman Hawkins began working in Los Angeles nightclubs such as the Trocadero, Ciro's, and The Streets of Paris on Hollywood Boulevard. At the same time, the nightlife on Central Avenue in the heart of the African-American neighborhood attracted both blacks and whites. However, competition over jobs and housing along with the fear of racial mixing exacerbated racial conflict. As a result, some ballrooms and clubs established "white-only" policies. Likewise, in New York City (the swing capital), southern and northern white soldiers were threatened by desegregation. At that time, it was not uncommon for white GIs to attack African-American musicians physically in swing clubs on 52nd Street. Such brawls led many club owners to fear a race riot, which prompted police abuse of African-Americans and mixed couples. In the end, however, clubs on 52nd Street and in Harlem remained open to both races.[18]

Following the war's end in August 1945, the swing industry continued to boom. Musicians who had served in the military began returning home from overseas and resumed their lives as professionals. A number of band-leaders quickly assembled new orchestras with brief rehearsals and scheduled tours of one-night engagements before accepting location jobs. Numerous location jobs were available because new clubs and ballrooms were growing rapidly around the country. Once again music fans were able to enjoy and dance to the sounds of their favorite bands in older venues as well as newer ones. In turn, a number of former sidemen who returned from military duty and wanted to lead their own bands swung into action and took advantage of the booming business. For example, Ray Anthony, Hal McIntyre, and Jerry Gray started their own bands along with Buddy Rich, Mercer Ellington, and songwriter Hoagy Carmichael. In addition, Glenn Miller's widow selected Tex Beneke to reorganize and lead the Miller band.[19]

Big bands received royal treatment, with heavy promotion from record companies, radio networks, and ballroom and theater operators, which resulted in lucrative one-night engagements and location jobs across the country. It is important to point out that recordings were not quite as important to the bands as live radio broadcasts at that time. Furthermore, swing bands did not need recordings for promotion as today's musicians do. Current music groups have technology to help them produce polished recordings. Musicians in the forties and fifties depended solely on the mastery of their instruments and their ability to sight-read music skillfully to make quality recordings. In fact, swing bands were sometimes expected to record from four to six sides in just three hours. Nevertheless, recordings were important enough to make or break the big band business. Although there were a number of recording companies in operation during the era, the three major labels (Columbia, Decca, and RCA Victor) recorded most of the big bands. Most bandleaders understood the promotional value of recordings. On the other hand, AFM president Caesar Petrillo believed that recordings had no financial advantages for union musicians. The result was an AFM strike on August 1, 1942, in which Petrillo ordered the union to stop recording if record companies did not pay them for the use of their recordings played on radio programs and in jukeboxes. The major labels thus recorded only vocalists (mostly with choral backgrounds) and no instrumentalists for over a year. The strike forced Decca to reach an agreement with the union in September 1943. Columbia and Victor finally joined Decca in November 1944 and agreed to pay union musicians royalties for all records distributed on the market. Although Petrillo claimed victory for the labor movement, big bands suffered, and singers ended up taking over the recording field.

Big bands received most of their exposure and publicity from live remote radio broadcasts in the early forties. Remote broadcasts, which originated in the thirties, came from venues such as Frank Dailey's Meadowbrook in New Jersey, the Palomar in Los Angeles, the Hollywood Palladium, Chicago's Sherman Hotel, as well as New York's Glen Island Casino, Arcadia Ballroom, Lincoln Hotel, Roseland Ballroom, Paramount Theater, Savoy Ballroom, Apollo Theater, Harlem's Cotton Club, and the Hotel Pennsylvania's Manhattan Room, to name a few. In fact, there were literally hundreds of nightspots around the country that featured name bands and semi-professional music organizations. Bandleaders understood the importance of these remote broadcasts and competed heavily for extended engagements in venues with radio outlets. Bands even accepted these jobs at low wages to gain enough national recognition for tours that included one-nighters and theater jobs where they could make more money. Many of these bands worked such odd hours as 11:00 A.M. and noon on Sundays to get network exposure. However, most remote broadcasts occurred at night between 11:00 P.M. and 1:00 A.M. on CBS and NBC and from 11:00 P.M. to 2:00 A.M. on the Mutual Radio Network.

Big bands headlined some of the most popular radio shows at that time. The strongest supporters of top-name bands were cigarette companies such as Raleigh-Kool, Philip Morris, and the American Tobacco Company. For example, the latter company sponsored *Kay Kyser's College of Musical Knowledge* and a series called *The Lucky Strike Hit Parade. The Lucky Strike Survey* polled the songs each band played, which became more important than the bands themselves as listeners waited with anticipation until the end of each show for the number-one tune. Disc jockeys also broadcast music shows that attracted large audiences and provided bands with exposure. For example, New York's Martin Block on WNEW and KFRB's Al Jarvis in Los Angeles set up broadcasts from their "make-believe ballrooms." Other disc jockeys around the country followed the same model and emulated broadcasts from "ballrooms" through recordings.[20] However, the early forties witnessed a struggle between the radio networks and the American Society of Composers, Authors and Publishers (ASCAP). Basically, ASCAP wanted more money from the networks for licensing its music than they were willing to pay. The networks banned all ASCAP music from their programs until the two groups reached an agreement. In the meantime, the networks created their own collection agency, Broadcast Music, Inc. (BMI), by offering attractive terms to ASCAP defectors and new writers. At first, the quality of music played over the air did not compare with songs by such ASCAP writers as Cole Porter, the Gershwins, Johnny Mercer, Rodgers and Hart, Harold Arlen, and Jerome Kern. However, the quality of BMI's music improved within a few years, especially after ASCAP and the networks reached a treaty. Despite the struggle, radio programs continued to feature big bands throughout World War II and immediately following the war. Many of these music shows were built around bandleaders such as Harry James, Vaughn Monroe, and Kay Kyser. Even Horace Heidt emerged from retirement in 1947 and launched a *Talent Show* sponsored by Philip Morris, which became highly successful. By the late forties, remote broadcasts from hotels and ballrooms began to deteriorate and lost their effectiveness as television gradually became the primary broadcast medium.

The forties saw attempts to re-create big band shows on television, but most of them only lasted for one or two seasons. Shows were broadcast on a weekly basis from dance locations in many major cities such as New York and Los Angeles. Lawrence Welk's show, broadcast from the Aragon Ballroom in Santa Monica, California, achieved moderate success, while Ina Ray Hutton's all-female band enjoyed more success than did most of its male counterparts by formulating a popular West Coast television show. The Hollywood Palladium broadcast a weekly show from its bandstand, featuring name bands that survived for about two or three seasons. It later tried a *Weekly Dance Party* in 1955 that did not make the grade. Frank

Dailey's Meadowbrook on the East Coast also tried television remote broadcasts from its ballroom in the early fifties and, subsequently, created *The Cavalcade of Bands* as a one-hour sponsored show in 1955. It, too, was unable to survive. Other television shows were created in the fifties to help keep big bands alive and achieve the level of success they once enjoyed on radio. For example, television star Jackie Gleason was a devoted dance band fan who supported the Dorsey Brothers until their deaths. Similarly, noted jazz journalist Leonard Feather created *Music 55* for television that featured Stan Kenton to promote progressive jazz. Given all the attempts to promote and support the top bandleaders on television, Lawrence Welk ended up achieving more success than any others on both television and radio. His show, which originated in 1952 at the Aragon Ballroom, barely held on until it eventually attracted a sponsor. After a few slow periods, Welk decided to expand the show, and it survived in the ballroom and on television. The Dodge Motor Company began sponsoring the show in 1955, and it went on to achieve national prominence.[21]

Like radio, Hollywood's movie industry had been cashing in on dance bands for over a decade before the war by featuring such leaders as Benny Goodman in *Hollywood Hotel*, Artie Shaw in *Dancing Co-Ed*, the Woody Herman band and Gene Krupa in *Ball of Fire*, and Tommy Dorsey in *Las Vegas Night*. Movie producers and directors naturally cast the leaders and their bands in plots that were often strange, to say the least. Charlie Barnet, Harry James, Jimmie Lunceford, Sammy Kaye, Freddie Martin, Glenn Miller, Alvino Rey, Jack Teagarden, and many other popular leaders and their bands appeared before the cameras in the summer of 1941. After the movie moguls realized that it was better to simply let the bands play rather than weave them into ridiculous plots, their films finally made some sense. *Stage Door Canteen*, for example, featured the bands of Count Basie, Benny Goodman, Xavier Cugat, Guy Lombardo, Freddie Martin, and Kay Kyser in straight-ahead musical settings. A similar version entitled *Jam Session* presented the bands of Louis Armstrong, Charlie Barnet, Jan Garber, Glen Gray and the Casa Loma Orchestra, Teddy Powell, and Alvino Rey with Jo Stafford and the Pied Pipers in a more natural setting that resulted in a good movie. By late 1942, war restrictions had hurt the dance bands' one-nighters, and Petrillo's union strike put a damper on their promotional efforts through recordings. Consequently, a number of popular bands stayed in Hollywood to take advantage of employment opportunities in the film industry. After two years, the movie industry had released only a few decent band movies, and the two professions gradually parted company.[22]

Throughout the swing era, jazz and dance coexisted as synchronized entertainment in the same way that pop music and dancing are unified today. Most current dance styles with two individuals consist of what Pener refers to as "formless booty-shaking freestyle dancing." On the other hand, "swing dancing [was] an electric communication between two partners, an unspoken dialogue of individual impulses moving into harmony."[23] Swing dancing, the Lindy Hop, or jitterbugging are all words that refer to a popular and exciting dance style that actually began in the mid-twenties and survived through rock-and-roll in the sixties.[24] The Lindy Hop originated in one of New York City's uptown African-American neighborhoods known as Harlem. Some of the most popular uptown nightspots were the Cotton Club, the Apollo, and the famed Savoy Ballroom where people danced to big band music. Legendary dancer Shorty George Snowden christened the Lindy Hop at the Savoy. A reporter once questioned Snowden about his dancing style at the ballroom. Snowden, who had not named the dance at that point, simply named it "the Lindy Hop" after Charles Lindbergh's famous solo flight across the Atlantic in 1927. Ironically, Lindy's long-distance flight across the ocean only seemed like a hop in many people's minds at the time.[25] The Lindy Hop, based on African movements, became popularized and refined at the Savoy Ballroom, with its Charleston kicks, aerial features, and swinging bounces in the knees. Like jazz, the hop is improvisatory in that it offers dancers the space to create new movements spontaneously. The jitterbug, a less Afrocentric version of the Lindy Hop, evolved in the late thirties as swing made its way over to the white mainstream.[26]

Unfortunately, some journalists in the forties and fifties felt that dances like the Lindy Hop had sexual overtones and accused swing music of contributing to moral degradation in various newspapers. On the positive side, some major magazines such as *Collier's, Look,* and *Esquire* covered big bands and jazz regularly. Industry magazines such as *Billboard* and *Variety* also covered bands regularly, while others such as *Baton, Preview,* or *Bandleaders* spoke to the interests of dance fans but were unable to survive. There were, however, three monthly trade magazines—*Orchestra World, Metronome,* and *Downbeat*—that covered swing bands thoroughly, with the two latter sustaining the most credibility. *Metronome* covered national music news and dedicated a considerable amount of space to columns that ranged from instrumental instruction to tips on arranging and composing for large ensembles. Some of its staff writers during the Later Swing Era included noted journalists Barry Ulanov, Leonard Feather, Barbara Hodgkins, and George Simon. This informative magazine began in the 1880s and lasted into the 1960s. Starting out as a "sensation sheet" in Chicago, *Downbeat* later developed into a quality magazine that included national music news and informative articles by such noted writers as Marshall Stearns, John Hammond, George Hoefer, Charles Edward Smith, Dave Dexter, John S. Wilson, and Mike Lewin. It also featured instructional columns and reviews of live performances as well as recordings of swing bands and individual musicians. Miraculously, it is still in publication.[27]

Although jazz journalism provided a valuable communication link between musicians and their listeners, it had its problems during the forties and fifties (as it does today) with critics who did not fully understand the music. George T. Simon summarizes this issue quite clearly in the following statement:

> More than anything else it was the uninformed comments by writers that irked the big band leaders and musicians. Few dailies had any men on their staffs who had either a feeling for or a knowledge of popular music, swing in particular. Time and again, reviewers versed only in classical music were sent to cover performances of swing bands. Time and again, they came up with nonsensical pieces.[28]

As noted by Simon, many jazz writers had problems judging swing music accurately. His colleague Barry Ulanov suggested three principles in the forties that jazz writers could follow to guide their thinking and writing—"profundity, freshness, and skill." In discussing his three principles, Ulanov stated, "The three elements must be joined together by some reactive force which assures a tight reciprocal relationship among them." He added, "As it [the reactive force] operates in each musician as an individual it can be called *intuition*. As it operates among a group of musicians playing together it can be called *tension*."[29] Ulanov also described the relationships between his three principles and the reactive force(s) (intuition and tension) that critics or journalists must discern to understand jazz and write about it effectively:

> When, then, skilled jazzmen can summon up fresh and profound ideas by using their intuitive resources, and can, beyond their individual contributions, contact the intuitive resources of their colleagues, you get that highly agreeable tension, that motion of minds expressed through instruments or human voices, which we call first rate jazz. The means are many: they may be melodic, rhythmic, or harmonic; they are always at least two of the three and often all three. Whatever the means, however many musicians you have playing, their end is nothing unless it is produced with an unmistakable tension, the product, in turn, of individual intuition.[30]

Ulanov's ideal profile of a credible critic is one who has adequate knowledge of the art form, "which parallels the jazz musician's right down the melodic line and up the harmonic chord, and always on the beat." The critic should also have intuition similar to that of a jazz musician and be able to understand and appreciate the three aforementioned principles. Without intuition, the critic can only perform his or her needed clerical duties and function merely as an accountant by adding figures and making misleading numerical judgments about musicians. In addition, the critic must be creative and have the ability to "describe the next development in jazz before the musicians have reached it." In effect, the true critic's "work takes on a freshness and profundity, intuitively directed, in which musicians can find inspiration and their audiences a trustworthy guide."[31] Although Ulanov's wise suggestions for improving jazz journalism were written in 1949, it was a challenge for the press to find qualified journalists to cover the music adequately during the Later Swing Era. Unfortunately, that same problem (to a lesser extent) still exists in jazz today.

After the war, the swing industry's prosperity started to show signs of decline. The money that supported much of the business came from the defense industries. Attendance at nightclubs and ballrooms began to decrease because people decided not to spend as much money as they had during the war. Instead, Americans began to concentrate on starting families, buying homes, and acquiring material goods that became available after wartime restrictions. The swing industry's downward spiral resulted from the fact that many clubs and ballrooms were forced to cancel numerous one-night engagements and reduce their weekly operating schedules to four or five nights. Some venues had to book entertainment only on weekends.[32] Months later some of the top bandleaders like Woody Herman, Les Brown, Harry James, Benny Carter, Tommy Dorsey, Cab Calloway, and Charlie Barnet disbanded.[33] There were other reasons for the music industry's economic downturn. For example, a 30 percent cabaret tax established during the war increased the price of entertainment and remained in effect after the war's end. With the high cost of entertainment, many people simply stayed at home and watched television. Moreover, music styles began to change. Many big bands such as Stan Kenton's changed their style from dance music to "progressive jazz" that was better suited for concerts. Couples who had previously felt the emotional security of dancing and listening to the lyrics of love songs were not interested in the newer progressive styles.[34] Moreover, swing musicians such as Dizzy Gillespie became innovators and/or proponents of bebop. This new jazz style was not suitable for dancing, thus creating a split between the two entities.

The music industry also experienced a split between jazz and popular music. When dance bands dominated the industry before and during the war, vocalists did not hold the same level of importance as bandleaders or sidemen. Most singers simply sat next to the band, stood up to sing one or two choruses, and returned to their seats. Singers, however, gradually became more visible after Frank Sinatra left Tommy Dorsey's band and established himself as a solo artist in a command performance at New York's Paramount Theater in 1944. Other vocalists like Nat "King" Cole, Peggy Lee, Frankie Laine, and Patti Page jumped on the bandwagon and reaped handsome rewards from their solo singing careers. The result was a shift from jazz to popular music that created a role reversal, with bands serving mostly as a backup for singers.[35] After the war, most of the swing industry's supporters, such as cigarette and soft drink companies, that previously supported bands now sponsored vocalists who were featured regularly on radio programs. Radio, which had survived the Great Depression with the help of swing, played it safe by responding favorably to audience ratings and advertising rates. In other words, radio executives replaced their previous big band music shows with vocalists and disc jockeys, because audiences had lost interest in orchestras. Furthermore, singers had gained popularity and were much cheaper than bands. Before the change, networks had featured top swing musicians regardless of race and, in some cases, mixed bands that played modern jazz. By 1947, radio networks such as CBS only featured vocalists like Dinah Shore and Frank Sinatra or singing bandleaders such as Vaughn Monroe.[36]

While many bandleaders realized that major changes were taking place in the swing music industry, some refused to give up. Harry James, for example, saw the impending economic downturn and tried to rectify the situation. He reduced his fees so that promoters could lower admission prices and make it possible for everyone to survive in the business. Many of James's fellow leaders disagreed with his reasoning and made it difficult for him to reverse the trend. With many leaders outbidding each other for the best sidemen during the war, musicians' salaries had reached an all-time high. Around 1947, as the big band market continued to decline, the only way a number of bandleaders could make a profit was to disband briefly and then reorganize with smaller bands. These bandleaders also had to pay their sidemen much lower salaries compared with wartime pay. During the war, many top-name bands featured loud brass sections and increasingly emphasized the concept of jazz as concert music. A sizeable number of the newer bands also followed that same concept, while others changed their direction to music that was softer and danceable. Jan Garber, who had fronted a large swing band since 1942, led the way and completely reorganized by returning to his original "sweet music" style. Other leaders such as Vaughn Monroe, Eddy Howard, Dick Jurgens, and Russ Morgan continued with (or changed to) a smooth style of music. In fact, only the established big bands were able to survive the economic recession following the war. Unfortunately, live music continued to diminish, and disc jockeys replaced remote live radio broadcasts. Disc jockeys also played fewer big band records on the radio, and record companies recorded fewer big bands.[37]

As big bands gradually declined, vocalists became even more popular. Practically all of the bands had vocalists when they dominated the American music scene. Some musicians and committed jazz lovers were barely tolerant of singers, but they served as an important communication link between the big bands and their customers. In many cases, band vocalists were paid lower wages than instrumentalists, mainly because they had no union protection and the supply outweighed the demand. In addition, male singers doubled as music librarians, helped out with instruments, and/or assisted with travel arrangements to protect their jobs. Furthermore, vocalists had no control over most circumstances that affected the way they sounded. Such circumstances ranged from being forced to sing outside their vocal range to having a new song introduced to them for the first time in a recording studio. According to many successful band singers, however, the disadvantages did not outweigh the advantages. For example, both Doris Day and Peggy Lee said that they learned discipline, the value of rehearsal, and how to deal with people through big band work. It is also a well-known fact that Frank Sinatra learned the concepts of breath control and musical phrasing from his ex-boss, Tommy Dorsey. Some vocalists were as popular as the bands before the musician's union strike in 1942 actually paved the way for them to exceed the bands' popularity. Some female band singers who emerged as big stars were Ella Fitzgerald, Peggy Lee, Doris Day, Jo Stafford, Kay Starr, Sarah Vaughn, Anita O'Day, Lena Horne, Dinah Washington, and June Christy, to name a few. Some of the male singers included Frank Sinatra, Billy Eckstine, Perry Como, Vaughn Monroe, Joe Williams, Merv Griffin, and Mike Douglas.[38] Near the end of the forties, many popular singers still performed swing music, but most of their engagements were in lounges and nightclubs rather than dance halls. There were some opportunities, however, for singers to perform in larger settings such as the Newport Jazz Festival and Norman Granz's Jazz at the Philharmonic concerts.[39]

As vocalists gained popularity, small swing groups moved into the limelight. In fact, vocalists who led small groups such as Nat "King" Cole and Louis Jordan became quite popular. Cole's national hits such as "Straighten Up and Fly Right," "The Christmas Song," "Mona Lisa," and "Nature Boy" established him as a leading popular singer who eventually became the first African-American to host his own network television series.[40] Additionally, former Chick Webb saxophonist-vocalist Louis Jordan rose to prominence after the war and sold millions of records as a "jump blues" artist. Jordan led a five- to seven-piece combo that accompanied his vocal and saxophone work on some of his greatest hits such as "Caldonia" and "Choo Choo Ch' Boogie." Count Basie's fast-moving Kansas City blues sound influenced the jump blues style popularized by Jordan, and Pener describes the style as "a powerful hard-rocking mix of jazz arrangements and solos with the deep soul of the blues."[41] The new style featured singers shouting the lyrics and a front line of horns playing background riffs and solos, while rhythm sections pushed the music with a strong backbeat.[42] Small groups such as Jordan's combo not only gained popularity during the forties but they later became the primary performing units in popular music, and that fact still exists today.[43] This trend began when several big band leaders formed small swing groups with their musicians that were commonly referred to as "bands within bands." For example, the Benny Goodman trio, Bob Crosby's Bobcats, and Artie Shaw's Gramercy Five were formed with some of the musicians from these leader's big bands. Music styles also changed with the rise of small groups. As noted earlier, Dixieland or traditional jazz returned as a result of the revival movement. Bebop continued to develop in nightclubs on New York City's 52nd Street. As swing, Dixieland, and bebop musicians vied for first place in the popular music field, another style quietly emerged that became known as the "cool" school.[44] The jump blues, a hybrid of swing and blues, was yet another contender.

As vocalists and small groups rose to prominence and music styles changed, big bands continued to decline in the 1950s, although bands that styled their music for dancing managed to survive the hard times. Some of the top record companies tried to jumpstart the band business by promoting commercial-styled big bands. RCA Victor, for example, released a record series called *Here Come the Dance Bands Again* and aggressively promoted Ralph Flanagan's band in the spring of 1950. After an extended tour of one-nighters and location jobs, Flanagan claimed the title of "America's Number-one Band" by the end of 1951. Capitol, Mercury, and other record labels followed Victor's example. Capitol promoted Billy May's band; Mercury launched a heavy promotion campaign in 1951 for Ralph Marterie's new band; and Victor repeated its promotional blueprint with Buddy Morrow's band. In addition, ballroom operators formed an alliance known as the National Ballroom Operators of America (NBOA) to help support the big band business. The NBOA had a few success stories, but most of its long-range goals proved too difficult to attain.

Though the dance band business had major problems, some of its name bandleaders like Flanagan, Guy Lombardo, and Sammy Kaye made gross incomes approaching $1 million. After these incomes became public in 1951, top musicians such as Sy Oliver, Lee Castle, Don Terry, King Guion, Shorty Rogers, Maynard Ferguson, Buddy Rich, Sonny Dunham, and Neal Hefti formed new big bands between the fall of 1951 and the spring of 1952. Unfortunately, only a few of them were able to succeed. Although many name bands found it tough to maintain their national visibility, the activity of numerous territory bands increased in ballrooms and hotels throughout the Midwest, South, and Southwest. In effect, territory bands literally became prosperous because ballroom and hotel operators across the country found it difficult to pay name bands and make a profit. Consequently, territory bandleaders like Ray Pearl, Tiny Hill, Teddy Phillips, Chuck Foster, Jimmy Palmer, Paul Neighbors, and Leo Peiper took advantage of the opportunities. Despite the gloom-and-doom in the big band business during the early fifties, there were still some successful organizations as mentioned earlier. A number of well-established veterans such as Guy Lombardo, Freddy Martin, Jan Garber, Wayne King, Sammy Kaye, Charlie Spivak, Russ Morgan, and Lawrence Welk continued to please dancers and enjoy lucrative careers. For example, the Dorsey Brothers reunited in 1953 and remained successful until their deaths. Harry James hired drummer Buddy Rich, which helped the leader maintain national visibility. The Glenn Miller Band (under Ray McKinley) and Les Elgart's orchestra also survived the 1950s.[45] In addition, Count Basie reorganized his orchestra in 1952, at the encouragement of Billy Eckstine, and continued to deliver his swinging big band sounds for the next thirty years.[46]

In sum, the 1940s and the first half of the 1950s witnessed dramatic changes in the country's socioeconomic climate and music styles. Similarly, sexual and racial tensions reached a point that brought new and exciting challenges to the nation's traditionally accepted social practices. World War II eventually forced the country to reshape its economic priorities, which opened up greater opportunities for more people to live the "American dream." Many big bands did not survive these changes, while vocalists and small groups breathed fresh air into the popular music industry. Although these changes forced large numbers of big bands to disband, they opened up ways for more individual musicians to create new musical pathways. Whereas the emphasis had been on competent music-reading skills and section playing in large ensembles, small groups provided musicians with more freedom to widen the boundaries of creative improvisation. As a result, instrumentalists and vocalists were able to develop unique sounds in jazz and, therefore, take the music to a higher level of creativity. On the other hand, the connection that existed between the big bands and the public throughout most of the Swing Era provided jazz with a popular support from the masses that is unparalleled in the history of American music.

NOTES

1. Leo Walker, *The Wonderful Era of the Great Dance Bands* (New York: Doubleday and Co., 1972), pp. 89–91.

2. Lewis A. Erenberg, *Swingin' the Dream: Big Band Jazz and the Rebirth of American Culture* (Chicago: The University of Chicago Press, 1998), p. 185.

3. Ibid.

4. Ibid., pp. 182–185.

5. Walker, *The Wonderful Era*, pp. 89–101.

6. Erenberg, *Swingin' the Dream*, p. 198.

7. Sherrie Tucker, *Swing Shift: "All-Girl" Bands of the 1940s* (Durham, NC: Duke University Press, 2000), pp. 35–43.

8. Quoted in Erenberg, *Swingin' the Dream*, p. 200.

9. Ibid., pp. 200–201.

10. Tom Scanlan, *The Joy of Jazz: Swing Era, 1935–1947* (Golden, CO: Fulcrum Publishing, 1996), p. 55.

11. Ibid.

12. Ibid., pp. 55–56.

13. Ibid., p. 56.

14. Ibid., pp. 56–57.

15. Erenberg, *Swingin' the Dream*, p. 202.

16. Quoted in Erenberg, *Swingin' the Dream*, p. 202.

17. Ibid., pp. 203–205.

18. Ibid., pp. 206–208.

19. Walker, *The Wonderful Era*, p. 103.

20. George T. Simon, *The Big Bands* (New York: Schirmer Books, 1981), pp. 50–59.

21. Walker, *The Wonderful Era*, pp. 175, 178–186.

22. Simon, *The Big Bands*, pp. 66–69.

23. Pener, *The Swing Book*, p. 66.

24. Ibid.

25. Ibid., pp. 16–17.

26. Ibid., pp. 66–67.

27. Simon, *The Big Bands*, pp. 70–72.

28. Ibid., p. 71.

29. Barry Ulanov, "The Function of the Critic in Jazz," *Metronome* 65, no. 8 (1949): 16.

30. Ibid., pp. 16–17.

31. Ibid., p. 17.

32. Walker, *The Wonderful Era*, pp. 107–108.

33. Pener, *The Swing Book*, p. 30.

34. Arthur Jackson, *The World of Big Bands* (New York: Arco Publishing Co., 1977), p. 65.

35. Pener, *The Swing Book*, pp. 31–32.

36. Erenberg, *Swingin' the Dream*, pp. 217–218.

37. Walker, *The Wonderful Era*, pp. 108–110.

38. Simon, *The Big Bands*, pp. 33–39.

39. Pener, *The Swing Book*, p. 32.

40. Leonard Feather and Ira Gitler, *The Biographical Encyclopedia of Jazz* (New York: Oxford University Press, 1999), p. 139.

41. Pener, *The Swing Book*, p. 32.

42. Ibid., pp. 32–33.

43. Gunther Schuller, *The Swing Era: The Development of Jazz 1930–1945* (New York: Oxford University Press, 1989), p. 806.

44. James L. Collier, *The Making of Jazz: A Comprehensive History* (New York: Dell Publishing Co., 1978), p. 409.

45. Walker, *The Wonderful Era*, pp. 113–127.

46. Feather and Gitler, *Encyclopedia of Jazz*, pp. 43–44.

Chapter 2

♪

Four Masters of Swing

The Later Swing Era witnessed an abundance of talented bandleaders, composer-arrangers, vocalists, and instrumentalists who mastered the art of swing. Many of these musicians were duly recognized for their achievements, whereas even more of them received little or no acknowledgment at all for their mastery of the music. Numerous artists who began their careers before or after World War II made significant contributions as swing artists throughout the forties and fifties. Unfortunately, it is impossible to recognize all of them and discuss their musical accomplishments within the confines of this single volume. Nevertheless, the following paragraph names some of these masters who created a large body of music that will continue to inspire generations of musicians and jazz aficionados.

Many jazz historians who have documented the work of Swing Era artists reserve noble titles such as the "King of Swing," "Count," and "Duke" for big band leaders such as Benny Goodman, William Basie, and Edward Kennedy Ellington. However, there were prominent musicians in that era who excelled in areas other than leading big bands. Vocalists, composer-arrangers, instrumental soloists, and/or small group leaders also played major roles in shaping swing music and deserve similar recognition. Therefore, musicians from all of these categories are represented in this chapter as masters of swing. Some of the major bandleaders who mastered swing music include Count Basie, Duke Ellington, Benny Goodman, Lionel Hampton, Tommy and Jimmy Dorsey, Jimmie Lunceford, and Artie Shaw. It is important to point out that most of these leaders were accomplished instrumentalists and, some—Ellington, Fletcher Henderson, Sy Oliver, Neal Hefti, Henry Mancini, and Nelson Riddle—were excellent composer-arrangers as well. Vocalists like Nat "King" Cole, Doris Day, Sarah Vaughn, and Perry Como, and instrumentalists such as Louis Armstrong, Coleman Hawkins, Red Norvo, Lester Young, Pee Wee Russell, Charlie Shavers, Henry "Red" Allen, Ben Webster, and Jack Teagarden were among an elite group of soloists who mastered the art of swing.

The four masters presented in this chapter represent a cross section of multi-talented musicians who made unique contributions to swing music. Although all four of these individuals received recognition for their work in varying degrees during their careers, a discussion of their lives, music, and accomplishments is included here to illuminate further the contributions of these artists. Ella Fitzgerald, Woody Herman, Billy Strayhorn, and Teddy Wilson represent a diverse group of musicians who achieved substantive and widely different musical and professional goals during the Later Swing Era.

Vocalist Ella Fitzgerald recorded her first million-seller with Chick Webb's band and later became one of the leading scat singers in the history of jazz. Clarinetist-saxophonist Woody Herman was one of the most successful bandleaders of the era and led swing big bands throughout his life. Billy Strayhorn was probably the most highly skilled composer-arranger-song-writer in the forties and fifties. He not only had the ability to write great music cooperatively with Duke Ellington, he wrote some of his own music that has easily endured the test of time. Like Strayhorn, Teddy Wilson was a great musical mind who helped Billie Holiday reach stardom. His consummate skills as a pianist, arranger, and bandleader were incomparable in the world of swing. The lives and music of these four artists are discussed in this chapter.

ELLA FITZGERALD

Ella Fitzgerald was born in Newport News, Virginia, on April 25, 1917, and was raised in Yonkers, New York, by her mother. As a youngster, she enjoyed dancing, singing, and sneaking off from junior high school at lunchtime to hear vocalist Dolly Dawn at a local theater. Ella also enjoyed listening to the Boswell Sisters on radio, and Connie Boswell was one of her favorite singers. Fitzgerald originally wanted to be a dancer, and most of her friends in Yonkers thought she could dance quite well. On one occasion, she and two of her friends drew straws to decide which one of them would try to enter the Apollo's amateur hour contest. Although she preferred dancing at the time, she entered the contest as a singer and won. Benny Carter and John Hammond were in the audience and arranged an audition for Ella with Fletcher Henderson, who apparently was not impressed. Subsequently, CBS Radio contracted with her to appear on the Mike Tracy Show, but her mother passed away and she was unable to be a guest on the program.[1] Despite her loss, she continued to win contests on the amateur hour circuit and finally landed her first professional job at the Harlem Opera House with Tiny Bradshaw's band. According to Ella, "Everyone had their coats on and were ready to leave when Tiny introduced me. He said, 'Ladies and gentlemen...here's the young girl that's been winning all the contests,' and they all came back and took off their coats and sat down again."[2]

Chick Webb's band followed Bradshaw's at the theater. So Benny Carter and Bardu Ali (Webb's male vocalist) recommended Ella to Chick, but he was not interested. Carter and Bardu hid her in Chick's dressing room and, of course, he ended up listening to her. At the time, she knew only three songs she had learned from Connie Boswell—"Judy," "The Object of My Affection," and "Believe It, Beloved." Webb reluctantly agreed to take her to Yale University for a one-night gig the following day. Bradshaw and the Apollo's chorus girls chipped in to buy Ella a gown for the event. She opened with Webb at the Savoy around 1935, and her professional career was born.[3] Fitzgerald became close friends with Webb, who took her under his tutelage, provided her with the guidance she needed to succeed, and eventually became her legal guardian. She toured the country with Webb's band and recorded "A-Tisket, A-Tasket" in 1938, which became their million-seller. When Chick died in 1939, Fitzgerald took over the leadership of his band, which lasted for about two or three years. Unfortunately, World War II and the military draft practically dismembered the band.[4] After the Webb band folded, Fitzgerald began a solo career. Because she had already recorded with Webb for Decca, she continued with that label from 1942 to 1955.

Decca's founder, Jack Kapp, believed in recording many of the label's artists together to integrate jazz and pop. As a result, some of Fitzgerald's recordings made during the forties include artists as diverse as Louis Armstrong, the Ink Spots, Louis Jordan, and the Mills Brothers. Although projects of this kind can be stifling to creative artists, these collaborations resulted in some of Fitzgerald's most successful recordings. For example, the songs she recorded with Louis Armstrong have an outstanding quality. In "Dream a Little Dream of Me," Fitzgerald and Armstrong are both featured as vocal soloists. Interestingly, she sings a scat obligato around a portion of Armstrong's vocals, and both of them sing a brief and effective duet on the coda. In one of the selections, Fitzgerald and Armstrong hold a dialogue in which she tells him to put his horn down and asks if he has ever been in love. Of course, Armstrong's trumpeting is elegant, and the dialogue has a surrealistic quality to it. Near the end of the piece, both vocalists sing a brief and exquisite duet. Sy Oliver's orchestra accompanied both of these songs.

Fitzgerald's work with the Ink Spots is equally appealing. The quartet's members (Bill Kenny, Charles Fuqua, Deek Wilson, and Happy Jones) turn in one of their best performances throughout the sessions. At times, it appears that Ella's girlish voice is overpowered by the four male singers, but she soars above the quartet during most of her solo flights. "I Still Feel the Same About You" showcases Fitzgerald's voice with the group's lead singer in alternating solo spots and duet sections. In this particular song, Ella's singing over the quartet's doo-wop accompaniment is the highlight of this project. The vocal blend between Fitzgerald's solo voice and the group's background harmonies is most attractive.

Similarly, Ella and Louis Jordan are timeless. For this project, Fitzgerald is accompanied by Jordan's Tympani Five, which was, at the time, a septet. The group's personnel included Aaron Izenhall on trumpet, Josh Jackson or Eddie Johnson on tenor sax, Bill Davis at the piano, Carl Hogan on guitar, Jesse Simpkins or Dallas Bartley on bass, and Eddie Byrd or Chris Columbus on drums. On "Petootie Pie," both Fitzgerald and Jordan turn in an enthusiastic and lively performance. Both singers are in excellent voice, but Ella's scat vocals alternating with Jordan's alto sax for two-bar phrases is a treat for the listener. Here, Fitzgerald performs as if she is another wind instrumentalist. Obviously, the musical empathy between Jordan and Fitzgerald was contagious, and it is sustained throughout their renditions of "Baby, It's Cold Outside," "Don't Cry, Crybaby," "Ain't Nobody's Business but My Own," and "I'll Never Be Free." Similarly, Fitzgerald's collaboration with the Mills Brothers was just as spectacular as the three previously mentioned projects. This collaboration yielded some unforgettable sides such as "I Gotta Have My Baby Back," "I've Got the World on a String," and "You'll Have to Swing It" that displayed the technical flexibility and rich tonal quality of her voice.

At the time of the Decca projects, bebop was gaining a foothold. Fitzgerald incorporated this new language into her own personal style and established herself firmly among jazz modernists with an all-scat performance on "Flying Home" in 1945. She also employed modern bop licks on "Lady Be Good," which was a favorite among her fans, and blended phrases from swing and bop on "How High the Moon." Fitzgerald's twenty-year association with Decca reached its highpoint when she recorded a Gershwin duet album with pianist Ellis Larkins in 1950, and another one that included a variety of songs in 1954. Her interpretation of Gershwin songs such as "Someone to Watch over Me," "Soon," "How Long Has This Been Going On?" and "I've Got a Crush on You" laid the foundation for her future beyond the swing era, and it closed the history books on the quickly fading big-band vocal style.[5]

During the last decade of her Decca years, Fitzgerald often toured with Norman Granz and his Jazz at the Philharmonic in Europe and Japan. From 1947 to 1954, she was usually accompanied by a trio under the leadership of bassist Ray Brown (her husband at the time). It was the JATP concerts that provided her with the opportunity to develop her style further by mimicking the other musicians. In fact, Fitzgerald's scat vocal style was derived from the instrumental solos of virtuosos such as Art Tatum, Roy Eldridge, Charlie Christian, Oscar Peterson, Lionel Hampton, Benny Goodman, Charlie Parker, and Dizzy Gillespie. She actually developed a vocabulary of wordless syllables that expressed the essence of improvised melodies and made sense musically. In effect, Fitzgerald became a musical virtuoso.[6] Examples of Fitzgerald's scat-singing were recorded live during her JATP years at Carnegie Hall in New York City on September 8, 1949, and September 17, 1954. She was accompanied by a trio consisting of Ray Tunia or Hank Jones on piano, Ray Brown on bass, and Buddy Rich on drums in the 1949 concert. These performances showcase Fitzgerald's singing style to great effect. For example, her authentic delivery of the melody from "Robbin's Nest" reminds the listener of a wind instrumentalist's interpretation of the tune. She sings the lyrics convincingly, but it is her horn-like melodic phrasing that sets her far apart from her peers. Here, she sings the thirty-two-bar melody and solos (or scats) like a horn player for sixteen bars before returning to the melody for the remaining sixteen measures. This solo displays Fitzgerald's acute ear for intervallic relationships as well as her thorough knowledge and understanding of motivic development. This same concert features an all-scat performance of "Flying Home." Trumpeter Roy Eldridge and trombonist Tommy Turk were added on this tune, along with saxophonists Charlie Parker, Lester Young, and Flip Phillips. Fitzgerald again performs like another horn player as she scats the theme and solos effectively with accompanying background riffs from the horn section. Flip Phillips follows with a wailing tenor sax solo, while Charlie Parker is mainly hidden in the background. The highpoint of the concert is Fitzgerald's brilliant impersonation of Louis Armstrong during her performance of "Basin Street Blues." She sings the verse in her normal vocal range but imitates Armstrong's gravel-like voice in the chorus by singing the lyrics and scatting in her lower register. This crowd-pleaser is outstanding.

In the 1954 concert, we hear a more mature Ella. Her vocal delivery of the melody and lyrics in "Hernando's Hideaway," for example, is more focused. Moreover, her scat-singing style sounds even closer to the improvised solos of wind instrumentalists. This tune, which contains both Latin-tinged and swing-style sections, displays Fitzgerald's ability to interpret the two idioms effectively with superb vocal improvisation. Fitzgerald's most exciting performance in this concert, however, is her rendition of "Later"—an up-tempo blues piece. After an introduction by the rhythm section, she scat-sings the theme and continues with a dazzling solo in bop style. Her solo makes full use of her vocal range and consists of wide interval leaps, broken chords or arpeggios, and accurate scale-wise melodic passages. She also holds sustained high notes in certain parts of the solo to build intensity. She ends the solo with a call-and-response dialogue with pianist Ray Tunia. Fitzgerald concludes the tune with the statement "It's later for you daddy!" Needless to say, this was a rousing ending to that concert.

On the other hand, we cannot dismiss the other side of Ella—her ability to sing a ballad. Her interpretation of "My Bill" not only displays the warmth of her singing but also demonstrates her ability to sing extended phrases across the barline.

In 1955, Norman Granz became Fitzgerald's manager, and she began recording for his new Verve record label. Granz was instrumental in organizing concerts and recordings for Fitzgerald with such jazz luminaries as Duke Ellington, Count Basie, Louis Armstrong, Oscar Peterson, and Joe Pass. Her most notable recordings for Verve were the highly regarded *Song Book* albums featuring the music of the Gershwins, Cole Porter, Duke Ellington, Jerome Kern, and Johnny Mercer. These albums helped establish Fitzgerald with a wider audience.[7]

Ella Fitzgerald's illustrious career spanned over fifty years, and she received a long list of honors that include: thirteen Grammy Awards; the Kennedy Center for the Performing Arts' Medal of Honor Award; the Pied Piper Award; the National Academy of Recording Arts and Sciences' Lifetime Achievement Award; the American Society of Composers, Authors, and Publishers' highest honor—The George and Ira Gershwin Award for Outstanding Achievement; the National Medal of Art awarded by former President Ronald Reagan; the first Society of Singers Lifetime Achievement Award; and a number of honorary doctorates.[8] During the last decade of her life, she performed only occasionally, because of declining health, until her death in 1996. The essence of Fitzgerald's brilliant contributions to music is captured by Wynton Marsalis' description of her as the "Apotheosis of American Singers."[9] Ella Fitzgerald not only left her legacy as the "First Lady of Song," she was also an undisputed master of swing.

WOODY HERMAN

Instrumentalist-vocalist-bandleader Woody Herman was born in Milwaukee, Wisconsin, on May 16, 1913.[10] He began singing and dancing in local theaters and clubs at age six and started playing saxophone at age nine.[11] By age eleven, Herman had started studying clarinet while working in the old Orpheum circuit as a "Boy Wonder of the Saxophone." He later played in Joel Lichter's band in Milwaukee at age sixteen as a high school student. After performing in vaudeville for about two years, Herman attended Marquette University before touring and recording with Tom Gerun's band in 1931. One year later, Herman made his first recording as a vocalist with Gerun. He left Gerun in 1934 and returned to Milwaukee, where he worked with the bands of Harry Sosnik and Gus Arnheim. Around 1935, Herman joined the famous Isham Jones Orchestra before Jones retired from the organization a year later for health reasons.[12]

After Jones' retirement, some orchestra members wanted to keep the organization intact. The result was a cooperative unit in which the members were equal shareholders and took the name "Woody Herman Orchestra." Within the corporate structure, Herman was president, Joe Bishop was first vice president, Walt Yoder was second vice president, and Neil Reid was treasurer. The orchestra made its debut at the Roseland in Brooklyn and was broadcast over the air by the Mutual Broadcasting System. The next job, at New York's Roseland, also received airtime and helped boost the band's popularity. By 1937, the orchestra had begun performing at top venues, including an appearance at the Schroeder Hotel in Herman's hometown of Milwaukee. For the next two years, the corporate unit, which called itself "The Band that Plays the Blues," struggled and received some harsh criticism along the way. Despite the struggle, the band recorded "Doctor Jazz" in 1937, which was considered one of its best records. The band continued with its blues formula and recorded "Woodchopper's Ball" in 1939, which became a major hit and the band's most requested chart. Engagements followed at some of the nation's top venues such as the Glen Island Casino, the New Yorker Hotel, Chicago's Hotel Sherman, and New York's Famous Door on 52nd Street.

By 1941, the Woody Herman Orchestra had finally made it to the top. They played an engagement at the Hollywood Palladium and drew a crowd of 4,800 on opening night that was, at the time, second only to Glenn Miller's audience of 5,200. Herman's band was, however, the first to play a "holdover" engagement there, when it had been originally scheduled for only six weeks.[13] Some of Herman's cooperative band members who had played with Isham Jones were flugelhornist Joe Bishop and guitarist Chick Reeves, who doubled as arrangers, trumpeters Clarence Willard and Kermit Simmons, saxophonist Saxey Mansfield, violinist Nick Hupfer, trombonist Neil Reid, bassist Walt Yoder, and drummer Frank Carlson.[14] Nevertheless, the band's personnel changed completely during the war.[15] After the military draft created personnel difficulties for Herman, he hired some of Duke Ellington's sidemen, including Johnny Hodges, Juan Tizol, Ben Webster, and Ray Nance, to record with the band. Herman also hired Dave Matthews (an Ellington-style arranger) to write for the band, which also played some of Dizzy Gillespie's charts. Herman realized that his band needed to change its style, although the music it played during 1943 and part of 1944 had a limited audience because of the recording ban. He recorded some excellent V-Discs, however, that included selections such as "Apple Honey," "Caldonia," "Goosey Gander," and "Your Father's Mustache," which were available at least to military personnel.

By early 1945, the Herman organization was practically a new band. The rhythm section now consisted of pianist-arranger Ralph Burns, vibist Marjorie Hyams, guitarist Billy Bauer, bassist Chubby Jackson, and drummer Dave Tough. The saxophonists were Flip Phillips, John LaPorta, Sam Morowitz, Pete Mondello, and Skip DeSair. Ralph Pfiffner, Bill Harris, and Ed Keifer made up the trombone section. The trumpet section included arranger Neal Hefti, Charlie Frankhauser, Ray Wetzel, Pete Condoli, and Carl Warwick. In addition, Burns and Hefti wrote some modern-sounding charts for the band's library.[16] Excellent examples of the band's sound are Herman's "Apple Honey" and his "Goosey Gander," which were recorded in 1945. "Honey" is an up-tempo tune based on "I Got Rhythm" (A-A-B-A) chord progressions. The theme follows an eight-bar introduction with unison saxes in the first two [A] sections. Harmonized trumpets play the melody in the bridge [B], with unison saxes playing a countermelody. The last [A] section features muted and harmonized trumpets playing the theme. Flip Phillips plays a smooth Ben Webster–style solo, with harmonized brass in the background. The second solo is played by Harris, who is accompanied by unison saxes and a few vocal chants from the rest of the band. Vibist Hyams and Herman split the third solo chorus, and the full band follows with two exciting shout choruses over excellent playing by the rhythm section. The band also turns in an energetic performance of "Gander." The rhythm section's brief introduction is followed by Herman's throaty clarinet playing the twelve-bar blues melody in a call-and-response pattern with unison saxes. Again, Phillips and Harris are deservedly the featured soloists. Their outings are followed by the full ensemble playing two consecutive shout choruses that include some screaming high-note trumpet playing. Unison saxes restate the melody with Herman's responses before the band proceeds to the coda.

Near the end of 1945, Herman's band had reached the pinnacle of success in the world of swing. The band was recording for Columbia, and record sales were favorable. The band won both the *Downbeat* and *Metronome* polls, while Phillips, Harris, and Tough were recognized as three of the nation's top instrumentalists. The band also attracted record-breaking audiences at ballrooms and theaters. To top it off, the "First Herd" and its vocalist Frances Wayne recorded a big hit entitled "Happiness Is a Thing Called Joe."[17] Herman also had a small group called the "Woodchoppers," made up of players from his big band. A 1945 edition of the small group included trumpeters Sonny Berman and Shorty Rogers, trombonist Harris, tenorist Phillips, pianist Jimmy Rowles, guitarist Bauer, bassist Jackson, drummer Don Lamond, and vibist Red Norvo. In 1946, the group recorded "Steps" and "Four Men on a Horse." The Woodchoppers' rendition of "Four Men" is a humorous two-beat excursion at a relaxed medium tempo. The arrangement effectively utilizes a call-and-response format in both the introduction (muted brass and vibraphone) and in the thematic section (A-A-B-A) between Herman's clarinet and muted brass. However, the bridge [B] employs a different format, with the vibraphone carrying the melody over a unison horn countermelody. Harris, Phillips, and Rowles each play brief eight-bar solos, and Herman returns with the last eight bars of the melody. The group follows with the coda, and Herman plays a brief cadenza before the final chord.

With two high-quality bands (big and small), successful record sales, poll-winning soloists, and large audiences, Herman's ten years of struggling as a bandleader finally paid off. He had finally reached the top. To everyone's surprise, however, he decided to disband in December 1946 and spend some time with his family. During his break from bandleading, he worked as a disc jockey for radio station KLAC in Hollywood, played golf, and recorded some sides with a pick-up band. Anxious to return to bandleading, Herman formed the Second Herd in mid-October 1947.[18]

The Second Herd featured a group of saxophonists (three tenors and one baritone) who became known as the Four Brothers. The original players were Stan Getz, Zoot Sims, Herbie Steward, and Serge Chaloff, but Al Cohn later replaced Steward and became a permanent member of the famous quartet. In recognition of their individual solo abilities and well-knit section playing, Jimmy Giuffre composed "Four Brothers," which blended musical elements from both swing and bop.[19] The composition has a thirty-two-bar structure in A-A-B-A form. The theme is played by the four saxes with full band accompaniment. Giuffre's arrangement is most interesting without overexposing the four soloists. For example, the first tenor soloist plays sixteen bars (A-A) and the baritonist solos for the next sixteen bars (B-A) to complete one solo chorus. The two remaining tenorists also share one solo chorus. Two shout choruses by the full band follow the two solo choruses. The first one features unison saxes for sixteen bars, and Woody's clarinet over the full ensemble during the next sixteen measures. The second shout chorus showcases the full ensemble during the three [A] sections and the sax section (harmonized) on the bridge [B]. Another brief tenor sax solo follows before the four saxes lead the band to the coda. In Al Cohn's "The Goof and I," the band plays in a convincing bebop style. Cohn's A-A-B-A theme features unison saxes (A), unison saxes with harmonized accompaniment by the brass section (A), harmonized trumpets with a unison sax countermelody (B), and unison trumpets with a unison sax countermelody (A). The first solo chorus is played by baritonist Chaloff, with a harmonized brass background. The second solo chorus features trombone for sixteen bars (A-A) and Woody's clarinet for the next sixteen measures (B-A). The full band follows with an exciting shout chorus that changes keys before the ensemble proceeds to the coda. In addition, the Second Herd's vocalist, Mary Ann McCall, sings "P.S. I Love You" in a style that suggests Billie Holiday. Burns' arrangement of this song also features Herman on clarinet, with full band accompaniment. In addition to the aforementioned saxophonists and McCall, band members included Ernie Royal, Bernie Glow, Stan Fishelson, Irving Markowitz, and Shorty Rogers on trumpet. Earl Swope, Ollie Wilson, and Bob Swift made up the trombone section. Pianist Fred Otis, guitarist Gene Sargent, bassist Walter Yoder, and drummer Don Lamond completed the rhythm section. At various times, the band also included Shadow Wilson, Red Rodney, Billy Mitchell, Lou Levy, Gene Ammons, Jimmy Raney, Oscar Pettiford, and other distinguished musicians. Although the Second Herd was not as popular as the first band, it had a higher level of creativity and displayed considerable solo and ensemble talent. Herman recognized the Second Herd's creative ability and held it together as long as he could, despite the low financial return. The Second Herd disbanded in 1949, and Herman continued performing with a small group that included Conte Condoli, Bill Harris, Milt Jackson, Dave Barbour, Red Mitchell, and Shelly Manne. From December 1949 to January 1950, the group toured the United States and Cuba.

In the spring of 1950, Herman formed the Third Herd. Initially, the band's personnel included Urbie Green, Carl Fontana, Bill Perkins, Dave McKenna, Red Mitchell, and Milt Jackson. Later, Shorty Rogers, Ernie Royal, Al Cohn, Bill Harris, and Chubby Jackson rejoined Herman. Other members were Kai Winding, Frank Rehak, and noted pianist-arranger Nat Pierce, who contributed some excellent Basie-style charts to the band's library.[20] By 1954, the personnel (with the exception of Pierce) were totally different. The trumpet section consisted of Dick Collins, John Howell, Al Porcino, Reuben McFall, and Bill Castagnino. Bass trumpeter Cy Touff led the trombone section, which included Dick Kenney and Keith Moon. The saxophonists were Jerry Coker, Dick Hafer, Bill Perkins, and Jack Nimitz. The rhythm section consisted of Pierce, bassist Thomas "Red" Kelly, and drummer Art Mardigan.[21]

In 1954, the latter edition of the Third Herd recorded Bill Holman's "Mulligan Tawny" and Cohn's "The Third Herd." Holman's "Tawny," with its haunting minor-key theme, is played at a medium tempo after being introduced by bass and drums. The melody is stated by one trumpeter, while Nimitz's baritone plays the countermelody before the full ensemble restates the theme. An outstanding tenorist takes the first solo, and Herman follows on clarinet. After a brief full-band interlude, a trumpet solo follows before the melody is played by the trumpet section in unison with a harmonized accompaniment by the saxophones. The theme is restated by the full band in another key and is followed by a coda featuring the original trumpet and baritone sax dialogue. Cohn's "Third Herd" is a bebop style up-tempo composition based on "I Got Rhythm" chord changes. Herman leads the harmonized reed section through the first sixteen bars of the melody, with brass accompaniment. The bridge is played with unison reeds and harmonized brass, whereas the last eight bars are scored like the first sixteen. The first solo chorus is shared by the baritonist and a tenorist, who both take noteworthy outings. A brief band interlude introduces Touff's bass trumpet solo for sixteen bars in the second chorus. The eight-bar bridge features a call-and-response interchange between Touff and the band, and Herman solos on clarinet for the remaining eight bars. A shout chorus follows that features some exciting high-note trumpet playing over the ensemble and a very musical tenor sax solo on the bridge. The full band returns in a different key to complete the shout chorus, and it modulates again in the coda before an effective drum solo break. The ensemble concludes the chart in a slower tempo with a harmonious ending on the final chord. These two sides reveal the Third Herd as a hard-swinging band with an outstanding rhythm section and excellent tenor saxophone soloists. Although the band's ensemble playing was not at the same level as that of the Second Herd, it was a much more musical and swinging unit. In fact, it can be said that this particular Herd was probably the most swinging Herman-led band in the Swing Era. This same band toured Europe in 1954 and South America (sponsored by the U.S. State Department) in 1958 before its demise.[22] Moreover, it is important to note that the Third Herd won the *Metronome* poll in 1953.[23]

After the Swing Era, Herman continued to lead small groups and big bands with young musicians well into the 1980s. Some of these bands, including the Fourth Herd and the Swingin' Herd, toured the United States and abroad. From 1971, Herman became part of the emerging jazz education movement in this country and gave numerous workshops and performances at educational institutions. In recognition of his contributions, the University of Houston established the Woody Herman Music Archives in 1974. In 1976, a Carnegie Hall concert marked his fortieth year as a bandleader. He also received an honorary doctorate from Berklee College of Music in 1977, and he served as "King of the Zulus" for the 1980 Mardi Gras in New Orleans.[24] Throughout Herman's career as a bandleader, he was often taken for granted as an instrumentalist. According to Simon, "He did not always match the modern styles of some of his band's top players, but he always adapted his playing to the styles in which his bands played."[25] On the other hand, his leadership style was such that musicians liked working for him. His longtime pianist-arranger Nat Pierce once said, "We never feel we're actually working for the man. It's more like working with him. He appreciates what we're doing, and he lets us know it. And the guys appreciate him and respect him. So they work all the harder." Drummer Jake Hanna added, "Woody's flexible. He goes along with the way the band feels instead of sticking strictly to the book. That makes it always interesting and exciting for us. If a man's really blowing, Woody doesn't stop him after eight bars because the arrangement says so. He lets him keep on wailing."[26] Herman's flexibility, in large part, contributed the most to his success. His ability to adjust to the various personalities and talents of his musicians made it possible for him to lead effectively without asserting his dominance as a leader. His flexibility in adjusting his music to the times always kept his bands sounding fresh throughout his fifty-year history as a bandleader. Furthermore, the most important aspect of Herman's leadership ability was his organizational skill. He once told jazz journalist Gene Lees, "I'm a good organizer and a good editor."[27] In fact, his leadership ability was his most outstanding trait and contribution to jazz. As with noted drummer and bandleader Art Blakey, Woody Herman's bands served the jazz world as a traveling college or university in which large numbers of musicians received their professional music training. According to Schuller, "The list of Herman alumni reads like a *Who's Who* of modern jazz."[28] In sum, Walker states, "Herman has to be rated as one of the musical giants of the swing era, and probably deserves a special award for durability."[29] When one listens to Herman's bands from the era, one will undoubtedly conclude that Woody Herman was a true master of swing.

BILLY STRAYHORN

Composer-arranger-pianist Billy Strayhorn was born on November 29, 1915, in Dayton, Ohio, and was raised in Hillsboro, North Carolina, before his family moved to Pittsburgh, where he attended school.[30] Both of his parents were born in the South. His mother attended Shaw University in North Carolina and his father, a laborer, grew up in a family that had been exposed to art and music. As a result, Strayhorn's inclination for culture and music became evident at a young age. His mother encouraged him to pursue his talent in music because it could lead to a career that most African-American men were unable to attain at the time.[31] Strayhorn, with his family's support, studied music extensively and developed his ability to write both music and lyrics. As a Westinghouse High School student, he was known as a pianist and composer who had an interest in European music. In fact, he performed Grieg's *Piano Concerto in A Minor* at his high school graduation.[32] Shortly after graduation, he wrote a musical called *Fantastic Rhythm* that the school performed in 1935. The show was obviously influenced by Gershwin, and the Strayhorn standard, "My Little Brown Book," came from the musical. However, Strayhorn wrote his most famous song, "Lush Life," in 1936. According to author Gerald Early, "With this song, Strayhorn showed that he could write popular songs with original and clever melodies, as well as lyrics that could combine sophistication with emotional weight."[33] By this time, Strayhorn had developed an interest in jazz with the help of two friends—Bill Esch, who taught him arranging, and Mickey Serima, with whom he performed. Strayhorn also led a band that worked around Pittsburgh in both black and white establishments. At this juncture, we must remember that jazz attracted young musicians commercially, artistically, and socially in the thirties. Therefore, Strayhorn was able to meet other ambitious and artistic young people like himself.[34]

As Strayhorn's interest in jazz developed further, he listened mainly to the recordings of Duke Ellington.[35] Strayhorn had established himself as a pianist and composer in Pittsburgh by the age of twenty-three, and many local people thought it was time for him to branch out and meet some stars in the business. This finally happened on December 1, 1938, when Strayhorn was introduced to Ellington by one of his friends who was the nephew of Gus Greenlee. Greenlee was a big-time African-American entrepreneur in Pittsburgh who knew Duke Ellington.[36] Strayhorn played some of his songs for Ellington, who was impressed and later hired Strayhorn as his protégé to write lyrics for some of his tunes. After joining the Ellington fold, Strayhorn's first assignment was to write arrangements for a Johnny Hodges–led small-group recording session. Following that session, Ellington assigned his entire small-group arranging duties to Strayhorn, who also ended up writing charts for the band's vocalists.[37] Afterward, Strayhorn became "Ellington's chief arranger, associate composer, and musical alter ego."[38] Strayhorn and Ellington had a long and productive working relationship that allowed Strayhorn the freedom to write what he wanted for Ellington's orchestra. According to Strayhorn, during a 1956 interview with *Downbeat*, "There are no restrictions on my writing....There are no restrictions either on material or on length. That's why I like working for Duke." Strayhorn further indicated that he and Ellington had occasional disagreements but were always able to resolve their issues amicably.[39] The main reason Strayhorn had the freedom to write whatever he wanted was that Ellington was not only his boss and collaborator but also his patron, and fully supported him. For example, during the ASCAP ban of 1941, Strayhorn collaborated with Mercer Ellington and composed a new book for the orchestra. The result was one of Strayhorn's most famous tunes, "Take the 'A' Train."[40]

Strayhorn's collaborative work with Ellington produced some of America's most important music, such as "A Drum Is a Woman," "Such Sweet Thunder," and "The Far East Suite."[41] Although Strayhorn had the freedom to write whatever he wanted, there were some restrictions regarding his collaborations with Ellington. For example, Strayhorn always had to respond to Ellington's sudden phone calls when he was traveling on the road with his orchestra. One such call took place when Ellington had to complete a suite commissioned by the Great South Bay Jazz Festival. During that phone call, Ellington said, "We're writing this suite," and Strayhorn replied, "We are?" Ellington said, "I need three or four minutes in D-flat. Do it."[42] With only three days to complete the assignment, Strayhorn met Ellington's deadline. When the band arrived at the festival to perform the suite, there was no opportunity for a rehearsal. The parts were distributed to the musicians backstage, who studied them individually just before they went onstage to perform the suite. Strayhorn had written the middle section of the three-part suite and, as the band played that section, Ellington laughed while he conducted. In the audience, Strayhorn laughed along with him, because his section was actually a development of the theme Ellington had written in the suite's first section. Ellington once remarked about the unique empathy between them by stating: "And then Strayhorn came along and he broke the code."[43]

The musical empathy between Strayhorn and Ellington was exceptional, and many people felt that it was difficult to distinguish between the arranging and composing styles of these two individuals. However, some musicians and historians have a different view. For example, bassist Aaron Bell, a one-time Ellingtonian, once pointed out that the band could always tell the difference between Ellington's and Strayhorn's compositions. According to Bell, "There's so much more sensitivity and complexity in Strayhorn's compositions than Ellington's."[44] Noted journalist Stanley Dance added, "Where Ellington tended to rely more heavily on the blues, Strayhorn was thoroughly schooled in impressionists like Debussy and Ravel." Dance further described the stylistic difference between Ellington and Strayhorn:

> Part of the joy of Ellington compositions like "Rockin' in Rhythm" or "Dancers in Love" is the devil-may-care fashion in which one section almost randomly follows one another, in the stop-and-start tradition of the great stride pianists. In Strayhorn's pieces, everything fits together much more organically. And although Strayhorn's music could stomp, moan, and swing no less convincingly than Ellington's (particularly in his most famous composition "Take the 'A' Train"), there was always a greater tenderness.[45]

Schuller agrees with both Bell and Dance and describes four characteristics that identify Strayhorn's work as follows: His writing makes use of brighter and leaner orchestral textures that emphasize high-register sounds and distinct voicings. Strayhorn's arrangements tend to emphasize lightweight densities that result from transparent instrumental voicings and a subtle use of dynamics. He employs a staccato writing style in faster tempos, especially for the brass section, to punctuate his bright sonorities. Much of Strayhorn's writing was influenced by early twentieth-century French composers, such as Ravel, Debussy, and Darius Milhaud. This influence also included Occidental contrapuntal styles, which are reflected in Strayhorn's compositions such as "On a Turquoise Cloud," "I Let a Song Go out of My Heart" and "Fugue-a-ditty."[46]

As we look further into Strayhorn's own individual creativity, we see that he viewed lyric writing and music composition as one complete process. During an interview with Stanley Dance in 1967, Strayhorn was asked whether he wrote music or lyrics first. He replied, "When I write lyrics, I write music and lyrics together. Because, you know, you have to bend them. Or I do. And not at the piano, but when I'm walking along the street. That's the time to polish off a phrase, when you're walking, and it sings well, naturally." Strayhorn also believed that tune titles are significant. He once said, "They're kind of psychological." In describing the derivation of "Take the 'A' Train," Strayhorn told Dance the following:

> The reason we gave it that title was because they were building the Sixth Avenue subway at that time, and they added new trains, including the "D" Train, which came up to Harlem, to 145th St., and then turned off and went to the Bronx, but the "A" Train kept straight on up to 200-and-something St. People got confused. They'd take the "D" Train, and it would go to Harlem and 145th St., but the next stop would be on Eighth Avenue under the Polo

Grounds, and the one after that would be in the Bronx. So I said I was writing directions—take the "A" Train to Sugar Hill. The "D" Train was really messing up everybody. I heard so many times about housewives who ended up in the Bronx and had to turn around and come back.[47]

It is important to note that Strayhorn's original idea of "'A' Train" was inspired by the work of Fletcher Henderson. Strayhorn pointed out the fact that Henderson "wrote so many wonderful arrangements," and added, "One day, I was thinking about his style, the way he wrote for trumpets, trombones, and saxophones, and I thought I would try something like that."[48] "Take the 'A' Train," of course, is Strayhorn's [crowning] achievement. Schuller's comments about this composition are most complimentary. He states, "Its unforgettable theme line is truly inspired, with, among other things, that fetching augmented chord in the third and fourth bars, and the whole piece has a sense of inevitability that marks the true masterwork...And, remarkably, one never tires of hearing it."[49]

Another example of Strayhorn's considerable skill as a composer is his advanced harmonic treatment of "Chelsea Bridge," one of his finest compositions. The first part of the "Chelsea" theme is supported with "floating" chromatic harmonies that reveal the influence of impressionism on Strayhorn's writing.[50] Gerald Early commented on Strayhorn's exposure to Occidental music theory and popular songs as well as his ability to write both melody and lyrics, concluding that "Strayhorn was a remarkable technician and a craftsman of exceptional skill."[51] And along with his technical mastery of music, Strayhorn demonstrated in "Take the 'A' Train" the true essence of swing. As Schuller points out, it became "Ellington's band theme, ushering in thousands of concerts, dances, and club engagements." Furthermore, Schuller raises the following question: "But what other bandleader and composer would have ceded the band's theme spot to another composer?"[52] From this question, we can easily conclude that the quality of Strayhorn's music speaks for itself.

Despite Strayhorn's immense contributions as a composer-arranger for the Ellington band, he rarely appeared in public with the ensemble, except for a European tour in 1950. He occasionally played piano duets with Ellington, mostly at private parties or gatherings. They also recorded their original piano duet composition, "Tonk," at an RCA recording session and at a two-piano session for Mercer Records.[53] And Strayhorn occasionally recorded with the band. Two examples are "Flamingo," recorded in 1940, and "Rocks in My Bed" in 1941. Both of these recordings featured vocalist Herb Jeffries. Surprisingly, Strayhorn recorded more frequently with Ellington's sidemen.[54] Strayhorn also rarely recorded as a leader. His first album, *The Peaceful Side*, was recorded in 1961 in Paris for Capitol Records. The album consists of ten tunes that had been recorded previously by the Ellington band. These tunes were reworked and include duo versions of "Passion Flower" and "Something to Live For." One of the album's highlights is a beautiful string arrangement of "A Flower Is a Lonesome Thing." Strayhorn's second recording as a leader, entitled "Lush Life," was recorded in 1964–1965 for Red Baron and produced by Duke and Mercer Ellington. The CD contains twenty-one tracks that feature the Ellington big band, a small group, Strayhorn's solo piano, and a duo in which Strayhorn accompanies vocalist Ozzie Bailey. The most notable track is "Lush Life," on which Strayhorn accompanies his own vocals. According to Andrew Gilbert, this CD "is absolutely essential for those interested in Strayhorn or Ellington."[55] Dance adds, "Almost every aspect of Strayhorn's creativity is to be found in this set. The lyricist, the singer, the composer, the arranger, the piano player (as soloist and accompanist) are all here."[56]

The 1980s saw a resurgence of Strayhorn's work. Artists such as Toshiko Akiyoshi, Art Farmer, and Marian McPartland dedicated full albums to Strayhorn that featured his compositions. In 1991, Joe Henderson recorded a CD entitled *Lush Life* that featured Strayhorn's music with trumpeter Wynton Marsalis, pianist Stephen Scott, bassist Christian McBride, and drummer Gregory Hutchinson. It is important to note that after a number of years as one of jazzdom's top tenor saxophonists, Henderson finally won a Grammy with *Lush Life*. More importantly, Strayhorn's unique contribution to music as an arranger in the mid-forties was duly recognized by *Esquire* with two Silver Awards.[57] However, as Leonard Feather states, "The extent to which he gained recognition during his years with us was never commensurate with his contribution." In describing some of the reasons why Strayhorn did not receive wider recognition, Feather states,

> Billy Strayhorn remained, in terms of worldwide fame, virtually unrecognized, not because of his association with Duke Ellington but in spite of it. The true reason was the nature of the man. He never chased after fame of the famous, nor after rainbows or pots of gold. This sensitive, gregarious, witty, modest little man was impressed neither by royalty nor by royalty statements. He was neither anxious to stay in the background nor eager to push himself into the foreground. "Who wrote that arrangement?" I would ask him. "You or Duke?" The answer was always predictable. It would be, "Oh, that was done around 1963 in San Francisco," or some similar evasion.

In concluding his thoughts, Feather writes, "For most creators in jazz, music to one degree or another is profession, business, livelihood. To Strayhorn… music remained forever a passion—his one and only love."[58]

Unfortunately, Strayhorn's passion for music ended when he passed away in 1967 at the age of fifty-one after having been diagnosed with cancer two years earlier.[59] During Strayhorn's relatively short life, he created a body of work during the Swing Era that has had a significant impact on American popular music. By all accounts, he was a humble individual with a great talent for music and a keen appreciation for the arts. It goes without saying that Billy Strayhorn was not only a gentle giant, he was also a consummate master of swing.

TEDDY WILSON

Pianist-arranger-bandleader Teddy Wilson was born in Austin, Texas, on November 24, 1912 and grew up in Tuskegee, Alabama. His father served as head of the English department at Tuskegee University, where his mother was the chief librarian.[60] He began studying piano at age six and took up violin later. After realizing that the piano was not as difficult to play as the violin, he returned to it and learned the fundamentals by the time he reached his early teens. Wilson discovered jazz during high school and began learning recorded solos by Earl Hines and Fats Waller on the piano while playing oboe and clarinet in the school band. After high school, he studied music at Talladega College, where he learned about harmony, composition, and the discipline of European music. At that point, he began to relate the music of Hines and Waller to the basic rules of theory and harmony.[61] Wilson made a visit to Chicago in 1928 and became influenced by the jazz he heard. Afterward, he decided to embark on a career in music and returned to Chicago, where he joined Speed Webb's big band a year later.[62] Wilson subsequently replaced Art Tatum in Milton Senior's quartet in Toledo, Ohio, where he had met Tatum. He later had the opportunity to play with Tatum and learned his approach to the piano, which became a major influence on his style. Wilson traveled to Chicago as a member of Senior's band and remained there in 1931 to work with Erskine Tate and other local bandleaders. He later recorded and toured with Louis Armstrong in early 1933 and returned to Chicago again to work with Jimmie Noone a few months later.[63]

Wilson subbed for Earl Hines at the Grand Terrace Ballroom in 1933. During a live broadcast from the ballroom, noted producer John Hammond heard Wilson and realized that he "was absolutely unique, with a cleaner and more elegant sound, never flashy but swinging, with an excellent left hand."[64] From that point, Hammond became Wilson's biggest supporter and recommended him to Benny Carter. Wilson moved to New York to join Carter and recorded with his small group, the Chocolate Dandies, and with his big band in September 1933. A year later, Wilson worked with Willie Bryant's big band until 1935, when Hammond arranged recording dates with Benny Goodman and Red Norvo. Hammond also introduced Wilson to Billie Holiday, which resulted in a number of recordings that were made between 1935 and 1942 and are now considered jazz classics. Wilson made significant contributions to Billie Holiday's success by selecting repertoire, organizing and rehearsing small groups, and arranging music that fit her unique vocal style. The various small ensembles he formed for Holiday's recordings contained some of the most prominent musicians of the Swing Era, including Lester Young.[65] Hammond reintroduced Wilson to Benny Goodman in 1935, and the two musicians played together informally during a jam session at a private party. Wilson joined Goodman's trio a year later and became the first African American to play in the clarinetist's group as a regular member. As the reader can well imagine, this caused quite a stir and generated a great deal of publicity.[66] Nevertheless, Wilson remained with Goodman's trio (with Gene Krupa) and quartet (with Lionel Hampton) until February 1939.[67] Wilson's tenure with Benny Goodman obviously helped to enhance his stature with a wide audience. Wilson's high level of visibility in the music world and his modern piano style made him one of the most celebrated musicians in the Swing Era.

With respect to Wilson's piano style, it was noted earlier that his approach was strongly influenced by the work of Earl Hines and Art Tatum. In comparing Wilson's playing to that of Hines and Tatum, James Collier states,

> His manner was much lighter and thinner than Hines'. He eschewed the broken figures and cross-rhythms that were so big an element in Hines' playing, concentrating almost entirely on developing long lines of single notes, with occasional forays into patterns of right-hand octaves. His bass, too, is simpler than Hines', at times consisting of single notes walked up and down the keyboard. Later on, he came under the influence of Art Tatum, and began using long right-hand runs, especially downward, in the Tatum manner. Occasionally, there are traces of rhythmic stiffness in his work, but he is neither flashy nor sentimental. His is a light, direct style, and it had great appeal for other young pianists.[68]

Wilson's incomparable work as a pianist with Goodman and as music director for Billie Holiday inevitably led to the next step of forming his own big band in 1939. The band won an excellent reputation among musicians and prompted Billy Strayhorn to say that Wilson's band was "the most musical and cleanest big band outside of Ellington's."[69] However, the band did not survive because of the leader's reserved personality.[70] In fact, Wilson himself admitted that the band had little commercial impact because of "a lack of showmanship."[71] From that point, he concentrated mostly on leading small groups with which he had excelled during his earlier collaborations with Billie Holiday. In 1940, Wilson formed a sextet with trumpeter Bill Coleman, clarinetist-saxophonist Jimmy Hamilton, trombonist Benny Morton, bassist Al Hall, and drummer Yank Porter. The group first performed at New York's Café Society in July and opened the second Café Society uptown later that same year. Except for a brief return to the Goodman quartet for about a month or so in 1941, Wilson continued to lead his own sextet. The group underwent some personnel changes during the same year. Emmett Berry replaced Coleman, and Israel Crosby became the group's bassist. Shortly thereafter, bassist Johnny Williams replaced Crosby, and later that year, Edmond Hall succeeded Hamilton and J. C. Heard took

Porter's slot as the drummer. Except for a few additional changes in personnel, the sextet continued, with long stands at both Café Society establishments alternating with tours. In May 1944, Wilson disbanded the sextet
and worked with Benny Goodman's sextet until 1945.[72]

Wilson continued to record as a leader and assembled another sextet
(Teddy Wilson and his All-Stars) for a studio session in August 1945 for
Musicraft Records. The group's personnel consisted of trumpeter Buck
Clayton, tenorist Ben Webster, guitarist Al Casey, bassist Al Hall, and
drummer J. C. Heard. The sextet recorded five sides, including "If Dreams
Come True," "I Can't Get Started," "Stompin' at the Savoy," and Wilson's
"Blues Too." The session opens with Buck Clayton embellishing the melody
of "If Dreams Come True" and Ben Webster playing a countermelody within
the tune's formal structure (A-B-A-B). Webster plays the first solo with
melodic phrases that literally flow across the barlines. His characteristic
robust sound displays a dark and lovely timbre. Wilson plays the second
solo, which leans more in Art Tatum's direction, with descending single-
line runs in the right hand. The full ensemble plays a shout chorus based
on a riff in the first [A] section, and Hall plays a walking bass solo on the
bridge. The band returns with the shout chorus for the next [A] section,
which is followed by a four-bar drum solo in the last [B] section. The final
four bars are played via group improvisation to conclude the song.

Casey opens "I Can't Get Started" with an effective unaccompanied intro-
ductory statement. Webster embellishes the melody for sixteen bars (A-A),
and Clayton plays in a similar manner on the bridge, with Webster carrying a
simple countermelody. Webster solos with a flowing melodic line for the
last eight bars (A) of the tune's structure (A-A-B-A). Wilson solos for twenty-
four bars (A-A-B) with a fine balance of single-line phrases in the right hand
and left-handed chordal accompaniment. The full band returns with the last
[A] section, where Clayton stays pretty close to the melody until the last bar.

"Stompin' at the Savoy" is played up-tempo, with Clayton and Webster
sharing the melody for sixteen bars (A-A). Webster solos on the bridge [B],
and the last [A] section returns with trumpet and sax at the helm. Wilson
plays the first solo with single-line phrases in the [A] sections and Hines-styled
chordal playing in the bridge [B]. Webster solos during the next chorus in his
usual relaxed and highly melodic manner. Buck Clayton plays his first full
solo chorus here with acute skill and aplomb. The sextet returns with a
riff-style shout chorus in the tune's three [A] sections and an articulate bass
solo on the bridge [B]. The piece ends in the last measure of the third
[A] section.

Wilson's "Blues Too" is basically a solo vehicle for piano, trumpet, guitar
and saxophone, with one twelve-bar chorus for each. Al Casey's guitar solo
shows that he is on par with the rest of the group. In the last twelve bars,
Clayton plays a commonly known blues riff, with Webster answering during
the first four bars; the last eight bars are concluded with group improvisation

to round out the tune. The group's high performance level at this session is obviously a reflection of Wilson's consummate skill as a bandleader.

In 1946, Wilson accepted a studio position with CBS Radio in New York while leading his own trios from 1949 to 1952. He also taught at the Metropolitan and Julliard music schools from 1945 to 1952 as one of the country's first premier jazz artists to work at major music institutions. He toured Europe between 1952 and 1953 before returning to CBS as a radio show host and leader of a trio with Milt Hinton and Jo Jones. Wilson invited various guest artists to the show until he left CBS at the end of the Swing Era.[73] As we look closely at his career, it is clear that he was one of the most talented and versatile musicians of the entire Swing Era. He successfully synthesized elements from the piano stylings of Hines, Tatum, and Waller into his own distinct and elegant style. Wilson's symmetrical melodic lines and efficient use of tenths in the left hand made him one of the most influential pianists of the era.[74] On the other hand, Wilson's venerable skills as an arranger and bandleader have been mostly overlooked. If we consider his contributions to Billie Holiday's creative output alone, it is easy to recognize that his talent in these two areas is certainly deserving of wider recognition.

Teddy Wilson continued to make lasting contributions in jazz beyond the Swing Era. He was featured as himself in the film *The Benny Goodman Story* and toured with his trio in the late fifties. He also rejoined Goodman for reunions at the Newport Jazz Festival, which became the Kool Jazz Festival when it moved to New York, and for tours in the Soviet Union during the sixties and seventies. Concurrently, he performed throughout the United States, as well as in Europe, Japan, South America, and Australia. He also continued to record during this period and appeared in several films. Wilson performed again in Japan in 1980 and played with Benny Carter occasionally between 1978 and 1981. Wilson later appeared on the *Swing Reunion* television shows in 1985 and in *Benny Goodman: Let's Dance: All-Star Reunion* in 1986 prior to his death that same year.[75] Hopefully, future jazz historians will review Teddy Wilson's work during the Swing Era in depth and further document the numerous contributions he made to jazz history. After all, during the height of Wilson's career in 1939, Benny Goodman called him "the greatest musician in dance music today, irrespective of instrument."[76]

NOTES

1. Leonard Feather, "Ella Today (And Yesterday Too)," *Downbeat* 32, no. 24 (1965): 21.

2. Quoted in Feather, "Ella Today," p. 21.

3. Ibid.

4. Hannah Wong, "LC Collection Tells Ella Fitzgerald Story," *LC Information Bulletin* 56, no. 13 (1997): 199–200.

5. Gary Giddins, *Visions of Jazz: The First Century* (New York: Oxford University Press, 1998), pp. 197–200.

6. John McDonough, "What Becomes a Legend Most: Ella Fitzgerald," *Downbeat* 60, no. 6 (1993): 24.

7. Feather and Gitler, *Encyclopedia of Jazz*, p. 226.

8. Wong, "Ella Fitzgerald Story," pp. 276–277.

9. Lolis Eric Elie, "The Defining of Miss Ella," *The Times-Picayune*, June 24, 1996: B-1.

10. Steve Knopper, ed., *Music Hound Swing: The Essential Guide* (Farmington Hills, MI: Visible Ink Press, 1999), p. 140.

11. Frank Stacy, "Herman's Is Finest Ofay Swing Band," *Downbeat* 12, no. 5 (1945): 9.

12. Knopper, *Music Hound Swing*, p. 140.

13. Leo Walker, *The Big Band Almanac* (New York: Da Capo Press, 1989), pp. 186–191.

14. George T. Simon, *The Big Bands*, pp. 247–248.

15. Walker, *The Big Band Almanac*, pp. 190–191.

16. Simon, *The Big Bands*, pp. 249–251.

17. Ibid., p. 252.

18. Ibid., pp. 254–255.

19. Barry Kernfeld, ed., *The New Grove Dictionary of Jazz*, vol. 2 (New York: Macmillan Press, 2002), p. 226.

20. Ibid., pp. 226–227.

21. Stan Brit, liner notes to *Woody Herman: Blowin' Up a Storm* (Affinity AFS 1043, 1987).

22. Kernfeld, *The New Grove Dictionary* (2002), 2:227.

23. Leonard Feather, *The Encyclopedia of Jazz* (New York: Bonanza Books, 1960), p. 253.

24. Kernfeld, *The New Grove Dictionary* (2002), 2:227.

25. Simon, *The Big Bands*, p. 250.

26. Ibid., pp. 245–247.

27. Ibid., p. 247.

28. Gunther Schuller, *The Swing Era: The Development of Jazz, 1930–1945* (New York: Oxford University Press, 1989), p. 744.

29. Walker, *The Big Band Almanac*, p. 191.

30. Feather and Gitler, *Encyclopedia of Jazz*, p. 626.

31. Gerald Early, "Passion Flower," *The New Republic*, September 30, 1996: p. 44.

32. Feather and Gitler, *Encyclopedia of Jazz*, p. 626.

33. Early, "Passion Flower," p. 44.

34. Ibid.

35. Feather and Gitler, *Encyclopedia of Jazz*, p. 626.

36. Early, "Passion Flower," p. 44.

37. John S. Wilson, "Billy Strayhorn: Alter Ego for the Duke," *New York Times*, June 6, 1965: 13X.

38. John S. Wilson, "The Duke's Alter Ego," *New York Times*, June 25, 1967: D21.

39. Frank Tracy, ed., "Swee'pea," *Downbeat* 23, no. 11 (1956): 15.

40. Early, "Passion Flower," p. 42.

41. Ibid., p. 45.

42. Wilson, "Billy Strayhorn," p. 13X.

43. Ibid.

44. Quoted in Will Friedwald, "Silent Partner," *New York Times*, July 14, 1996: 8.

45. Ibid.

46. Schuller, *The Swing Era*, p. 134.

47. Stanley Dance, "An Interview with Billy Strayhorn," *Downbeat* 34, no. 4 (1967): 19.

48. Ibid.

49. Schuller, *The Swing Era*, p. 136.

50. Ibid., p. 135.

51. Early, "Passion Flower," p. 45.

52. Schuller, *The Swing Era*, p. 136.

53. Feather and Gitler, *Encyclopedia of Jazz*, pp. 626–627.

54. Ian Carr, et al., eds., *Jazz: The Rough Guide* (London: Penguin Books, 1995), p. 615.

55. Andrew Gilbert, *Music Hound Swing*, p. 287.

56. Stanley Dance, liner notes to *Billy Strayhorn: Lush Life* (Red Baron AK 52760, 1992).

57. Feather and Gitler, *Encyclopedia of Jazz*, pp. 626–627.

58. Leonard Feather, "Feather's Nest," *Downbeat* 34, no. 15 (1967): 12.

59. Friedwald, "Silent Partner," p. 18.

60. Carr, *The Rough Guide*, p. 703.

61. John McDonough, "Teddy Wilson: History in the Flesh," *Downbeat* 44, no. 4 (1977): 17.

62. Carr, *The Rough Guide*, p. 703.

63. Kernfeld, *The New Grove Dictionary* (2002), 3:969.

64. Carr, *The Rough Guide*, p. 703.

65. Kernfeld, *The New Grove Dictionary* (2002), 3:969.

66. Carr, *The Rough Guide*, pp. 703–704.

67. Kernfeld, *The New Grove Dictionary* (2002), 3:969.

68. James L. Collier, *The Making of Jazz*, p. 214.

69. Carr, *The Rough Guide*, p. 704.

70. Kernfeld, *The New Grove Dictionary* (2002), 3:969.

71. Carr, *The Rough Guide*, p. 704.

72. Kernfeld, *The New Grove Dictionary* (2002), 3:969–970.

73. Ibid.

74. Feather and Gitler, *Encyclopedia of Jazz*, p. 703.

75. Kernfeld, *The New Grove Dictionary* (2002), 3:970–971.

76. Carr, *The Rough Guide*, p. 704.

Chapter 3

♪

Big Bands

Big bands dominated the American popular scene at the beginning of World War II with performances in the country's top venues and regular, commercially sponsored, remote radio broadcasts. Even during the war, when gas and tire rations made travel difficult, big bands retained their popularity with the American public. The war industries pumped large sums of money into the economy, and Americans spent a lot of their disposable income on entertainment and amusement. However, things started to shift when the American Federation of Musicians (AFM) initiated a strike against the recording industry in 1942. The strike eventually had an adverse effect on big bands and on instrumental musicians in general. Nevertheless, conclusion of the AFM strike and a rebound in the economy after the war gave big bands a boost toward regaining some of their popularity. By the mid-forties, however, this popularity had begun to fade, with another slump in the economy and changing music styles. These economic and musical style changes made it possible for vocalists and small groups to take the place of big bands and eventually dominate the music industry.

On the other hand, a number of big bands survived the 1940s and retained their success beyond the Swing Era. Many new and established bands failed, while others became even more successful in the 1950s. A number of bandleaders faced the economic times by lowering their performance fees and the salaries of their sidemen. Other leaders changed or maintained their styles and played music suitable for dancing. At one end of the spectrum, some leaders adapted the music of European composers to their overall styles and promoted the concept of concert jazz. On the opposite end, several leaders played hard-swinging jazz that pleased both dancers and listeners. A few leaders even formed big bands that played bebop, while others created a swing style that included elements of bebop and/or Western concert music. Still another group of leaders formed a style that resulted from a marriage between swing and rhythm and blues. In effect, the forties and fifties saw swing bands branch out into several different stylistic directions. This diversification had a positive effect on jazz, despite the fact that these large organizations decreased significantly in number.

The bands discussed in this chapter represent a wide variety of music styles played between 1942 and 1955, as well as race and gender differences among some of the leaders and musicians. In some cases, discussions of different band styles consist of statements made by the leaders themselves during interviews with jazz journalists. Some interviews reveal information about the music and business philosophies that contributed to the success of these bandleaders. In addition, this chapter contains information from reviews of pertinent recordings and live performances at some of the nation's top ballrooms, hotels, and nightclubs. This chapter also presents a discussion of different bandleaders and their bands' styles, arrangements/compositions, soloists, and performances during the era. The variety of viewpoints discussed here is provided to enable the reader to form his or her own conclusions about big bands in the Later Swing Era. Furthermore, it is important that jazz journalism document balanced viewpoints about some of the contributions big bands made during the era. These bands now hold a special place in history, because they served as a training ground for numerous musicians who eventually made notable contributions to a variety of modern music genres.

RAY ANTHONY

Ray Anthony started his band in 1946 in New York City. Before forming one of the most disciplined and well-dressed bands of the time, Ray began his career as a professional musician at the age of fourteen with Al Donahue's band. In 1941 he joined Glenn Miller and, after several months, moved on to Jimmy Dorsey's band, where he remained until signing up for the navy early in World War II. During the war, Anthony became the leader of one of the best military bands in the Pacific.[1] Anthony's civilian band became one of the most popular postwar bands in America primarily because of his philosophy as a bandleader. He had a businesslike attitude and believed that big bands should play music that is danceable and entertaining. Of course, his philosophy was based on the reality that music is a business. According to Anthony himself, "There are three ways to make it in the band business. One is to crusade and go broke enough times so that luck has to turn in your favor. Second is to come in on a boom time in the business with a moderate amount of luck on your side. The third way is to take an accepted style, gain acceptance with it and then begin your insertion of the modern simultaneously."[2]

The accepted style Anthony refers to was that of Glenn Miller. The most significant aspect of this style is the clarinet-led reed section. Anthony's trumpet section, led by Jack Laubach, was one of the best at the time, and the trombone section was considered full and exciting. In fact, at that time, Bill Coss believed that "Ray [had] one of the most musical bands in the country."[3] Anthony's style is summarized by Ken Burke, who wrote, "His band style consisted of reed-oriented, Glenn Miller–era standards with [the] brassier new pop sounds of the growing rock-n-roll scene."[4] Ray Anthony shared a more in-depth description of his style with *Metronome* during an interview in 1952:

> The primary reason for my having the type of band which I have is that I have always believed, ever since my days with Glenn Miller, in having a universal appeal to the public. We play good music, but we stay down the middle. With Lombardo at one extreme and Stan Kenton at the other extreme, our aim is to stay halfway between. We try to give the public the melody, written in good, musical arrangements, the melody with a strong beat. As a result, our jump arrangements are generally written in two-beat, but not a corny two-beat. We have followed up on some of the Lunceford two-beat style. We have used the clarinet lead sound in the reeds on ballads because we felt that it is a sound which the public wants to hear. We have, however, combined the reed sound with modern brass sounds to create the ballad style which has been identified with Ray Anthony. I feel that by staying down the middle, playing good music, and strong arrangements, we are able to reach the largest portion of musical tastes in the public today.[5]

The sound of Anthony's band was due, in part, to the work of arranger George Williams (who wrote all the charts) and instrumentalists such as saxophonists Buddy Wise and Billy Usselton. Anthony's Harry James–styled trumpet playing also added to the successful sound of the band, which reached its height with hits such as "Sentimental Me," "Count Every Star," and "Harbor Lights" for Capitol Records in 1950. In fact, "The Bunny Hop" really hit it big by inspiring a national dance craze. Anthony's own popularity reached even greater heights when he co-wrote the theme for the hit television show *Dragnet* in 1953. His popularity later moved with him to Hollywood, where he appeared in over fifteen movies in the fifties. He continued leading his big band through the late fifties, until he found maintaining it too difficult.[6]

TEX BENEKE

Tex Beneke's career began with territory bands in Texas and Oklahoma. In 1938, Beneke's life changed dramatically when Glenn Miller hired him to join his orchestra on the recommendation of Gene Krupa. In a relatively short period of time, Beneke became a prominent figure in the Miller band, where his saxophone playing was featured on "In the Mood," and his singing on "Chattanooga Choo Choo." He also sang duets with the band's vocalist, Marion Hutton, appeared with the band in a 1941 film, and became popular as an individual musician. When Miller disbanded in 1942 to serve in the army, Beneke toured with the Modernaires before joining the navy and directing a dance orchestra in Oklahoma.[7] After the war ended, Glenn Miller's widow selected Beneke to resurrect and lead the Miller band in January 1946. At that time, the Miller sound was still quite popular among music lovers, and the band regularly played to large audiences. For example, when the band opened at the Hollywood Palladium in 1947, there was a record-breaking crowd of 6,750 dancers on the floor.[8]

Understandably, Beneke was proud of the fact that he fronted one of the most successful dance orchestras in the forties and early fifties. In a 1948 interview with George Simon, Tex asserted, "The band is one thousand percent better now than it was when we first started!" He added, "The trombones were always good; now they're the best section. The trumpets with Pete Condoli in there are better than they ever were. The saxes are the tail end. What's more, it swings more than ever, much more than the old Miller civilian band ever did. That band never swung!" In response to Beneke's statement, Simon commented, "The Miller band never did swing too much, to be sure, but, judging from what Beneke and his boys have been putting down on wax, they swing even less. Just about all you hear, in fact, is one ballad after another, each one done in very much the same way." In fairness to Beneke, however, Simon's conversation with the band's arrangers, Norm Layden and Perry Burgett, revealed the following explanation for its style:

> A large part of our records have been influenced by the man at Victor (Eli Oberstein). It's a matter of past associations. That's why you find us getting those tunes. They throw any song about anything west of the Mississippi at us and expect us to make it sound good. They all scream that we have to stick to the old Miller style. Even the ballroom operators kick if we don't have the trumpets playing "boo-wah, boo-wah" all the time. We've got to make money. We can't afford to try to be progressive or anything like that. There are too many people in our organization for us to take chances.[9]

In spite of front-office control of the Miller band, Beneke served as a good leader as his own reputation continued to grow. In the early fifties, he decided to terminate his contract with that organization and lead his own band, known as "Tex Beneke and His Orchestra, Playing the Music Made Famous by Glenn Miller."[10] Although the Beneke organization was a commercial success, some critics felt that the band did not grow artistically because it was always looking back at Glenn Miller.[11] Miller, on the other hand, always looked ahead and strived to develop his band and musical style as an astute entrepreneur-musician.[12]

TINY BRADSHAW

Tiny Bradshaw formed his first big band in 1934 and continued to lead large and small ensembles into the fifties. Bradshaw, a vocalist and drummer, attended Wilberforce University in Ohio, where he sang with the Collegians, directed by Horace Henderson. In 1932 Bradshaw moved to New York and played with Marion Hardy's Alabamians, the Savoy Bearcats, and the Mills Blue Rhythm Band as a drummer before joining Luis Russell as a singer.[13] Bradshaw later formed his own big band, which made its debut at the Renaissance Ballroom in New York and recorded for the Decca record label. The band also performed in Philadelphia, Chicago, and on some southern tours. Although the band's activity was concentrated mostly on the East Coast and in the Midwest, it gained national prominence with several hit records.[14] When the United States entered World War II, Bradshaw was commissioned as a major and led a large military band that toured the United States and overseas to entertain the troops.[15] In 1944 his civilian big band, which included alto saxophonist Sonny Stitt, resumed recording on the Blue Star, Manor, and Regis labels.

On the Decca recordings (1934–1942), Bradshaw's early style as a vocalist-bandleader resembled in some ways that of Cab Calloway. The style and format generally consisted of the main theme (sung by Bradshaw), a scat solo, instrumental solos, and restatement of the theme. Schuller commented on this "narrow" format by stating that "a lot of good jazz managed to occur" despite Bradshaw's interspersed shouting to urge the instrumental soloists to greater emotional heights. Although many of the band's charts, such as "Darktown Strutters' Ball" and "Ol' Man River" were played in the same tempo, Schuller added that "Bradshaw and his band were a rhythmically exciting, hard-swinging group [and] committed to a strong propulsive swing as the essence of jazz—at a time when so many bands could not swing at all or reserved it only for special up-tempo instrumental numbers."[16] Bradshaw made his last big band recording in 1945 and, in the late forties, moved over into the rhythm-and-blues field and signed with King Records.[17] Along with an increase in the demand for R&B came a rise in Bradshaw's popularity, and between 1949 and 1952, he had hits such as "Gravy Train," "Soft," and "Well Oh Well."[18] Bradshaw, who was quite successful in bridging a connection between blues and jazz, suffered from heart problems and died in 1958. His legacy is best summarized by Schuller, who wrote, "Perhaps the finest tribute to Tiny Bradshaw we can make was that, with jazz and blues always at his side, he was swinging long before swing arrived in full force and long after it had disappeared."[19]

LES BROWN

Les Brown started his first professional band, a twelve-piece orchestra, in New York City in 1938. His orchestra opened at New York's Edison

Hotel in October of that year for a three-month stand at the encouragement of Eli Oberstein, who signed Brown to RCA Victor's Bluebird label. The twelve-piece unit was not overly successful, but it appealed to the hotel's management and booking agent, Joe Glaser, who provided it with his backing and full financial support. Both Oberstein and Glaser saw the potential in Brown and spent a great deal of time and energy promoting his career.[20] As a result, the band played in many of the top theaters and dance venues throughout the East Coast and later in the Midwest.[21] As with most bands at the time, the military took its toll on Brown's orchestra by drafting some of its best musicians. Les was once quoted as saying, "It got so you wouldn't hire a guy unless you weren't sure he was 4-F." In spite of this, the band continued to improve and finally hit its "commercial groove" during a long engagement at Chicago's Blackhawk Restaurant starting in late 1941. The band continued with extended engagements at places such as Chicago's Hotel Sherman, New York's Prestige Room, and the Hotel Pennsylvania; it was also a big hit at the Palladium in Hollywood.[22]

Vocalist Doris Day joined the band in 1939, but left after only a year and returned in 1943. Day's return was a major turning point for Brown. With Day back in the band, the two of them collaborated on "Sentimental Journey," a featured vocal that they recorded in 1944. Of course, the following year, the "Band of Renown" became a national hit. After a couple of highly successful years, Day left the band again in September of 1946 to pursue a movie career, and Brown broke up the band for a couple of months to get some rest.[23] Even though he had originally planned a year's leave from the business, Brown reorganized the band in March 1947 because of contractual obligations with the Palladium. In 1948 Bob Hope recruited Brown to join his high-profile radio and television shows. This association included all of Bob Hope's musical tours. All through the fifties, Brown enjoyed a highly successful career, winning *Downbeat*'s "best dance band" poll and *Billboard*'s "favorite band of 1958" poll, and was voted Number One by *Metronome*.[24]

The sound of Brown's band was achieved by the highly competent arranging skills of Frank Comstock and Bob Higgins.[25] In an interview with educator Mark Fonder in 1990, Les Brown agreed that Comstock and Higgins helped "immeasurably" in developing the band's sound. Brown himself summarized his sound and style best:

> If I had done my own arrangements, I would never have been successful. In the early days we had a heavy four-beat swing but admired the Jimmie Lunceford style and the things Sy Oliver wrote for the Tommy Dorsey band. Our band's sound was never distinctive like Glenn Miller's or Guy Lombardo's with that big vibrato. We strove for a cleanliness and a certain conservativeness that was commercially successful. It was an out-and-out, middle-of- the-road swing. For the most part we played ballads on the pretty side, rather than swinging them

like Benny Goodman did. The critics gave us credit for our clean playing, intonation, and the way we attacked and ended together. Although I started with a 12-piece band in 1938 that has grown and shrunk in size over the years, the instrumentation never went through radical changes. Instead of the four bones we used in 1942, we use three today. We started with three trumpets, but to compete with Goodman and Dorsey, we hired a fourth. The rhythm section was piano, bass, guitar, and drums back then, but today I don't use a guitar at all. I love the sound, but for the work we do now it's superfluous. [26]

Although Brown never referred to himself as a direct contributor to his band's sound and style, his years of experience undoubtedly prepared him to be an effective bandleader.

BILLY ECKSTINE

Vocalist-instrumentalist Billy Eckstine led one of the most innovative big bands in the Later Swing Era. Prior to organizing the band, he gained several years of experience performing in Pittsburgh, Washington, D.C., Buffalo, Detroit, and Chicago before working with Earl Hines' band as a singer and occasional trumpeter from 1939 to 1943.[27] After Eckstine's departure from the Hines band, he performed as a single and included some trumpet playing in his act. At venues such as the Yacht Club on 52nd Street in New York City, he worked opposite the bands of Trummy Young and Dizzy Gillespie. After the Club folded, Gillespie and Budd Johnson urged Eckstine to "get [y]our own band." So in 1944, the Billy Eckstine Orchestra was formed and included several members of the 1943 Earl Hines band—Charlie Parker, trombonist-arranger Jerry Valentine, trumpeters Gail Brockman and "Shorty" McConnell, and saxophonist Tommy Crump. Because of the draft, plans to recruit trombonist Bennie Green and drummer Shadow Wilson did not materialize, and Tommy Crump followed them into the military after only two band rehearsals. Before Eckstine's band was formed, however, he recorded for DeLuxe records as "Billy Eckstine, vocal, accompanied by the DeLuxe All-Stars," which was a studio band. The recording did well, largely because of Eckstine's singing, and he received a one-year contract with DeLuxe before embarking on a southern tour with his band in June 1944.

The original band's trumpet section consisted of Gillespie, Brockman, McConnell, and Eckstine. Charlie Parker and Robert Williams were on alto sax, Lucky Thompson and Gene Ammons were the two tenors, and Leo Parker played baritone. Valentine, Howard Scott, Arnett Sparrow, and Rudy Morrison were the trombone section, while pianist John Malachi, guitarist Connie Wainwright, bassist Tommy Potter, and Art Blakey made up the rhythm section. Eckstine shared the vocal duties with Sarah Vaughn. The aforementioned tour started down the east coast of Florida and proceeded over to Texas, up to Kansas City, and on to St. Louis at the Club Riviera.

According to Eckstine, "It was in St. Louis that we whipped the band together."[28] During that period, the band worked at night and rehearsed all day, playing the arrangements of Gillespie, Valentine, Tadd Dameron, Gil Fuller, and Budd Johnson. Eckstine also picked up some charts from Count Basie and Boyd Raeburn before the tour. The band became a hit with the singing of Eckstine and Sarah Vaughn and grossed $100,000 during its first six months as a unit.[29]

Eckstine's band recorded only one session for DeLuxe, which resulted in two good tracks: Jerry Valentine's "Blowing the Blues Away" and John Malachi's "Opus X." Between May 1945 and late 1946, Eckstine recorded eight sessions for National Records, and over forty tracks have been released from these sessions. Some ardent listeners of Eckstine's music from that period have questioned the quality of those recordings. However, a live recording at the Club Plantation in Los Angeles during February and March of 1945 that captured the band's true quality is available. McCarthy comments on the quality of Eckstine's band in the live recordings:

> The sound is better than that achieved by the studio recordings and, though, a fair proportion of numbers are devoted to vocals by Eckstine or Sarah Vaughn, the backgrounds can be heard. Despite the contingent of modernist soloists, the sound of the band comes essentially from the Late Swing Era. The section scoring is generally conventional. Unlike the Dizzy Gillespie band, which was really far more bop oriented, Eckstine's has high quality ensemble and individual section work...no doubt [due] partly [to] the work of musical director Budd Johnson.... Ensemble interludes are performed cleanly and with fine intonation, leaving no doubt that this was a very good band indeed.[30]

The National sessions were released again in the mid-seventies as "the Savoy Sessions." This writer agrees with McCarthy's opinion of the questionable quality of National's studio recordings. Despite the problems in these mid-forties recordings, however, one can still ascertain the high quality and professionalism of Eckstine's band. These recordings also reveal Eckstine as a competent valve trombonist. Unfortunately, because of the high costs of keeping a big band together, Eckstine disbanded in 1947 and signed with MGM as a single.[31] Drum legend Art Blakey, who stayed with the big band until the end, later stated that "It was one of the most venturesome and stimulating of all modern big bands."[32]

LES ELGART

During the Later Swing Era, Les Elgart fronted two different big bands. The first was started around 1947 and survived until late 1949. The second was organized in 1952 and officially broke up in 1958. Elgart spent his early career in the bands of Bunny Berigan, Hal McIntyre, Charlie Spivak, Woody Herman, and New York's CBS studios before joining the navy.[33]

After military service, Les and his younger brother Larry, who played lead alto sax, formed the first band, with the goal of developing a new sound. Arrangers such as Nelson Riddle, Bill Finnegan, and Ralph Flanagan were recruited to help meet that goal. The band appeared at popular venues such as the Hotel New Yorker and the Pelham Heath Inn at Virginia Beach. There were also performances in Wildwood, New Jersey, and at army camps, as well as a lot of one-nighters, several radio broadcasts, and some recordings. The late forties were tough times for many big bands, and the Elgarts disbanded near the end of the decade. After the band folded, Les worked as a sideman in various bands, made record dates, and served as a contractor for a few singers. Larry also freelanced on record dates, worked with Bobby Byrne, and played for quite a while in the pit band for *Top Banana*.[34]

In 1952, Les, Larry, and saxophonist-arranger Charlie Albertine started the second and more successful band. According to Les, "We felt there was a big need in music for a band that could be aimed at the largest possible segment of the public—a band that could make the best hotel and location jobs without sounding like a society band or an imitation of Glenn Miller." In describing the band's sound, Les stated, "We spent many hours developing our unique sound that emphasized brass and reeds. Our simplistic, clean sound is what made us popular, both on records and on the dance floors."[35] Leo Walker adds that "Les' unique sound was partially due to the fact that no piano was used."[36] According to Larry, he and Charlie actually did most of the work in developing the band's sound:

> Charlie Albertine and I spent many hours a day for months developing my own concept of sound and tonality, with emphasis on bass trombone. We brought in such arrangers as Al Cohn, Bill Finnegan, and John Murtaugh and spent much time developing our sounds in the studio of Rudy Van Gelder, over in Jersey. So, when I did raise some money to cut a record of what became *Sophisticated Swing* in 1953 on Columbia Records, Les actually was not part of it. It was an idea to do a band thing; to do something else in another direction. With *Sophisticated Swing*, we used the name Les Elgart because at that time I had no real interest in being a bandleader, and Les, of course, always did. *Sophisticated Swing*, Les Elgart, *College Prom Favorite* went out and we started what turned out to be a very successful career on Columbia Records. They tried to bring other bands in, but we were the one band that really did sustain them.[37]

The Elgart bands were always associated with Les' name because he fronted the first band, and this prominence was largely because of a family affair. Les was five years older than Larry, and their father thought that the older brother should be the leader. However, Les was the business type, who could relate to industry executives, and Larry was basically the music director of both bands. In effect, the family partnership worked because the second band was a best seller, especially during the Columbia years. The band

subsequently recorded with RCA and later for MGM. In 1955, Larry and Charlie recorded *Barefoot Ballerina* for Decca Records and *Impressions of Outer Space*. Their third recording, *New Sounds at the Roosevelt*, received a Grammy nomination. It is also interesting to note that, at one point, Les approached the producer of *American Bandstand* about recording a theme song for the show. The producer was interested in the idea, so Larry and Charlie Albertine co-wrote "Bandstand Boogie," which became the show's theme song, later inherited by Dick Clark when he became the host.[38]

The second band included some of the country's top musicians. Les, Stan Fishelson, Phillip Sunkel, and John Wilson formed the trumpet section. The trombones were Eddie Bert, Danny Repole, and Bart Varsalona. Larry, Charlie Albertine, Wally Bettman, Sam Morowitz, and John Murtaugh made up the saxophone section. In the rhythm section were Jimmy Raney on guitar, bassist Russ Savakus, and drummer Ted Sommer. Eleanor Russell, the band's vocalist, brought a great deal of experience from the orchestras of Jerry Wald, Charlie Barnet, and Jimmy Dorsey to the Elgart band.[39] The band was promoted heavily by the Music Corporation of America (MCA) and was strongly supported by Julie Wintz, who enlisted the band with his agency before his death. In fact, Wintz continually asked about the band and listened repeatedly to *Sophisticated Swing* while on his deathbed. With MCA's support, the Elgart band played a danceable style that appealed to a lot of people. Les Elgart summarized the band's popular style:

> We want to play for ALL dancers.... That's how we have styled the band. Too many other bands forget about them. We're trying to make it as easy as possible for them. Take our emphasis on a two-beat. It's more or less in the Lunceford groove—maybe even a little more obvious. Originally, we'd planned a Basie-type thing, using lots of open rhythm, only without any piano for fill-ins. But when we started playing more for the dancers, we evolved our new style.[40]

DIZZY GILLESPIE

One of the founders of bebop, Dizzy Gillespie, organized a band in 1945 that performed throughout the United States and made several European tours, until disbanding around 1950.[41] Prior to starting his own band, he gained experience playing with Teddy Hill, Cab Calloway, Benny Carter, Charlie Barnet, Earl Hines, Duke Ellington, Billy Eckstine, and others until 1945.[42] During that period, Gillespie became a national celebrity, with an *Esquire* "New Star" award as "best trumpeter of the year." Consequently, trumpeters everywhere imitated his playing and mannerisms. In fact, many established musicians on practically every instrument were playing his musical ideas, including Woody Herman's entire trumpet section in unison.[43] In any event, Gillespie organized his first band and toured for five or six months but disbanded and made his first bebop recording with an all-star quintet. He also led a sextet that toured in California for two months.

Because bebop was still relatively new to the general public, Gillespie re-formed his big band in 1946 and resumed recording and touring.[44] A full year of hard work paid off when Dizzy finally whipped the band into shape. The band achieved the smoothness, playing ease, and polish necessary for a top-ranking big band, and it was voted as *Metronome*'s Band of the Year in 1947.[45] In early 1948, the band toured for two months in Sweden, Denmark, Belgium, and France. Despite management issues in some of the venues, road manager Milt Shaw pointed out that "People were paying the equivalent of three and four dollars to see the band, and the promoters sometimes grossed as much as $15,000 a day!"[46] In June of the same year, journalist Barry Ulanov wrote about the band's opening at the Royal Roost in New York City. He indicated, "Two things were obvious at that opening: that Dizzy's band was important enough at this point to attract almost everybody who was anybody in the music business to its first Broadway opening; and that the musicians in it were good, singly and as an ensemble." He also indicated that the club was so crowded that at night "It was impossible to tell whether you were stepping on your own feet or on someone else's."[47] Obviously, Ulanov gave the band a very positive review.[48]

Gillespie's band recorded for the Musicraft label in 1946, and tunes such as Tadd Dameron's "Our Delight," "Ray's Idea," "Things to Come," and "Emanon" were waxed. Although there were some personnel changes during the 1946 sessions, the trumpet section consisted of Gillespie, Dave Burns, Raymond Orr, Talib Daawood, and John Lynch. The trombone section included Leon Cormenge, Charles Greenlee or Gordon Thomas, and Alton Moore. Howard Johnson and John Brown were on alto sax, Lucky Warren and Ray Abrams or James Moody were on tenor, and Pee Wee Moore played baritone. The rhythm section had John Lewis on piano, Ray Brown on bass, and Kenny Clarke on drums. Alternates for the recording sessions included trumpeters Kenny Dorham and Elmon Wright, alto saxo-phonists Sonny Stitt and Scoops Carey, and baritonist Leo Parker. On "Our Delight," the band played brilliantly, with fine ensemble work and superb solos by Gillespie, Milt Jackson, and Ray Abrams. The technical difficulty of Dameron's arrangement is noteworthy, especially for the trumpet section. Quite frankly, with the breakneck speed of the chart's tempo, it is amazing that any big band could play it with the level of precision displayed by Gillespie's unit. The band's rendition of "Ray's Idea," arranged by music director Gil Fuller, was played with fine ensemble work in swing style featuring a bebop solo by Gillespie.

In 1947, Gillespie changed record labels, securing a contract with RCA Victor. In McCarthy's opinion, Dizzy's big band "was always at its best on the RCA Victor releases," but it was not always recorded well. Furthermore, there were people who claimed that the band's full impact was not captured on record.[49] The 1947 recordings featured tunes such as "Two Bass Hit," "Stay on It," "Cool Breeze," and Gillespie's scat bop vocal "Oop-Pop-A-Da." In the late forties, Latin American music began to influence jazz, and the band recorded Dizzy's "Manteca" and George Russell's "Cubana Be, Cubana Bop" featuring famed Cuban percussionist Chano Pozo. Gillespie's big band obviously had a major impact on the jazz world. Like Billy Eckstine's band, it was ahead of its time. All of the elements of a Later Swing Era band can be heard in its ensemble playing and in the bouncing pulsation of its rhythm section. Daring unison passages written for the trumpet section, as well as some fine bop solos by people such as Ray Brown, Kenny Clarke, Sonny Stitt, James Moody, and Cecil Payne, definitely helped usher in a new era in jazz.

INTERNATIONAL SWEETHEARTS OF RHYTHM

The International Sweethearts of Rhythm was formed in 1937 and became the most popular all-female jazz band in the Later Swing Era. The band was started as a fund-raising effort for the Piney Woods School in Mississippi by its principal, Dr. Lawrence C. Jones. Piney Woods was a boarding school for poor and orphaned African-American and other minority children that depended on donor contributions for its existence. While on a trip to Chicago, Jones heard Ina Ray Hutton and the Melodears and decided to organize a similar group at Piney Woods to play at local functions and help raise money for the school. Jones was a serious recruiter of young people, and he expended a great deal of energy and work to build the band.[50] At its inception, other minorities in the band were Mexican-American, Asian-American, and Native American, the main reason for including "International" in the band's name. The name also had an "exotic" sound and later helped deflect some of the racist harassment inflicted on the band by white policemen in the South.

When the band was formed, the average age of the girls was fourteen or fifteen, and they were selected for their musical abilities as well as their striking appearance. A few of them could read music, and others were just learning to play their instruments. Their initial inspiration came from imitating their teachers' phrases and melodies. As the band developed, the girls learned to read "stock" arrangements of standards such as "Stardust" and "How Long, Baby." Their first tour included small towns near and around Piney Woods; however, the band's tour schedule later increased to as many as twelve to fourteen dates within a sixteen-day period.[51] It is not clear who first directed the band, but it rehearsed for a brief period under the direction of teacher Lawrence Jefferson after Jones assembled it. The band's chaperone was Ella Gant and its tutor was Vivian Crawford. As the band members gained more experience and began to sound professional, Lawrence Jones hired Rae Lee Jones, a social worker from Nebraska, to replace Gant. Mrs. Jones (no relation to Lawrence) kept a watchful eye on the girls and saw to it that they were properly groomed and maintained good eating habits.[52]

Once the Sweethearts' fund-raising efforts began to take them outside of Piney Woods and the surrounding area, Lawrence Jones provided them with a bus that included bunk beds and other amenities. It was difficult to find hotel accommodations for a racially mixed group at that time; therefore, the girls ate, slept, practiced, prepared their lessons, and dressed on the bus. During a one-week period in October 1939, the band performed in Kansas City, Omaha, Des Moines, and Chicago. Their performance in Chicago at Earl's Club House was reviewed as follows:

> Sixteen girls, best known in music circles as the "International Sweethearts of Rhythm" who hail from Piney Woods, Mississippi, right in the heart of the Delta, invaded Chicago Saturday night and gave jitterbugs, swing fans, and hep cats something to talk about. They beat out a bit of mellow jive, sang the latest song hits, then started a swing session that caused the dance lovers to stop in their tracks and listen to the hot sounds that blared out from the instruments played by these Mississippi girls. Together for two years, these girls handle their instruments like veterans and can rightfully take a place among the leading male aggregations.[53]

As a result of such reviews and the Sweethearts' increasing popularity, Daniel Gary, who represented the Amusement Corporation in Washington, D.C., began booking the band in 1940. Gary, a friend of Rae Lee Jones, promised the Sweethearts more work, and by 1941, they were earning as much as $3,000 a month for Piney Woods' fund-raising campaign.[54] At this point, it is important to note that the Sweethearts owed part of their success to band member and solo trumpeter-arranger Edna Williams, who contributed some excellent arrangements to the band's repertoire.[55] Once Dan Gary came into the picture, the Sweethearts terminated their relationship with Piney Woods and set out on their own as the International Sweethearts of Rhythm, Inc. They relocated to Arlington, Virginia, and moved into a ten-room house named "Sweetheart House." Rae Lee Jones, who was designated as trustee of Sweethearts, Inc., told the band members that they owned shares in the house. Because the band was not quite at the level of its exposure, it rehearsed many hours a day for several months to improve its performance skill. To help the Sweethearts develop further, guitarist-trombonist-arranger Eddie Durham (formerly with Count Basie and Jimmie Lunceford) was hired as music director. He arranged music that highlighted the band's strong points and circumvented its technical limitations. Because most of the soloists' improvisational skills were underdeveloped, Durham wrote out solos that were within the musicians' skill range but sounded as if they were being improvised. Vocalist Anna Mae Winburn was also brought in to sing and "front" the band as its showpiece. As the band toured the country, its personnel began to change; other professional musicians joined, bringing the Sweethearts more experience and substance. Once the band reached a higher level of skill and professionalism, they played the famed Apollo in 1941 and became a hit. They were invited back to the Apollo every year after their initial performance.[56] From that point on, life for the Sweethearts was spent mostly traveling on the road playing one-nighters, except for gigs at the major clubs in large cities, which usually lasted a week or two. In 1943 an important change took place when Eddie Durham left his position as arranger-music director. He was concerned that more than half of the band members' salaries were taken by Gary and his partner, Al Dade. Jesse Stone succeeded Durham.[57]

Like Durham, Stone was highly respected and successful in the world of top-notch African American swing bands. He made several major changes in the band by hiring new musicians such as Lucille Dixon (bass), Marjorie Pettiford (Oscar's sister, on alto sax), Johnnie Mae Stansbury (trumpet), Amy Garrison (sax), and Roxanna Lucas (guitar). These talented musicians had advanced musical skills, and they helped raise the performance level of the entire band. Stone also taught the girls to play with better ensemble precision and cleaner attacks and to listen to improve their intonation. Stone formed a vocal quartet from within the band that would go down in front during part of the show and sing. This had great audience appeal. During Stone's first year, the band's overall ensemble sound was smoother and more mature. There were more challenging arrangements, the individual musicians' skills improved markedly, and the band members learned more about music in general. On the other hand, Stone, like Durham, was concerned that the young women were performing for inadequate wages, and he left after fulfilling his two-year contract.[58]

Shortly after Stone's departure, Maurice King came from Detroit to replace him as music director. Around the time of King's arrival, the Sweethearts became the first integrated female band when alto saxophonist Rosalind "Roz" Cron from Boston joined it after a stint with Ada Leonard's band. Cron was impressed with Maurice King's ability to train and polish the band. He led the band through long and hard rehearsals. For example, he would show the girls how to phrase a passage four bars at a time in an arrangement and rehearse it repeatedly until it jelled. King also wrote specialty charts for the band such as "Vi Vigor," "Slightly Frantic," "Don't Get It Twisted," and "Diggin' Dirt" (which became the band's dance stopper). According to King, when playing a dance stopper, "we'd end the tune, pause, and then start it all over again. We'd do this several times. It was a big number."[59]

From the mid- to late forties, the Sweethearts were at the height of their popularity. For example, when they performed at clubs such as the Rhumboogie in Chicago, there were three shows a night and seven shows a day. Crowds were turned away many times. The Sweethearts would often tour with other bands, such as those of Jimmie Lunceford and Fletcher Henderson, and the shows were billed as the "Swing Battle of the Sexes."[60]

In addition to grueling road tours, the Sweethearts recorded for RCA Victor and Guild Records in New York and made some short films in various Hollywood studios. In 1945 they became USO entertainers and toured throughout Europe entertaining the troops. Incidentally, during this time, the girls received the highest pay they had ever received as members of that band, because Maurice King instructed the USO to deposit the girls' paychecks in U.S. banks.[61] The Sweethearts were highly successful overseas with the GIs and returned to the United States with money in the bank for the first time in their lives. They continued performing throughout the country in top venues, receiving rave reviews in some of the nation's most visible newspapers and in magazines such as *Billboard*. However, Rae Lee Jones, the band's lifeline, had become ill and could no longer travel and work with the young women.[62] The band had become one of the most successful in the forties, but it died along with Mrs. Jones in either late 1948 or early 1949. Unfortunately, both of these events closed one of the most exciting and unusual chapters in the history of jazz.

BUDDY JOHNSON

Pianist-vocalist Buddy Johnson led one of the most popular big bands in the Later Swing Era and had a major impact on the rise of rhythm and blues. Johnson's band popularized the walking rhythm and featured several notable soloists, such as saxophonist Purvis Henson, vocalist Ella Johnson (Buddy's sister), and legendary singer Arthur Prysock. Johnson, a talented songwriter, wrote a number of pop standards that were later recorded by such artists as Lou Rawls, Ruth Brown, Annie Laurie, and Muddy Waters. Johnson recorded for Decca Records from 1939 to 1952 and made his first big band recordings in the early forties. In 1952 he signed with the Mercury label and continued to make hit records well into the early days of rock and roll. Some of Johnson's hit songs were "Walk 'Em," "Since I Fell for You," "Baby, You're Always on My Mind," and "Satisfy My Soul."[63]

Johnson's band toured regularly, playing numerous one-nighters and serving many long residencies at the Savoy Ballroom in New York City.[64] During the band's earlier years, its personnel included trumpeters Frank Brown, Dupree Bolton, Johnny Wilson, and Willis Nelson. Bernard Archer, Leonard Briggs, and Gordon Thomas were in the trombone section. Altoists Joe O'Laughlin and Alfonso Robinson, tenorists David Van Dyke and Jimmy Stansford, and baritonist Teddy Conyers made up the saxophone section. Guitarist Jerome Darr, Johnson, bassist Leon Spann, and drummer Teddy Stewart were in the rhythm section. Between the mid-forties and the early fifties, several of the band's records sold more than half a million copies. This was largely because of Buddy's ability to adapt his band's sound to current music styles. As a result of the band's immense popularity, it kept a busy schedule on the road and in the recording studios.[65]

Johnson was also a highly skilled composer-arranger of instrumental music and wrote a large number of popular compositions that appealed to jazz buffs and the dancing public. During the early stages of his big band career, he recorded some danceable compositions that featured modern instrumental soloists and fit comfortably into the swing music genre. For example, his "South Main" was a medium-tempo swing tune that could easily get most patrons at the Savoy Ballroom on the dance floor. This particular arrangement contained short sixteen-bar solos for piano and trumpet and a thirty-two-bar tenor saxophone outing. The piano and trumpet solos were closed with a simple two-bar background phrase played by the trumpet section. The saxophone solo had the benefit of a longer background or accompaniment played by the trombones. A shout chorus followed the solos, with the trombone section carrying the melody and exchanging some call-and-response phrases with the trumpets. The saxophone section played the ending. The theme of this sixteen-measure composition was written for saxes in unison for the first eight bars and harmonized for the second eight bars. "One of Them Good Ones," commonly referred to as a "riff tune," follows a call-and-response format for the saxes and brass section. A saxophone solo is played between the theme and an interlude, with the full ensemble navigating skillfully through some modulations. A trumpet solo follows with a repeat of the interlude in the middle before it ends. The call-and-response theme returns to conclude the tune. One of Johnson's most famous compositions, "Walk 'Em," recorded in November of 1945, foreshadowed rhythm and blues with Buddy's catchy vocals and the walking rhythm that made him famous. This arrangement features an introduction by the rhythm section, some bluesy thematic statements by the tenor saxophone with band accompaniment, and a trumpet solo backed by unison saxes. The tenor sax returns after a brief band interlude with some bluesy statements, and the piano closes the arrangement.

As for Johnson's songwriting skill, his "Since I Fell for You" is probably his most famous song. Recorded in November 1945, it featured vocalist Ella Johnson singing its attractive and bluesy melody in a style reminiscent of Billie Holiday. The song was written in a thirty-two-bar form (A-A-B-A) and uses chord progressions similar to those in "I Got Rhythm." This recording also features an alto sax solo that sticks pretty closely to the original melody that Ms. Johnson sang so well. Similarly, the band and its male vocalist, Arthur Prysock, recorded Johnson's "I Wonder Where Our Love Has Gone" in January 1947. Prysock's rich baritone voice stands out distinctly in this ballad as he sings the melody in a musical and bluesy fashion. Johnson used the band sparingly in this arrangement and, except for a brief saxophone solo, Prysock is featured throughout until the full band closes with a short statement at the end.

Throughout the forties, Johnson's band experienced only some minor personnel changes and, in 1947, the lineup included trumpeters Frank Royal,

Andrew Wood, Willis Nelson, and Calvin Strickland. Steve Pulliam, Bernard Archer, and William Harrison were the trombone section. Purvis Henson replaced Jimmy Stansford on tenor saxophone, and guitarist Bernard Mackey and drummer Emmanuel Simms completed the rhythm section. Although Johnson composed and arranged most of the repertoire, the band recorded a few charts by other composers. For example, a composition entitled "Pullamo" by band members Steve Pulliam and Willis Nelson was recorded in December 1947. It opens with trumpets playing a fanfare before the saxes play in rubato. This opening is followed by vocal scatting of the theme in the three [A] sections, while the full ensemble plays throughout the bridge [B]. A tenor saxophonist, probably Purvis Henson, solos for a full chorus (A-A-B-A) and is followed by an interlude featuring the saxophone section. A trumpeter solos for sixteen bars before an eight-bar trombone solo on the bridge, and is followed by soft unison saxes in the final [A] section that leads to the ending. This composition displays the band's ability to swing and show off some of its solo talent.

Although the band continued to record, it gradually reduced its busy touring schedule in the late fifties. Subsequently, Johnson disbanded, led a small group in the early sixties, and made his last recordings in 1964. Shortly thereafter, he retired from the music business because of illness and spent the last ten to twelve years of his life involved in church and welfare work.[66] As a bandleader, Johnson was keenly aware of the need to satisfy the musical tastes of his audience and provide his band with the artistic freedom to swing and be creative. His ability to develop a wide-ranging style that reached dancers, listeners, and musicians alike earned him a unique place in the history of swing. Unfortunately, most music journalists and historians have overlooked Johnson's musical contributions, but the enduring quality and popularity of his songs alone will help keep his name alive.

STAN KENTON

Stan Kenton began his career in the 1930s as a pianist and arranger in various theater and dance bands.[67] He also worked in Everett Hoagland's aggregation.[68] Kenton premiered his first band, The Artistry in Rhythm Orchestra, in the summer of 1941 at the Rendezvous Ballroom in Balboa, California. After receiving critical acclaim, he performed at the Hollywood Palladium in early 1942 and traveled to New York for engagements at the Roseland Ballroom and Frank Daily's Meadowbrook. A few months later, Kenton's orchestra was established among the top-name bands in the country.[69]

In late 1941, Kenton's initial recordings on the Decca label were popular, with charts such as "Adios," "Taboo," and "Gambler's Blues."[70] He signed a contract with newly formed Capitol Records in 1942, and his was one of the first bands to record for that label. He gained additional visibility when

Bob Hope selected his orchestra to replace Skinnay Ennis on the Pepsodent radio show during Ennis' stint in the military until the end of World War II.[71] By 1943, Kenton had a different band, with the exception of three musicians from his earlier unit. The newer band had more experienced players, and the recordings were more popular, with charts such as "Eager Beaver" and the theme "Artistry in Rhythm." A year later, the band gained more momentum with the addition of saxophonists Stan Getz and Dave Matthews (who wrote some of the band's arrangements). During this same period, Anita O'Day joined the band and recorded some of its most famous songs such as "And Her Tears Flowed Like Wine" and "Are You Livin' Old Man?" After a year, O'Day left Kenton and was replaced by June Christy, who recorded such commercial hits as "Tampico" and "Willow Weep for Me." After the war ended, more musicians were available, and Kenton's band improved, along with its popularity. The orchestra was well received at Chicago's Sherman Hotel and New York's Paramount Theater. The improvement in Kenton's music was due in part to the addition of chief arranger Pete Rugolo in 1945, whose arrangements gave the organization a distinctive and identifiable sound. In addition, instrumentalists such as trombonist Kai Winding, saxophonist Vido Musso, bassist Eddie Safransky, and drummer Shelly Manne joined the band and made important contributions to one of its biggest hits, "Artistry Jumps." Kenton continued to enjoy popularity, with successful recordings and bookings in high-profile establishments. In January 1946, the editors of *Look* magazine chose his band as "Band of the Year," and a year later, *Metronome*'s editors accorded it the same honor, although they had been highly critical of Kenton's music.[72] At the same time, his style had changed completely, to what he labeled "progressive jazz." He disbanded in 1947 for health reasons.

Kenton returned to the road in early 1948 and attempted to play only concert dates, but his promoters disregarded his request.[73] In spite of this, he performed in Carnegie Hall with a twenty-piece orchestra in 1949.[74] However, he returned to the Rendezvous in Balboa in 1950 with a band that played dance music.[75] Shortly after, Kenton organized the forty-three-piece Innovations in Modern Music Orchestra, complete with a large wind section and strings, for two nationwide tours in 1950–1951. This project ended up being too costly, and he returned to the conventional big band format.[76] Kenton continued to lead bands and experiment with his concept of concert jazz for the next fifteen years. Except for a period of semi-retirement, he returned to bandleading with a new "creative jazz" orchestra in the early seventies, playing one-nighters and several international tours until 1977.

Throughout Kenton's career as a bandleader, he attracted numerous top-flight musicians for his organizations. In addition to some of the instrumentalists and vocalists mentioned earlier, several sidemen included Howard Rumsey, Buddy Childers, Chico Alvarez, Gerry Mulligan, Bud Shank,

George Roberts, Shorty Rogers, Jack Nimitz, Art Pepper, Bob Cooper, Max Bennett, and Maynard Ferguson, to name a few.[77] Kenton was deeply respected by his musicians, and they were dedicated to quality performances of his music. Shelly Manne, who played with Kenton's band for several years, made the following comments: "He was personal, always one of the fellows and yet nobody ever lost any respect for him. If the guys needed money, Stan would lend it to them. Everybody really wanted to work for what he was working. And the spirit of the band was wonderful. It was such a clean atmosphere. You always felt you were working for something that mattered, instead of just jamming 'Tea for Two' or 'Perdido.'" Manne continued, "The way Stan encouraged everybody was so wonderful, too. He was always encouraging young arrangers. If a guy joined the band, he'd never judge him on first appearances, the way most leaders do. He'd let him play for a while until he settled down. Then Stan would make up his mind. And he was so wonderful with the public too. He never fluffed anybody off."[78]

Stan Kenton strongly believed that jazz is concert music and should be played in respectable places at decent hours and for affordable prices. He also believed that his music should provide more than just a background for drinkers' conversations in bars and dancers' shuffling feet. At one point, he sought the support of other top-ranking bandleaders such as Dizzy Gillespie, Woody Herman, Duke Ellington, Gene Krupa, and Ray McKinley, among others to help improve working conditions for jazz bands.[79]

Although Kenton was admired by his musicians and by jazz fans, he was a controversial figure. Some media critics thought that he was headstrong, verbose, and overly confident. They also felt that his band played too loudly and did not swing.[80] Shelly Manne, who greatly respected Kenton, once left the band and complained that playing with it was "like chopping wood." After a brief hiatus, however, he rejoined the orchestra.[81] Despite the criticism, Kenton's bands were always well rehearsed, polished, and professional. Additionally, Kenton's music style continually changed during the forties and early fifties. Throughout this period, his style can be loosely categorized into two periods as pre-Rugolo (1941–1945) and post-Rugolo (1945 and beyond). During the first period, Kenton made several popular recordings, as mentioned earlier. Some fine examples of the band's swing style can be found in the original radio recordings of 1944–1945 and released on the Hindsight record label around 1980. These recordings also feature the vocals of both Anita O'Day and June Christy.

The Hindsight release features charts such as "The Man I Love" and "Blow Jack," arranged and composed by alto saxophonist Henry "Boots" Mussulli, and "Fine Fine Deal" arranged by Dave Matthews. On "The Man I Love," Mussulli is the soloist, with the band providing tight ensemble backgrounds and dynamic contrast in the beginning slow portion. In the up-tempo portion of the arrangement, the full ensemble continues, with clean and precise passages on top of a driving rhythm section that emphasizes beats one and three (better known as the "strong beats"). Mussulli's "Blow Jack" employs Sy Oliver's favorite technique of scoring saxes in unison against alternating harmonized brass figures in the theme. Trumpeter John Carroll and Kenton share solos on the first chorus, with ensemble backgrounds before an eight-bar interlude of full ensemble (tutti) passages and a brief drum solo by Jim Falzone. Saxophonist Emmett Carls' sixteen-bar solo before a harmonized sax soli on the bridge alternates with the full ensemble to close his solo. Mussulli's alto sax also alternates with the ensemble before he solos on the bridge and is followed by the full band to conclude the chart. The Hindsight release features June Christy and Anita O'Day singing the blues. "Fine Fine Deal" opens with a somewhat slow full-band introduction that includes the "Salt Peanuts" motif. When Christy enters, the band changes to a medium up-tempo, and she phrases the melody tastefully. The next twelve bars consist of alternating harmonized saxes and unison trumpets. Christy returns with a few bars of stop-time (in the rhythm section) before she scats for a few bars until the end. O'Day sings a blues piece written by Kenton. Similarly, this chart begins slowly, with O'Day singing the melody before the band changes to an up-tempo swing beat. After two choruses by O'Day, the ensemble enters with alternating harmonized saxes and unison trumpets. O'Day returns with another chorus before a twelve-bar trumpet solo. She ends the chart with four bars of melody over a stop-time rhythm, followed by the full ensemble for eight bars to the end. There is a close resemblance between the vocal styles of O'Day and Christy, with O'Day obviously having the more mature voice.

   Now let us turn to the post-Rugolo Kenton style and, particularly, innovations in modern music. Two Rugolo compositions ("Conflict" and "Mirage") are noteworthy. They were recorded in 1950 and later released on Kenton's Creative World Records label with a twenty-piece band, two French horns, tuba, ten violins, three violas, and three cellos. Both compositions consist of many elements contained in the music of Ravel and Stravinsky. Rugolo was obviously a well-trained composer-arranger. His work relied heavily on European music, which was in direct opposition to the concept of swing at the time. Nevertheless, many of the chord structures and voicings employed by Rugolo in Kenton's style brought some newer sounds to jazz that eventually made their way into the language of a number of today's successful jazz musicians. In addition to Kenton's musical contributions, he established the first of his "jazz clinics" in 1959 at Indiana University and Michigan State University. He also formed his own publishing and recording companies, Creative World Music and Creative World Records, and received three honorary doctorates. Along with his talents as a pianist, arranger, and bandleader, Kenton probably made his greatest contribution to jazz as an educator who encouraged hundreds of college-trained musicians to pursue careers in jazz.[82]

ELLIOT LAWRENCE

Elliot Lawrence's career as a bandleader began after he graduated from the University of Pennsylvania, where he studied conducting with Leon Bragin.[83] Lawrence gained experience at the university by conducting the football band. He ultimately received the Art Achievement Award, which was only the second time the university had granted this award to a musician.[84]

In 1945 he became music director at radio station WCAU in Philadelphia, where his father was the general manager. Lawrence's big break came when CBS began network broadcasts of the WCAU band around the country. As a result, the band became very popular and received an offer to play in the Café Rouge at the Hotel Pennsylvania in New York. The engagement was so successful that Elliot left his steady job at the radio station in 1946 to enter the band business full-time. His father, Stan Broza, also left his longtime position at WCAU to become his manager.[85] Subsequently, Lawrence's band played engagements at New York's Paramount Theater, Frank Dailey's Meadowbrook in New Jersey, the Sherman Hotel in Chicago, and the Palladium in Hollywood. In addition to these important bookings, he played many college dates, and his band ended up becoming one of the most popular in the country to play for college proms.[86] The popularity of Lawrence's band also made it possible for him to get a recording contract with Columbia. The Artists & Repertoire (A&R) person who worked with the band when it recorded was Mitch Miller, who also played oboe on some of the sides. The recordings helped publicize the band around the country. Lawrence was an excellent composer-arranger who penned "Heart to Heart," "Five O'Clock Shadow," "Brown Betty," "Sugar Beet," "Once upon a Moon," "Sugar Town Row," and his most popular chart, "Elevation." Lawrence contributed the most music to the band's repertoire, but other arrangers, such as Al Cohn, Tiny Kahn, Johnny Mandel, Gerry Mulligan, and Nelson Riddle also wrote for the band.

Columnist Stan Woolley pointed out in his article that Elliot Lawrence led "one of the finest bands, if not the finest" in the country for two years during the early fifties.[87] At various times, the trumpet section included Charlie Frankenheimer, Bernie Glow, Al Porcino, and Stan Fishelson. The trombone section consisted of three Woody Herman alumni, Bob and Earl Swope and Ollie Wilson. The saxophone section included Sam Morowitz, Al Cohn, Phil Urso, and Gerry Mulligan.[88] The rhythm section was completed by drummer Tiny Kahn and bassist Buddy Jones. The vocalists were Rosalind Patton and Danny Ricardo. *Metronome* columnist Bill Coss reviewed the Lawrence Band in 1952, and a portion of his review follows:

> This is an interesting band to listen to. Tiny and bassist Buddy Jones do a good job as two thirds of the rhythm section during Elliot's absences. Johnny Mandel, Ollie Wilson, and Al Robinson may suffer in comparison to the

Herman section, but their ensemble work is note perfect and Robinson's soloing is a handsome thing. The reed section is the star group of the band. Al Cohn does most of the tenor work, playing with more of a beat than ever before. For the rest, Al Steele, Sam Morowitz, Hal McKusick and Steve Perlo play the rolling ensemble stuff for which Sam is famous, perfectly in tune, a joy to hear. It is in the trumpet section that something is lacking. Nick Travis, Al Porcino, Al DeRisi and Dick Sherman are capable trumpeters with attack and precision. But the joie de vivre of the trumpets is missing. The sound is most often dull. There is a brilliance missing except in their mute work that, I think, hurts the punch that the band should have. Nick's work, however, is an eloquent example of the trumpet's nobility. Such tunes as "Tenderly" and "You Took Advantage of Me" were high points in the art. Rosalind Patton is still with the band, giving to it the only constantly distinctive, identifying sound aside from Elliot's piano for the listeners' ears. On ballad or jump numbers, Roz continues to be my idea of a band vocalist. In the male department, Danny Ricardo impresses with a big natural voice. There were a few moments when intonation or beat suffered a bit, but his is a thoroughly musical sound so seldom found today.[89]

Coss also commented on the fact that Lawrence was experimenting with the sound of two curved soprano saxes, one alto, one tenor, and baritone. At one time, the band also used French horns, but Lawrence felt that they did not project well and opted for bass trumpets instead of the horns.[90] Simon agrees with Coss' overall assessment of the band by summarizing that the band "sounded musical," and its "musicianship was always outstanding."[91]

Around 1955 Lawrence gave up the band business and spent the next ten years in the theater conducting Broadway shows. His training and experience were particularly helpful to him as a conductor on Broadway. He worked mostly in television for the following twenty-five years and later became a music supervisor for a major New York advertising agency. He also served as music director for the annual Tony Awards.[92] Although Elliot Lawrence may not be a household name, he brought a great deal of competence and talent to swing and show music. He surrounded himself with some of the top musicians in the business and experimented with various instrumental combinations utilizing curved soprano saxophones, French horns, and bass trumpets. Lawrence's achievements have had a positive impact on the sound of modern jazz.

HAL McINTYRE

Alto saxophonist-clarinetist Hal McIntyre led his first swing band for about a year and played with Glenn Miller's orchestra for four years before starting his own professional band in 1941.[93] McIntyre, a close friend of Miller, was able to get his financial backing and support to start the band. As with Miller, McIntyre's engagement at the Glen Island Casino catapulted his band into the national spotlight. Shortly afterward, it was voted "the most promising new orchestra" in a college poll conducted by *Billboard* magazine in 1942 and 1943. McIntyre's band performed in top venues, such as Frank Dailey's Meadowbrook, the Hollywood Palladium, and many theaters and hotel ballrooms in the country from the early forties until the mid-fifties. Notably, the band performed for President Roosevelt's Birthday Ball at the Statler Hotel in Washington, D.C., in January 1945. In May of that same year, McIntyre undertook an overseas tour to entertain military personnel during World War II.[94] He had to reorganize the band for the tour, however, because some of the musicians did not meet army and USO requirements. Obviously, the band could not perform at its previous level of quality during the tour, but it was well received, and the tour ended up a success.[95] Following the overseas tour, McIntyre and his band appeared in two films for Paramount Pictures and performed regularly in the Midwest, the South, and on the East Coast.[96] In fact, the band worked an average of fifty-two weeks a year from about 1945 to 1952.[97]

Such a busy work schedule speaks to the quality and musicality of McIntyre's organization, although it was not one of the more commercial bands in the Later Swing Era. Schuller comments, "This then was one of the truly fine bands of the era. Its excellence is attested to by its ability to survive the decline of the big bands, working well into the 1950s. On the other hand it cannot be said that the McIntyre band achieved top-level popularity or the critical acclaim it surely deserved. For that it was too musicianly, played too tastefully, resisted commercialism too stubbornly, and recorded too few pop tunes."[98] One of the strengths of McIntyre's band was its sound, which was due, in no small part, to the style and quality of its arrangements. Some of the top arrangers in the band business, Dave Matthews, Howard Gibeling, Danny Hurd, Sid Schwartz, and Billy May, wrote for the band. Furthermore, all of them were familiar with the style of Duke Ellington, which was an identifiable element of the McIntyre organization. Although the band did not necessarily play a large number of Ellington compositions, it did play numerous arrangements that employed what Billy Strayhorn referred to as the "Ellington effect."[99] In a review of the McIntyre band's memorable engagement at the Glen Island Casino, George Simon commented on the arrangements' "imaginative voicings," "variety of tonal effects," and "fine rhythm figures." He also pointed out that the band paid close attention to dynamics and contrast. Another aspect of the band's sound was the quality of its personnel, who were handpicked by McIntyre. At one point, the trumpet section included Paul McCoy, Clarence Willard, Billy Robbins, and Steady Nelson (who doubled on vocals). Vic Hamman, Howard Gibeling, and Don Ruppersberg were in the trombone section. On saxophones were McIntyre (lead), Dave Matthews, Gene Kinsey, Bob Poland, and Johnny Dee. Pianist Danny Hurd, bassist Ed Safransky, drummer Ralph Tilken, and guitarist-vocalist Jack Lathrop made up the rhythm section. Completing the quartet of vocalists were Penny Parker and Carl Denny.

In Simon's aforementioned review, he gives us an interesting glimpse into the inner workings and/or contributions of the four instrumental sections and the four vocalists. For example, in his assessment of the trumpet section, he referred to it as "an exceptionally adaptable section." Paul McCoy and Clarence Willard were described as two good lead men, with Willard having the warmer sound for ballads. Billy Robbins was considered an "impressive" jazz soloist, and Steady Nelson lived up to his name as a section player. With regard to the trombones, Vic Hamman played good lead, whereas Gibeling and Ruppersberg blended well to form a consistent section. McIntyre was credited with providing "lovely" lead for the saxophone section, and Dave Matthews was praised for drilling it into a "formidable" quintet. Hal's solo work was linked to that of Johnny Hodges, whereas Matthews' tenor passages, influenced by Ben Webster, produced "a warm, exciting intimacy on slow numbers and a fine, rhythmic kick on faster tunes." The rhythm section was also described as a tight-knit unit, and bassist Ed Safransky was hailed as its most impressive member, with "a wonderfully warm tone and a strong, definite beat." Pianist Danny Hurd played "tasty piano bits," and drummer Ralph Tilken seldom did anything that did not fit into the scheme of things. Guitarist Jack Lathrop, who rounded out the rhythm section, was praised as a good singer of novelty tunes. McIntyre was cited as having a strong "vocal department," with Penny Parker "who does certain songs wonderfully well" and "sings higher than most girls do." Carl Denny, who sang most of the ballads, had the vocal equipment and was "not scared to let out." Trumpeter Steady Nelson, the fourth singer, added "pleasant variety" to the quartet started by Lathrop. In sum, the above-mentioned excerpts from Simon's comments made in 1942 revealed a great deal of excitement about and enthusiasm for the McIntyre band.[100]

A decade later, *Metronome* caught the band during its return to New York City in July of 1952 to appear on NBC's *Saturday Night Dance Party* and record some sides for Decca Records. Prior to that year, the band's activities had been restricted mostly to the Midwest and southern parts of the country. Again, the band was reviewed with the same enthusiasm displayed ten years earlier and was referred to as "one of the top bands in the country today." The band's style was said to have "the light buoyancy of much of Les Brown's music," "some of the modern touches...of Elliot Lawrence's band," and "the easy danceability of Billy May's Lunceford-like scores." This style was due, in large part, to the arrangements written by trumpeter Walt Stewart. Hal McIntyre added, "Bassist Ernie Taylor has also been writing some great things, especially ballads." The saxophone section was considered by *Metronome* to be the best, with McIntyre on lead alto, Harvey Nevins on alto/flute, tenor saxophonists Johnny Hayes and Eddie Martin, and "gutty baritonist" George Harris. Stewart and Don Eisman shared lead duties in the trumpet section, which included Johnny Twaddell and Ernie Bernhart. Trombonists Larry Valentino (on lead) and "exciting soloist" Lou Skeen were mentioned, along with "brilliant pianist" Harry Crisp, "exceptionally fine bassist" Taylor, and "kicking" drummer Frank DeVito. Vocalist Jean McManus had "a good jazz feeling," and Ernie Bernhart sounded "fine when letting out."[101]

It is also important to point out that McIntyre's orchestra was capable of high-spirited performances. For example, his earlier outfit was recorded live in a performance of Danny Hurd's arrangement of "Singin' in the Rain" for recuperating military patients on Long Island. The performance, recorded on V-Disc, opened with a slow introduction featuring muted brass accompanied only by Safransky's bass. McIntyre plays the melody, with muted brass and bass accompaniment, before the arrangement shifts to a faster tempo, with the leader playing the first solo. His solo, accompanied by full rhythm section and muted brass, was followed by a brief harmonized saxophone section interlude. Tenor saxophonist Johnny Hayes' solo was also accompanied by muted brass and was followed by the same brief interlude after McIntyre's solo; this gave way to Joe Wiedman's trumpet solo. The harmonized accompaniment, played by the saxes, preceded a brief shout chorus by the full band to the end. The ensemble work was precise, with fine solos and particularly exciting bass playing by Safransky. Schuller adds,

> McIntyre's orchestra played more jazz—and more consistently so—than any number of more famous and critically acclaimed orchestras (for example, Dorsey, Shaw, James), one clear manifestation of that being the great amount of solo space provided in its arrangements.... Moreover, the McIntyre band played more jazz instrumentals than most—even their relatively few vocals and popular songs were definitely couched in jazz terms—and it consistently swung more than most.[102]

The McIntyre organization disbanded as the Late Swing Era ended. McIntyre subsequently relocated to the West Coast and, in May 1959, died from injuries sustained in a fire at his Los Angeles apartment. According to Simon, Hal McIntyre was "one of the really nice guys of the big bands."[103]

RAY McKINLEY

Drummer-vocalist Ray McKinley teamed with trombonist Will Bradley to form a big band in 1939 that achieved commercial success by recording boogie-woogie-style arrangements that were quite popular at the time.[104] The band played top bookings in such venues as the Paramount Theater and New York's Famous Door. The organization, managed by William Alexander, was heavily promoted, and it received a lot of coverage in music trade journals and the press.[105] McKinley composed and sang some of his biggest hits, such as "Beat Me Daddy Eight to the Bar," "Bounce Me Brother with a Solid Four," "Scrub Me Mama with a Boogie Beat," and "Fry Me Cookie with a Can of Lard." In 1942 he and Bradley parted company, and McKinley formed his own big band.[106] He immediately began searching for young talent, and once he found the musicians he was looking for, he rehearsed them for several weeks in Patchogue, Long Island, away from the distractions of New York City.[107] When McKinley felt the band was ready, he introduced it in the New York area at the Commodore Hotel and Frank Dailey's Meadowbrook. George Simon, who was excited about the new band, made the following comments:

> It was a swinging outfit, featuring Mahlon Clark, the brilliant clarinetist who had followed Ray from Will's band, a fine seventeen-year-old trumpeter named Dick Cathcart, a swinging young pianist named Lou Stein, a very pretty and very good singer named Imogene Lynn, and two veterans: trombonist Brad Gowans and tuba player Joe Parks, who instead of burping with the rhythm section, played right along with the brass, to which he added an unusually full, rich sound.[108]

McKinley's band recorded some successful sides for Capitol Records, such as "Hard-hearted Hannah," which featured Ray's vocals. The band also had some successful bookings in California, where it was part of a movie entitled *Hit Parade of 1942* that featured Count Basie and Tony Martin. Unfortunately, the organization only lasted briefly because McKinley was soon drafted into the service.[109] Around 1943 he became a member of Glenn Miller's Army Air Force Band in Atlantic City, New Jersey, which was transferred to New Haven, Connecticut, in April of that same year.[110] The band was sent overseas in June of 1944 and was stationed in England for about six months, where McKinley led Swing Shift, a small group from within the Miller band. In December 1944, following Miller's death, he and Jerry Gray co-led the band in Europe until McKinley finished his tour of duty.[111]

After discharge, McKinley formed another big band in early 1946 and recruited arrangers Eddie Sauter and Dean Kincaide to write new repertoire. According to Simon, "Sauter's wonderfully inventive scores were musically superb. But they were difficult to play, requiring intensive rehearsing and concentration. The results were sometimes good, sometimes not so good." Subsequently, Simon added, "As the McKinley band mastered the magnificent Sauter arrangements, it developed into one of the most musically exciting groups of all time, one that combined artistic creativity, color and wit with a true swinging beat."[112] Leo Walker agreed with Simon, stating, "Musically it was rated as a top flight organization."[113] Some of Sauter's arrangements such as "Sandstorm," "Tumblebug," "Borderline," and "Hangover Square" were favorites among many musicians. McKinley also continued to develop his commercial appeal by singing successful hits such as "Red Silk Stockings" and "You've Come a Long Way from St. Louis."[114] In addition to Ray's singing and arrangements by Sauter and Kincaide, the band's enthusiastic musicians contributed a great deal to the organization's quality and success. The trumpet section included Nick Travis and Joe Ferrante, and two of the trombonists were Vern Friley and Irv Dinkin. The woodwind section included Peanuts Hucko on clarinet/tenor saxophone and Ray Beller on alto saxophone.[115] In the rhythm section were guitarist Mundell Lowe, pianist Lou Stein, bassist Paul Kashion, and drummer Johnny Chance.

McKinley's band made a number of recordings, including six Sauter originals for the RCA Camden label.[116] The Sauter charts were "Caesar and Cleopatra," "Harold in Italy," "McKinley for President," "The Seventh Veil," "Idiot's Delight," and "Cyclops." Sauter's compositional style draws heavily on the work of several European composers and is similar in some ways to that of Pete Rugolo. However, Sauter's style displays humor at times, as in "Harold in Italy" and "McKinley for President." In both pieces, Sauter uses muted trumpets to express his humor. In "McKinley for President," he employed various tempo changes, different alternating instrumental combinations, and brief clarinet and trombone solos that alternate with full-ensemble passages. "The Seventh Veil" featured altoist Ray Beller in a haunting ballad in which Sauter again alternated muted brass passages with woodwinds. Beller played a cadenza that alternated with intermittent full-ensemble passages, and his musical phrasing on this chart is certainly a highpoint. In "Idiot's Delight," Sauter utilized some semi-pointillistic compositional techniques, and his theme is centered around the use of fourths. He also employed contrapuntal devices, while the tempo floated without a steady beat. "Cyclops," on the other hand, was mostly straight-ahead in a more traditional swing vein that featured a muted trumpet solo before brief piano, trombone, and alto sax solos. In this writer's opinion, Sauter, like Rugolo, was moving in the direction of concert jazz, but with a little more of a swing feel to it. On the Camden recording, the other side contains six standards, which feature the vocals of McKinley and Dale Nunnally in two of the selections. These arrangements are on the commercial side, in comparison with Sauter's originals, and are treated in a more relaxed and light swinging manner.

McKinley's orchestra had several strengths. It was polished, played with musical taste, and developed a style that appealed to a wide-ranging audience. Nevertheless, McKinley broke up the band for health reasons in 1951 to relax for a while.[117] For the next few years, he worked as a disc jockey and on a television show before he was asked to replace Tex Beneke as leader of the Glenn Miller band in 1956. McKinley fronted the band for ten years and toured the United States, Europe, and Japan. After tiring of the road, he handed the band over to Buddy DeFranco and worked in radio and television commercials until semi-retirement in the mid-seventies.[118]

LUCKY MILLINDER

Lucky Millinder's career as a bandleader began when he took over the Mills Blue Rhythm Band in 1934 as it replaced Cab Calloway at the Cotton Club.[119] The band broke up in 1938, and Millinder worked with Bill Doggett before forming his own band in September 1940.[120] Millinder knew how to spot talent and selected some of the best musicians for his band. He was also an excellent organizer, a consummate showman, and well respected by other musicians.[121] Millinder was known to have a retentive ear for music and could conduct difficult scores after only one hearing. In fact, he studied the scores diligently and stayed up all night when necessary to learn them thoroughly. According to Dizzy Gillespie, Millinder was "the best conductor I've ever seen."[122] The Millinder band had a large following of African-Americans in the North and other urban centers, where a lot of work was available in wartime factories that operated around the clock. During and following World War II, rhythm and blues became increasingly popular in urban America, and Millinder was smart enough to capture that market.[123] His band played a fine blend of jazz, blues, and R&B and accompanied solo singers, vocal groups, and dancers. Millinder was also a singer and dancer who understood show business and crafted a musical style that reached his audiences, especially at the Savoy Ballroom and the Apollo in Harlem.[124]

One of the outstanding features of Millinder's band was vocalist Sister Rosetta Tharpe, who was primarily a gospel singer and second only to Mahalia Jackson. But Tharpe had a powerful mezzo-soprano voice and a hard-swinging style that was influenced by Cab Calloway. She also played guitar in the style of Leadbelly. In fact, Tharpe was a "crossover artist" long before the expression was coined. The first records Millinder made in 1941–1942 featured Sister Tharpe's vocals on "Trouble in the Mud," "Rock Daniel, Rock Me," "I Want a Tall Shining Papa," "Shout, Sister, Shout!" and "That's All." Her performances on these six tracks are energetic and striking, with the band providing a high-spirited musical accompaniment. Vocalist Wynonie Harris was also featured with the band, and he was one of the great blues vocalists at the time. He recorded "Hurry, Hurry!" and "Who Threw the Whiskey Down the Well?" in the forties, and his voice displays a relaxed yet confident sound with down-home musical phrasing. In addition to Tharpe and Harris, vocalist-guitarist Trevor Bacon and singer Annisteen Allen were featured with the band in the forties. Millinder's band also had a number of fine instrumentalists who were prominent during the era. Two arrangers were Chappie Willett and alto saxophonist Tab Smith. At various times, the trumpet section consisted of Freddy Webster, Archie

Johnson, Nelson Bryant, and Dizzy Gillespie. George Stevenson, Donald Cole, and Eli Robinson played in the trombone section. The woodwind section included Tab Smith, Buster Bailey, Sam "The Man" Taylor, Eddie Davis, Ben "Bullmoose" Jackson, Dave Young, and Ernest Purce. The band's outstanding rhythm section consisted of pianist Bill Doggett, bassist George Duvivier, and drummer Panama Francis. Other Millinder rhythm sections included pianists Ellis Larkins and Sir Charles Thompson and bassist Al McKibbon.[125]

From 1941 to 1947, the band recorded for the Decca label before moving over to RCA Victor for a while, and later recording for King Records around 1950. McCarthy believes that Millinder made his best records for Decca in the early forties.[126] Along with the vocal numbers mentioned above, instrumentals such as "Mason Flyer," "Little John Special," and "Shipyard Social Function" are exciting and well-played charts that reflect a tight-knit ensemble and a swinging rhythm section. Although recording techniques in the early forties had a long way to go, Millinder's band had a clean and professional sound that was second to none in the Later Swing Era. Millinder also had a keen ear for picking top-notch soloists who were also excellent section players. Some of the band's soloists were Dizzy Gillespie, Freddie Webster, Tab Smith, Buster Bailey, Dave Young, and Bill Doggett. On "Ride, Red, Ride," Buster Bailey plays a sparkling clarinet solo on the up-tempo portion of the chart that dazzles the listener's ear. Additionally, the trumpets and trombones display some fine section work during their solo outings on this exciting flag-waver. On "Mason Flyer," composer Tab Smith's alto solo displayed his command of the swing language in the early forties. Dizzy, who played the second solo, showed signs that he would move in another direction and adopt a new musical language. Stafford Simon's tenor sax solo revealed a thorough grounding in Swing Era language. His solo also had a driving and straight-ahead feel to it that could easily stir listeners' emotions and dancers' feet. The rhythm section definitely played swing style, and every beat was "in the pocket." Another notable side recorded by Millinder was "Little John Special," which again showed that Tab Smith's alto sound was influenced by Johnny Hodges. On this selection, in particular, Dizzy actually revealed his knowledge of the bebop language. In fact, his solo stands heads above the other solos with regard to modern improvisational techniques, and it was a forecast of things to come. The tenor saxophone solo on this tune is also noteworthy. The liner notes that accompany these sides indicate that Stafford Simon is the soloist, but this writer hears a totally different approach to that of Simon and believes that it is Dave Young. In fact, McCarthy pointed out in *Big Band Jazz* that some sources suggest that tenorist Dave Young is actually the soloist.[127] In any event, the solo is a hard-swinging outing that grooves from beginning to end. Overall, the band provides an exciting performance of this chart, with excellent solos, precise ensemble work, and a swinging rhythm section.

Although all of Millinder's bands are notable for a high technical level, the early Decca recordings are undoubtedly the best, according to McCarthy. Around the mid-forties, the Millinder band drifted more toward rhythm and blues featuring several vocalists. However, his recordings with the King label after 1950 saw commercial success until 1952, when he decided to disband. After about a year or so of working in nonmusical jobs, he began fronting big bands for periodic tours and specific club or theater engagements. Millinder spent his later years leading bands occasionally and working as a disc jockey and publicist until he passed away in 1966.

Lucky Millinder had all of the elements necessary for a career as a high-profile bandleader. He was an excellent conductor, a singer and dancer, an astute businessman, and an exciting showman. However, the contributions he made to the Later Swing Era remain mostly in the African American community. Despite Millinder's talent, effort, and hard work, he never made it to the world's bright lights. Therefore, according to McCarthy, "one must assume that his full potential as a leader was not realized."[128]

VAUGHN MONROE

Vocalist-trumpeter Vaughn Monroe became interested in music when he started out on trumpet in grade school. Although Monroe became a respectable trumpeter, he achieved considerable success as a vocalist and bandleader. He cut his teeth as the leader of one of Jack Marshard's society bands in the Boston area and started his own organization around 1940 in Wayland, Massachusetts. His band began to attract national attention in 1941, and during the war, he toured the country playing one-nighters, ballrooms, and theaters. In 1945, his RCA Victor recording of "There, I've Said It Again" topped the charts by selling over a million copies. Other hits such as "Let It Snow, Let It Snow, Let It Snow," "Ballerina," "Cool Water," "Someday," "Ghost Riders in the Sky," and "Somebody Else Is Taking My Place" followed, and Monroe made it to the *Camel Caravan* radio show.[129]

Most of the band's repertoire was based on the singing of Monroe, Marilyn Duke, Ziggy Talent, the Murphy Sisters, and the Moonmaids. Their theme song was entitled "Racing with the Moon."[130] Monroe was a very popular singer and had a dynamic personality. Although some music critics at the time were not too impressed with his singing, an interviewer once described him as "one of the most polite, pleasant and peaceful citizens in the music business—a very normal person in a very crazy world."[131] Monroe surrounded himself with talented musicians, such as trumpeter Bobby Nichols and trombonist-arranger Ray Conniff, but all of his popular recordings were built around his singing. Monroe was not totally comfortable with this situation. He once said, "Don't think I like the idea of making all those vocal records. We have plenty of good jazzmen in the band, and I'd like to do some instrumentals. But [RCA] Victor tells me to keep right on singing."[132]

Monroe, nevertheless, was realistic about the music industry. During an interview, he stated, "The band business isn't an artistic thing. It's a business. I could name four or five bands that aren't doing very well today because they don't do what people ask for. I can't feel sorry for them. You've got to justify what you're doing; you can't fool a promoter more than once or twice. And you've got to be right in there working all the time."[133] Obviously, his bandleading philosophy was on target, because he was one of the biggest box office attractions in the music business. His stature in the industry was equal to that of Harry James, Tommy Dorsey, and Benny Goodman. But Monroe went a step further and became one of the most popular stars of television commercials and made his first movie, entitled *Singing Guns*. He made other movies, and his band was featured on the first color television shows. After Monroe disbanded in 1953, he continued as a solo artist, performing throughout the United States and abroad. In between appearances, he managed his own restaurant in Framingham, Massachusetts, and by the mid-sixties, began spending most of his time in semi-retirement in Florida. After a lingering illness, he passed away in May 1973.[134] Monroe's contribution to the Later Swing Era was his popularity as a vocalist-bandleader. He was one of the few bandleaders of the forties and fifties who clearly understood that music is a business, and he made it to the top of both the music and media industries.

BOYD RAEBURN

Saxophonist Boyd Raeburn began his career as a professional bandleader in 1933 after winning a college band contest sponsored by the Sherman Hotel in Chicago. For nearly a decade, he led a commercial dance band in the Midwest before changing over to swing, and he established a good reputation during an engagement at the Chez Parie in Chicago in 1940. He took his band to New York City in 1942 for a brief period and returned to Chicago for a year's engagement at the Bandbox.[135] In 1944 he switched over to a "progressive jazz" style and reorganized his band with several Sonny Dunham alumni. At the time, young musicians such as trumpeters Sonny Berman and Marky Markowitz, trombonists Earl Swope and Tommy Peterson, saxophonists Johnny Bothwell and Emmett Carls, and drummer Don Lamond filled the ranks of the new Raeburn organization.[136] With a new band, Raeburn returned to New York City for an extended engagement at the Lincoln Hotel and started to impress jazz fans with his modern sounds. His sound and style were due, in no small part, to the band's arrangers. Until that point, the chief arranger had been Ed Finckel, who contributed some popular charts to the band's library. Arrangements such as "Two Spoos in an Igloo," "Bernie's Tune," and "Whispering" helped shape the Raeburn sound.[137] According to Simon, "His 1944 band was ahead of the times. Perhaps the times would have caught up with the band. But before there was a chance, a fire at Palisades Amusement Park in New Jersey destroyed the band's music library, some of its instruments, and most of its momentum."[138] In that same year, Finckel left Raeburn to join the Gene Krupa Orchestra.[139]

In 1945 Raeburn organized another band that played even more modern sounds. The new chief architect of that band's sound was George Handy, a Julliard alumnus and former student of Aaron Copeland. Handy's charts included many compositional devices from composers such as Stravinsky, Ravel, and Bartok. Of particular interest was Handy's treatment of "There's No You" and "Out of This World." Jazz critic Barry Ulanov commented, "The introduction to 'There's No You,' all by itself, is a handsome composition, bizarre chords and progressions filtered through the brightest tones the enthusiastic Raeburn musicians could manage."[140] Likewise, Allen Scott applauded Handy's arrangement of "Out of This World," penned for the band's male vocalist, David Allen. According to Scott, "The arrangement attracted instant acclaim and was indicative of the route that the band was taking. Polyrhythms and strange harmonies may have confused America's dancing public, but drew praise from critics and jazz insiders."[141] The 1945 band consisted of vocalists David Allen and Barbara Cox and saxophonists Lenny Green, Hal McKusick, Frankie Socolow, Hy Mandell, and Raeburn. The trombone section included Jack Carman, Johnny Mandel, and Rodney Roberts. The trumpets were Alan Jeffrey, Carl Berg, Dale Pearce, and Tommy Allison. Rounding out the rhythm section with pianist Handy were bassist Joe Burriesce and drummer Irv Kluger. Barry Ulanov heard the band in the Rose Room of the Palace Hotel in San Francisco and praised some of the soloists. He referred to tenorist Frankie Socolow as "a brilliant tenor man," altoist Hal McKusick "as able a lead man as Johnny [Bothwell]" who "plays a Lester Young alto," Tommy Allison as "a brilliant trumpeter," and Johnny Mandel as a trombonist "who had some absolutely new sounds to contribute" and was a "first rate arranger." Ulanov also said that the rhythm section "jumps all the way."[142]

In the late forties, Raeburn continued to enjoy some of the remaining fruit of the big band era with his third and last chief arranger Johnny Richards, who was considered a romanticist who wrote advanced yet lush and inventive charts. Journalist Allen Scott was particularly impressed with Richards' writing for the reed section, which sometimes involved doubles with oboe, bassoon, English horn, flutes, and clarinets.[143] Richards, an experienced musician and multi-instrumentalist, worked in dance bands and served as Victor Young's assistant at Paramount Studios in the 1930s. Most of Richards' scores for Raeburn's band were not recorded. However, "Prelude to the Dawn" featuring alto saxophone and "Man With a Horn" written for Raeburn on English horn were recorded.[144] It is important to note here that Johnny Mandel, Tadd Dameron, and Budd Johnson also wrote a number of charts for Raeburn's orchestra. To Raeburn's credit, he was one of the few white bandleaders in the Swing Era to hire African American musicians such as Dizzy Gillespie, Oscar Pettiford, Roy Eldridge, Trummy Young, Britt Woodman, and Lucky Thompson for radio broadcasts, recording sessions, and guest appearances.[145]

Much has been written about the "modern sound" of Raeburn's bands in the forties. In 1946 one particular recording, entitled the *Jubilee Performances*, captured the Raeburn sound and featured the charts of Finckel and Handy. "Tonsillectomy" by McKusick-Handy is a humorous composition that highlights the tight-knit and polished ensemble work of the band. "A Night in Tunisia" features Dizzy Gillespie as a guest soloist, and the theme is played beautifully by one of the band's trombonists. Handy's "Yerxa" displays how a big band can deliver an eerie but beautiful orchestral sound. In another example, Finckel's "Boyd Meets Stravinsky" is an unusual blues chart with some interesting interludes and background passages for soloists. His contrapuntal writing for the three wind instrument sections (trumpets, trombones, and saxophones), along with the use of bitonality, is particularly engaging for the serious jazz listener. Handy's "Dalvatore Sally" features some interesting tempo changes and arranging techniques using the harp, whereas "Hey Look—I'm Dancing" showcases oboes, French horns, harp, and bassoon.[146] Raeburn's modern sound impressed jazz critics, a Midwest businessman (who invested $100,000), and Duke Ellington (who contributed $15,000) in the late forties.[147] Unfortunately, Raeburn's "progressive jazz" style did not appeal to the public at large, and by 1948, he was unable to sustain a major impact on the big band scene. Many of his best musicians began to leave the band, and he finally decided to disband later that year.[148] Raeburn worked off and on around New York with various pickup bands until 1952, when he left music for the furniture business. In the mid-fifties, he and his wife, vocalist Ginnie Powell, moved to the Bahamas, where she died in 1959.[149] Unable to cope with her death, Raeburn remained in obscurity until he was injured in an automobile accident in Texas. Subsequently, on August 2, 1966, he died in Lafayette, Louisiana, at age fifty-two.[150]

As an instrumentalist, Raeburn started out on tenor saxophone and later switched to baritone. Arranger Ed Finckel reportedly encouraged him to play the rarely seen bass saxophone, which "was a natural attention-getter." According to Allen Scott, Raeburn, a very personable individual, was once quoted as saying, "For a musician idiot, I've got a great band!"[151]

BUDDY RICH

Drummer-bandleader Buddy Rich began his musical career as a young drummer in vaudeville with his family. He also learned to dance, but not from his family's touring vaudeville act. According to Rich, he "picked up dancing from being around with colored boys; they were full of rhythm!"[152]

He started in the band business when bassist Artie Shapiro invited him to sit in with Joe Marsala's sextet at the Hickory House in New York. Rich joined Marsala in 1938 and, later that year, switched over to Bunny Berigan's band before leaving to join Artie Shaw. In 1939 Rich joined Tommy Dorsey's orchestra and remained until 1942, prior to entering military service as a marine for two years. In late 1944, he rejoined Dorsey's band for another two years.[153] Rich formed his first big band in 1946 with financial backing from Frank Sinatra and got off to an "impressive" start according to journalist George Simon. The band's library included some modern charts by noted arrangers Ed Finckel, Tadd Dameron, Turk Van Lake, and Billy Moore, Jr. In addition, booking agent Sonny Werblin secured engagements at some of the country's top venues, such as the Hotel Sherman in Chicago, the Palladium in Hollywood, and the Arcadia Ballroom in New York City.[154] Rich's band employed some of the most accomplished musicians in the music industry. At one point, the trumpet section included Stan Fishelson, Tommy Allison, Phil Gilbert, and Bill Howell. Earl Swope, Bob Ascher, Johnny Mandel, and/or Chunky Koenigsberg played in the trombone section. The saxes were Eddie Caine, Jerry Thirkeld, Allen Eager, Mickey Rich (Buddy's brother), and Harvey Levine. Pianist Harvey Leonard, guitarist Gene Dell, bassist Tubby Phillips, and drummers Stanley Kay and Rich made up the rhythm section. Linda Larkin and Rich were the band's vocalists.[155]

The sound of Rich's band reflected his philosophy of swing. During an engagement at the Strand Theater, Barbara Hodgkins interviewed him during an intermission, and he stated, "I like swing; I like the message it gives. But I don't understand this new trend toward real frantic stuff. It has no conception of melody. If you're playing the blues you want to have a semblance of the blues, don't you? This writing down a lot of notes and putting a tempo to it is overestimated."[156] Obviously, Rich referred to the ultramodern bands that were moving in the direction of concert jazz performance that evolved during the Later Swing Era. He further expressed his thoughts on the subject:

> And another thing...I'm going to keep right on playing the kind of music we're doing now, in spite of all the leaders who think jazz is on the way out. You have to be able to feel an audience and feel what they want you to play. As long as there are kids who want me to play jazz, I'm not going to try to change the band. You're all right if you have people to write for you who're accepted as the right writers of new jazz. I like ballads with a beat; they're listenable and danceable. We're not trying to be a novelty band; we don't want any weird sounds or weird instruments—no French horns or English horns or oboes or any of that stuff.[157]

During Rich's first year as a bandleader, jazz journalists began to take notice of his singing. He never thought of himself as a vocalist, but Frank Sinatra heard him sing "Aren't You Glad You're You?" at one of the band's first rehearsals and suggested that he start singing with the band. During the aforementioned interview with Hodgkins, Rich pointed out that two of his favorite singers were Nat "King" Cole and Sinatra. After hearing Buddy sing "Baby, Baby All the Time," Hodgkins commented, "As far as I can see, this was singing as great as Nat's or Frank's: it certainly had a relaxed beat, a real feeling for jazz and a sense of intimacy for the listener."[158] Bill Gottlieb, who reviewed one of the band's performances at the Arcadia Ballroom added, "[Rich's] voice is a winner." In Gottlieb's review, he also discussed a few aspects of the band's quality and style. He felt that it was too early in the band's career to appraise it fairly at that point. However, in referring to Bill Channon's ballad arrangements and Ed Finckel's up-tempo numbers, Gottlieb indicated that the arrangers "will ultimately have to create some distinctive style to make the Rich orchestra recognizable as such." Gottlieb, on the other hand, identified one of Finckel's scoring devices that gave the band an identifying sound: "The use of trumpet and sax sections to the exclusion of trombones, with the first horn playing in unison with the first reed, the second horn with the second reed, and so on,…gives a soft, pretty effect." Gottlieb also recognized the solo work of Lester Young–influenced tenorist Allen Eager and trombonist Bob Asher, whereas lead trumpeter Stan Fishelson was cited for handling "his burdensome job extremely well."[159]

Despite excellent musicians, strong financial support, and bookings in some of the top performance venues in the country, the band never reached the public at large. The biggest problem was the lack of an organized plan to promote and publicize the band. It is difficult to determine the reason because MCA, personal manager Lou Mindling, and band manager Harvey Perskey were firmly behind Rich's organization.[160] In any event, after a couple of years, Rich disbanded and toured with Norman Granz and Jazz at the Philharmonic. During the fifties, Rich worked for Harry James and Tommy Dorsey while leading his own bands intermittently. He took a break from the band business in 1959 for health reasons but rejoined Harry James in 1961 and remained with that band until early 1966. Shortly after leaving James, Rich formed another big band that played exciting and modern-sounding arrangements. This band, with its rock-influenced commercial appeal, began to reach young listeners and eventually became successful.[161] The summer of 1967 saw Rich's band hit the big time when it was chosen for Jackie Gleason's summer replacement TV series as well as one of Frank Sinatra's concert tours. Rich also became somewhat of a TV personality, primarily because of frequent appearances on Johnny Carson's *Tonight Show*. For about a decade, Buddy Rich had one of the most exciting and popular big bands in the country. Rich was forced to reduce his band to a sextet after being warned by doctors to slow down; however, after regaining his strength, he started another big band with young musicians, which continued to perform into the eighties.[162] Although Buddy Rich's success as a bandleader came a decade after the Later Swing Era, his bands of the mid- to late forties did have an impact on many musicians and journalists at that time. However, he had more of an impact as a drummer through his work with Tommy Dorsey and Harry James.

CLAUDE THORNHILL

Claude Thornhill's career as a bandleader began in 1940 when he started his first band in New York City. He arrived in the Big Apple in the early thirties after studying at the Cincinnati Conservatory and the Curtis Institute in Philadelphia. Thornhill's talent as a pianist-composer was soon recognized by such bandleaders as Hal Kemp, Freddy Martin, Russ Morgan, Ray Noble, and Benny Goodman, with whom he eventually played and/or recorded. In the mid-thirties, Thornhill served as pianist-arranger for Andre Kostelanetz. Subsequently, Thornhill received some national attention after he arranged and recorded "Gone with the Wind" and "Loch Lomond," which featured singer Maxine Sullivan. Success opened its door even more for Thornhill when he served as music director for Skinnay Ennis' band on *The Bob Hope Show* during the summer of 1939. Six months later, with forty new arrangements, Thornhill formed his first big band. During its infancy, the band subbed several times for Glenn Miller at the Pennsylvania Hotel and for Sammy Kaye's orchestra at the Commodore in New York City. Some rocky starts followed, however. For example, Thornhill's first engagement in Virginia Beach fell through because the venue caught on fire the night before the opening. His band migrated to the West Coast for an engagement at Balboa Beach, but the club's manager reneged on the deal. Another job at a San Francisco hotel was not successful, because Thornhill's piano style was much different than expected. He ended up back on the East Coast at a club in Hartford, Connecticut, but that job lasted only two nights, because the club manager closed the place and disappeared with the money. In March 1941, things finally shifted for Thornhill during a two-month stint at the Glen Island Casino. His band included some fine musicians, such as trumpeters Conrad Gozzo and Rusty Deadrick, clarinetist Irving Fazola, trombonists Tasso Harris and Bob Jenney, and vocalists Betty Claire and Dick Harding.[163] The band's arranging staff consisted of Bill Borden, Andy Phillips, Gil Evans, and Thornhill himself.[164]

With a talented band and top-flight arrangers, Thornhill developed a unique style that raised the eyebrows of jazz critics such as George Simon, who wrote, "Truly, it is an amazing aggregation...for not only has it struck upon a style that's musically unique and thrilling, but it also shows a flair for commercialism that's lacking even in most bands whose only claim to fame is cow-towing to the public's demands." Simon continued,

> Of all its qualities of fine musicianship, the one that set the band several notches above almost all others was its magnificent use of dynamics. It would

achieve a soft, mellow mood, either through Claude's extremely delicate, one-fingered piano solos or through six delicately blown unison clarinets; then suddenly it would burst forth into a gorgeous, rich full ensemble sound, highlighted by the brilliance of Conrad Gozzo's lead trumpet.[165]

There were two main factors that contributed to Thornhill's unique style in the early forties. First, because of an ASCAP ban of all the band's copyrighted material, Thornhill transformed some of the popular works of Western composers such as Tchaikovsky, Grieg, and Dvorak into dance arrangements. Traditional tunes such as "Auld Lang Syne," "Londonderry Air," and "Stick of Barley" also served as prime vehicles for popular big band charts. In addition, Thornhill's own compositions, such as the tone "poem-let" "Snowfall," were similar in style. Second, Thornhill employed the use of clarinets (sometimes as many as seven), French horns, and tuba for an expanded ensemble.[166]

Between 1940 and 1942, Thornhill's orchestra established itself on the national scene. However, it became increasingly difficult for him to keep his organization intact, because the draft kept taking musicians to help defend the country. Finally, Thornhill himself entered the navy on October 26, 1942, at the rank of apprentice seaman. He served for three years as a musician in the military, where he played in Artie Shaw's band and organized special shows and dance bands in the Pacific. In fact, Thornhill worked with Admirals Nimitz and Halsey and was a respected advisor on musical matters. In 1946 Claude Thornhill returned to civilian life and started another band with a number of his former sidemen. Four of his five saxophonists, all three trumpeters, both trombonists, and one of two French horn players came back to the band along with arrangers Evans and Borden. The rhythm section included bassist Iggy Shevach and drummer Billy Exiner, while Fran Warren and Gene Williams were the vocalists. Fortunately, Thornhill's first band had recorded some excellent sides, and his popularity remained buoyant on the U.S. mainland during his tour of duty.[167] In effect, he was able to continue where he had left off, but this time with Gil Evans as the band's chief arranger.[168]

The band's postwar style evolved to another level with Gil Evans' arrangements, which often adapted small-group compositions to a big band sound. Bebop compositions such as "Anthropology," "Donna Lee," and "Yardbird Suite" featured modern jazz soloists such as Red Rodney and Lee Konitz. However, the public preferred the band's ballad sounds on recordings such as "For Heaven's Sake," "Lover Man," and "Let's Call It a Day."[169] Thornhill's orchestra offered both dancers and listeners a potpourri of both traditional and modern arrangements along with compositions that resulted in an identifiable sound. Moreover, the continued use of clarinets, French horns, and tuba in the ensemble contributed to the band's overall sound. The clarinet, while used to add a wider range to the band, created some intonation problems when played in its upper register. Thornhill probably employed clarinets as a substitute for violins. Nevertheless, the clarinets added to the band's tonal color and range. The French horns and tuba, of course, added more depth and weight to the overall ensemble sound.

The sound of Thornhill's band is captured vividly in its recording of "Robbin's Nest" arranged by Evans. The band's expanded tonal range is evident in this chart, which employs full-ensemble passages in the theme and background behind Danny Polo's clarinet solo. A tenor sax solo and a brief call-and-response section follow the clarinet solo. Afterward, the full ensemble proceeds with some interesting tonal colors and combinations before a brief solo by Thornhill. Evans' scoring of muted brass within the rest of the ensemble in the final passages rounds out the arrangement. This arrangement is probably one of the most modern-sounding pieces written in the forties. On the more traditional side, we hear Evans' subtle yet modern treatment of "Polka Dots and Moonbeams," which certainly must have appealed to Thornhill's dancing fans. It is primarily an instrumental backdrop for Thornhill's simple and effective piano style. Again, the French horns and tuba add resonance and depth to the ensemble's sound. As with many of the commercial dance bands in the forties, the rhythmic feel here is subtle. Similarly, Thornhill's "Snowfall" is a rather misty-sounding composition for slow dancing, with ensemble colors that are pleasing to the jazz listener's ear. This chart features Thornhill's piano throughout and is, in some ways, similar to European concert music.

Returning to Thornhill's modern bop side, Evans' arrangement of Charlie Parker's "Donna Lee" replicates the sound of a jazz quintet, with the melody stated by reeds and muted trumpets in unison over the rhythm section. This chart features solos for tenor sax, trombone, and guitar. Barry Galbraith's guitar solo especially stands out on this chart. Following Galbraith's solo, the band's shout chorus near the end of this arrangement displays Evans' talent for scoring beautifully shifting tonal colors in tutti passages. This chorus, along with the tag, clearly foreshadows the sound of Miles Davis' "Birth of the Cool" sessions that followed a few years later. Thornhill's 1947 recording of Evans' arrangement of Parker's "Anthropology" also simulates the small bop group with the melody played by muted trumpets and reeds after a piano introduction and solo. Evans' treatment of the full ensemble is tasteful, for it follows a brief trombone solo with an interlude that adds spice and color to the arrangement. Lee Konitz's alto solo follows the interlude with full-ensemble accompaniment before a second brief interlude introduces a guitar solo by Barry Galbraith. Thornhill adds some sparse fill-ins behind Galbraith's noteworthy outing before the theme or melody is restated by muted trumpets in unison with reeds.

Claude Thornhill's band was one of the most original-sounding ensembles in the forties. Unfortunately, it was unable to reach the heights of popularity and wealth enjoyed by many of the more commercial orchestras. Thornhill was simply a skilled composer-arranger who utilized the talents of arrangers such as Bill Borden, Gerry Mulligan, and Gil Evans to create a big band sound that had a major impact on modern jazz. Thornhill disbanded in 1948 but returned to the music scene a few months later and made occasional appearances with temporary big bands that featured arrangements by Gerry Mulligan and jazz solos by Tony Scott, Hal McKusick, Bob Brookmeyer, and others. In the mid-fifties, Thornhill began leading small groups off and on in the South up to his death in 1965. Claude Thornhill's years as a big band leader were rather brief, in comparison with many bandleaders, but his contribution to modern music was indeed large. A few days after Thornhill's death, Duke Ellington called his widow to express his condolences and concluded his conversation by saying simply, "He was a beautiful man."[170]

COOTIE WILLIAMS

Trumpeter Cootie Williams' career as a professional bandleader started in late 1941 when he assembled his first big band.[171] Williams brought a great deal of experience to the front of his band after working with Fletcher Henderson, Benny Goodman, and Duke Ellington. This experience served Williams well, because he was able to keep a big band together for almost a decade in the forties.

Williams' orchestra made its first New York appearance at the Apollo Theatre in May 1942 and received a highly complimentary review by columnist Barry Ulanov. He wrote, "The first appearance of Cootie Williams and his band in New York was an exciting and auspicious one. Few bands, colored or white, make inaugural appearances this fine in every way. But then, few bands have a star of the magnitude of Cootie Williams to head them, and few leaders have support of the quality that Mr. Williams has." Ulanov further complimented Williams' trumpet playing by stating, "His trumpet, open, plungered, buzz-muted, or hand-muted paraded through everything the band did." He added that Williams "led a band that showed forthright and unmistakable musicianship in everything it played." The reviewer recognized the high-quality soloists in the band: pianist Kenneth Kersey, alto saxophonist-vocalist Eddie "Cleanhead" Vinson, trumpeter Joe Guy, trombonist R. H. Horton, and tenor saxophonist Bob Dorsey. Vocalist Pearl Bailey was cited as having a "fine jazz voice," a solid beat, and fine all-around showmanship. Eddie Vinson was described as "a thrilling altoist in the Hodges tradition" and a "fine blues singer" who was visually the highpoint at the Apollo that night. Vinson's facial and body gestures revealed the true meaning of "Cherry Red" and "Outskirts of Town," which hit a home run with the audience.[172] In addition to Williams' appearances at the Apollo, he secured bookings in major venues such as New York's Paramount and the Savoy Ballroom. Williams' orchestra also contributed to the war effort by entertaining troops in numerous camps, hospitals, and USO spots. This was done in spite of the fact that he, like many other bandleaders at the time, had difficulty keeping his band intact because of the military draft.[173]

A few months later, Barry Ulanov wrote another review of Williams' performance at the Savoy Ballroom in New York City in October 1942. This particular review was more in-depth and complimentary than the first one. Not only was Williams' trumpeting recognized, but his singing, bandleading, and handling of an audience was regarded as "big time." More importantly, Ulanov commented on the quality of the band's musicianship, well-rehearsed sections, precise ensemble playing, and good intonation. The trumpet section included Milton Fletcher, Joe Guy, and Louis Bacon. Ed Burke, Jones Walker, and R. H. Horton were in the trombone section. The saxes were Eddie Vinson, Bob Dorsey, Charlie Holmes, Sam Taylor, and Greely Walton. Pianist Fletcher Smith, bassist Norman Keeman, and drummer Butch Ballard rounded out the rhythm section. Bacon, Vinson, and Williams doubled on vocals. Ulanov rated the trumpets as the top section under Cootie Williams' lead, and the trombones were described as a solid section that played evenly with a good trio sound. The saxes were labeled a fine section, and the three-person rhythm team was cited for being steady and giving the band maximum support.[174]

One of Williams' strong points as a bandleader was his willingness to foster the talent of younger musicians such as Pearl Bailey, Eddie Vinson, Thelonious Monk, and Bud Powell. For example, Williams had to exercise a great deal of patience in helping Bailey develop her talent because of her recalcitrant attitude at the time. In another example, Eddie Vinson was afraid to relocate from Texas to New York City. Consequently, Williams fed and housed Vinson for a while and bought him a new saxophone. As a result of Williams' encouragement, both Bailey and Vinson went on to become major artists in the music industry. Williams also recognized Bud Powell's talent and gave Bud his first big band job when he was only sixteen.[175] Williams also supported the work of younger composer-arrangers and premiered Thelonious Monk's "Epistrophy" in 1942 and "Round About Midnight" in 1944. Other young instrumentalists, such as pianist Ken Kersey, saxophonist Sam Taylor, and trumpeters Joe Guy, Gene Redd, and George Treadwell entered the music profession through Cootie Williams' orchestra.

Referred to as a "transitional band" by Schuller, the Williams organization played a combination of both swing and bebop styles.[176] On one hand, "the band was resident at New York's Savoy Ballroom and was popular with the dancers who formed the major part of its clientele," according to McCarthy.[177] Therefore, it played with "a strong danceable rhythmic beat" that appealed to the Savoy's dancing crowd.[178] On the other hand, the band foreshadowed bop by performing works written by composers such as Monk and featuring soloists including Bud Powell, Charlie Parker, and Bennie Harris. Furthermore, during part of the band's existence, vocalist Eddie

Vinson added a blues style to its overall identity, which gave it an eclectic sound. Such a sound was referred to as "unidentifiable" by some jazz historians, but that sound can also be considered unique because it existed during the forties when most big bands were commercial. The sound of Williams' band is available on sides recorded by Capitol in the mid-forties. For example, the band's recording of "House of Joy" is a medium up-tempo flag-waver that undoubtedly appealed to the Savoy's dancing patrons. It has all of the excitement and energy necessary to lift the spirits of dancers and listeners alike. Eddie Vinson's alto sax solo is exuberant, with flaring background passages played by the brass section. Cootie's solo follows with the same level of intensity over unison saxes in the [A] sections and harmonized backgrounds in the bridge [B]. An equally exciting shout chorus by the full ensemble follows before the end. "Echoes of Harlem" by Duke Ellington features Cootie's muted trumpet in a somber minor key. There is also an attractive call-and-response section between Williams and vocal utterings by the rest of the band. Les Hite's "That's the Lick" is a riff tune that features solos by tenorist Sam "The Man" Taylor and Cootie Williams. Taylor's solo swings throughout, and Williams' intense outing showcases his high-note playing, while the full ensemble riffs continuously to the end. Williams' band helped to forecast the bebop era with its rendition of Monk's "Fly Right" (Epistrophy) that featured Cootie's trumpet. Likewise, the same composer's "Round Midnight" showcased Williams' trumpet stating the melody with a full-ensemble background. Although this piece demonstrated an original sound at the time, it also served as an appropriate vehicle for slow dancing. Cootie's muted trumpet stated the melody with band accompaniment throughout the theme. His famous growls are quite evident here along with a tenor sax solo accompanied by plunger-muted brass passages. Following is a trombone solo with a plunger for one chorus before Bud Powell's piano solo that fuses bop with swing quite successfully. After the solos, the full band plays a grooving tutti section to the final chord.

The Cootie Williams big band chapter was closed in 1948, but he led a small rhythm-and-blues band from 1950 to the mid-sixties before he returned to Duke Ellington's orchestra. With the exception of his big band recordings that featured some all-star musicians he assembled in 1958, he spent the rest of his big band years with Duke and Mercer Ellington until his death in 1985.[179] Although Cootie Williams did not achieve the success of many commercial big band leaders in the forties, jazz historians may well recognize him in the future as a pioneer of jazz fusion.

GERALD WILSON

Trumpeter-arranger-composer Gerald Wilson became a bandleader in 1944 when vocalist Herb Jeffries asked him to organize a big band for his show that was scheduled to open at Shepp's Playhouse in Los Angeles.

Unfortunately, Jeffries left town, but Wilson was offered the job without Herb. Wilson decided to keep the band together and took the job. Subsequently, he and the band became quite successful after working with Joe Williams in St. Louis for six weeks, recording with Dinah Washington, and obtaining a contract with Excelsior Records. The band also played in Salt Lake City, Dallas, St. Louis, Chicago, and at the Apollo in New York City.[180] By 1945, Wilson's orchestra had recorded over fifteen sides for Excelsior. The personnel included Wilson, Snooky Young, Hobart Dotson, Joe "Red" Kelly, and James Anderson on trumpets. Melba Liston, Isaac Livingstone, Ralph Bledsoe, and Robert Huerta were the trombone section. The saxophone section consisted of Floyd Turnham and Leo Trammel on alto, Vernon Slater and Eddie Davis on tenor, and Maurice Simon on baritone. The rhythm section consisted of Jimmy Bunn on piano, Benny Sexton on guitar, Robert Rudd on bass, and Henry Tucker Green on drums. Two of the more interesting charts recorded that year were Wilson's arrangements of Duke Ellington's "Come Sunday" and Dizzy Gillespie's "Groovin' High."

"Come Sunday" features Wilson's muted trumpet on the melody for sixteen bars during the two [A] sections, accompanied by a small ensemble of muted brass and soft saxophones. The saxes continue with the bridge [B] in harmony, and Hobart Dotson plays the last eight bars of the theme with open trumpet over an eight-bar harmonized background played by the saxophone section. Pianist Jimmy Bunn plays a brief eight-bar solo (A) and, without playing the next [A] section, Melba Liston proceeds directly to the bridge [B] and solos for eight bars, using a mute with harmonized accompaniment by the saxophones (incidentally, this is one of her first recorded solos). Wilson returns with the final eight bars of the melody, playing muted trumpet over a subdued full-ensemble accompaniment. The band easily captured the Ellington mood with sensitive phrasing and musicianship. As a matter of record, Wilson's band actually recorded this song before Duke Ellington did.

Gillespie's "Groovin' High" opens with a twelve-bar introduction that consists of different variants of the theme that showcases each of the three instrumental sections. The saxes play the first sixteen bars of the tune with alternating unison and harmonized phrases. The introduction is repeated here as an element of surprise, and it is followed by Dotson's sixteen-bar driving trumpet solo. Tenorist Eddie Davis (no relation to "Lockjaw") plays a swinging full thirty-two-bar solo over brass accompaniment. Bunn solos for sixteen bars and is followed by a twelve-bar interlude that displays the band's technical facility as it quotes from the tag of Gillespie's "A Night in Tunisia." The end of the interlude signals a modulation to another key, and the trumpet section plays the melody over harmonized backgrounds in the saxophone and trombone sections for the first sixteen bars of the tune. The saxophone section then plays the theme for the last sixteen bars, with brass accompaniment before the final chord. This chart features screaming brass, and it has all of the bells and whistles that one finds in an exciting big band arrangement.

In 1946, Wilson's band recorded for the Black & White label with most of the aforementioned personnel, except that altoist Gus Evans replaced Leo Trammel, and Elijah "Buddy" Harper took over on guitar. Among the tunes recorded were Liston's "Warm Mood" and Wilson's "Cruisin' with Cab." Floyd Turham's alto saxophone is featured on "Warm Mood" with band accompaniment, which shows off Liston's unique ability to write a ballad for big band with considerable skill and harmonic sensitivity. Wilson's fast-moving "Cruisin' with Cab" features unison saxes in the three [A] sections of the tune, and in harmony during the bridge [B], with accompanying punch figures played by the brass. Tenorist Davis plays two full solo choruses, with muted brass accompaniment in the second chorus. The third solo chorus is shared by either Dotson or Young on trumpet and Bunn's piano. The full band returns with the theme played by harmonized brass and unison saxes. Evans solos on the bridge before the band concludes with the song's last eight bars and the final chord. In 1946, A. S. Otto wrote of Wilson's band:

> The hours of rehearsal are plainly evident, for this is a weighty, powerhouse ork which executes passages with perfection. A smooth, balanced tone seems to be the desired effect, rather than the common succession of solos with background scoring. The sax section, faintly reminiscent of the Lunceford blending which Gerald absorbed for three years is great. There are sufficient solos, however, for interesting listening. Hobart Dotson shares trumpet honors with the leader. Melba Liston, femme trombonist, blows excellent choruses and so does Ralph Bledsoe. The rhythm section lays down a reliable beat on hot and sweet selections alike, and pianist Jimmy Bunn plays more than acceptably. It is remarkable that a band can be as versatile as this one.[181]

With excellent reviews (such as Otto's) and two tours around the country, Wilson's orchestra reached its peak of popularity and commercial success in 1947. It had numerous bookings and lucrative contracts when Wilson suddenly decided to disband. To say the least, his booking agent was disappointed. Wilson dissolved his band because he felt that he needed to study and refine his knowledge of harmony and orchestration.

However, Wilson continued to perform and arrange charts for other bandleaders, such as Duke Ellington, Dizzy Gillespie, and Count Basie. In fact, he played with Basie in 1948, and in Gillespie's big band in 1950 with Paul Gonsalves, Jimmy Heath, and John Coltrane. Wilson also continued to write for Ellington, Ella Fitzgerald, and Al Hibbler.[182] As a result of his studies, Wilson became one of the most active arrangers in jazz and popular music in the late forties and fifties. He went on to write for Nancy Wilson, Sarah Vaughn, Ray Charles, Julie London, Carmen McRae, Bobby Darin, and many others after the Swing Era. Wilson reorganized another big band in the early sixties, wrote scores for movies and television, composed and orchestrated for symphony orchestras, and taught at three universities in the Los Angeles metropolitan area for over twenty years. He recorded with Pacific Jazz for a number of years and began recording for MAMA Records in the nineties. His 1995 *State Street Sweet* CD received a Grammy nomination as Best Large Ensemble Jazz Performance. He was also honored at the Chicago Jazz Festival on his eighty-third birthday and received a similar honor from the city of Los Angeles.[183] In sum, Gerald Wilson has experienced one of the longest and most successful careers in the history of American music.

NOTES

1. Leo Walker, *The Big Band Almanac*, p. 5.
2. Bill Coss, "Ray Anthony," *Metronome* 68, no. 3 (1952): 21.
3. Ibid., p. 11.
4. Ken Burke, "Ray Anthony," in *Music Hound Swing*, p. 5.
5. Ray Anthony, "The Anthony Statement," *Metronome* 68, no. 3 (1952): 11, 21.
6. Burke, "Ray Anthony," p. 5.
7. Barry Kernfeld, ed., *The New Grove Dictionary of Jazz*, vol. 1 (New York: MacMillan Press, 1988), p. 96.
8. Walker, *The Big Band Almanac*, p. 34.
9. George Simon, "Tex Beneke," *Metronome* 64, no. 5 (1948): 15.
10. Walker, *The Big Band Almanac*, p. 34.
11. Simon, "Tex Beneke," p. 16.
12. Schuller, *The Swing Era*, pp. 661–677.
13. Kernfeld, *The New Grove Dictionary* (1988), 1:143.
14. John Chilton, *Who's Who of Jazz: Storyville to Swing Street* (Philadelphia, PA: Chilton Book, Co., 1978), p. 44.
15. Walker, *The Big Band Almanac*, p. 47.
16. Schuller, *The Swing Era*, pp. 423–424.
17. Albert McCarthy, *Big Band Jazz* (New York: Exeter Books, 1983), pp. 274–275.
18. Knopper, *Music Hound Swing*, p. 32.
19. Schuller, *The Swing Era*, p. 425.
20. Simon, *The Big Bands*, pp. 101–102.
21. Walker, *The Big Band Almanac*, p. 54.
22. Simon, *The Big Bands*, pp. 103–104.
23. Walker, *The Big Band Almanac*, p. 54.
24. Ibid., p. 58.
25. Schuller, *The Swing Era*, pp. 758–759.
26. Mark Fonder, "Les Is More: A Sentimental Journey with Les Brown," *The Instrumentalist* 45, no. 2 (1990): 36.
27. Eileen Southern, "Conversation with William Clarence 'Billy' Eckstine," *The Black Perspective in Music* 7, no. 2 (1979): 183–198.
28. George Hoefer, "The First Big Bop Band," *Downbeat* 32, no. 16 (1965): 23.
29. Ibid., p. 24.

30. McCarthy, *Big Band Jazz*, pp. 222–224.

31. Walker, *The Big Band Almanac*, p. 113.

32. Hoefer, "The First Big Bop Band," p. 24.

33. Richard Palmer, "Les Elgart," *Cadence* 12, no. 11 (1986): 17–18.

34. Frank Tracy, ed., "The Elgart Brothers and How They Grew," *Downbeat* 21, no. 20 (1954): 7.

35. Palmer, "Les Elgart," p. 18.

36. Walker, *The Big Band Almanac*, p. 114.

37. Richard Palmer, "Larry Elgart: Interview," *Cadence* 11, no. 9 (1985): 9.

38. Ibid., pp. 8–10.

39. Tracy, "The Elgart Brothers," p. 8.

40. George Simon, "Latest Prescription: More Dancing, Les Elgart," *Metronome* 70, no. 10 (1954): 14.

41. Walker, *The Big Band Almanac*, p. 141.

42. Leonard Feather, "Dizzy Is Crazy Like a Fox," *Metronome* (July 1944): 16.

43. Leonard Feather, "Dizzy—21st Century Gabriel," *Esquire* (October 1945): 91.

44. Carr, *The Rough Guide*, pp. 234–237.

45. Band of the Year: Dizzy Gillespie, *Metronome* 64, no. 1 (1948): 17–18.

46. Leonard Feather, "Europe Goes Dizzy," *Metronome* 64, no. 5 (1948): 19.

47. Barry Ulanov, "Dizzy Atmosphere," *Metronome* 64, no. 8 (1948): 13.

48. Ibid., p. 18.

49. McCarthy, *Big Band Jazz*, p. 225.

50. Linda Dahl, *Stormy Weather: The Music and Lives of a Century of Jazz-women* (New York: Limelight, 1989), pp. 53–54.

51. Marcia Froelke Coburn, "Sweethearts of Swing: The Rise and Fall of an All-Girl Band," Institute of Jazz Studies–Rutgers University File Folder 32, 34.

52. Marian McPartland, *All in Good Time* (New York: Oxford University Press, 1987), pp. 143–145.

53. Ibid., p. 145.

54. Coburn, "Sweethearts of Swing," p. 34.

55. Dahl, *Stormy Weather*, p. 55.

56 Coburn, "Sweethearts of Swing," pp. 34, 36.

57. Ibid., p. 36.

58. McPartland, *All in Good Time*, pp. 150–151.

59. Ibid., pp. 152–153.

60. Coburn, "Sweethearts of Swing," p. 38.

61. Ibid., p. 48.

62. McPartland, *All in Good Time*, p. 156.

63. Knopper, *Music Hound Swing*, pp. 162–163.

64. Chilton, *Who's Who of Jazz*, p. 167.

65. Anatol Schenker, liner notes to Buddy Johnson & His Orchestra 1942–1947 (Classics CD 1079, 1999).

66. Anatol Schenker, liner notes to Buddy Johnson & His Orchestra 1947–1949 (Classics CD 1115, 2000).

67. Kernfeld, *The New Grove Dictionary* (1988), 1:648.

68. Simon, *The Big Bands*, p. 293.

69. Walker, *The Big Band Almanac*, p. 239.

70. Simon, *The Big Bands*, p. 295.

71. Walker, *The Big Band Almanac*, p. 239.

72. Simon, *The Big Bands*, pp. 295–297.

73. Walker, *The Big Band Almanac*, pp. 239–240.

74. Kernfeld, *The New Grove Dictionary* (1988), 1:648.

75. Walker, *The Big Band Almanac*, p. 240.

76. Kernfeld, *The New Grove Dictionary* (1988), 1:648.

77. Walker, *The Big Band Almanac*, pp. 238–240.

78. Simon, *The Big Bands*, p. 294.

79. Barry Ulanov, "He's In and He's Out!" *Metronome* 65, no. 1 (1949): 15–16.

80. Barry Ulanov, "What's Wrong with Stan Kenton?" *Metronome* 64, no. 2 (1948): 17, 32–33.

81. Jack Tracy, "Is 'Kenton Era' End for Stan?" *Downbeat* 22, no. 5 (1955): 6.

82. Kernfeld, *The New Grove Dictionary* (1998), 1:648.

83. Stan Woolley, "Elliot Lawrence—Forgotten Big Band Leader," *Jazz Journal International* 50, no. 5 (1997): 8.

84. Simon, *The Big Bands*, p. 318.

85. Woolley, "Elliot Lawrence," p. 8.

86. Walker, *The Big Band Almanac*, pp. 255–256.

87. Woolley, "Elliot Lawrence," pp. 8–9.

88. Ibid.

89. Bill Coss, "Elliot Lawrence: In Person," *Metronome* 68, no. 8 (1952): 19.

90. Ibid.

91. Simon, *The Big Bands*, pp. 318–319.

92. Woolley, "Elliot Lawrence," pp. 9–10.

93. Simon, *The Big Bands*, pp. 340–341.

94. Walker, *The Big Band Almanac*, p. 277.

95. Simon, *The Big Bands*, pp. 341–342.

96. Walker, *The Big Band Almanac*, p. 277.

97. George Simon and Barry Ulanov, eds., "The Band that Came Back!" *Metronome* 68, no. 9 (1952): 16.

98. Schuller, *The Swing Era*, p. 763.

99. Ibid., p. 760.

100. George Simon, "Review of Hal MacIntyre's performance at the Glen Island Casino," *Metronome* 58, no. 3 (1942): 12, 22.

101. Simon and Ulanov, "The Band That Came Back!" p. 16.

102. Schuller, *The Swing Era*, pp. 761, 763.

103. Simon, *The Big Bands*, p. 342.

104. Carr, *The Rough Guide*, pp. 426–427.

105. Walker, *The Big Band Almanac*, p. 280.

106. Carr, *The Rough Guide*, pp. 426–427.

107. Burt Korall, "Ray McKinley: Swing Pioneer," *Modern Drummer* 10, no. 4 (1986): 82.

108. Simon, *The Big Bands*, pp. 343.

109. Ibid., pp. 343–344.

110. Korall, "Ray McKinley," pp. 82–83.

111. Feather and Gitler, *Encyclopedia of Jazz*, p. 453.

112. Simon, *The Big Bands*, p. 345.

113. Walker, *The Big Band Almanac*, p. 280.

114. Simon, *The Big Bands*, p. 345.

115. Korall, "Ray McKinley," p. 83.

116. Walker, *The Big Band Almanac*, p. 280.

117. Korall, "Ray McKinley," p. 83.

118. Simon, *The Big Bands*, p. 345.

119. Carr, *The Rough Guide*, p. 441.

120. Knopper, *Music Hound Swing*, p. 219.

121. McCarthy, *Big Band Jazz*, p. 291.

122. Carr, *The Rough Guide*, p. 441.

123. Schuller, *The Swing Era*, p. 390.

124. Stan Britt, liner notes to Lucky Millinder and His Orchestra: Apollo Jump (Charly/Affinity AFS 1004, 1983).

125. Ibid.

126. McCarthy, *Big Band Jazz*, p. 291.

127. Ibid.

128. Ibid.

129. Walker, *The Big Band Almanac*, pp. 300–301.

130. Simon, *The Big Bands*, p. 374.

131. Ibid., p. 373.

132. Ibid., p. 374.

133. Ibid.

134. Walker, *The Big Band Almanac*, pp. 301–302.

135. Ibid., p. 350.

136. Simon, *The Big Bands*, pp. 398–399.

137. Scott, "Rediscovering Boyd Raeburn," pp. 13–14.

138. Simon, *The Big Bands*, p. 399.

139. Scott, "Rediscovering Boyd Raeburn," p. 14.

140. Barry Ulanov, "The Early Boyd," *Metronome* (September 1945): 17.

141. Scott, "Rediscovering Boyd Raeburn," p. 14.

142. Ulanov, "The Early Boyd," p. 37.

143. Scott, "Rediscovering Boyd Raeburn," p. 13.

144. Stan Woolley, "The Forgotten Ones: Boyd Raeburn," *Jazz Journal International* 37, no. 2 (1984): 19.

145. Leonard Feather, "Fate Finally Smiles on Bandleader," *The Times Picayune*, November 14, 1980.

146. Max Harrison, liner notes from Boyd Raeburn and His Orchestra: Jubilee Performances 1946 (HEPCD 1, 1995).

147. Scott, "Rediscovering Boyd Raeburn," p. 13.

148. Woolley, "The Forgotten Ones," pp. 18–19.

149. Scott, "Rediscovering Boyd Raeburn," p. 13.

150. Feather, "Fate Finally Smiles," p. 11.

151. Scott, "Rediscovering Boyd Raeburn," p. 14.

152. Barbara Hodgkins, "That's Rich!" *Metronome* 62, no. 10 (1946): 19.

153. Walker, *The Big Band Almanac*, p. 362.

154. Simon, *The Big Bands*, p. 405.

155. Bill Gottlieb, "Review of Buddy Rich's performance at the Arcadia Ballroom," *Downbeat* 14, no. 11 (1947): 14.

156. Hodgkins, "That's Rich!" p. 42.

157. Ibid.

158. Ibid., pp. 19, 42.

159. Gottlieb, "Review of Buddy Rich," p. 14.

160. Ibid.

161. Walker, *The Big Band Almanac*, p. 362.

162. Simon, *The Big Bands*, p. 406.

163. Ibid., pp. 433–435.

164. Schuller, *The Swing Era*, p. 755.

165. Simon, *The Big Bands*, p. 435.

166. Schuller, *The Swing Era*, pp. 755–756.

167. Simon, *The Big Bands*, pp. 437–438.

168. Schuller, *The Swing Era*, p. 757.

169. Simon, *The Big Bands*, p. 438.

170. Ibid., p. 439.

171. Schuller, *The Swing Era*, p. 403.

172. Barry Ulanov, "Review of Cootie Williams' performance at the Apollo Theatre on May 21, 1942," *Metronome* 58, no. 6 (1942): 20.

173. Gretchen Weaver, "Good Music…That's All!" *Bandleaders* 2, no. 2 (1944): 40–41.

174. Barry Ulanov, "Review of Cootie Williams' performance at the Savoy Ballroom," *Metronome* 58, no. 10 (1942): 11, 24.

175. Dance, "The Immutable Cootie Williams," *Downbeat* 34, no. 9 (1967): 35–36.

176. Schuller, *The Swing Era*, p. 403.

177. McCarthy, *Big Band Jazz*, p. 302.

178. Schuller, *The Swing Era*, p. 403.

179. Ibid., p. 405.

180. Zan Stewart, "Orchestral Man: Gerald Wilson Excites with His Complex Sounds," *Downbeat* 69, no. 2 (2002): 40–42.

181. A.S. Otto, ed., "Riding on a Meteor: Gerald Wilson," *Clef* 1, no. 2 (1946): 13–14.

182. Stewart, "Orchestral Man," p. 42.

183. Ibid., p. 43.

Chapter 4

Vocalists

At the beginning of the Later Swing Era, most vocalists were employed as big-band singers. Many big bands had one male or female vocalist, whereas others used two (male and female) singers. In addition, it was not uncommon for some bands to feature small vocal groups of three or four singers. Regardless of the various combinations, vocalists were generally integral parts of big-band personnel, their level of importance, in some ways, the same as that of instrumentalists. Within some big bands, however, singers held a somewhat lower status than instrumentalists. Many big-band vocalists experienced a rise in popularity after the American Federation of Musicians ordered its instrumental musicians to stop recording in 1942. This strike had an adverse effect on big bands but paved the way for vocalists (who were still being recorded) to gain a foothold toward independence in the music industry. In fact, vocalists began to dominate the music scene by the mid-forties as solo artists and/or leaders of their own small groups. At the same time, music styles began to change as jazz and popular music started moving in different directions. These changes favored vocalists who were in a position to appeal to a wider audience because they had the advantage of delivering lyrics.

The economic climate in the country changed after the war and made it possible for singers to obtain more work as solo artists, for they were less expensive than big bands. As a result, radio and television networks focused their attention on vocalists and featured them instead of big bands in their live broadcasts. Many singers even ended up hosting their own radio and television shows. This high level of visibility increased the singers' popularity even more, and some of them eventually became movie stars. Though singers such as Mel Tormé and Helen Merrill achieved national prominence with nominal big-band experience, mostly those who became big-name solo artists were the vocalists who sang with swing orchestras. A number of successful vocalists who sang in the forties and fifties are presented in this chapter as an overview of the stylistic diversity that represented the era. These singers' careers ultimately took widely different paths, but they all made major contributions toward the growth and development of jazz and popular music in the Later Swing Era.

CAB CALLOWAY

Cab Calloway, one of the most popular vocalists in the entire Swing Era, was born in Rochester, New York, on December 25, 1907. He was raised in Maryland where he occasionally sang with the Baltimore Melody Boys during his childhood years.[1] The family later relocated to Chicago, where his sister Blanche participated in a theater troupe and Cab sang in the chorus while studying law at Crane College. Calloway obtained his law degree, but he was more interested in show business and began to develop his musical skills during an engagement at Chicago's famous Sunset Café. He later decided that he wanted to become a bandleader and made his debut at the Sunset. After his name became known outside of Chicago, the Savoy Ballroom in New York called for his services in 1929. Calloway failed at the Savoy, and his band, The Alabamians, broke up. Subsequently, he managed to get a job in an all-black musical and established himself as a vocalist on opening night after singing "Ain't Misbehavin'."[2] While featured in the musical, he worked simultaneously with The Missourians, which became Cab Calloway and His Orchestra in 1930. Afterward, Calloway and his organization spent a successful year at the Cotton Club in 1931–1932 and soon replaced Duke Ellington as the house band. Calloway recorded "Minnie the Moocher" in 1931, which became a big hit and propelled him into the national spotlight as the "Hi-De-Ho Man."[3] Calloway and his band's recordings and network radio broadcasts gained the group even more national exposure.[4] From that point on, Calloway's orchestra toured Europe, the United States, and Canada while recording frequently and appearing in several films including *The Big Broadcast* in 1932, *The Swinging Kid* in 1936, and the classic *Stormy Weather* in 1948. Throughout most of the thirties and forties, Calloway was one of the most successful vocalists–bandleaders in the country.[5] In addition to Calloway's "Minnie the Moocher," some of his other popular sides recorded in the forties were "My Gal," "St. James Infirmary," "I Want to Rock," "I'll Be Around," "Honey Dripper," "Hi-De-Ho Man," "Jungle King," and "The Calloway Boogie."

In 1948, Calloway disbanded the orchestra and formed a sextet called the Cabaliers, and he performed with it and other small groups until 1951. During that same year, he reorganized the orchestra for a European tour and performed in musical theater and as a single in nightclubs. From June 1952 to August 1954, he assumed the role of Sportin' Life (modeled after Calloway) in Gershwin's *Porgy and Bess* in a New York City revival. Calloway resumed touring in the mid-fifties, mostly as a single in nightclubs, until the late fifties when he formed big bands for special events and brief residencies in New York City and Las Vegas.[6]

Unfortunately, jazz critics and historians have sometimes considered Calloway more of an entertainer than a jazz performer. According to Schuller, "This is eminently unfair and historically unjustifiable on several counts."[7] Schuller comments on Cab Calloway's performance ability as follows:

> First of all, Calloway was a magnificent singer, quite definitely the most unusually and broadly gifted male singer of the thirties. Second, considering his enormous popularity, and therefore the temptation to cater to the basest of mass tastes, Calloway's singing—and even his choice of material (when all is said and done)—is of far higher caliber than any other male vocalist's (with the exception of Jimmy Rushing and some of the great blues singers of the period). Moreover Calloway, amazingly, even in his most extravagant vocal antics, never left the bounds of good taste. It was as though he had a built-in mechanism that kept him from turning corny. Third, he was a true jazz musician and as such surrounded himself with a real jazz orchestra, something no other band-leading vocalist cared (or managed) to do. In that regard, though he had every excuse to do otherwise, his performances—especially in clubs and dances, as opposed to recordings with their absolute time limits— were always liberally sprinkled with instrumental solos and ensembles, more so the more popular he became (in this respect a deliberate reversal of the usual trend).[8]

Referring to Cab's vast range, Schuller adds, "Calloway had a phenomenal voice. Its range is extraordinary: from low B to the highest tenor range and, by means of excellent 'mixing' and falsetto, even quite beyond that into the soprano range. Like Sarah Vaughn in our time, who also had three voices— soprano, alto, and baritone—Calloway is at once bass, baritone, and tenor, with soprano available when needed."[9] Schuller further states, "His technique extends beyond timbre to a perfectly controlled coloratura, quite natural and impeccable breath support, and above all incredible diction. Cab's voice in its heyday was as clear as a bell, capable by virtue of its purity of remarkable projection."[10] In addition to Calloway's memorable recordings mentioned earlier, other examples of his vocal qualities as described by Schuller can be heard in "Hey Now–Hey Now" (1946) and "Oh Grandpa" (1947). The full spectrum of Calloway's work was recorded on the Brunswick, Victor, Vocalion, Okeh, Columbia, and Epic labels.

As a bandleader, Calloway was one of the best in the thirties and forties. According to critic Barry Ulanov, who wrote in 1943, "How many people realize what a great band Cabell is leading right now, a band extraordinary in every aspect, in its clean musicianship, its jazz kicks and its brilliant showmanship. Here's one of the magnificent bands of our time!"[11] George Simon adds, "Yet that band, with its rich, clean ensemble sounds, its brilliant soloists, and its persuasive swing and great spirit, must go down as Calloway's greatest contribution to American music."[12] It is also important to note that Calloway helped further the careers of many great musicians who played in his band such as Dizzy Gillespie, Chu Berry, Cozy Cole, Jonah Jones, and Milt Hinton, to name a few.[13] Calloway continued to perform, record, and appear in films and on television for more than thirty years after the end of the Swing Era. His career spanned over sixty years. On a personal note, this writer had the opportunity to perform with Calloway in the early eighties, and it was the most fun and uplifting show I have ever played.

JUNE CHRISTY

June Christy was born Shirley Luster on November 20, 1925, in Springfield, Illinois. She started singing with a local society band led by Benny Strong while she was a high-school student. After gaining experience in her hometown, she changed her name to Sharon Leslie and began working in Chicago in the early forties with some local bands. She worked with Boyd Raeburn's band in 1944 for four months but became ill with scarlet fever. After recuperating, she joined Stan Kenton in March 1945, immediately following Anita O'Day's one-year stint with the band. At the beginning, Christy's style was similar to that of O'Day's, and she basically sang the same repertoire originally arranged for Anita by trumpeter-arranger Dave Roland. Kenton later paved the way for Christy to develop her own style, however, and Roland arranged a number of charts for her that became hits, including the band's second million seller "Tampico." As an aspiring jazz singer, Christy had mixed feelings about the success of "Tampico" because it was a commercial song. Nevertheless, she was happy that the song was a best-seller because it established her as a professional vocalist. Christy remained with Kenton for about four years, until he temporarily disbanded in 1948. During that period, she recorded other hits arranged by Roland such as "I Been Down in Texas," "Shoo Fly Pie and Apple Pan Dowdy," "Ain't No Misery in Me," and Neal Heft's arrangement of "How High the Moon." Christy played no small role in Kenton's great popularity in the late forties. After Kenton's 1948 breakup, she immediately became successful as a solo artist on the West Coast nightclub circuit.[14] When Kenton re-formed his band in 1950, Christy rejoined for special tours and concerts while involved with her own solo career.

As a soloist, Christy preferred to work with a rhythm section. In a 1956 interview with John Tynan, she stated, "I love working with a rhythm section in a small room. It seems to bring me much closer to the people in an arrangement like that, naturally the piano man is your right hand."[15] Some of her favorite pianists were Benny Aronoff, Jimmy Lyon, Claude Williamson, and Gerald Wiggins.[16] George Simon, who heard June Christy in a solo appearance at Bop City in New York, stated, "She's a very sleek, slick little performer. Unlike other jazz singers, she looks clean and refreshing and her warm smile and graceful motions make a fine impression on everyone."[17] Simon added, "She looks forward to working with soft backgrounds in clubs, preferably with a trio or quartet like the Nat Cole group with which she worked at Bop City."[18] During an interview with Simon, Christy said, "A quieter group always means a quieter audience! And that's great! Since working with Nat, I really enjoy singing ballads, something I've never especially enjoyed before."[19] Christy's solo recording career began with a single, "Everything Happens to Me," recorded by Capitol in 1949. Bob Graettinger was the arranger for the session that was conducted by Christy's husband, saxophonist Bob Cooper, with a studio orchestra of West Coast musicians. Her first album, *Something Cool*, was also recorded by Capitol and released in 1954. It contains eight songs arranged by Pete Rugolo. The highly acclaimed album was reissued a year later with three additional tracks and is considered her most memorable solo recording project.[20]

Christy's solo work took her around the world for performances in Europe, South Africa, Australia, and Japan with Ted Heath, Bob Cooper, and others. In the mid-sixties, she went into semi-retirement and continued performing occasionally in nightclubs in Los Angeles and San Francisco. In 1972, Christy made a guest appearance with Kenton at the Newport Jazz Festival in New York.[21] She later performed with an all-star West Coast band led by Shorty Rogers that performed at several international jazz festivals in 1985.[22] Although Christy enjoyed performing as a solo singer for three decades, her four years with Stan Kenton established her as one of the most important jazz vocalists in the Later Swing Era. In reviewing two of Christy's solo albums, *Something Cool* and *The Misty Miss Christy*, Cook and Morton summarized her vocal style by stating that "Christy's wholesome but particularly sensuous voice is less an improviser's vehicle than an instrument for long, controlled lines and the shading of a fine vibrato. Her greatest moments—the heartbreaking 'Something Cool' itself, 'Midnight Sun,' 'I Should Care'—are as close to creating definitive interpretations as any singer can come."[23]

BILLY ECKSTINE

Billy Eckstine, who led a highly acclaimed big band from 1944 to 1947 (see Chapter 3), embarked on a career as a solo singer shortly after his orchestra disbanded. In 1949, he became the most popular vocalist in the country and obtained a lucrative five-year contract with the MGM record label. Eckstine, however, had previously recorded a blues hit, "Jelly Jelly," when he was with the Earl Hines band in 1940. Although Eckstine liked the blues, he considered himself a ballad singer. Nearly ten years later, MGM recognized this fact and capitalized on his ability to deliver a ballad. As a result, he became the first African-American male vocalist allowed to sing ballads or love songs.[24] He introduced songs such as "Skylark" over network radio and recorded hits such as "A Cottage for Sale," "Prisoner of Love," "I Surrender Dear," "Everything I Have Is Yours," "My Foolish Heart," "Caravan," and "Body and Soul."[25] Despite the racial barriers in the forties and fifties, Eckstine was the first African-American vocalist to become a national sex symbol who appealed to both black and white audiences. Consequently, he recorded a string of hits that were million-selling records.[26] He, in fact, had become such an American icon that "Hip young men copied his style of dress, shirts with rolled collars and jackets draped off the body," according to Coates.[27] Before MGM struck gold with Eckstine, he had already recorded ballads such as "I'm in the Mood for Love" in 1945 with his big band, demonstrating his ability to sing ballads. Here, he delivered the melody in a flowing manner with impeccable diction. Likewise, in "You Call It Madness" (1945) and "My Silent Love" (1946) Eckstine phrased the melodies smoothly with a resonance that subtly impacted the listener.

Although Eckstine preferred ballads to blues, the October 1946 recording of "Jelly Jelly" displays his penchant for singing the blues in a manner similar to that of Billie Holiday. Furthermore, he also began to demonstrate his knowledge of the jazz language. For example, in his May 1945 recording of "I Love the Rhythm in a Riff," he demonstrated his versatility by scat-singing some bebop phrases played by many instrumentalists at the time. Since Eckstine played the trumpet and valve trombone, he was familiar with all of the current jazz licks and phrases. In fact, he was a competent and well-grounded musician. Although Eckstine's later MGM recordings were sung with the accompaniment of an orchestra and strings, he toured with all-star jazz bands and developed his own nightclub act as a single. In the latter setting, he sang ballads, played trumpet and guitar, did impersonations, and performed soft-shoe dances.[28]

Eckstine toured internationally as a soloist with accompanists such as Bobby Tucker and other jazz musicians like Charlie Persip from the fifties through the seventies.[29] Living in Las Vegas, he also performed in the casino circuit regularly.[30] He continued to perform as a single into the early nineties.[31] As an international star, Eckstine brought the ballad style to a wide audience and influenced singers such as Tom Jones, Englebert Humperdinck, and Elvis Presley.[32] Unfortunately, Eckstine suffered a stroke in the summer of 1992 and moved from Las Vegas to his hometown in Pittsburgh for treatment. He passed away on March 8, 1993, as a result of cardiac arrest.[33] Like Cab Calloway, Eckstine was a successful vocalist and bandleader who helped a large number of jazz musicians establish themselves as professionals. As a rich baritone-voiced ballad singer, Eckstine's contributions to American music are second to none.

BILLIE HOLIDAY

Billie Holiday, born Eleanora Fagan in Baltimore on April 7, 1915, was the daughter of Sadie Fagan and guitarist Clarence Holiday who played with McKinney's Cotton Pickers and Fletcher Henderson's orchestra in the thirties. Her early childhood in Baltimore was spent with relatives after her mother moved to New York. During that time, she listened to singers such as Bessie Smith and Louis Armstrong. In 1928 Billie joined her mother in New York at age fifteen, and her professional career began around 1930 when she was hired as a singer at a small club in Brooklyn.[34] After about a year, she moved on to Pods' and Jerry's, a Harlem nightclub that was popular with jazz enthusiasts, and other uptown establishments including The Log Cabin.[35] She later began working at Monette's, another Harlem club, in 1933, where she was discovered by producer John Hammond who arranged her recording debut with Benny Goodman and booked her in a number of New York clubs through 1935. From that point on, she recorded regularly with studio bands under the direction of Teddy Wilson until around 1942.[36] In the meantime, Holiday worked with Count Basie in 1937 and Artie Shaw in 1938. Her work with Basie and Shaw (including her recordings with Teddy Wilson) brought her national recognition and an engagement at New York's Café Society from 1939 to 1941. Subsequently, she became a featured solo artist at some of the nation's top clubs while recording regularly and earning more than $1,000 a week.[37]

Holiday's recordings produced by Hammond for Columbia from 1933 to 1942 were among the best of her career. Her first Columbia session with Teddy Wilson in the summer of 1935, for example, included some of the country's top jazz musicians such as Benny Goodman, Roy Eldridge, and Ben Webster. Four songs were recorded, and three of them, "I Wished on the Moon," "What a Little Moonlight Can Do," and "Miss Brown to You," became highly successful. The first of her own sessions followed a year later, with pianist Joe Bushkin, Bunny Berigan, and Artie Shaw as soloists. In 1937 another Wilson-led date found Holiday with Goodman and five members of Basie's band (the rhythm section, Lester Young, and Buck Clayton) in an ensemble that recorded "This Year's Kisses" and "I Must Have That Man." This date established a special musical empathy that developed between Holiday and Young, who nicknamed her "Lady Day." Throughout the Columbia years, Holiday's vocal style revealed a strong resemblance to that of Louis Armstrong whom she admired. From Armstrong she learned to swing, adapt a tune to her vocal range, and project herself emotionally like an instrumental soloist. The blues-tinged tone quality of her voice was undoubtedly influenced by Bessie Smith.[38] Holiday's recordings during this period were highly successful musically because of her unique style and the fact that she was accompanied mostly by small bands with top-ranked instrumental soloists. Many of their obbligatos, which supported her vocals as well as their ensemble and fine solo work, were of the highest order. However, it was Holiday, the vocal improviser, who attracted listeners with her honest emotional expression.[39]

After 1942, Holiday recorded "Travelin' Light" with Paul Whiteman, which became a hit. She later recorded for Commodore with written band arrangements that did not particularly complement her singing style. Decca took a gamble, however, and recorded her with strings, which was a first for a jazz vocalist. As a result, Decca and Holiday made history with notable recordings of "Lover Man," "Good Morning Heartache," "I Loves You, Porgy," "Don't Explain," "Ain't Nobody's Business," "No More," and the memorable "God Bless the Child." The setting for these recordings was rather sedate in comparison with her small-group recordings, but she met the challenge of the situation with her exemplary musicianship.[40]

During Holiday's Verve years from 1952 to 1959, some jazz columnists felt that her singing career was headed downward because of some health-related issues. Furthermore, one point of view was that she had lost her voice and musicianship and that all she had left was feeling and "compelling talent for dramatic recitative." Columnist Martin Williams disagreed, however, by stating, "The Billie Holiday of the 1950s was not only a great dramatic performer but also an even greater jazz singer because she was a greater musician."[41] Williams clarified his point as follows:

> Oddly, her musicianship had little to do with her vocal equipment, and her voice and her range were small from the beginning. But the extremely personal quality of her sound, so arresting and even shocking the first time one hears it, was absolutely appropriate to every other aspect of her act. That was true in the beginning and it remained true even as her voice thickened and deteriorated, as untrained voices (and some trained ones) are apt to do.[42]

In all of the Verve albums except one, Holiday was recorded with small groups of exemplary improvisers, as in her Columbia recordings. Here, she is once again Billie Holiday, the improviser and great musician who had the ability to realize her art through variations, captured in her 1952 recording of "These Foolish Things."[43] In spite of her declining health, Holiday continued to perform whenever possible and made her last public appearance just two months prior to her death in July 1959. The emotional breadth and depth of her singing and her legacy of recorded work have set the standard for jazz musicians even today.[44] According to Feather and Gitler, "She is considered by many to be the most important and influential female singer in jazz history."[45]

HERB JEFFRIES

Herb Jeffries was born in Detroit, Michigan, on September 24, 1916, of a part-black mother and a white father. This was not an optimal family situation at that time. He literally had to hobo around Detroit, Chicago, and New York as a kid. As fate would have it, he ended up getting the opportunity to appear with Erskine Tate's orchestra in Chicago at age fourteen. Earl Hines heard Jeffries, contracted him for the Grand Terrace Revue, and hired him later to sing with his band.[46] Jeffries stayed with Hines from 1931 to 1934 and later joined Blanche Calloway for a brief period.[47] After leaving Calloway, he went to Hollywood and appeared in a number of all-black Western films as a singing cowboy star.

Duke Ellington remembered Jeffries from his days with the Grand Terrace Revue and hired him in 1940. He remained with Ellington for two years and, during that time, became successful with songs such as "Flamingo," "I Don't Know the Kind of Blues I've Got," "The Brownskin Gal," and "Jump for Joy." The 1940 recording of "Flamingo" displays Jeffries' rich and resonant baritone voice, smooth phrasing, and superb diction. Here, he demonstrates a vocal range that extends from a deep bass-baritone up to a crystal clear falsetto voice on the coda. In "Brownskin Gal" (1941) he again demonstrates his ability to deliver smooth phrasing of the melody with impeccable intonation in his lower baritone range. Although Jeffries has a clear legato style, his articulation in "Jump for Joy" (1941) is slightly detached but clean and precise in this medium-tempo song. Along with his precise articulation, he displays clear diction and wonderful intonation. Probably the most impressive aspect of Jeffries' vocal style is his ability to sing a melody with mature musical taste and, at the same time, display an infectious humor that was rare for the early forties.

When Jeffries left Ellington in 1942, he settled in Los Angeles and became a successful entrepreneur with a nightclub called The Black Flamingo. He continued to sing in some of LA's other clubs for about three years before signing a contract with Exclusive Records, a black-owned independent company. He recorded the *Magenta Moods* album for Exclusive, which contains singles such as "My Blue Heaven," "Body and Soul," "Jungle Rose," and "What's the Score" accompanied by arranger-conductor Buddy Baker's band.[48] Between 1945 and 1956, Jeffries performed in Hollywood clubs and recorded several times as a leader with Lucky Thompson, Eddie Beal, Bobby Hackett, and Russ Garcia's orchestra. Jeffries remained active both as a vocalist and actor during the seventies and formed his own record company, United National Records, in 1978.[49] He continued to perform in the eighties and nineties on jazz cruises and in nightclubs.[50] Jeffries surprised several nightclub patrons on one occasion when they found out that he was part African-American. Jeffries, a very proud man, responded by saying, "Imagine, if a few drops of Negro blood, beside all that white blood, make me a Negro, imagine how valuable that Negro blood must be!"[51] Regardless of Jeffries' hue, Ulanov wrote the following in reference to his vocal ability: "Maybe you'll hear why an opera singer, a wonderfully-talented one just arrived in America to make a highly successful Metropolitan debut, exclaimed on hearing Herb's records, after a large dose of the famous records of the famous names of popular singing, 'Ah, now, there at last is a singer!'"[52]

PEGGY LEE

Singer-songwriter Peggy Lee was born Norma Delores Egstrom in Jamestown, North Dakota, on May 27, 1920, and began performing professionally at age fourteen. She appeared on a local radio station and was employed later by WDAY in Fargo where the station manager christened her Peggy Lee. After high-school graduation at age eighteen, she worked as a vocalist (and at various odd jobs) in Los Angeles, Minneapolis, and St. Louis, and at Chicago's Ambassador Hotel with a vocal group between 1938 and 1941. She joined Benny Goodman's band in August of that same year and recorded "Why Don't You Do Right?" a year later, which became a big hit. She married Goodman's guitarist, Dave Barbour, and left the band in 1943 to settle down with her new family in Los Angeles. After a break from public performance, she began her solo career and signed with Capitol Records in 1944.

Lee co-wrote a number of hits with Barbour including "I Don't Know Enough About You," which they recorded in 1945 using a studio orchestra he conducted. Her approach to this song encompasses a laid-back style with a light and airy vocal delivery. After a brief introduction by guitar and rhythm section, she sings the melody with ease as she establishes its overall mood in a subtle manner that exhibits rhythmic assurance. In the second chorus, after an eight-bar statement by the orchestra, she reenters with the melody and follows effectively with a few bars of spoken words before the end. She also recorded Joe McCoy's "Why Don't You Do Right?" again in 1947 with Barbour. The orchestra plays an introduction to this twelve-bar minor blues piece before Lee sings three choruses, placing accents on certain words and syllables (e.g., "get-me some mon-ey too") in the lyrics that create a light and solid swinging effect. Her rhythmic placement of these accents forces the listener's attention to her easy-going and precise vocal delivery, which, in essence, is what made Peggy Lee great. She also wrote and recorded other hits including "It's a Good Day," "You Was Right, Baby," "What More Can a Woman Do?" and "Mariana."

After recording and appearing on radio with personalities such as Jimmy Durante and Bing Crosby in the late forties, Lee relocated to New York in 1951 following a divorce from Barbour. She performed in nightclubs and worked with Steve Allen while acting in films such as *The Jazz Singer* in

1952 and *Pete Kelly's Blues* in 1955. She also provided her voice for characters in Walt Disney's *Lady and the Tramp* and continued performing until she recorded her most popular hit, "Fever," in 1959. Around 1960, Lee began to limit her schedule of public performances.[53] Nevertheless, during her career, she had a reputation as a meticulous performer and learned the value of thorough rehearsal from Benny Goodman, who was known as a taskmaster who knew how to get the most from a band. She also thought of Victor Young as another major influence who taught her orderliness. Columnist John Tynan, who observed Lee in rehearsal, indicated that she had an unusual way of communicating with her musicians and that they always understood exactly what she wanted.[54] As a songwriter, Lee believed that lyrics were her forte because rhyming was easy for her. She closely checked her lyrics and music for ease of singing for herself as well as other vocalists. It is a little-known fact that she wrote several hundred songs during her long career.[55] She continued to perform intermittently into the nineties as a popular singer-songwriter and collaborated with major jazz artists such as Quincy Jones, Lou Levy, and Benny Carter.[56] In sum, Peggy Lee had one of the most successful and multifaceted careers in American music.

CARMEN McRAE

Carmen McRae was born in New York City on April 8, 1920, and grew up listening to the music of Duke Ellington and Louis Armstrong in her parents' home. She took piano lessons from age eight to thirteen. At fifteen she was playing and writing songs when she met Irene Wilson (Teddy Wilson's wife), a pianist and songwriter. Ms. Wilson taught her own songs to Carmen who, in turn, would sing them for Billie Holiday, whom she met through Irene. If Billie liked the songs, she would record them. Needless to say, Holiday was the earliest and most influential vocalist on McRae.[57] Just before McRae met her idol, she had won an Apollo Theater amateur-night contest at age seventeen and written a song entitled "Dream of Life." As it turned out, Irene Wilson persuaded Holiday to sing and record McRae's song in 1939. Afterward, McRae began working in the chorus line for music shows in Atlantic City, and she would entertain her colleagues backstage by singing and playing the piano for them.[58] One of her colleagues encouraged her to become a performer, but club work was slow in the early forties; so, she worked intermittently as a pianist-vocalist while working full-time as a secretary.

In 1944 McRae worked with Benny Carter for a while, then moved on to Count Basie's band. She later worked with Mercer Ellington in 1946–1947 and made her recording debut with him.[59] A turning point in her fledgling career came when she moved to Chicago in the late forties. Luckily, her Atlantic City chorus-line friend, Lulu Mason, had also moved to

Chicago.[60] Mason knew Harold Johnson, a club owner, and arranged an audition for McRae with him at the Archway. She was given a job as a pianist-vocalist that lasted for seventeen weeks. McRae gained the confidence she needed to expand her repertoire and learned to sing and play in different keys while at the Archway. Afterward, she became an intermission pianist at The Hi Note and The Air Liner before moving on to work at other clubs in Chicago for over three years.

Encouraged to pursue a recording career, McRae returned to New York City in 1952 and started working at a club in Brooklyn where she met Dutch accordionist Mat Mathews. A record company offered Mathews a recording date and wanted a female vocalist for two sides. He took McRae to the session, and she recorded "Tip Toe Gently" and "Old Devil Moon," which were released on the Venus label. Fortunately, those two sides are available on Bethlehem Records along with six other titles. When listening to "Old Devil Moon," for example, it is obvious that McRae has a strong and clear voice with exact phrasing that flows smoothly across the bar lines. On "Tip Toe Gently," she restrains her strong voice and opts for a light swinging style that matches the song's lyrics. After the recording session with Mathews, McRae's fame began to spread, and Bob Thiele of Coral Records heard about her. He offered to record her in 1953, but she chose what she thought was a better deal with Len Frank of the Stardust label. Although the recording turned out well, the company's distribution was either limited or nonexistent, because the records were not available in stores. Luckily, the disc jockeys played her records, which helped increase her visibility. In 1954 McRae hit the jackpot when Milt Gabler signed her with the Decca label. She recorded four sides with an orchestra directed by Jack Pleis and a vocal group led by Dave Lambert.[61] In the same year, she was named Best New Female Singer by *Downbeat*.[62] Afterward, she gradually ascended to the top echelon of jazz vocalists and received international recognition.[63]

McRae was one of the few vocalists who remained dedicated to art and resisted the temptation for commercialism.[64] With several years of piano training, she was a well-grounded musician with impeccable phrasing, acute intonation, and the ability to manipulate a melody. According to McRae, "You have to improvise. You have to have something of your own that has to do with that song. And you have to know where you are going when you improvise."[65] Obviously, she knew where she was going because her professional career spanned approximately fifty years. She toured nationally and abroad in Europe and Japan. She appeared in the film *Hotel*, in two documentaries, *The Story of Jazz* and *Lady Day*, and as an actress in *Roots*. She continued to record as a leader and with Betty Carter, George Shearing, and pianist-vocalist Shirley Horn.[66] In 1994 McRae passed away and left a large body of recorded work that will serve as a model for serious up-and-coming jazz vocalists who are trying to find their own style.

ANITA O'DAY

Anita O'Day, born Anita Belle Colton in Chicago, Illinois, on October 18, 1919, grew up in a musical family that gave her piano and voice lessons at an early age.[67] As a young teenager she participated as a contestant in dance marathons and was encouraged, along with other contestants, to sing. In one marathon, she was accompanied by Erskine Tate's orchestra, and, at that time, she made the decision to become a professional singer.[68] At age seventeen, a musician friend introduced her to recordings by female vocalists like Billie Holiday, Mildred Bailey, and Ella Fitzgerald.[69] Anita changed her surname to O'Day and began singing professionally in Chicago nightclubs by her late teens.[70] In 1939 she worked at the Three Deuces for about a year with the Max Miller combo.[71] Gene Krupa happened to hear O'Day during a club performance and promised to hire her if he ever had an opening. Krupa eventually called her in 1941, and she remained with him until 1943. His band became a big hit when O'Day and Roy Eldridge recorded a duet entitled "Let Me Off Uptown." She also recorded a wordless vocal on "That's What You Think" that became popular. O'Day worked with Stan Kenton's band in 1944 and 1945 and recorded another hit, "And Her Tears Flowed Like Wine." She rejoined Krupa in 1945 and stayed with the band for a year before moving on to a solo career.[72]

O'Day recorded several albums as a soloist for Verve in the mid-fifties that were successful collaborations with such artists as Billy May and Oscar Peterson.[73] She also made appearances around the country with local rhythm sections and was accompanied regularly by drummer John Poole.[74] Poole, a close friend of O'Day's, played a major role in helping her secure bookings in top jazz venues such as the Half Note in New York City.[75] For O'Day's solo Verve recordings under the supervision of Norman Granz, mostly standards were selected. When speaking of her early recording days to columnist Alan Surpin, she referred to an experience that took place in a Hollywood bar the day before she recorded four tunes for a small record label. O'Day had the freedom to pick the four songs, and she had already decided on two standards and a pop tune. She talked with the bartender one night about the fact that she needed another tune when a drunk at the end of the bar overheard the conversation. The drunk told O'Day he was a songwriter and invited her to his place, where he played three of his songs on the piano. She bought one of his songs for five dollars, which turned out to be "Vaya Con Dios," that she sold later for $10,000.[76] In any event, after the successful Verve recordings, O'Day made a memorable appearance at the Newport Jazz Festival in 1958 that was documented in a film entitled *Jazz on a Summer's Day*. She later toured Japan in the mid-sixties, Europe in the early seventies, and Japan again in the mid-seventies. She also established her own record company in 1972, Emily Records, and gave a concert at Carnegie Hall in 1985 to celebrate her fiftieth year in jazz.[77] During O'Day's career, she received the *Esquire* Silver Award in 1945, two *Downbeat* awards in 1944–1945, and a National Endowment for the Arts Jazz Masters Award in 1997. She appeared in *The Gene Krupa Story*, *Zig Zag*, and *The Outfit*, and she was interviewed on *60 Minutes* in 1980 about her forthcoming autobiography entitled *High Times, Hard Times* (1981).

In describing her own style, O'Day once stated, "I started out learning riffs, and I used to try to put a riff into everything I did until I got to where I could really do it. And then somebody said, 'Hey, we've got a jazz singer here.' So I guess that's where I am."[78] Kernfeld adds, "O'Day excels at improvisation; whether scat singing or skillfully interpreting a song text she allows herself all the liberties of instrumental jazz performance in refashioning a popular song."[79] Over four decades later, *New York Times* columnist John Wilson referred to her in 1989 as "funny, swinging and convincingly the best jazz singer performing today."[80] O'Day was a major influence on many singers who followed her, especially June Christy, Chris Connor, and Helen Merrill.[81]

JIMMY RUSHING

Jimmy Rushing, born in Oklahoma City on August 26, 1903, grew up in a musical family. His mother played piano in church and sang in the choir, while his father played trumpet in the Knights of Pythias band. Young Rushing sang in church choirs, school glee clubs, and operatic companies. He enjoyed vaudeville, however, and listening to some of his favorite singers such as Ethel Waters and Bessie Smith. He especially enjoyed singing the blues and playing honky-tonk piano at parties, but Rushing's parents objected to his performing secular music and insisted that he study violin.[82] Although he wanted to sing, he continued to improve his musicianship by studying music theory in high school and at Wilberforce University in Ohio.[83] With a strong urge to sing, he left Ohio for California at age twenty and made his professional debut at the Quality Night Club, a popular meeting place for Hollywood movie stars.[84] Around this same time, he performed at private parties with Jelly Roll Morton and traveled widely as an itinerant musician, including a brief tour with Walter Page in 1925.[85] Shortly after the tour with Page, Rushing returned home for about two years to help his father with his café. The singing urge hit Jimmy again, however, and he joined Walter Page's Blue Devils from 1927 to 1929. Rushing referred to his tenure with Page as a "wonderful experience." In fact, all of Page's band members were friends and would help each other pay bills to keep their families afloat, because the band did not make much money in those days. Rushing traveled with the band throughout Oklahoma, Texas, Missouri, Tennessee, and Colorado. Although the band had a lot of fun on the road, some of its members had trouble dealing with the difficulty of traveling in the South at that time. In any event, a highpoint occurred for Rushing when he made his first record in 1928 with the Blue Devils in Kansas City.

Page disbanded his orchestra a year later, and Rushing joined Bennie Moten's band, which created a new opportunity for him to return to Kansas City. At that time, during Prohibition, Kansas City was a jazz musician's paradise. Bands from the East Coast and other parts of the country would travel there to perform at the Muehlebach Hotel and other venues. After work, the visiting musicians would go to the nightclubs and sit in with the Kansas City musicians, who would often change the keys of certain tunes to test their visitors' performance skills. In fact, the local musicians would often play tunes through all twelve keys, and some of the visitors could not keep up, packed their instruments, and left the clubs disappointed. These kinds of jam sessions were referred to as "cutting contests," and scores of jazz musicians became great players by surviving the competitions. Rushing remained with Moten in Kansas City until the leader's death in 1935.

In that same year, Rushing joined Count Basie's band and began a long, fruitful relationship with one of the top bands in the Swing Era. Rushing experienced the excitement of performing with Basie's band in New York, along with touring and appearing in movies that brought the singer international renown. In addition, he recorded tunes with the band that became jazz classics such as "Goin' to Chicago," "Good Mornin' Blues," "Baby, Don't Tell on Me," "Evenin'," and "Harvard Blues."[86] Rushing also recorded other tunes such as "Jimmy's Blues" with Basie that highlighted his vocal skill and featured his upper vocal range and mature melodic phrasing. Rushing and Basie's band also recorded "For the Good of Your Country," arranged by Don Redman, to support the troops during World War II. This particular tune is interesting in that it finds Rushing outside of his blues element. It is in A-A-B-A form and basically follows "I Got Rhythm" chord progressions, except for the bridge that continues with the normal I-vi-ii-V chord changes in another key. As expected, Rushing's interpretation of the melody is delightful and humorous, while Redman's arrangement is obviously first rate. Rushing was mainly a ballad singer during his early days, but Basie insisted that he sing mostly blues and popular songs in a bluesy style. In doing so, Rushing took blues singing to a sophisticated level that Schuller describes as follows:

> To be sure, he was not the typical male blues shouter of old: baritonal, untrained, and more declamatory than singing. Rushing's high, clear, silver-toned voice and clean execution gave his blues singing a distinctive clarity— one might say a certain propriety—that blues shouting had never had before. Remarkably, Rushing's voice was both warm and penetrating, and when he sang/shouted his wailing "Baaaaay-bay, bay-aaay-bay" (as Ellison has translated it), the anguish and passion of it were often overwhelming.[87]

When the Basie band folded around 1950, Rushing led his own small group until 1952 and discovered that he was not a bandleader. He began working as a single and, with the public's renewed interest in the early blues style, his solo career was born. His popularity increased in the mid-fifties when he performed at the Newport Jazz Festival and recorded mainstream jazz albums for the Columbia and Vanguard labels. From that point on, he toured Europe, Australia, New Zealand, Japan, and the United States with major artists such as Buck Clayton, Benny Goodman, Thelonious Monk, and Harry James.[88] Rushing won the British critics' poll in 1957 and was voted the number-one male vocalist by *Downbeat*'s critics' poll in 1958 and 1959. His long, successful career included acting roles in films such as Olsen and Johnson's *Funzapoppin'* and Gordon Parks' *The Learning Tree*, as well as appearances on some major television shows.[89] One of Rushing's last appearances was with the Al Cohn-Zoot Sims Quintet at the Half Note in New York City before his death in 1972.[90] Feather concluded in 1960 that, "Several experts in recent years have spoken of [Jimmy Rushing] as the greatest living male jazz singer."[91]

FRANK SINATRA

Frank Sinatra was born on December 12, 1915, in Hoboken, New Jersey, to Italian immigrants who stimulated his interest in the bel canto singing style.[92] Against his parents' wishes, he quit school early to pursue a music career and made a breakthrough when he won a Major Bowes Amateur Hour radio contest in 1935.[93] Because Sinatra was determined to reach his professional goal, his mother reconciled with him and found him a job singing at the Rustic Cabin in Englewood, New Jersey, in the late thirties. More radio appearances followed, including work on WNEW's *Dance Parade*, which enabled him to attract the attention of nationally recognized musicians. Harry James hired Sinatra in 1939 as a featured vocalist for his newly formed band. A year later, Sinatra left James to join Tommy Dorsey's band and recorded "I'll Never Smile Again."[94] Other early recordings with Dorsey included "The Sky Fell Down," "Too Romantic," and "Shake Down the Stars." During Sinatra's tenure with Dorsey, he listened carefully to Tommy's trombone playing and learned how to breathe and phrase properly. Sinatra adopted an instrumentalist's approach to breath control by carrying or holding a musical phrase across bar lines and breathing at its beginnings and cadence points. Of course, Sinatra had the natural talent to perfect this kind of style because he had what musicians refer to as "natural time," along with a rich baritone voice and excellent intonation. The result was a "horn"-like approach that perfectly complemented Dorsey's "vocal" approach on the trombone.[95]

Sinatra's singing style not only earned him the respect of his fellow musicians but also attracted sold-out audiences at New York's famous Paramount

Theatre and screaming bobby-soxers as well. His popular success became so great that Dorsey resented the fact that his singer received a better reaction from audiences than the band.[96] Sinatra's success made it possible for singers around the country eventually to dominate popular music to the point that most big bands became secondary by serving mostly as vocal accompaniment.[97] In any event, Sinatra left Dorsey's band in 1942 and started a solo career.[98] Columbia reissued Sinatra's 1939 recording of "All or Nothing at All" (with Harry James) in 1943, and it became a hit as Sinatra had attained worldwide fame.[99] He was in constant demand for live performances, radio appearances, and recordings to the point that it took a toll on his voice, and his career went into a decline around 1947. He continued to record mostly ballads, however, for Columbia until around 1952.[100] A year later, he made a comeback with a non-singing role in the film *From Here to Eternity* that won him an Oscar and a new recording contract with Capitol.[101] The deal with Capitol placed Sinatra in a comfortable jazz-oriented setting with excellent arrangements for big band and strings by Billy May, Nelson Riddle, and Gordon Jenkins. These arrangers captured the essence of Sinatra's style and changed his image to that of a "swinger."[102] This change is particularly evident in Billy May's arrangements on "Come Fly with Me" in 1957 and "Come Swing with Me."[103] As Sinatra dominated the popularity polls again, important roles in films and musicals followed with *Guys and Dolls* in 1955, *High Society* in 1956, and *Can-Can* in 1960.[104] Fully established and at the height of his career, he left Capitol and formed his own record company, Reprise, in 1961. Again, he recorded projects that utilized jazz arrangers such as Neal Hefti, Quincy Jones, and Johnny Mandel, as well as May and Riddle during the sixties. These projects included recordings with Count Basie, Duke Ellington, and Antonio Carlos Jobim.[105]

Sinatra retired in 1971 but gradually returned to perform concerts in 1973. From that point on, his career returned to full bloom with national and international tours, television appearances, and more recordings.[106] He usually performed live with a big band, sometimes augmented by a string section. Two of his notable recordings are a live album, *The Main Event*, backed by the Woody Herman band, and *L.A. Is My Lady*, with Quincy Jones who assembled an all-star band with Lionel Hampton, George Benson, the Brecker brothers, and others.[107] Sinatra continued singing into the mid-nineties until his performing activities were curtailed by illness.[108] Although he was best known as a popular singer, he was well respected in the jazz community. In fact, Sinatra was most comfortable in a jazz setting with big bands/strings and top-flight arrangers and conductors. This fact is clearly substantiated by the kinds of recordings he made on his own record label in the sixties. In addition to Tommy Dorsey, Sinatra cited Louis Armstrong and Billie Holiday as major influences.

During Sinatra's career, he won numerous awards from *Downbeat*, *Metronome*, and *Playboy* and received the coveted Presidential Medal of

Freedom in 1985. Furthermore, countless books, an unauthorized biography, discographies, and articles have been written about him, as well as a complete guide to his music. Sinatra transcended the role of the "boy" or "girl" singer in the Swing Era who sat near big bands and waited his or her turn to stand up and sing. In fact, he played a major role in shifting the focus of music lovers from big bands to vocalists during the forties and early fifties. After one of the most successful careers of any vocalist, Sinatra passed away on May 14, 1998, in Hollywood. He not only left a legacy as an American icon but is considered the master of American popular song.[109]

KAY STARR

Kay Starr was born Katherine Laverne Starks to Native American parents in Dougherty, Oklahoma, on July 21, 1922. Her family moved to Dallas, Texas, when she was three, and she began singing as a child to chickens in the family-owned henhouse. An aunt recognized Starr's talent and entered her in an amateur contest at age twelve, and she won.[110] After winning more contests, she was given her own fifteen-minute radio show. Her family moved to Memphis, Tennessee, where she worked with local hillbilly bands during her high-school years and was discovered by bandleader Joe Venuti. Venuti convinced Kay's parents to let her sing on weekends with his band at Memphis' Claridge Hotel. Venuti was impressed with Starr's talent and persuaded her parents to let her go on the road with him for a summer. Kay's big break came when Bob Crosby's band manager heard her and talked Venuti into letting her join Crosby. She appeared with Crosby and Johnny Mercer on the *Camel Caravan* and, while in New York, was hired by Glenn Miller to sub for Marion Hutton for two weeks at the Glen Island Casino. Starr also got the opportunity to record "Baby Me" and "Love with a Capital A" with Miller.[111]

Following the two aforementioned opportunities in New York, Starr returned home to finish high school. Upon receiving her diploma, she rejoined Venuti and remained with his band until it was depleted by the war. Once again, Starr returned home before relocating to the West Coast where Wingy Manone, who had heard about her, invited her to rehearse with his band at Music City in Hollywood. Charlie Barnet, who was looking for a vocalist, found out about Starr and invited her to audition, and she won the spot.[112] Starr replaced Lena Horne in Barnet's band in 1943 and remained with him until 1945. During that time, she recorded with Wingy Manone in 1944 and "If I Could Be with You" with the Capitol Jazzmen in 1945. The Jazzmen, an all-star band, included Nat "King" Cole, Bill Coleman, Benny Carter, Buster Bailey, Coleman Hawkins, and Max Roach.[113]

After spending two years with Charlie Barnet's band, Starr took a break when a throat specialist advised her against singing with a big band. After she was able to sing again, she began her solo career in 1946 by working in various clubs on the West Coast with pianist Bob Laine and signed a contract with Capitol Records.[114] Some of her hits in the late forties include "So Tired" and Pee Wee King's "Bonaparte's Retreat." Her 1947 recording of "You've Got to See Mama Ev'ry Night" finds her in the company of an orchestra conducted by Dave Cavanaugh. Her expressive phrasing of the melody as well as her rhythmically precise exchanges with the orchestra reflect Starr's confidence in her vocal ability in front of a large ensemble. Some of her jazz recordings as a leader included Venuti and Barney Bigard in 1946, Red Norvo in 1947, and Red Nichols in 1947 and 1949 as sidemen.[115] Starr was also a versatile pop/jazz vocalist who scored a number of hits in other genres such as country, rock and roll, the waltz, and the polka.[116] In describing her versatile vocal style to Barbara Hodgkins during a 1949 interview Starr stated,

> I've run the gamut from hillbilly to jazz to just plain modern music to ballads, and though I might not sing them all well, I feel them. And if I can sing them well, I attribute that to the fact that I have sung hillbilly stuff. Contrary to what people say, it's a hard style to sing, and it made my voice flexible enough so that I'm able to have my own style. The nicest compliment I ever had paid to me was when I was told that I sing like a fellow playing an instrument.[117]

Starr's professional career, like her vocal style, was also versatile. Throughout the late forties and fifties, she appeared on radio shows with Bing Crosby, the Great Gildersleeve, and Spike Jones. She also starred on the *Chesterfield Supper Club* twice a week and landed her own radio show on ABC where she often served as master of ceremonies, singer, writer, producer, and/or director.[118] After the fifties, she recorded with jazz luminaries Ben Webster in 1961 and Count Basie in 1968, and she continued to work occasionally as a vocalist for several years. During the eighties, she worked with small swing bands in New York and London.[119] Starr remained active until the nineties, having influenced some of the country's most popular singers including Rosemary Clooney, Vic Damone, Jack Jones, and Liza Minnelli.[120] Kay Starr was one of the few popular vocalists in the Later Swing Era who successfully formed a vocal style that encompassed jazz, country, blues, and rock and roll. Moreover, she was able to reach a wide audience with her own radio show and spread her musical contributions to the listening public.

SARAH VAUGHN

Sarah Lois Vaughn was born in Newark, New Jersey, on March 27, 1924, and grew up in a musical family. Her father, Asbury Vaughn, was a carpenter who enjoyed playing guitar and singing folk songs, whereas Ada, her mother, sang in a Newark church choir. In fact, the Vaughn home was always filled with sacred music. Obviously, Sarah was influenced by religious music during her youth, and she would often sing along with her parents. She began studying piano and organ at age eight and became a church organist at twelve. The Vaughn family was deeply religious and encouraged Sarah to remain committed to the church. Like many teenagers, she gravitated toward secular music by singing popular songs at parties and playing piano in the high-school orchestra. Persuaded by her friends, she entered an amateur contest at the Apollo Theatre and won first prize after singing "Body and Soul." Like many African-American families at the time, the Vaughns were not happy about Sarah's desire to be in show business. Her mother wanted her to continue in school and become a teacher or a choir director. Sarah, who was once recognized as a fine pianist, decided to pursue a career in popular music.[121] Vaughn's music career began in April 1943 when she joined Earl Hines' band as a vocalist and second pianist when Billy Eckstine was a member of that organization. Eckstine left in 1944 to form his own big band, and Vaughn joined him a few months later.[122] In December 1944, Leonard Feather organized Vaughn's first recording session for Continental Records, wherein she was accompanied by Dizzy Gillespie's septet. She recorded a vocal version of Gillespie's "Night in Tunisia" during that session, and another recording followed a few months later—the well-known version of "Lover Man" that included Dizzy and Charlie Parker.[123] Vaughn left Eckstine after about a year to work with John Kirby's sextet during the winter of 1945–1946. Afterward, she began her solo career and was eventually featured with various instrumental combinations ranging from small groups to symphony orchestras.[124]

In 1947, her first hit record was "It's Magic," and George Treadwell, her husband, became her manager. At that point, she revised her stage appearance and repertoire and went on to win popularity polls and to perform on radio and television. She signed a five-year contract with Columbia in 1949 and toured Europe in 1951. As her reputation grew, she received more lucrative performance fees and began to record popular music with string orchestras, which reached the commercial market.[125] The result was her biggest hit ever, "Broken-Hearted Melody," which was recorded in 1958.[126] Although Vaughn had achieved considerable commercial success, she continued to record with jazz trios and outstanding solo artists such as Cannonball Adderley, Miles Davis, and Clifford Brown. In addition, she recorded with the orchestras of Ernie Wilkins and Count Basie.[127] These sessions were recorded by the Roulette, Mercury, and Columbia labels between 1960 and 1967. After taking a five-year break from the studios, she resumed her recording career in 1971, making popular albums and some occasional dates with small jazz groups.[128] Vaughn continued to record and perform throughout the seventies and eighties and ultimately won a Grammy for her music achievement in 1989. She was diagnosed with cancer that same year and passed away in 1990.[129]

Sarah Vaughn, known as "The Divine One," is considered a legendary jazz singer. According to Maria Jurkowska, "She had a voice of operatic dimensions; of exceptional range spanning four octaves, from baritone to lyrical soprano, powerful and beautiful in tone quality. Her consummate skill, superb control, harmonic instinct, and improvisatory talent evoked respect and admiration of her musician colleagues."[130] Quincy Jones added that "Sarah Vaughn was among the most powerful, influential and soulful voices of all time, a perfectionist with an astonishing vocal range and a genius for conveying emotion through her music."[131] Some of Vaughn's most enduring work are her interpretations of standards, such as "If You Could See Me Now," "I Cover the Waterfront," "Body and Soul," "Tenderly," "Everything I Have Is Yours," "I'll Remember April," "Here's That Rainy Day," "I Remember Clifford," "Don't Blame Me," "Misty," and "Send in the Clowns."[132] In addition, some Brazilian favorites are "I Love Brazil," "Copacabana," and "Brazilian Romance." George Gaffney, Sarah Vaughn's music director during the last decade of her life and career, concluded, "Her voice was a Stradivarius, one of the finest instruments God ever created."[133]

EDDIE VINSON

Vocalist–alto saxophonist Eddie "Cleanhead" Vinson was born in Houston, Texas, on December 18, 1917, and began his music career on alto saxophone in 1934. A year later, he joined Chester Boone's big band, along with Arnett Cobb and Illinois Jacquet, in which he sang and played saxophone. Vinson remained in the band under three leaders (including Milt Larkin and Floyd Ray) until 1941. He toured in the South with blues musicians Lil Green and Big Bill Broonzy for about a year before joining Cootie Williams' big band in 1942.[134] Williams discovered Vinson at a roadhouse outside of San Antonio. Williams originally went to Texas to recruit Arnett Cobb but found out that Cobb's wife did not want him to leave town. At the roadhouse where Cobb and Vinson were playing, the band would split up during the intermission so that half would play while the other half rested. When hanging out with some of the band members in the kitchen, Williams heard Vinson, who was kidding around singing the blues (the band never featured him as a vocalist), and exclaimed, "That's what I want!" In a state of surprise Eddie asked, "Are you sure you want me?" "Of course," said Williams, and the rest is history.[135] During Vinson's tenure with Williams (1942–1945), their recordings of "Cherry Red Blues" and "Somebody's Got to Go" became hits and marked Vinson's emergence as a popular vocalist.[136]

In 1945 Vinson formed his own sixteen-piece band and established himself as a leader with big hits such as "Kidney Stew Blues" and "Juice Head Baby." He also worked at the Club Zanzibar on Broadway around 1947 and was featured regularly on remote NBC radio broadcasts from the club. In addition, he signed with the new Mercury label that had gained national distribution at the time. With national recognition, Vinson toured regularly around the country between 1947 and 1949. He had to tour with a small group, however, because of the economic problems in trying to survive with a big band in the late forties. In 1948 he changed over to King Records after the second musicians' union strike and recorded "Person to Person," which also became a hit. Vinson recorded prolifically for King, but only a few sides were released. He continued to work mostly as a single with small groups until 1954, when he rejoined Williams for a brief period. Vinson later relocated to Chicago for about a year and worked with Johnny Griffin, Junior Mance, and Wilbur Ware. After Vinson's popularity waned, he returned to his Texas hometown and played occasional gigs while working a day job at a hospital to support himself. In 1957 he recorded an album for Bethlehem in which his old material was modernized with arrangements by Ernie Wilkins and played by members of Count Basie's band.[137]

In referring to Vinson's vocal style, Kernfeld points out that "His blues singing was characterized by an intentionally broken falsetto with which he punctuated line endings, and he performed his earthy, humorous lyrics in a deliberately understated manner."[138] Foster adds, "As a vocal-instrumental performer he successfully bridges the cross-over areas of jazz, blues, R&B, and manages to appeal to a wide (including rock) audience."[139] An excellent example of Eddie Vinson's powerful singing in the blues idiom can be heard on "Stingy Blues," recorded by the Cootie Williams orchestra in January 1946. On this side, Vinson delivers the soulful lyrics in an extroverted and uplifting manner. In referring to his own blues singing style, Vinson states, "I do a different kind of blues ... I try to make it a little happy, have a little truth in it, with a message in it, but not that depressing thing. I don't have that background."[140]

After the Swing Era, producer Bob Thiele recruited Vinson for a successful Bluesway session in 1967, and his career re-emerged with national and international tours during the seventies and most of the eighties. He also continued to record in this country and abroad, which resulted in his receipt of the Grand Prix award by the Hot Club of France and the International Jazz Club.[141] After becoming ill in the late eighties, Vinson still performed until his death in 1988 in Los Angeles where he had settled two decades earlier. Eddie Vinson was one of the few musicians who could sing, play the saxophone, and compose. He was comfortable as a performer and composer in the blues, R&B, and jazz idioms. In fact, many musicians have acknowledged Vinson as the actual composer of two jazz classics, "Tune Up" and "Four," that are usually associated with Miles Davis. These two classics are still being played by jazz musicians and heard by music lovers all around the world.[142]

DINAH WASHINGTON

Dinah Washington was born Ruth Lee Jones on August 24, 1924, in Tuscaloosa, Alabama, but was raised in Chicago. She played piano and often performed duets with her mother at St. Luke's Baptist Church for the congregation. Ruth became known as a child prodigy and won a talent contest at the Regal Theater by singing "I Can't Face the Music." Influenced by Billie Holiday, she began singing in nightclubs at fifteen—secretly because of her age and family pressures to perform sacred music. At sixteen (in 1940), she became the pianist for Sallie Martin's gospel choir and worked the gospel circuit with Reverend C. L. Franklin, Roberta Martin, and Mahalia Jackson for two years.[143] Afterward, Ruth returned to performing secular music in some of Chicago's top nightclubs such as the Downbeat Room, the Rhumboogie, and the Garrick Stage Bar, where critics and talent scouts recognized her talent and ultimately recommended her to Lionel Hampton.[144] She joined Lionel Hampton's band in 1943, changed her name to Dinah Washington, and remained with that organization until 1946.[145] In 1943 while with Hampton, jazz critic Leonard Feather organized Washington's first studio session for the Keynote record label to record a program of his blues compositions. Two of Feather's tunes, "Salty Papa Blues" and "Blow Top," became hits and laid the foundation for Washington's later success. In 1945 she recorded for the Apollo label in Los Angeles with a band organized by Lucky Thompson that included Gene Porter, Charles Mingus, and Milt Jackson.

In 1946 Washington signed a long-term contract with Mercury Records, which showcased her ability to sing repertoire that included "Embraceable You," "I Can't Get Started," and "The Man I Love." In the following years, she recorded with several different bands led by Gus Chappell, Gerald Wilson, Tab Smith, Cootie Williams, and others.[146] Her 1946 recordings reveal a young, high-spirited, and musical voice that delivers a melody with fine intonation and lyrics with clear diction. For example, in her rendition of "The Man I Love," her phrasing of the melody is particularly striking with the ornaments she adds at various cadence points. It is also interesting to point out that it is unusual for a twenty-two-year-old vocalist to express herself with the kind of feeling and emotion she displayed in her early recordings. Kernfeld adds, "Washington's singing was characterized by high-pitched, penetrating sounds, precise enunciation, contrasts between tender understatement and gospel-inspired intensity and an entrancing languor."[147] The results were some exciting and swinging sessions that represent one of the most fertile periods in her recording career. Later on, Mercury wanted to expand Dinah's audience by recording her with studio ensembles, including strings conducted by Jimmy Carroll or Mitch Miller. The company also wanted to satisfy Washington's large jazz audience by recording her with high-profile instrumental soloists such as Clark Terry, Clifford Brown,

Cannonball Adderley, Ben Webster, and Max Roach.[148] Until the mid-fifties and the rock-and-roll explosion, her recordings always reached the top ten R&B charts. She recorded a wide range of songs including ballads such as "I Only Know" and "It Isn't Fair," the pop tune "Wheel of Fortune," the classic blues song "Trouble in Mind," and Hank Snow's "I Don't Hurt Anymore."[149]

By the end of the Later Swing Era, Washington had exhausted most of the classic jazz repertoire and become a national success story as an R&B vocalist. She took an even bigger step in 1959 when she collaborated with rock arranger Belford Hendricks. With a rhythm section and strings, he helped create Dinah Washington's biggest hit ever, "What a Difference a Day Makes," which took her to the top of the lucrative pop charts. Shortly afterward, she teamed up with Brook Benton and the rhythm and strings format to record "Baby You Got What It Takes." The Washington-Benton duo followed up with "Rocking Good Way" a year later, and the result was, according to Kurt Mohr, "Two tracks that nobody has ever been able to top."[150] Influenced by Billie Holiday and Bessie Smith, Washington successfully forged a link between both gospel and jazz styles that provided her with the foundation to become one of the top female vocalists in the history of American music. Like many talented artists, she passed away at a young age of thirty-nine during the height of her career. The queen (as she was called) can still be heard through the vocal work of successors such as Nancy Wilson, Aretha Franklin, and Patti LaBelle.

JOE WILLIAMS

Joe Williams was born in Cordele, Georgia, on December 12, 1918, and moved with his family to Chicago at age three. Like many African Americans, he grew up in poverty and worked at menial jobs as a teenager to survive. He was determined, however, to become a professional singer and made his debut at age nineteen with clarinetist Jimmie Noone.[151] Williams later performed with Coleman Hawkins and Lionel Hampton in the early forties, and he made his first recording while on tour with Andy Kirk and his Clouds of Joy during 1946 and 1947. Williams had opportunities to perform intermittently with some high-profile bandleaders in the forties, but he continued to struggle while working odd jobs as a laborer in Chicago. He sang briefly with the Albert Ammons–Pete Johnson and Red Saunders bands in the late forties, worked with trumpeter Hot Lips Page, and performed at Chicago's Brass Rail for ten weeks with Count Basie's septet in 1950. Williams recorded "Everyday I Have the Blues" in 1951 with King Kolax, and it became a minor hit.[152]

After struggling for a few more years, Williams' luck changed forever when he sang with Count Basie's big band on Christmas Day in 1954.

Williams recorded "Everyday I Have the Blues" with Basie in early 1955, and the thirty-seven-year-old veteran vocalist practically became an overnight success.[153] The hit tune is included on the Verve album *Count Basie Swings, Joe Williams Sings*, along with "The Comeback," "In the Evening," and "Alright, Okay, You Win." The entire session, produced by Norman Granz, contains tight and swinging band arrangements and Williams' distinctive bass-baritone voice. This album is generally considered the definitive Williams-Basie work.[154] Williams received a lot of credit for the band's renewed popularity as it experienced one capacity crowd after another while touring across the country. He remained with Basie until 1960 and, during that period, ended up with the title of "blues king."[155] He later expanded his scope of repertoire, however, and developed himself into a well-rounded singer and superior balladeer.[156] In fact, Bob Weir states, "Williams re-shaped the role of the big band singer and brought it up to date without sacrificing his innate taste and musical imagination."[157]

After Basie, Williams maintained a solo career by appearing in clubs, on television, and at major national and international festivals.[158] He first appeared as a soloist with the Harry Edison Quintet from 1961 to 1962 and later worked with his own trios led by pianists Junior Mance and Norman Simmons.[159] Williams also recorded and/or toured with many big-name musicians such as George Shearing and Cannonball Adderley, and appeared at occasional reunions with Count Basie.[160] It is important to point out that television played a major role in the success of Williams' career. For example, in 1994 he held the record for the most network television appearances of any jazz musician. He appeared over sixty times on *The Tonight Show* and other shows hosted by Merv Griffin, Mike Douglas, Art Linkletter, and Steve Allen. According to Joe Williams, "That exposure was absolutely essential for my career. I think my many appearances made me more acceptable to the public."[161] He also played acting parts on Bill Cosby's television show and in the film *The Moonshine War*.

Williams continued to record and perform well into the nineties on international concert tours, jazz cruises, and at golf tournaments. He was recognized by *Downbeat* many times as the "Best Jazz Singer." In 1983 he received the National Academy of Recording Arts and Sciences' Governor's Award and a Grammy for his album *I Just Want to Sing*. He was also honored at an all-star concert in 1991 by the Society of Singers and received an American Jazz Masters Award in 1993 by the National Endowment for the Arts.[162] Although Williams' professional career actually began during the Later Swing Era, he did not become famous until the end of that era. He indeed struggled a great deal during that time, but he had a great sense of dignity in the way he presented himself and his music. Anyone who had the opportunity to witness him in performance can attest to the fact that he brought a high level of sophistication to American music. The jazz world is indeed fortunate to have had him in its midst.

NOTES

1. Feather and Gitler, *Encyclopedia of Jazz*, p. 106.
2. Margaret E. Winter, "Hi De Ho!" *Bandleaders*, no. 8 (1944): 6, 46.
3. Feather and Gitler, *Encyclopedia of Jazz*, p. 106.
4. Carr, *The Rough Guide*, pp. 96–97.
5. Kernfeld, *The New Grove Dictionary*, 1:182.
6. Feather and Gitler, *Encyclopedia of Jazz*, p. 106.
7. Schuller, *The Swing Era*, p. 329.
8. Ibid., pp. 329–330.
9. Ibid., p. 330.
10. Ibid.
11. Quoted in Simon, *The Big Bands*, p. 111.
12. Ibid., p. 110.
13. Feather and Gitler, *Encyclopedia of Jazz*, p. 106.
14. Stan Woolley, "The Misty Miss Christy," *Jazz Journal International* 40 (October 1987): 18–19.
15. John Tynan, "That Misty Miss Christy," *Downbeat* 23, no. 22 (1956): 13.
16. Ibid.
17. George T. Simon, "June's in Tune!" *Metronome* 65, no.7 (1949): 20.
18. Ibid.
19. Ibid.
20. Woolley, "The Misty Miss Christy," pp. 18–19.
21. Feather and Gitler, *Encyclopedia of Jazz*, p. 123.
22. Woolley, "The Misty Miss Christy," pp. 18–19.
23. Richard Cook and Brian Morton, *The Penguin Guide to Jazz on CD*, 3rd ed. (New York: Penguin Books, 1996), 243.
24. Kernfeld, *The New Grove Dictionary* (1988), 1:322.
25. Claudia Coates, Billy Eckstine Obituary, *The Times-Picayune*, March 9, 1993.
26. John Swenson, "R&B/Jazz," *Saturday Review* (January/February 1986): 94.
27. Coates, Eckstine Obituary.
28. Kernfeld, *The New Grove Dictionary* (1988), 1:323.
29. Carr, *The Rough Guide*, p. 186.
30. Swenson, "R&B/Jazz," p. 94.
31. Feather and Gitler, *Encyclopedia of Jazz*, p. 201.
32. Swenson, "R&B/Jazz," p. 94.
33. Coates, Eckstine Obituary.
34. Dahl, *Stormy Weather*, p. 137.
35. Feather and Gitler, *Encyclopedia of Jazz*, pp. 324–325.
36. Kernfeld, *The New Grove Dictionary* (1988), 1:533.
37. Dahl, *Stormy Weather*, p. 138.
38. Giddins, *Visions of Jazz*, pp. 370–371.
39. Whitney Balliett, "Jazz Records: Miss Holiday," *New Yorker* (March 1960): 1–2.
40. Giddins, *Visions of Jazz*, pp. 372.
41. Martin Williams, "Billie Holiday: Triumphant Decline," *Saturday Review* (October 31, 1964): 68.

42. Ibid.

43. Giddins, *Visions of Jazz*, pp. 374.

44. Dahl, *Stormy Weather*, pp. 139–140.

45. Feather and Gitler, *Encyclopedia of Jazz*, pp. 324–325.

46. Barry Ulanov, "Not Just a Singer's Singer-But Everybody's!" *Metronome* 64, no. 4 (1948): 19.

47. Kernfeld, *The New Grove Dictionary* (1988), 1:612.

48. Ulanov, "Not Just a Singer's Singer," pp. 19, 30.

49. Kernfeld, *The New Grove Dictionary* (1988), 1:612.

50. Feather and Gitler, *Encyclopedia of Jazz*, p. 354.

51. Ulanov, "Not Just a Singer's Singer," p. 19.

52. Ibid., p. 30.

53. Kernfeld, *The New Grove Dictionary* (2002), 2:565.

54. John Tynan, "Peggy Lee," *Downbeat* 24, no. 6 (1957): 13.

55. Eliot Tiegel, "Riffs: Peggy Lee," *Downbeat* 57, no. 6 (1990): 13.

56. Feather and Gitler, *Encyclopedia of Jazz*, p. 407.

57. Krystian Brodacki, "Carmen McRae," *Jazz Forum*, no. 123 (February 1990): 17.

58. Bruce Crowther, "Carmen McRae," *Jazz Journal International* 48, no. 4 (1995): 19.

59. Feather and Gitler, *Encyclopedia of Jazz*, p. 457.

60. James T. Jones, "Cut the Crap," *Downbeat* 58, no. 6 (1991): 25.

61. George T. Simon, "Carmen McRae," *Metronome* 70, no. 12 (1954): 17.

62. Kernfeld, *The New Grove Dictionary* (1988), 2:72.

63. Feather and Gitler, *Encyclopedia of Jazz*, p. 457.

64. Crowther, "Carmen McRae," p. 19.

65. Jones, "Cut The Crap," p. 24.

66. Feather and Gitler, *Encyclopedia of Jazz*, p. 457.

67. Alan Surpin, "Dawn of a New O'Day," *Downbeat* 36, no. 23 (1969): 16.

68. Knopper, *Music Hound Swing*, p. 231.

69. Surpin, "Dawn of a New O'Day," p. 16.

70. Kernfeld, *The New Grove Dictionary* (1988), 2:264.

71. Surpin, "Dawn of a New O'Day," p. 16.

72. Feather and Gitler, *Encyclopedia of Jazz*, p. 503.

73. Knopper, *Music Hound Swing*, pp. 231–233.

74. Carr, *The Rough Guide*, p. 479.

75. Bunny Matthews, "Music Brings Her 'High Times' Today," *The Times-Picayune*, June 25, 1982.

76. Surpin, "Dawn of a New O'Day," p. 38.

77. Antonio Garcia, ed., "1997 NEA Jazz Masters," *Jazz Educators Journal* 29 (January 1997): 19.

78. Feather and Gitler, *Encyclopedia of Jazz*, p. 503.

79. Kernfeld, *The New Grove Dictionary* (1988), 2:265.

80. Feather and Gitler, *Encyclopedia of Jazz*, p. 503.

81. Carr, *The Rough Guide*, p. 480.

82. Helen McNamara, "The Odyssey of Jimmy Rushing," *Downbeat* 32, no. 8 (1965): 22.

83. Kernfeld, *The New Grove Dictionary* (2002), 3:472.

84. McNamara, "The Odyssey of Jimmy Rushing," p. 22.

85. Kernfeld, *The New Grove Dictionary* (2002), 3:472.

86. McNamara, "The Odyssey of Jimmy Rushing," p. 23.

87. Schuller, *The Swing Era*, p. 240.

88. Kernfeld, *The New Grove Dictionary* (2002), 3:472.

89. Feather and Gitler, *Encyclopedia of Jazz*, p. 405.

90. Kernfeld, *The New Grove Dictionary* (2002), 3:586.

91. Feather and Gitler, *Encyclopedia of Jazz*, p. 405.

92. Kernfeld, *The New Grove Dictionary* (2002), 3:586.

93. Richard S. Ginell, "Frank Sinatra Biography," *All-Music Guide* (2000), http://www.sonicnet.com/artists.

94. Knopper, *Music Hound Swing*, p. 274.

95. Schuller, *The Swing Era*, p. 689.

96. Knopper, *Music Hound Swing*, p. 274.

97. Schuller, *The Swing Era*, p. 688.

98. Knopper, *Music Hound Swing*, p. 274.

99. Feather and Gitler, *Encyclopedia of Jazz*, p. 605.

100. Kernfeld, *The New Grove Dictionary* (2002), 3:586.

101. Feather and Gitler, *Encyclopedia of Jazz*, p. 606.

102. Kernfeld, *The New Grove Dictionary* (2002), 3:586.

103. Ginell, "Frank Sinatra Biography," p. 2.

104. Kernfeld, *The New Grove Dictionary* (2002), 3:586.

105. Ginell, "Frank Sinatra Biography," p. 2.

106. Kernfeld, *The New Grove Dictionary* (2002), 3:586.

107. Ginell, "Frank Sinatra Biography," p. 2.

108. Feather and Gitler, *Encyclopedia of Jazz*, p. 606.

109. Ginell, "Frank Sinatra Biography," p. 2.

110. Knopper, *Music Hound Swing*, p. 282.

111. Barbara Hodgkins, "Starr Bright," *Metronome* 65, no. 8 (1949): 13.

112. Ibid., p. 31.

113. Kernfeld, *The New Grove Dictionary* (1988), 2:488.

114. Hodgkins, "Starr Bright," p. 31.

115. Kernfeld, *The New Grove Dictionary* (1988), 2:488.

116. Knopper, *Music Hound Swing*, p. 282.

117. Hodgkins, "Starr Bright," p. 13.

118. Ibid., p. 31.

119. Kernfeld, *The New Grove Dictionary* (1988), 2:488.

120. Knopper, *Music Hound Swing*, p. 284.

121. Barbara Gardner, "Sarah," *Downbeat* 28, no. 5 (1961): 19–20.

122. Kernfeld, *The New Grove Dictionary* (1988), 2:573.

123. Maria Jurkowska, "The Divine Sarah," *Jazz Forum* 123 (1990): 14–15.

124. Kernfeld, *The New Grove Dictionary* (1988), 2:573–574.

125. Jurkowska, "The Divine Sarah," p. 15.

126. Kernfeld, *The New Grove Dictionary* (1988), 2:573.

127. Jurkowska, "The Divine Sarah," p. 15.

128. Kernfeld, *The New Grove Dictionary* (1988), 2:573.

129. Knopper, *Music Hound Swing*, pp. 301–305.

130. Jurkowska, "The Divine Sarah," pp. 14–15.

131. Associated Press, Sarah Vaughn Obituary, *The Times-Picayune*, April 5, 1990.

132. Dahl, *Stormy Weather*, pp. 141–142.

133. Jurkowska, "The Divine Sarah," p. 15.

134. Kernfeld, *The New Grove Dictionary* (1988), 2:580.

135. Helen Dance, "The Immutable Cootie Williams," *Downbeat* 34, no. 9 (1967): 35.

136. Kernfeld, *The New Grove Dictionary* (1988), 2:580.

137. Larry Birnbaum, "Eddie Cleanhead Vinson," *Downbeat* 49, no. 10 (1982): 29–30.

138. Kernfeld, *The New Grove Dictionary* (1988), 2:580.

139. Lorne Foster, "They Call Him Mister Cleanhead," *CODA* 218 (1988): 7.

140. Birnbaum, "Eddie Cleanhead Vinson," p. 29.

141. Ibid., p. 30.

142. Feather and Gitler, *Encyclopedia of Jazz*, p. 666.

143. Giddins, *Visions of Jazz*, p. 428.

144. Kurt Mohr, liner notes to *The Complete Dinah Washington* 1946–1947, Vol. 2 (Official 3005).

145. Carr, *The Rough Guide*, p. 672.

146 Mohr, liner notes to *The Complete Dinah Washington* 1946–1947.

147. Kernfeld, *The New Grove Dictionary* (1988), 2:597.

148. Mohr, liner notes to *The Complete Dinah Washington* 1946–1947.

149. Larry Birnbaum, "Review of Dinah Washington's *A Slick Chick (On the Mellow Side): The Rhythm and Blues Years* (EmArcy 814184)," *Downbeat* 51, no. 5 (1984): 31.

150. Mohr, liner notes to *The Complete Dinah Washington* 1946–1947.

151. Barbara Gardner, "Is Joe Williams Really Joe Williams?" *Downbeat* 30, no. 32 (1964): 19.

152. Knopper, *Music Hound Swing*, p. 324.

153. Gardner, "Is Joe Williams Really Joe Williams?" pp. 19–20.

154. Knopper, *Music Hound Swing*, pp. 324–325.

155. Gardner, "Is Joe Williams Really Joe Williams?" pp. 19–20.

156. Feather and Gitler, *Encyclopedia of Jazz*, p. 696.

157. Kernfeld, *The New Grove Dictionary* (1988), 2:625.

158. Ibid., p. 624.

159. Carr, *The Rough Guide*, p. 697.

160. Kernfeld, *The New Grove Dictionary* (1988), 2:624.

161. David Zych, "Joe Williams: Celebrating Every Day," *Jazz Times*, March 1994, 45.

162. Feather and Gitler, *Encyclopedia of Jazz*, p. 696.

Chapter 5

Small Groups

As many big bands were fading from the music scene in the forties and fifties, small groups slowly increased in number and popularity. Small groups, for one thing, provided individual musicians with more freedom to develop their creative abilities as soloists. At the same time, vocalists were evolving as popular individual artists, and many of them preferred the small-group format as their primary accompaniment vehicle. Several instrumentalists also doubled as vocalists and led their own small groups. Furthermore, The financial difficulty of leading a big band after World War II forced many leaders to form small groups. By 1940, there were some jazz buffs who felt that swing music had become too commercial, and they wanted a return to traditional jazz. This laid the foundation for the Dixieland Revival Movement, and many musicians who had left the music profession to work elsewhere returned to the jazz scene and later became big-name artists. All of these crosscurrents created a healthy environment in which several different musical styles such as swing, Dixieland, bebop, cool, and the jump blues coexisted and helped foster the rise of small groups. As a result of this diverse activity, the American popular music scene flourished as the country once again witnessed the return of a high degree of musical creativity that had subsided in the thirties with big bands and the restrictions of structured ensemble arrangements.

Large numbers of big-band musicians later developed their solo capabilities in small groups. Such instrumentalists as Jonah Jones, Louis Jordan, Modern Jazz Quartet members John Lewis and Milt Jackson, Oscar Peterson, George Shearing, and Charlie Ventura either started out or worked in big bands. It was the small-group format, however, that allowed these musicians to achieve a degree of musicianship that might not have been possible had they continued performing in big bands. In addition, Dixieland musicians such as Bob Scobey, Wilbur DeParis, Wild Bill Davison, and Muggsy Spanier had worked in big bands during their early careers. However, they later became noted instrumentalists by playing traditional jazz in small groups. Swing musicians such as Roy Eldridge, Artie Shaw, Lester Young, Ben Webster, Jonah Jones, Chu Berry, and Benny Goodman continued playing swing in small groups whenever possible. Other instrumentalists such as George Shearing, Oscar Peterson, and Charlie Ventura carried the swing style a step further by mixing it with bop elements to produce their own hybrid yet individual styles. At the other end of the spectrum, pianist-vocalist Nat "King" Cole led a popular swing trio for a number of years before claiming the national spotlight as a popular vocalist. Similarly, saxophonist-vocalist Louis Jordan continued in the swing tradition and adapted Count Basie's hard-swinging Kansas City blues style to his musical approach with the Tympani Five. This combination of swing and jump blues styles provided Jordan with the musical formula he needed to become a popular artist who helped lay the foundation for rhythm and blues.

Naturally, there were reactions against the commercialism of swing. The first was the Dixieland Revival, which actually began in the late thirties and gained momentum in the early forties. The push for a return to older jazz resulted from the rediscovery of Jelly Roll Morton and Sidney Bechet along with some reissues of early Dixieland. The revival consisted of two different schools of musical thought. One school contained mostly white Midwesterners who had played jazz in the twenties under the influence of such bands as the New Orleans Rhythm Kings and the Original Dixieland Jazz Band. The second school resulted from the fact that younger musicians wanted to re-create the music of older black New Orleans bands like those of Morton, King Oliver, and Louis Armstrong.

The first school of musicians revolved around Eddie Condon, a guitarist who had worked with Bobby Hackett at Nick's club in Greenwich Village that featured traditional jazz. Condon was an average musician with an aggressive personality who organized jam sessions at Town Hall that were broadcast every week. These sessions played an important role in increasing the audience for traditional jazz. He also became the music director for Commodore Records and organized numerous recording sessions for the musicians. Condon became influential as a leader and opened his own jazz club in 1945 that became highly successful. Some of the musicians associated with him were Wild Bill Davison, George Brunis, Max Kaminsky, Pee Wee Russell, Edmond Hall, and Muggsy Spanier. These musicians were not revivalists. They simply continued playing the music they had played in the 1920s.

The second school consisted of true revivalists that comprised two sets of musicians. The first set was led by cornetist Lu Watters in the San Francisco area. After leading a big band for several years, Watters formed a small group that was devoted to the music of Morton and Oliver. The group, called the Yerba Buena Jazz Band, utilized the same traditional instrumentation of Oliver and Armstrong with two cornets, clarinet, trombone, and a rhythm section. Watters' band became popular on the West Coast and later developed a national reputation. Two of his band members, trombonist Turk Murphy and second cornetist Bob Scobey, formed their own groups after leaving Watters. Their groups became quite popular by recording and touring throughout the country playing at major music festivals and colleges. The second set of musicians emerged after William Russell and Frederic Ramsey, Jr., rediscovered traditional jazz pioneer Bunk Johnson in New Iberia, Louisiana, in 1939. Johnson began playing again and recorded in 1942 as a leader. He started working in northern jazz clubs in 1943 and rose to national prominence. In the same year, Orson Welles rediscovered Edward "Kid" Ory and presented Ory on his radio program. Once Johnson and Ory garnered public attention, the revival movement was under way. Johnson became the seminal leader of the movement, and he continued to perform until his retirement in 1948. His clarinetist, George Lewis, assumed leadership of the group and became even more popular than Johnson.[1] There were other musicians, including trombonist Wilbur DeParis, who also led revival bands that made notable contributions during the Later Swing Era.

Another reaction to swing was the bebop movement. This movement, referred to as "The Bop Rebellion" by Collier, had a more significant philosophical goal that extended far beyond music; it also reacted toward the socioeconomic situation that existed in this country at the time. Instrumentalists such as Charlie Parker, Dizzy Gillespie, and Thelonious Monk were not only visionary artists but were socially conscious and, in some ways, considered eccentric by mainstream America. Influenced by the sophisticated harmonic inventiveness of guitarist Charlie Christian, Parker and Gillespie played a major role in creating a musical language that was far ahead of its time. This new language was expressed in much the same way that African-Americans reacted to racial injustice in this country in the forties and fifties. Suffice it to say, bop was purely a black invention.[2]

Another movement, referred to as the "cool school," quietly made its way into the Later Swing Era as a fourth instrumental jazz style. This style was firmly rooted in European concert or "classical" music and gained momentum in the forties as a continuation of earlier experiments with "symphonic jazz" by Scott Joplin, James P. Johnson, Paul Whiteman, and George Gershwin. Big-band leaders such as Stan Kenton, Woody Herman, and Claude Thornhill had already extended the boundaries of swing with symphonic-styled compositions. As small groups increased in number, so did individual musicians who were interested in this style. Small-band leaders such as Dave Brubeck, John Lewis, Gerry Mulligan, and Lennie Tristano explored this hybrid style that combined swing with symphonic music and some elements of bop. Although Tristano might be considered somewhat of an underground leader of the movement, it was Brubeck, Lewis, Mulligan, and ultimately Miles Davis who became the leaders of this style.[3]

A fifth instrumental style evolved from Kansas City swing via the fast-swinging style of Count Basie's orchestra. One of the first small-group leaders to adopt this style was vocalist-saxophonist Louis Jordan who actually formed his group in the late thirties. Jordan's hard-swinging, blues-based music became known as the "jump blues" style in the early forties. This style became highly popular among the masses in the forties and fifties and laid the foundation for rhythm and blues, which ultimately influenced the rise of rock and roll. In sum, this chapter contains a sample of the different small groups and music styles that flourished and contributed to the diverse creativity that took place during the Later Swing Era.

JONAH JONES

Trumpeter Jonah Jones first played alto horn in a Louisville, Kentucky, community band at age eleven and switched over to trumpet two years later. While listening to records by Louis Armstrong and Fletcher Henderson, he played around Louisville with local bands.[4] At eighteen, he began playing professionally on a Mississippi riverboat and joined Horace Henderson a year later, working mostly in Cleveland and Buffalo. Jones performed around Buffalo with several bands for the next three or four years and ended up with Jimmie Lunceford in the spring of 1932. Later that year, Jones joined Stuff Smith until 1935. Between 1934 and 1935, Lil Armstrong served as the leader of Smith's band. Afterward, Jones worked with McKinney's Cotton Pickers briefly before rejoining Smith in 1936 for a four-year residency at New York's Onyx Club. He worked with Benny Carter and Fletcher Henderson from late 1940 to early 1941 and became a member of Cab Calloway's big band and Cab Jivers' group from 1941 to 1952.[5] After Calloway disbanded, Jones worked with Joe Bushkin's band, which included bassist Charles Mingus and Jo Jones on drums, at The Embers in New York City. During that year, Earl Hines assembled an all-star band with Jones, trombonist Bennie Green, tenorist Harold Clark, drummer Art Blakey, bassist Tommy Potter, and vocalist Etta Jones that lasted until 1953. Jones' next job was in the pit band for *Porgy and Bess* at the Ziegfeld Theatre for about a year. In 1954 he worked around New York with Stuff Smith, Urbie Green, and Big Chief Moore for a few months and later toured in Paris and Belgium as a solo artist. Jones returned to New York City in 1955 and ran into Sam Berk, who had been a booking agent for Duke Ellington and Cab Calloway. Berk advised Jones to forget about big bands, which were having a tough time, and encouraged him to take a small group into The Embers on George Shearing's night off. Jones formed a quartet with pianist George Rhodes (who later became Sammy Davis' music director), bassist John Browne, and drummer Harold Austin for the engagement. The group's repertoire consisted of a mix of jazz and show tunes. Jones played mostly with a mute and instructed Austin to use brushes. As a result, the club's manager was impressed and invited the group for a week-long engagement.

The quartet recorded an album for RCA Victor the following year entitled *Jonah Jones at The Embers,* which consisted of Broadway show tunes on one side and Dixieland on the other.[6] Throughout the album, the quartet plays in a light swinging style that is precise and very direct. The group's up-tempo rendition of "It's All Right with Me" opens with Jones stating the melody in its original form with a mute. Rhodes' solo for one chorus is followed by muted trumpet in the [A] sections and piano again for eight bars in the bridge [B]. The third chorus follows with Jones playing a quarter note on the first beat every other measure, while Austin plays a drum solo throughout using brushes. Jones returns with the last seven bars to conclude the tune. The band's treatment of "All of You" is similar to that mentioned above, but with a medium swing tempo. Again, Jones states the melody and is followed by a piano solo for one chorus. Jones solos on the second chorus and proceeds with melody notes on the first beat of every other measure over a drum solo for the third or shout chorus. Jones follows with another solo for sixteen bars and returns to the melody for the last sixteen measures. The band concludes with an eight-bar vamp over the dominant or B♭7 chord to the end.

The quartet's performance of "Basin Street Blues" is interesting in that it features Jones' Louis Armstrong–influenced singing. In the first four bars, the trumpet alternates with piano in the verse, followed by the group swinging for the next four measures, which is repeated for a total of sixteen bars. Jones plays a trumpet solo for the first chorus and follows by singing during the second chorus with clear diction and excellent intonation. This section is one of the highpoints of the album. Rhodes and Browne play eight bars apiece on the third chorus, with Rhodes quoting two bars of "Yankee Doodle." Jones returns with a trumpet solo over stop-time in the first six bars of one and a half choruses and swings for six bars during the next half chorus before playing an impressive cadenza as he proceeds to the end. The quartet's clean swinging style throughout the album effectively shows why it worked at The Embers from 1955 to 1964 for twenty weeks per year.[7] Throughout the sixties and until 1977, the band was extremely successful with several hit records and tours in Europe, the Far East, and Australia. Jones continued to perform at European jazz festivals in 1978 and worked occasionally into the nineties.[8] He was one of the most versatile and swinging trumpeters in jazz history.

LOUIS JORDAN

Louis Jordan began playing clarinet and saxophone at age seven under the tutelage of his father in Brinkley, Arkansas. While still in high school, he toured with the Rabbit Foot Minstrel's band led by his father.[9] At age fifteen, Louis played with the Ruby Williams Quintet in Hot Springs, Arkansas, and worked with other regional bands before relocating to Philadelphia to work with Charlie Gaines in 1933. After two years with Gaines, he moved to New York and worked briefly with drummer Kaiser Marshall. Jordan joined violinist Leroy Smith's orchestra for about a year and gained invaluable experience as an instrumentalist and vocalist. He later played with Chick Webb in 1936 where he had the opportunity to develop his instrumental and vocal skills further and gain some national exposure.

Jordan formed his own small group in 1938 and opened at the Elks' Rendezvous Club in New York City for a clientele that preferred entertainment instead of dance music. The group was first named Louis Jordan and His Elks' Rendezvous Band. Jordan signed a recording contract with Decca, and the first two sides he recorded for the label were released under the band's original name. Subsequent records, however, carried the name of the Tympani Five. Incidentally, the band's drummer, Walter Martin, was a proficient tympani player, and it was a part of the group's style during its first three years of existence. Hence, Tympani became a part of the group's permanent name, even when it was actually expanded to seven or eight players at various times. The Jordan name became popular in 1940 when Decca released a new record every month that featured him singing and playing along with a few instrumentals. He reached wide audiences with tunes such as "I'm Gonna Move to the Outskirts of Town," "Knock Me a Kiss," "What's the Use of Getting Sober," and the ever-popular "Five Guys Named Moe" until the recording ban in 1942. He returned to the studio in 1943 and recorded "Caldonia, Is You Is or Is You Ain't My Baby," "Beware," and "Saturday Night Fish Fry," which were million-sellers. "Choo Choo Ch' Boogie" was an even bigger hit and sold more than two million copies.[10]

With other hits such as "Ain't Nobody Here but Us Chickens" and "Don't Let the Sun Catch You Cryin," Jordan's band was one of the most popular small groups of the forties and fifties. He had hit the big time by reaching both the black and white markets, working the top clubs in the country, and achieving a high income. Jordan's accessible style was the obvious reason for his resounding success, and Leonard Feather offers us a glimpse into the Tympani Five's musical formulae below:

> The arrangements were never beyond the comprehension of the average bar-and-grill listener. Unison horns (trumpet and alto) and basic two-part harmony predominated in the instrumental sections with frequent use of the shuffle boogie rhythm that became Jordan's trademark. The group had a straight-ahead, clean-cut sound. When Jordan sang, there was often a strong suggestion of humor, not only in the content of the lyrics, but also in the use of spoken asides and even in his vocal timbre itself. Everything the Tympani Five played qualified as jazz, yet it was geared to elicit laughter as well as foot-stomping

and thunderous applause. Apollo Theater audiences went wild over the group.[11]

Jordan had an uncanny ability for writing hits as well as picking songs from publishers' shelves and turning them into popular hits. A good example of Jordan's ability to pick hit songs was his selection of Mike Jackson's "Knock Me a Kiss." This thirty-two-bar song written in A-A-B-A form is based on "I Got Rhythm" chord progressions with a simple eight-bar bridge. He sings with the rhythm section in the three [A] sections, and a muted trumpet plays background riffs in the bridge [B] to complete one thirty-two-bar chorus. During the next sixteen bars, Jordan plays an alto sax solo simultaneously with the trumpeter's solo for a Dixieland "contra-puntal" effect and resumes singing in the bridge. After singing in the last [A] section (eight bars) of the second chorus, the two horns solo again together for an eight-bar coda to end the song. Although the group's arrange-ment of this song is simple, it is unique and holds the listener's interest.

While Jordan was at the height of his fame, he made a sudden shift in his career and formed a big band in 1951. By all accounts, it was a top-notch ensemble but difficult to manage economically. After about a year, he returned to the small group. He continued to record with the Tympani Five for Decca as well as sessions with Ella Fitzgerald, Bing Crosby, Louis Armstrong, and others until 1953. Afterward, Jordan recorded for RCA and Mercury into the late fifties. He also worked during the sixties and in the early seventies intermittently until his death in 1975.[12] Jordan was one of the few musicians to combine musicianship and showmanship effectively during the Later Swing Era, and he played a major role in laying the founda-tion for generations of rhythm-and-blues musicians who followed him.[13]

MODERN JAZZ QUARTET

The Modern Jazz Quartet's seeds were sown when three of its original members (vibraphonist Milt Jackson, pianist John Lewis, and drummer Kenny Clarke) worked together in Dizzy Gillespie's big band in 1946. In fact, the three musicians and bassist Ray Brown played at least one tune as a quartet in each set to give Dizzy's band (especially the trumpet section) a brief rest from playing the ensemble's difficult and demanding arrangements. The four players later performed and recorded as the Milt Jackson Quartet in 1951. After bassist Percy Heath replaced Brown, the group became known as the MJQ, with John Lewis as its music director. In August 1954, the group began to perform regularly with bookings into jazz venues such as New York's Chantilly and Birdland. A year later, drummer Connie Kay replaced Clarke and established the group's long-standing membership. The quartet's recordings and international tours bolstered its public recognition, and the group became recognized as a superb ensemble. In addition to performing in some of the country's top jazz clubs, the MJQ appeared at the Newport Jazz Festival and twice in Town Hall during 1955. In 1956, they returned to Newport, served as artists-in-residence at the Music Inn in Lenox, Massachusetts, and toured Europe.[14]

John Lewis was raised in Albuquerque, New Mexico, and studied piano from age seven. He went on to study music and anthropology at the University of New Mexico, receiving a bachelor's degree in 1942. He served in the army from 1942 to 1945 and joined Dizzy Gillespie's big band in 1946 as pianist–arranger. Lewis also worked with Illinois Jacquet and freelanced with Charlie Parker, Ella Fitzgerald, Miles Davis, and the Milt Jackson Quartet prior to receiving a master's degree from the Manhattan School of Music.[15] Milt Jackson grew up in Detroit, Michigan, and became involved in music at age seven by singing gospel duets with his brother. Jackson later played piano and switched to the vibraphone in his teens before studying music at Michigan State University. Dizzy Gillespie heard Jackson in Detroit and brought him to New York in 1945 to play with his sextet and big band in 1946. Milt also worked with Tadd Dameron, Howard McGhee, Charlie Parker, and Woody Herman before leading his own quartet in 1951 and 1952.[16] Percy Heath was raised in Philadelphia and began studying the violin at age eight. After military service as a fighter pilot, he resumed his musical training on bass at Philadelphia's Granoff School of Music. He played his first job with Red Garland and served as house bassist at the Down Beat Club in Philadelphia in 1946. He moved to New York in 1947 and worked with Howard McGhee, Miles Davis, Fats Navarro, J. J. Johnson, and others before joining Milt Jackson's quartet in 1951.[17] Connie Kay began studying piano with his mother in Tuckahoe, New York, at age six. He switched to drums at age ten and played his first professional job with Fats Noel in 1939. Kay later worked with Sir Charles Thompson and Miles Davis at Minton's in 1944 and 1945, and with Lester Young between 1949 and 1950. Kay also freelanced with Charlie Parker and Coleman Hawkins before working with Stan Getz from 1950 to 1952, and returning to Lester Young between 1952 and 1955.[18]

Once Connie Kay joined the MJQ in 1955, its future course in jazz history was set. Moreover, with Lewis at the helm, the group's musical style was more or less defined. He was well trained in European concert music, especially in Renaissance and Baroque musical styles. As a result, he arranged and composed pieces that featured the group's improvisations in more formal structures. In fact, he once said, "The audience for our work can be widened if we strengthen our work with structure. If there is more of a reason for what's going on, there'll be more overall sense, and therefore, more interest in the listener."[19] The MJQ recorded some pieces in 1955 that utilized formal structures referred to by Lewis. In Jackson's "Ralph's New Blues," for example, the theme is built on a motive that is played in imitation and stretto by the vibes, bass, and piano. Jackson takes the first solo and plays a number of eighth-note phrases based on early bebop language, while Lewis accompanies him with chords in the left hand and simple melodic phrases using his right hand. Lewis follows with a solo that is sparse and combines aspects of both swing and bop.

The group's arrangement of Cole Porter's "All of You" leans more toward the jazz tradition. After a brief introduction, Jackson plays the theme over an ostinato for the first eight bars (A) and continues the next eight bars (B) in a walking-ballad style. The second [A] section (eight bars) is a repeat of the first eight, and the second [B] section is an imitation of the first [B]. Jackson solos for sixteen bars (A-B) using a shaded vibrato, and the full ensemble returns for the final sixteen bars (A-B). Jackson plays a tasty cadenza before the rest of the quartet ends on the final chord. Likewise, "I'll Remember April" receives traditional jazz treatment as the quartet plays it up-tempo after a four-bar introduction by Jackson. He solos for two choruses in bop style, and Lewis follows with his characteristic solo approach for three choruses. Jackson and Lewis exchange some eight-bar solos followed by four-bar solo statements before restatement of the theme. Lewis' "Concorde" is, however, at the opposite end of the musical spectrum. Once Heath plays the opening eight-bar statement, the listener will recognize that the composition is a fugue when Lewis and Jackson each enter with the same statement eight measures apart. Connie Kay's cymbal work during the fugue is unique and exciting, to say the least. The MJQ's innovative style closed the Later Swing Era, but it continued to develop until the group disbanded in 1974. The group reunited at various times in the seventies, eighties, and nineties, but it finally disbanded in 1997 and left its legacy as one of the most sophisticated and refined small groups in the history of American music.[20]

OSCAR PETERSON

Oscar Peterson began his musical training with his father in Montreal, Canada. Oscar's second teacher was his sister Daisy, who later became a noted piano teacher. Daisy and Oscar studied with Hungarian concert pianist Paul de Marky, who was trained by a student of Franz Liszt. Peterson won an amateur contest sponsored by the Canadian Broadcasting Corporation and received his own regular fifteen-minute radio program at age fourteen. Five years later, he began working in a local dance band led by Johnny Holmes. Peterson signed a contract with Canadian RCA Victor in 1945 and recorded during the next four years, mostly in a boogie-woogie style. He also led a trio at Montreal's Alberta Lounge, where many American musicians such as Coleman Hawkins and Ray Brown heard him during their visits. Peterson was encouraged to move to the United States by Jimmie Lunceford and Count Basie, but he was reluctant to pull up stakes at that point. Norman Granz heard Peterson over a broadcast from the Alberta Lounge and visited the club in 1949. As a result, Granz influenced him to relocate and scheduled him for an appearance at Carnegie Hall with Ray Brown and Buddy Rich as a trio for a Jazz at the Philharmonic (JATP) concert. In 1950 Peterson became a regular member of JATP and toured as a duo with Ray Brown before adding Irving Ashby on guitar to form a King Cole–styled trio. Barney Kessel later replaced Ashby and, by 1953, Herb Ellis became the guitarist to form one of the most popular trios in jazz history. Peterson's trio stayed together until 1958, when Ellis left and was replaced by drummer Ed Thigpen.[21]

During the forties, Peterson's style was influenced by Teddy Wilson, Nat "King" Cole, Art Tatum, and Erroll Garner. Peterson's style expanded later as he adopted the "locked-hands" or block chord approach developed by pianist-organist Milt Buckner. Peterson is an incredible musician with exceptional piano technique. According to Dobbins, "[he] is often compared to Art Tatum, with whom he shares a unique gift for inspiring awe from musicians, critics, and listeners alike."[22] In fact, Peterson is without peer as a pianist-bandleader. His skill is immediately apparent when one listens to the first few seconds of a performance by any of his trios. For example, his trio that included bassist Ray Brown and guitarist Herb Ellis was recorded live in a JATP concert in September 1953. The group played with absolute precision, and it swung harder than most groups with a drummer. At this concert, the trio's up-tempo rendition of Peterson's "Lollobrigida" (based on "I Got Rhythm" chord progressions) demonstrates a well-knit group with a high level of interaction among its members as it plays the theme. Peterson solos with some exciting single-line improvisations for two choruses. Ellis follows with two solo choruses and plays some swinging bebop melody lines. Peterson returns with another high-spirited solo for two choruses before the trio plays a shout chorus that leads to a restatement of the theme. When the group repeats the theme, the three musicians sound as if they actually "breathe" together in two-bar phrases before proceeding to the coda.

Next on the program is "Pompton Turnpike" by Rogers and Osborne, using the same formal structure (A-A-B-A) as the preceding tune. The trio opens with a sixteen-bar introduction. The theme follows, with Peterson harmonizing the melody using block chords and Ellis playing it in octaves. The group's arrangement features a sixteen-bar interlude with lush harmonies that foreshadows Horace Silver's early compositional style. Ellis continues with an effective solo that combines both swing and bop styles for sixteen bars. Peterson jumps right in on the bridge for a swinging eight bars, and Ellis returns to complete the last eight measures of the first solo chorus. Peterson plays the second solo chorus with right-handed, single-line phrases for sixteen bars before playing the bridge and the last eight bars, using Milt Buckner's "locked-hands" style. The trio follows with an ensemble chorus in block chords for twenty-four bars (A-A-B) before Brown completes the last eight bars of the theme in the style of Slam Stewart by simultaneously bowing and scat-singing the melody to the end of the tune. The group opens Cole Porter's "Love for Sale" with an eight-bar vamp, and Peterson follows with the theme during the first [A] section. He continues by improvising single-line phrases around the theme before playing block chords during the second half of the bridge [B]. After returning to the last [A] section with single-line phrases, he plays a full solo chorus before the trio vamps briefly to the final chord. This particular trio played with extraordinary musicianship, and it had an unusually mature sound.

After the Swing Era, Peterson changed his trio format to piano, bass, and drums and continued until 1965. A few years later, he began performing as a solo pianist and made many appearances with symphony orchestras throughout North America. He also performed and recorded with numerous established artists such as Dizzy Gillespie, Joe Pass, and Clark Terry, as well as in duo performances with notable bassist Neils Henning Ørsted-Pedersen.[23]

GEORGE SHEARING

Blind from birth, George Shearing began playing piano at age three, and he studied music formally between the ages of twelve and sixteen at the Linden Lodge School for the Blind in London.[24] At age eighteen, his teacher arranged an audition for him with an all-blind band sponsored by the Royal National Institute for the Blind. The band consisted of fifteen or sixteen musicians who played arrangements by Jimmie Lunceford and Duke Ellington, and the band members learned their parts from braille, although Shearing learned his music by ear. Shearing became interested in jazz as a member of the aforementioned band. Two of the band members collected jazz records, which gave him the opportunity to listen to many of America's top musicians. Shearing and his friends also had the opportunity to hear and meet musicians such as Fats Waller and Coleman Hawkins in some of London's jazz clubs. In fact, Waller encouraged Shearing to relocate to the United States.[25] Meanwhile, he listened to recordings by Earl Hines, Waller, Meade "Lux" Lewis, Art Tatum, and Teddy Wilson while leading his own groups in London during the late thirties and early forties.[26]

After Shearing learned the jazz language, he built a reputation as a soloist and was voted the top British pianist by several *Melody Maker* polls. He visited the United States in 1946 and, with the encouragement of his friend Leonard Feather, moved to New York City a year later. Shortly after the move, Shearing began to experience the bustling musical activity on 52nd Street by sitting in wherever he could and meeting many of his idols such as Art Tatum. While playing at clubs like Minton's with musicians such as swing drummer Sid Catlett, he began to assimilate the styles of Art Tatum and Teddy Wilson as well as the bebop language of Bud Powell.[27] By 1949,

Shearing had found the musical approach he was looking for—a combination of Milt Buckner's block chord or "locked-hands" style and the chordal sound of Glenn Miller's saxophone section. In the "locked-hands" style, each melody note is harmonized with a three-note chord in the right hand, while the left hand doubles the melody an octave below.[28]

Shearing formed his first quintet in 1949 with vibraphonist Margie Hyams, guitarist Chuck Wayne, bassist John Levy, and drummer Denzil Best, and the historic "Shearing sound" was established. In referring to his sound, Shearing himself stated, "We sat down and, frankly by accident, this sound was born.... Marjorie and Chuck just happened to play an octave apart, and I filled in all the blocks between and still played both their melodies with them."[29] Shipton adds, "By shifting all the rhythmic momentum of his group to the bassist and the drummer, Shearing could play melodic, chordal patterns across the beat,...creating an unusual, spacey texture which remained the foundation of his ensemble style into the twenty-first century."[30] Shearing's new quintet and its fresh approach to ensemble playing skyrocketed his name to fame by 1950. According to Pelletier, "Shearing's rapport with the new line-up was immediate and he decided to keep the group as his permanent accompaniment. This rapport was evident with the quintet's first recording session for MGM Records on February 17, 1949; of the four titles produced, "September in the Rain" sold over a million copies, and Shearing's reputation was established almost overnight."[31]

In "September in the Rain," the rapport within the group and the quality of its performance on the recording is obvious on the first hearing. The "Shearing sound" is heard immediately during the ensemble's statement of the thirty-six-bar theme composed in A-A-B-A form. The three [A] sections are played by the ensemble in block chord style, and Shearing solos in the bridge [B], playing single-line phrases with his right hand in bop style while "comping" with his left hand. After the band's statement of the theme, he solos for one full chorus using the same approach played in the bridge during the theme. Shearing continues soloing for the next twenty-four bars in the A-A-B sections in block chord style before the full ensemble returns with the last eight bars or [A] section of the theme and plays a coda to the end. The quintet also recorded "The Continental" in 1949 using a slightly different arrangement from the one described previously. Like "September in the Rain," "The Continental" is also composed in A-A-B-A form, and the group plays the theme in the three [A] sections in block chord style. However, Shearing plays the bridge [B] with "locked-hands" and the guitar and vibraphone play a countermelody in octaves against the harmonized melody for an interesting effect. The first solo chorus displays Wayne's tasty improvisations for eight bars and Hyams' bop-style eight-bar outing. Shearing begins his solo on the bridge [B] with single-line bop phrases and continues through the last [A] section in the first chorus. He also plays another chorus using block chords in swing style for sixteen bars in the first two [A] sections. The full ensemble enters on the bridge [B] and plays through the last [A] section before proceeding to the coda, which contains portions of the theme while fading out.

In 1949 Shearing's ensemble style was considered revolutionary. It utilized the "locked-hands" approach in ensemble playing with an amalgamation of swing and bebop solo styles by all five members of the quintet. Shearing, moreover, created his sound in a manner that was accessible to the average listener. With highly successful recordings such as "September in the Rain" and Shearing's own composition, "Lullaby of Birdland," the Shearing quintet remained highly popular until 1967. Shearing later led a trio for nearly three decades after leaving the quintet format, and he currently performs as a duo with bassist Neil Swainson. Although his rise to fame occurred during the last half of the Later Swing Era, he has continued to appeal to music lovers and musicians alike up to the present day.

ART TATUM

Art Tatum was born with impaired vision and raised in Toledo, Ohio, where he began playing on the family piano at an early age.[32] During his teens, he received formal training at the Toledo School of Music and learned to read music in braille as well as sheet music with the aid of glasses. He also learned to improvise from listening to recordings, piano rolls, radio broadcasts, and local musicians. Tatum's main influences were Fats Waller and popular radio pianist Lee Sims.[33] Tatum began playing professionally in Toledo at age seventeen and became a staff pianist for radio station WSPD. He was given his own regular fifteen-minute radio show, and his talent was duly rewarded when the program started being nationally broadcast.[34] He later became vocalist Adelaide Hall's accompanist in 1932 and traveled to New York where he raised the eyebrows of the jazz world. Most pianists were in awe of Tatum's musicianship. For example, Fats Waller who was performing at a club realized that Art Tatum was in the audience and announced to his listeners, "I play piano, but God is in the house tonight."[35] Without a doubt, the high esteem in which Tatum was held by his fellow musicians resulted from his extraordinary musicianship. He had exceptional technique on the piano and an incredible ear that was beyond absolute pitch. In essence, he had a "photographic ear" because, after hearing an arrangement twice, he could replicate it perfectly at the piano. Hughes Panassie adds, "Art Tatum holds a place apart among jazz pianists. Equipped with an astonishing instrumental technique, he scatters his solos with virtuosity, fireworks, and unexpected harmonies.... Moreover, one finds ideas in his choruses which reveal a fine inspiration."[36]

Tatum made his first recordings as a solo pianist in 1933. During the thirties, his reputation grew with frequent club performances around the country, in England, and on radio programs.[37] In addition, he (along with Billie

Holiday and Coleman Hawkins) had a popular following on New York City's famed 52nd Street. Although most of Tatum's career was spent as a soloist, he worked with small groups including his own legendary trio. He formed his trio in 1943 with bassist Slam Stewart and guitarist Tiny Grimes, who was later replaced by Everett Barksdale. Tatum's group was modeled after the successful Nat "King" Cole trio. Grimes and Stewart were both leaders on their instruments and consummate showmen. With Tatum's prodigious talent, the excitement and electricity generated by the three musicians' highly interactive group performances drew capacity audiences.[38] As a result, the trio became one of the most influential small groups in the forties.[39] Tatum's trio recorded seven sides in January 1944. The group's performances of "I Got Rhythm," "I Would Do Anything for You," "Honeysuckle Rose," "Moonglow," "Cocktails for Two," "Deep Purple," and "After You've Gone" provide the listener with a musical kaleidoscope of its style.

In "I Got Rhythm," Tatum opens with an eight-bar introduction based on the melody. The tune's three [A] sections consist of variations on the song's theme or melody played in chordal style by the guitar and piano over a walking bass, with Tatum soloing during the bridge. After the tune's thematic variations are stated, Tatum plays the first solo chorus with single-line phrases in the three [A] sections. He harmonizes the first three bars of the melody in the bridge and follows with single-line phrases for the last five measures. The second solo chorus is split between Grimes (A-A) and Stewart (B-A). As Stewart bows and sings simultaneously during his solo, Grimes taps the music's basic rhythmic pulse with his hands on the guitar for an interesting percussive effect. Tatum returns for the third solo chorus and plays his signature single-line phrases over substitute chord progressions in bars one through four in each of the three [A] sections. He plays the original chord changes in the bridge. The trio concludes with a shout chorus of harmonized riffs in the first four bars of each [A] section and a straight-ahead bridge before proceeding to the coda.

The trio's rendition of "Honeysuckle Rose" is totally different from that of the foregoing tune, except for the introduction. Again, Tatum plays the introduction based on thematic material. During the song's theme in A-A-B-A form, however, Tatum plays only two bars of the melody and improvises melodic variations for the next six measures in the first [A] section. He continues improvising for eight bars on the next [A] section before Grimes solos during the last sixteen bars (B-A) of the tune. Surprisingly, the group plays three full choruses of various harmonized ensemble passages over a walking bass in the tune's [A] sections with Tatum playing eight-bar solos in each [B] section. Afterward, the trio proceeds to the coda.

Tatum opens "Moonglow" with an eight-bar introduction based on variants of the melody. During the song with its (A-A-B-A) structure, Tatum plays only two bars of the melody in the first [A] section and improvises through the next [A] section to the bridge [B]. He plays the melody in bars one through four in the bridge and improvises during the remaining four measures. He completes the last eight bars of the tune with improvisation and no hint of the melody. Grimes and Stewart again split one solo chorus effectively with their two stylistic approaches. The trio returns to the melody, with Tatum playing only the first two bars of the melody, followed by six bars of improvisation in the first [A] section and the bridge [B]. The second [A] section is fully improvised, and Tatum plays the melody in the last [A] section as a landmark before concluding the tune with a coda. Similarly, the remaining four tunes recorded by the trio in January 1944 offer a great deal of variety and interest for the listener.

Although Tatum played solo piano throughout most of his career, his trio recordings from the forties are invaluable. They demonstrate his hidden talent as a bandleader and his ability to play effectively in a group setting. Undoubtedly, anyone who listens to Tatum's piano playing will instantly recognize the fact that he was a true genius. According to piano great Teddy Wilson, "Tatum was head and shoulders over all other jazz pianists and most classical pianists."[40] In spite of this fact, however, Tatum's trio was actually the vehicle that brought him his greatest commercial success.[41]

CHARLIE VENTURA

Saxophonist Charlie Ventura started out on the C-melody saxophone, played alto for a while, and settled on the tenor.[42] His first idol was Chu Berry, and he later became influenced by Charlie Parker. Ventura grew up in Philadelphia and worked as a clerk in the Navy Yard there during the day while working at night in a band that included Buddy DeFranco, Bill Harris, Lou Stein, and Teddy Waters. They also sat in at jam sessions at Nat Siegel's Downbeat Club with visiting musicians such as Dizzy Gillespie and Roy Eldridge. Eldridge recommended Ventura to Gene Krupa, and Charlie was invited to join Krupa's band in 1942. Ventura played with Krupa for a year and joined Teddy Powell when Krupa disbanded in 1943. In Powell's band, Ventura gained a great deal of solo experience and exposure since the band performed regularly on radio. When Krupa reorganized his band in 1944, Ventura returned as the main soloist in Gene's new big band and trio, where he remained until 1946.[43]

Ventura formed his own big band in 1946 but ended up finding more work as a small-group leader. He started another big band in 1948 but soon realized that it was more feasible economically to lead an octet that included trombonist Bennie Green, vocalist Jackie Cain, pianist/vocalist Roy Kral, and Ventura's brother Ben on baritone saxophone. At that time, Charlie used the slogan "Bop for the People," but the group was actually a swing band that played bop themes. Ventura's band had a unique style in that it performed arrangements that featured voices and instruments in unison.[44]

Ventura had first played along with vocalist Peggy Mann in Teddy Powell's band. However, Ventura later developed the concept by accident in Gene Krupa's band when vocalist Buddy Stewart was featured on "Summertime," and Ventura was asked to play cadenzas near the end of the tune. Since Ventura had to play his tenor passages after Stewart finished singing and the audience was about to applaud, he felt guilty about it. Ventura approached Stewart about changing the routine, and the result was Charlie playing and Buddy singing a coda in unison.

Ventura's 1948 band used the same approach when he and/or the other wind instrumentalists played along with Jackie Cain and Roy Kral (who wrote most of the group's arrangements in various combinations). The two featured instrumental soloists were Bennie Green and trumpeter Norman Faye, while the other two members in the rhythm section were bassist Gus Cole and drummer Ed Shaughnessy.[45] In fact, 1948 was a great year for Ventura, whose band was named the best small combo in *Downbeat*'s 1948 poll. He had an even better year in 1949 when he was voted the best tenor saxophonist and his band was named the best small band in *Metronome*'s polls.[46]

Without a doubt, Ventura had an outstanding band between 1948 and 1950. He and Bennie Green were strong soloists, the rhythm section could swing, and Kral wrote some clever arrangements that gave the band a big sound. Ventura's octet recorded a number of sides for Savoy in October 1948. One of his compositions, "Euphoria," has a bop theme that features Charlie, Jackie, and Roy carrying the melody in unison through the [A] sections and a harmonized horn background in the bridge [B]. Green plays the first chorus with his characteristic velvety sound and luscious phrasing. Ventura plays the second chorus and half of a third chorus where he phrases like Flip Phillips with a robust sound. The full ensemble returns on the bridge and then proceeds to the last [A] section with unison instruments and voices to the end of the piece. The octet's performance of "Deed I Do" features Cain in the first two [A] sections accompanied by the four horns playing harmonized background phrases without the rhythm section, and their sense of time is impeccable. The rhythm section enters on the bridge [B] with Cain and the four horns and accompanies them through the last [A] section of the song. A four-bar interlude follows and introduces a full chorus of a bop-style melody played/sung by Ventura's tenor and the Cain-Kral duo, with the three other horns playing a harmonized background. Ventura continues with a swinging tenor solo for one chorus, and the full ensemble returns with part of the theme and plays a beautiful coda at the end. In addition to vocal-instrumental combinations, the group sometimes played tunes such as "Sweet Georgia Brown," featuring only Ventura and Green with the rhythm section. Here, the tenor sax and trombone combination is quite effective and rather unique for the late forties.

Ventura unfortunately broke up the octet and led another big band between 1950 and 1951. He returned to the small-group format and led the Big

Four, a quartet that included Marty Napoleon, Chubby Jackson, and Buddy Rich in 1951. Ventura returned to Krupa's band in 1952–1953 and performed again with Cain and Kral in 1953. Ventura continued to work with Krupa at various times during the sixties and led and/or worked with small groups into the eighties until he passed away in 1992.[47] Charlie Ventura's hard-driving performances brought himself and hundreds of music lovers a great deal of satisfaction for over forty years. The contributions he made to the Later Swing Era with the octet of 1948–1950 and the vocal-instrumental unison style are noteworthy. None of this would have been possible, however, had he not left his $125 per week secure job at the Philadelphia Navy Yard in 1942 to play in Gene Krupa's band for $80 per week.

LU WATTERS' FOLLOWERS

Trombonist-bandleader Turk Murphy gained a foothold in San Francisco's classic jazz revival with Lu Watters' Yerba Buena Jazz Band beginning in 1937. After serving in the navy, Murphy resumed his career as Watters' trombonist until the band broke up in 1949.[48] Murphy recruited some former Yerba sidemen and formed his own band in the same year. In the fifties, Murphy's band gained a national reputation, performing in San Francisco, New York, and New Orleans.[49] While leading his band, Murphy became an articulate spokesman for traditional jazz and wrote regularly about the music in liner notes to recordings and in books.[50] He signed with Columbia Records in 1954, and his band made a large number of recordings during the following three decades.[51]

Columbia recorded Murphy and his band live at the New Orleans Jazz Festival in 1955. The band performed at the Municipal Auditorium, on board the S.S. *President* riverboat, and at the Delgado Museum of Art during the three-day festival. Columbia covered the performances with two engineers and the same equipment used to record the Philadelphia Orchestra a week before the New Orleans festival. Surprisingly, the quality of the recording is excellent. Murphy's band performed "Storyville Blues," "Just a Closer Walk with Thee," "Memphis Blues," "Big Butter and Egg Man," "Floatin' Down to Cotton Town," "Canal Street Blues," "Papa Dip," "Mecca Flat Blues," "Pineapple Rag," and "High Society." The ensemble played "Just a Closer Walk with Thee" in a "dead march" tempo, which the old New Orleans street bands played either at a graveyard or outside of a church. The group's interpretation of the hymn is authentic, and it plays with a full-ensemble sound during some harmonious chorale-like passages. "Floatin' Down to Cotton Town" features the first-rate banjo playing of Dick Lammi, while Murphy's trombone solo work stands out in "Big Butter and Egg Man." Here, Murphy's sound is resonant, and he paces himself economically as he develops thoughtful melodic statements during his solo. He returns with another well-paced solo spot before the final ensemble chorus. Murphy solos with a mute in "Canal Street Blues," while the rest of the band keeps a happy and bouncy two-beat feel throughout. The ensemble interplay in the final chorus is authentic and well played.

The band's repertoire consisted of 1920s jazz classics, original compositions, and well-known ballads. Murphy, himself, was a fine trombonist who played with a full-bodied sound and a consistently humorous style.[52] His band contained proficient musicians, and it played traditional jazz with commendable musicianship and spirit. Simply put, Murphy's talent as a bandleader was equal to his performing ability as an instrumentalist. As a staunch traditionalist, he made a major contribution toward furthering the revival movement.

Trumpeter-bandleader Bob Scobey grew up in Stockton, California. He began playing the cornet at age nine and switched to trumpet around age fourteen. His family relocated to Berkeley, where he later played with dance orchestras, pit bands, and in nightclubs during the thirties. From 1938 to 1940, he played in Lu Watters' big band at Sweet's Ballroom in Oakland. He played second trumpet in Watters' renowned Yerba Buena Jazz Band from 1940 to 1942, served four years in the military during 1942–1946, and rejoined Watters from 1946 to 1950.[53] Scobey formed his Frisco Jazz Band in 1950 and, soon after, landed a recording contract with the Good Time Jazz label. The band spent a three-year residency at Victor and Roxie's in Oakland and headlined at a number of major Dixieland festivals. A key element of the band's success was banjoist-vocalist Clancy Hayes who was co-billed with Scobey throughout the fifties. As Fairweather noted, "[Hayes'] lazy southern charm was central to the band's presentation."[54] The band's reputation became well known by the mid-fifties when it recorded with such stars as Bing Crosby and popular guests like Manny Klein, Frank Beach, Dick Cathcart, and Matty Matlock.[55]

After the twilight of the Swing Era, Scobey's band toured the Midwest and performed at Beloit College in Wisconsin, Northwestern University in Illinois, the University of Chicago, the National Council of Jewish Women at Chicago Heights, Purdue University, and a number of dance and nightclub engagements in Milwaukee. The band had the opportunity to prepare its program before the tour by playing for audiences at San Francisco State College, San Jose State College, and the University of California–Davis.[56] The music prepared for the tour consisted of twelve tunes, and Good Time Jazz recorded the program in March 1956. Half of the repertoire consisted of Clancy Hayes' vocals, including one of his originals, and the remaining six sides were instrumentals. Most of the tunes had been recorded by the Original Dixieland Band, King Oliver, Jelly Roll Morton's Red Hot Peppers, and bands from the Bix Beiderbecke period. The band's personnel were Scobey, trombonist Jack Buck, clarinetist Bill Napier, pianist Jesse "Tiny" Crump, Hayes, tubaist Bob Short, bassist Hal McCormick, and drummer Fred Higuera.

The recording displays Scobey's crisp ensemble playing, which shines through in the band's arrangement of "Ostrich Walk." He shares short solo breaks with clarinetist Napier in the thematic section that alternates with the ensemble's "contrapuntal" passages. Crump's piano solo is in the traditional jazz mold but includes melodic phrases one hears from swing band soloists. The full ensemble follows with Scobey exchanging brief solo breaks with Short's fine tuba playing and Higuera's propulsive drumming. The ensemble concludes with the preceding thematic section and a coda.

Hayes' folksy vocal style is featured on "Indiana," along with musically effective solos by Buck and Napier. Scobey's solo particularly pays homage to Oliver and Armstrong, but with a Beiderbecke twist. Scobey leans closer to Oliver, however, when he plays the melody in a fascinating arrangement of "Sobbin' Blues." Scobey's sensitive and musical phrasing is supported with richly harmonized background passages played by the horns and keyboard instruments. Crump's solo ability is displayed at its best on this piece, and the three-horn harmonized background played softly also encourages Crump's inspired solo. Scobey returns with the melody and inserts some effective call-and-response passages between himself, Short's tuba, and the rest of the ensemble before the coda. After a brief introduction, Hayes delivers a fine rendition of "Michigan Water Blues." Unlike "Sobbin'," this song is actually a twelve-bar blues. Hayes' buoyant singing style is captured effectively with harmonized three-horn background passages played softly for sensitive support. Scobey solos here with singing-style melodic phrases in an Armstrong vein. Hayes returns with the melody and handles the lyrics with clear diction. Crump enters unexpectedly and plays a brief coda with the rest of the rhythm section.

On "Just a Closer Walk with Thee," Scobey and company play the introduction in true hymn style. After a harmonious fermata, Scobey plays the melody with enthusiasm as the clarinet and trombone play sustained background passages. Scobey, Napier, Buck, and Crump all continue with ebullient solos over softly sustained horn background passages. Scobey returns with the theme (à la Armstrong) over traditional group improvisation, and the full ensemble concludes with the hymn. This recording spotlights Bob Scobey's fine musicianship and highly effective bandleading skill. His Frisco Band was one of the most disciplined and tight-knit Dixieland units to participate in the revival movement during the fifties.

BUNK JOHNSON ET AL.

Trumpeter-bandleader Bunk Johnson was born in New Orleans in 1889 and probably became active as a musician around the turn of the century.[57] He worked in New Orleans with bands led by Adam Olivier, Bob Russell, Buddy Bolden, and Frankie Dusen—usually as the second trumpeter. With regard to Johnson's role as a second player, Mutt Carey once stated that

"Bunk always stayed behind the beat—he wasn't quite the drive man that Joe Oliver and Freddie Keppard were."[58] Although Johnson was not considered a lead player, Louis Armstrong pointed out that "Bunk played funeral marches that made me cry!"[59] Johnson left New Orleans around 1915 and played throughout the South in bands, minstrel shows, theaters, and club performances with entertainers such as Ma Rainey, Louis Fritz, and Julia Lee.[60] He later worked with Sammy Price in Kansas City around 1931 and returned to Louisiana (New Iberia) where he joined the Banner Band.[61] A few years later, Johnson retired from music and supported himself by working as a laborer.

Frederick Ramsey and William Russell were researching a chapter on New Orleans for their book *Jazzmen* (1939) and were directed to Johnson by Louis Armstrong and Clarence Williams. The writers located Johnson, and a collaboration began that resulted in Johnson's rediscovery. With the help of producer David Stuart, Russell recorded the trumpeter in a room above Grunewald's Music Shop in New Orleans between 1942 and 1945. Nearly one hundred sides were recorded and praised as the true return of traditional jazz.[62] The first recording session took place in June 1942. Johnson's band consisted of trombonist Jim Robinson, clarinetist George Lewis, pianist Walter Decou, banjoist Lawrence Marrero, bassist Austin Young, and drummer Ernest Rogers. Billed as "Buck Johnson and His Superior Jazz Band," the group recorded nine sides: "Panama," "Down by the Riverside," "Storyville Blues," "Ballin' the Jack," "Make Me a Pallet on the Floor," "Bunk's Blues," and "Yes, Lord I'm Crippled." Johnson leads the ensemble throughout all of the selections in the 1942 session by playing either a song's melody or embellishments on its theme. During Johnson's thematic statements, the other two members on the front line play collective or group improvisation, while the rhythm section accompanies with a quarter note on each beat per measure. At other times, one can hear either Lewis or Robinson as the dominant soloist. When this does occur, Johnson usually lays out for eight or sixteen measures, and the other front-line player performs a secondary improvised melody along with the soloist. For example, on "Pallet on the Floor," Robinson's sixteen-bar solo is heard prominently while Johnson lays out and Lewis plays a secondary melody softly with the trombone. In another instance, Lewis' clarinet solo is heard reasonably well over Robinson's medium-soft melodic lines for sixteen bars, while Johnson takes a brief rest. Amazingly, the seven musicians played together as a group for the first time during the first recording session without the opportunity of a rehearsal, and the nine selections were recorded in just three hours. At that time, the racial situation in New Orleans made it impossible for African-American musicians to record in a professional studio. In spite of this restriction, however, Johnson's band played well throughout the recording session. In addition to the aforementioned nine sides, Johnson is interviewed during the recording session, and he summarizes his history as a musician prior to his rediscovery. This particular album is a true collector's item.

Although Johnson's return to music was vital to the revival movement, he still worked primarily as a laborer during the day and performed only occasionally. Between 1943 and 1945, however, he did have opportunities to play at San Francisco's Gary Theater, give concert lectures on Rudi Blesh's jazz radio series, record with Lu Watters' Yerba Buena Jazz Band, and work with the legendary Sidney Bechet at the Savoy Café in Boston.[63] Meanwhile, Johnson continued to record for Russell's American Music label in New Orleans and with Sidney Bechet in New York. Johnson's big opportunity finally arrived when he opened at New York's Stuyvesant Casino with Lewis, Robinson, Marrero, Alton Purnell on piano, Alcide "Slow Drag" Pavageau on bass, and Baby Dodds on drums in September 1945 for a four-month residency. After a two-month break, Johnson returned to the Casino in April 1946 for two months, with Don Ewell and Alphonse Steele replacing Purnell and Dodds on piano and drums, respectively. Afterward, the group disbanded, and Johnson continued working mainly as a soloist in Louisiana, New York, and Chicago. In October 1947, Johnson returned to New York and held a residency at the Caravan Ballroom with a new band consisting of clarinetist Garvin Bushell, trombonist Ed Cuffee, pianist Don Kirkpatrick, banjoist Danny Barker, bassist Wellman Braud, and Steele on drums. The group also recorded and played at the Stuyvesant Casino. Early in 1948, Johnson returned to New Iberia and played occasionally with a few local bands. Near the end of the year, he suffered two strokes and passed away in 1949.[64] With an authentic sound and a relaxed playing style, Bunk Johnson was considered the seminal figure of the revivalist movement.

Trombonist-bandleader Wilbur DeParis was born in January 1900 and began his career on alto horn around 1912. He performed with his father's circus band on the Theater Owner's Booking Association circuit.[65] In 1925 he led his own band, Wilbur DeParis' Cotton Pickers, briefly at New York's Cinderella Ballroom.[66] Afterward, he worked as a sideman for the next eighteen years with bands led by Leroy Smith, Noble Sissle, Edgar Hayes, Teddy Hill, Louis Armstrong, Ella Fitzgerald, and Roy Eldridge.[67] By 1943 DeParis had formed another band with his brother Sidney but left in 1945 to replace Tricky Sam Nanton in Duke Ellington's Orchestra. After two years with Ellington, DeParis finally formed his "New" New Orleans Band. As DeParis once said, "We try to play as the early New Orleans masters would if they were alive today."[68] In other words, the band wanted "to make discoveries within old traditions."[69] The group's repertoire consisted of light classics, folksongs, hymns, spirituals, blues, marches, and traditional jazz standards. According to Kenney, "[the band's] style evoked that of Jelly Roll Morton's Red Hot Peppers and at the same time had some of the rhythmic and harmonic characteristics of swing."[70] In 1951 DeParis' band began a record-breaking, eleven-year residency at Jimmy Ryan's in New York, then signed a lucrative recording contract with Atlantic in 1952.[71]

Wilbur's band personnel included his brother Sidney on trumpet and tuba, Omer Simeon on clarinet, Don Kirkpatrick or Sonny White on piano, Eddie Gibbs or Lee Blair on banjo, Harold Jackson or Wendell Marshall on bass, and Fred Moore or George Foster on drums. At times, Doc Cheatham played second trumpet.

Hailed as "perhaps DeParis' best album," *"New" New Orleans Jazz* was recorded in April 1955 with his brother, Simeon, White, Blair, Marshall, Foster, and Cheatham. The band recorded eight sides including five traditionals and three DeParis originals. DeParis' "Madagascar" has an asymmetrical structure in which the melody or theme is either played or embellished by the clarinet and followed by a four-bar drum solo of Afro-Cuban rhythms. The same scenario is repeated by muted trumpet in a truncated format. The piano follows suit before Sidney plays open trumpet solos throughout the original form of the tune. Next is a brief clarinet solo that precedes a trombone solo for only sixteen bars. The theme is played by the full ensemble in traditional style and followed by a coda. According to Wilbur, his "March of the Charcoal Grays" is a "comment on the Madison Avenue schoolboys in their gray suits."[72] "March" is an up-tempo humorous piece that opens with Sidney's trumpet carrying the melody over collective improvisation by clarinet and trombone. Spirited solos follow by Omer and Sidney (muted), respectively, with two-horn harmonized background riffs. A brief and effective drum solo follows before giving way to Blair's banjo on the melody, with Simeon's countermelody over the rhythm section. The full band returns with the theme in traditional ensemble style and ends with a characteristic drum break. DeParis' "Mardi Gras Rag" is a medium-tempo swing piece. After a four-bar introduction by the band, White introduces the theme before the full ensemble repeats it with two trumpets in harmony over countermelodies played by clarinet and trombone. The band continues with some stop-time breaks through the theme again. Simeon solos with banjo accompaniment for a portion of his outing, which is a unique sound. When the rest of the rhythm section re-enters for the remaining portion, the result is quite effective. Wilbur's trombone solo follows with phrasing that combines elements from both traditional and swing styles. The band continues with "Are You from Dixie?" in traditional New Orleans ensemble style with trumpet lead. Blair repeats the melody, while Simeon plays a countermelody over the rhythm section for a light and beautiful effect. Blair follows with a swinging solo that raises the band's intensity level up a notch. Wilbur plays a brief solo and bows to Sidney and Omer Simeon, who both turn in swinging outings. Afterward, they trade eight-bar solos with each other, and Wilbur plays a witty sixteen-bar solo. The full ensemble returns with two shout choruses before Marshall quotes the melody for eight bars. The ensemble follows for a few bars and takes the coda. The remaining four tunes on this recording are played by the band with similar inventiveness and clever aplomb.

Wilbur DeParis' band continued to record, made a U.S. State Department tour of Africa in 1957, appeared in the "Early Jazz" portion of a television series in 1958, and performed at the jazz festival in Antibes, France, in 1960.[73] After the group's long residency at Ryan's finally ended in 1962, DeParis continued performing with his band in other New York clubs until his death in 1973.[74] Wilbur DeParis was one of the most capable and imaginative bandleaders in the revival movement. His well-knit and hard-swinging band, as exemplified by its recordings, deserves much more recognition than it has received to date in revival history.

George Lewis, Bunk Johnson's heir, was born and raised in New Orleans at the turn of the twentieth century. He started out playing the flute at age seven and picked up the clarinet at around thirteen or fourteen years of age.[75] He began his professional career with the Black Eagle Band in Maudeville, Louisiana, and later worked with Buddy Petit and Joseph Rena during the early twenties in New Orleans. Lewis also formed the New Orleans Stompers that included Henry "Red" Allen. In the late twenties, Lewis worked with the Eureka Brass Band, Chris Kelly, Kid Rena, the Olympia Brass Orchestra, and with trumpeter Evan Thomas' band in 1931 that included Bunk Johnson. Like many early New Orleans musicians, Lewis worked infrequently during most of the thirties and appeared sometimes with De De and Billie Pierce.[76] Because it was during the Depression, Lewis worked full-time as a longshoreman to supplement his income.[77] As a result of the revival, Lewis recorded frequently with Bunk Johnson, Kid Shots Madison, and as a leader of his own groups from 1942 to 1945. Lewis also composed "Burgundy Street Blues" in 1944 for clarinet and rhythm section. His big break finally came when he performed with Johnson and Baby Dodds in New York from 1945 to 1946, thus achieving national recognition. At that point, he returned to New Orleans and formed the George Lewis Ragtime Band, which included trumpeter Elmer Talbert, drummer Joe Watkins, and the nucleus of Bunk Johnson's group of Jim Robinson, Lawrence Marrero, and Alcide "Slow Drag" Pavageau.

After Johnson's death, Lewis became the new major figure of the emerging revival movement. For example, *Look* magazine ran a feature article on Lewis in 1950, and his band was featured on New Orleans' Bourbon Street. By 1952 he had a new full-time manager, Dorothy Tait, and left New Orleans with his band.[78] Between 1952 and 1954, they toured in Ohio, Illinois, and California—performing at major venues such as San Francisco's Hangover Club and Beverly Cavern in Los Angeles with trumpeter Kid Howard who replaced Talbert.[79] During the tour, Lewis and his New Orleans Jazz Band recorded *George Lewis on Parade* on June 18, 1953. The program for the recording consisted of marches and spirituals. Five of the seven sides featured Howard and Watkins doubling as vocalists. For example, "Down by the Riverside" featured Watkins on vocals as the only soloist. Howard leads the ensemble on trumpet through the theme playing the melody with the other two horns playing countermelodies before Watkins' vocals, and he embellishes the melody during the final thematic statements. The band plays "Gettysburg March" throughout with group improvisation except for a brief drum solo to set up a faster tempo for the rest of this rendition. Similarly, "Panama Rag" is performed as an instrumental with group improvisation and a brief drum solo to signal the conclusion. The highpoint of the recording is "When the Saints Go Marching In." After a brief introduction by Purnell, Howard plays the melody over the ensemble and follows with some vocal choruses. The background consists of responses by the other two horns and vocal chanting by the rhythm section. Robinson and Lewis are featured as soloists between Howard's vocal choruses. Both instrumental soloists play exceptionally well here. The full band follows Howard's final vocal chorus with a different version of the theme before a brief drum solo and the coda.

During the rest of the fifties, as Ashforth points out, "[Lewis' playing] regained most of its timbral purity and exhibited a rapid filigree and seamless registral crossing, the hallmarks of his technically fluent and highly individual style."[80] Lewis continued playing at a high level throughout the remainder of his career with successful tours in England, Denmark, Sweden, and Japan. After touring, he led the Preservation Hall Jazz Band in New Orleans until his death in 1968.

Trombonist-bandleader Edward "Kid" Ory was born in La Place, Louisiana, just before the twentieth century. At age ten, while working odd jobs to help support his family, he realized that he wanted to play music. He and some of his friends made their own string instruments and formed a small band that played at local social functions. Ory earned enough money to purchase a valve trombone and, two years later, bought a slide trombone while visiting his sister in New Orleans. He taught himself to play the instrument while working as a laborer and performing part-time with his band at dances and picnics. In 1911, Ory took the band to New Orleans and worked regularly for street parades, lawn parties, funerals, and in Storyville cabarets. The band also performed on advertising wagons where he played with his trombone slide protruding over the tailgate, which was later referred to as the "tailgate" style. Ory and his band were successful in New Orleans for nearly a decade, but he decided to move to Los Angeles in 1919. After five years as a prosperous West Coast bandleader, Ory disbanded and moved to Chicago where he became the city's top tailgate trombonist. He performed and recorded regularly either as a leader or sideman with major artists such as King Oliver and Louis Armstrong.[81] With the Depression in the thirties, Ory returned to Los Angeles and worked outside of the music profession for about eight years. He resumed playing in clarinetist Barney Bigard's band in 1942, performed with Bunk Johnson a year later, and appeared on Orson Welles' radio program series in 1944.[82] At that point, Ory regained his prominence as a traditional jazz artist and moved to San Francisco, where he and his Creole Jazz Band made the famous Crescent recordings. The band's personnel included Mutt Carey on trumpet, Omer Simeon on clarinet, Buster Wilson on piano, Bud Scott on guitar, Ed Garland on bass, and Alton Redd on drums.[83] Ory also made numerous recordings for the Exner, Decca, and Columbia labels.

In 1948 Dixieland Jubilee Records recorded Ory live at the Shrine Auditorium in Los Angeles at a Dixieland festival organized by Frank Bull and Gene Norman. This unique recording contains an opening fanfare, "Shine," as well as "Eh La Bas" (featuring Ory's vocals), "12th Street Rag," Ory's "Blues for Jimmy Noone," "Tiger Rag," "Milenberg Joys," Ory's classic "Muskrat Ramble," "St. Louis Blues," and "Maryland, My Maryland." For this performance, the band's personnel consisted of Teddy Buckner on trumpet, Joe Darensbourg on clarinet, Lloyd Glenn on piano, Ed Garland on bass, and Minor "Ram" Hall on drums. The opening fanfare, played by the three horns in unison/octaves, set the stage for the rest of the night's performance. It is unbelievable that three wind instrumentalists actually stood on an auditorium stage and played with such a high level of excitement and intensity over fifty years ago. The band proceeded with "Shine" in a super fast tempo with traditional ensemble "counterpoint" around the melody. Darensbourg follows with a solo in the clarinet's lower register and builds up to an exciting climax in the upper register. Buckner's trumpet solo is musical and demonstrates that he had excellent technical facility. Glenn's piano outing shows the influence of Earl Hines and Fats Waller, while Kid Ory continues with a solo full of gutbucket phrases to keep the tradition alive. The group concludes the tune with collective improvisation.

"Eh La Bas," an old Creole song, features Ory's vocal work with background recitations by the rest of the band. Darensbourg again solos using the full range of the clarinet to build excitement. The group closes with characteristic Dixieland ensemble phrases. By the way, the enthusiastic crowd certainly approved of Ory's singing. Darensbourg's resonant clarinet sound is heard again on "12th Street Rag," with fine musical phrasing in the horn's lower register. Glenn's ragtime piano solo is particularly effective here. On this tune, Ory really opens up in gutbucket style with an assortment of growls and swoops to build the intensity level. The band retains its energy level by playing in stop-time (quarter notes played on the first beat of each measure), while Garland plays walking bass lines. The band continues in stop-time, while Hall solos in the style of a street march. Ory's performance on "Muskrat Ramble" proves that he was the undisputed master of tailgate trombone playing. His growls, use of flutter-tonguing, and highly rhythmic phrases using repeated notes excited the audience. The true highpoint of the program, however, was a stirring performance of "Maryland, My Maryland." The band opens in "contrapuntal" style and gives way to an interlude played only by trumpet and drums. Ory re-enters and plays the melody with two-horn contrapuntal accompaniment. Darensbourg solos for about eight bars and apparently leaves the stage. Ory follows with eight bars of the melody and gives the show to Garland and Hall. Garland solos in jest with quotes from "Yankee Doodle," the Ajax cleaner theme, and another novelty tune before passing the show over to Hall. Hall plays a series of modern drum cadences that reminds one of a contemporary marching band. To say the least, Hall's playing is impeccable as he proceeds to "roll off" and signal re-entry of the trumpet and percussion interlude. The full band returns with the theme and concludes the show. Needless to say, the audience's response was ecstatic. After this performance, Ory and his band continued to record while touring in the United States and abroad for nearly twenty years. In addition, Ory appeared in the film *New Orleans* in 1946, completed the soundtrack for *Crossfire* in 1947, and appeared in *The Benny Goodman Story* in 1955.[84] Kid Ory undoubtedly made a major impact on early Dixieland music and the revival movement. His hard-swinging trombone style and his unusual ability as a bandleader set him apart from his contemporaries. His lengthy and successful career as a professional musician rivals that of any trombonist in jazz history.

EDDIE CONDON'S DIXIELANDERS

George Brunis was born and raised in New Orleans, Louisiana. He began playing the alto horn at age eight and switched to trombone around age ten or eleven. At age eighteen, he moved to Chicago and worked with local bands and on a Mississippi riverboat. Afterward, he joined Paul Mares' Friars Society Orchestra, which later became known as the New Orleans Rhythm Kings.[85] Brunis joined clarinetist Ted Lewis' band in 1924 and remained until 1934. During the ten-year association with Lewis, Brunis toured extensively and made a number of recordings that brought him national exposure in the music industry.[86] He worked with Louis Prima, Bobby Hackett, Sharkey Bonaud, and Chauncey Morehouse between 1934 and 1938. Around 1935 or 1936, Brunis became active in New York and played at several clubs that featured Dixieland including Nick's. He later worked with Muggsy Spanier's Ragtimers in 1939. From 1940 to 1943, Brunis led bands and freelanced as a sideman, including work with Art Hodes.[87]

Brunis recorded as a leader in November 1943 as George Brunis and His Jazz Band. The group's personnel included Pee Wee Russell on clarinet, Wild Bill Davison on cornet, Gene Schroeder on piano, Eddie Condon on guitar, Bob Casey on bass, and George Wettling on drums. Milt Gabler of Commodore Records produced the session, which yielded four sides: "Royal Garden Blues," "Ugly Child," "Tin Roof Blues," and "That Da Da Strain." Brunis and company played "Garden" in a traditional up-tempo with a lively bounce. Russell solos with ease and fine technical skill. Davison's solo contains solid traditional phrasing with clean execution. Brunis plays in New Orleans tailgate style, and his energetic musical personality is quite apparent. Two ensemble choruses follow in the usual Dixieland "contrapuntal" style before Schroeder plays a brief piano break. The thematic section is repeated and followed by Wettling's effective drum break before the coda. Brunis leads the ensemble through the theme of "Ugly Child" in Dixieland style before he sings the lyrics with southern humor. The two-horn harmonized background is effective behind Brunis' vocal work. His trombone solo playing, however, is the highlight of this particular rendition of the tune. The full ensemble follows Brunis' instrumental solo with Davison as the dominant voice. Brunis returns with the final vocal chorus, and the ensemble concludes the piece.

On "Tin Roof Blues," Brunis leads the band through the theme and plays two solo choruses in gutbucket style throughout the full range of the instrument, which displays his best effort on the recording date. He uses a mute to good effect during the first chorus and plays with an open horn for the second to render some fine musical statements. Brunis leads the ensemble through the theme again, but in the trombone's lower register with cornet and clarinet in harmony before proceeding to the coda. Brunis again plays the melody as the cornet and clarinet play contrapuntal lines in "That Da Da Strain." Schroeder plays an excellent stride piano solo here, while Russell explores the different registers of his horn as he proceeds with his solo outing. Brunis solos in his characteristic humorous style before the full ensemble re-enters with the theme. Wettling follows with an exciting drum solo before the full ensemble returns and plays the coda. The overall session was successful due, no doubt, to the fact that each of the seven musicians was in familiar company. Around the time of the foregoing recording session, Brunis rejoined Ted Lewis and remained with his band until early 1946. Brunis worked with Eddie Condon from 1947 to 1949 and returned to Chicago where he led his own group. He worked again with Muggsy Spanier in 1949–1950, rejoined Hodes in 1950, and played an extended residency at Club 1111 from 1951 to 1959. Afterward, he led his own bands, rejoined Spanier in 1961, worked with Hodes again in 1968 at the New Orleans Jazz Festival, and performed until the early seventies.[88] Throughout Brunis' career, he helped define the trombone's role in a Dixieland ensemble and embodied "the sophisticated end of tailgate trombone," according to Fairweather.[89]

Cornetist-bandleader Wild Bill Davison grew up in Defiance, Ohio, and learned to play several different instruments during his youth. He toured with a local band as a teenager and later relocated to Chicago from 1927 to 1932.[90] He moved to Milwaukee in 1932, where he was billed as the "Trumpet King," and he remained there during the thirties.[91] As leader of his own groups, Davison's name began to spread after some of his recordings hit the market in 1940. As a result, he moved to New York in 1941 and, soon after, performed at Nick's and other clubs that featured Dixieland. At one point, he led his own group that included trombonist Brad Gowan, clarinetist Pee Wee Russell, and drummer Danny Alvin. Davison also led a band in

Boston around 1943 and at Jimmy Ryan's in New York City, with Gowan and James P. Johnson as sidemen.[92]

In November 1943, Davison recorded for the Commodore label as Wild Bill Davison and His Commodores. The group included George Brunis on trombone, Pee Wee Russell or Edmond Hall on clarinet, Eddie Condon on guitar, Gene Schroeder on piano, Bob Casey on bass, and Dave Tough or George Wettling on drums. They recorded twelve sides, with "That's A-Plenty," "Muskrat Ramble," "Panama," and "Clarinet Marmalade" clearly standing out over the remaining eight. Davison's ability as a cornetist is quickly recognizable as he leads the ensemble through "Plenty" with aggressive assurance. The group follows with consistency, and all of its members execute their parts with precision. Solos follow by Russell, Schroeder, Davison, and Brunis. Russell plays his characteristic melodious phrases that tell a coherent story, whereas Davison solos with flair and a big sound. Schroeder plays an authentic ragtime piano solo between outings by Russell and Davison. As usual, Brunis solos with excitement and fluency. The two-horn sustained backgrounds behind each of the three wind instrumental solos add some harmonious sounds to the band's arrangement. The ensemble plays "Muskrat Ramble" with humor and a full sound as it proceeds through the tune's theme. Russell again starts the solo chain with solid musical ideas. Davison follows with well-played melodic phrases and hands the baton to Brunis who demonstrates his familiarity with the old New Orleans trombone style. The band plays an exciting shout chorus before the characteristic Dixieland drum break that cues the listener for the coda.

"Panama" features traditional jazz-ensemble counterpoint during the thematic statement. Here, clarinetist Edmond Hall paces himself in a thoughtful manner and plays some well-conceived melodic lines. Schroeder continues with his usual consistency before Casey plays an exuberant walking bass solo under sustained harmonized backgrounds by the three horns. Brunis follows with a gutbucket style solo, and the full ensemble finishes the tune with a shout chorus that contains some effective harmonized phrases played by the horns. Edmond Hall is featured on "Clarinet Marmalade." After the ensemble approaches the theme in traditional style, Hall solos by stating a motive and developing it with continuously expanding phrases. His solo is made even more effective with harmonized sustained background passages played by cornet and trombone. Davison plays his solo, using strongly rooted traditional jazz language with considerable humor and confidence. As the ensemble concludes the tune, the overall sound of the band is mature and clean. On these four sides and the other eight, the rhythm section swings consistently throughout the recording.

After the aforementioned recording sessions, Davison spent two years in the army. After his discharge, he returned to New York where he joined the house band at Eddie Condon's club when it opened in 1945.[93] Davison worked at the club regularly during the rest of the forties and proved himself a strong and reliable cornetist, which worked well for the long grueling nights at Condon's.[94] Davison also led his own groups outside of Condon's for brief appearances and several recording sessions with Sidney Bechet. The cornetist was also an active participant in the radio series *This Is Jazz* hosted by Rudi Blesh.[95] By 1950 Davison took the initiative and integrated the band at Condon's club with Edmond Hall, who played there from 1950 to 1955. Davison also brought other African-American musicians into the band under his leadership until the club closed in 1957. Meanwhile, he continued to record and appeared at the first Newport Jazz Festival in 1954. After 1957, Davison toured as a leader or sideman nationally and internationally throughout the rest of his life. His resonant sound and fresh command of the cornet made him one of the most important figures in traditional jazz.

Cornetist Muggsy Spanier began his professional career in 1920 and worked with a number of bands in his hometown of Chicago. One of his most important jobs was in Ted Lewis' orchestra where he remained until 1935. Spanier joined Ben Pollack's group in 1936, but illness forced him to leave in 1938.[96] After a year's recovery, he organized Muggsy Spanier's Ragtime Band and went into Chicago's Sherman Hotel for a six-month stay, followed by an appearance at Nick's nightclub in New York. Afterward, the ragtimers recorded sixteen Chicago-style Dixieland pieces for Bluebird Records before they disbanded.[97] Spanier rejoined Lewis briefly before working with Bob Crosby between 1940 and 1941.[98] Subsequently, Spanier led his own big band from 1941 to 1943, which recorded seven sides before the infamous recording ban. Again, he returned to Lewis' band until 1944 when he joined Miff Mole, who often played at Nick's in New York.[99]

While in New York with Mole in April 1944, Spanier recorded eight sides for Commodore under the title of Muggsy Spanier and His Ragtimers. The musicians assembled for the sessions were Miff Mole on trombone, Pee Wee Russell on clarinet, Dick Carey on piano, Joe Grauso on drums, former Ragtimer's guitarist Bob Casey on bass, and Commodore's music director Eddie Condon on guitar. Baritone saxophonist Ernie Caceres replaced Mole, and Sid Weiss substituted on bass for the last four sides. The first four tunes displays the ensemble's characteristic Chicago-style Dixieland sound. For example, Spanier leads the ensemble through the thematic structure of "Angry" à la early Louis Armstrong, with Mole and Russell supplying the traditional accompaniment of contrapuntal lines. Mole solos in a fluid manner with Dixieland phrasing reminiscent of the older New Orleans street band trombonists. Russell follows with clean articulation and liquid melodic phrasing in what might be called or referred to as a "modern" Dixieland style. Muggsy returns to lead the ensemble through the final thematic statements before one of Joe Grauso's effective Dixieland tag drum endings. Spanier leads the ensemble again on "Weary Blues" (which is really not a blues) in a lively two-beat style bounce. Carey plays an authentic ragtime piano solo and hands the baton to Russell, who phrases his melodic statements like a true Dixielander. Spanier returns with his ensemble to play the "head" of the tune with solid musical humor.

"Snag It," on the other hand, is actually a twelve-bar blues in which Russell leads the ensemble on the old-style melody. The background is harmonized in two parts for cornet and trombone, which provides a solid sound palette for clarinet lead. Mole plays his solo with a big sound and authentic Dixieland blues phrasing. He uses the lower, middle, and upper registers of the trombone effectively to add musical interest to his playing. Conversely, Russell plays in a raw yet realistic bluesy style that reminds one of the old traditional New Orleans clarinetists. As Russell and the ensemble return with the tune's theme, one wonders if the title of this song is more appropriate for the previous piece and vice versa. As Spanier leads the ensemble through "Alice Blue Gown," his respect for King Oliver and Louis Armstrong is obvious. Spanier's phrasing is mellow with a full sound. As usual, Pee Wee Russell solos with consistency and musicality. Spanier is heard at his best when he solos with a mute as he does here. He employs a wide vibrato as he "sings" through his horn with melodic statements that are both happy and sad. In essence, the emotional content of Spanier's solo is on par with some of the great traditional New Orleans trumpeters.

After the foregoing recording session, Spanier continued working with Mole and leading his own groups for brief appearances and recording sessions until 1950. Throughout the fifties, he worked mostly on the West Coast where he finally settled in 1957. In the same year, he began working with Earl Hines at the Club Hangover, which resulted in a two-year residency.[100] At this juncture, it is important to note that Spanier's contributions to the revival must not be understated, for he knew how to lead an ensemble and solo effectively as a traditional jazz trumpeter. With regard to his ensemble playing, Fairweather states, "His cornet encapsulates the art of direct musical lead (a quality which King Oliver, one of Spanier's idols, put first) and, while Muggsy was never the most technically startling player, no one knew better how to lead a Dixieland band with perfect economy, power, time and note placement."[101] Likewise, Spanier's solo ability is noteworthy. According to Freddie Goodman, "I don't believe there was any other trumpeter to use a growl mute like he did.... Muggsy influenced a lot of players. He had a beautiful tone and he played with a kind of natural feeling. Bunny Berigan was the only other white guy with that kind of feeling."[102]

NOTES

1. Collier, *The Making of Jazz*, pp. 280–291.
2. Ibid., pp. 341–361.
3. Ibid., pp. 408–436.
4. Stanley Dance, *The World of Swing: An Oral History of Big Band Jazz* (New York: Da Capo Press, 1974), pp. 161–162.

5. Kernfeld, *The New Grove Dictionary* (2002), 2:448.

6. Dance, *The World of Swing*, p. 174.

7. Ibid., p. 175.

8. Kernfeld, *The New Grove Dictionary* (2002), 2:448.

9. Kernfeld, *The New Grove Dictionary* (1988), 1:637.

10. Leonard Feather, "Louis Jordan: The Good Times Still Roll," *Downbeat* 36, no. 2 (1969): 16.

11. Ibid.

12. Ibid.

13. Kernfeld, *The New Grove Dictionary* (1988), 1:637.

14. Kernfeld, *The New Grove Dictionary* (2002), 2:786.

15. Feather and Gitler, *Encyclopedia of Jazz*, p. 413.

16. Ibid., pp. 345–346.

17. Ibid., p. 308.

18. Ibid., p. 378.

19. Collier, *The Making of Jazz*, p. 422.

20. Kernfeld, *The New Grove Dictionary* (2002), 2:786.

21. Feather and Gitler, *Encyclopedia of Jazz*, p. 525.

22. Bill Dobbins, quoted in H. Wiley Hitchcock and Stanley Sadie, eds., *The New Grove Dictionary of American Music*, vol. 3 (New York: MacMillan Press, 1986), p. 544.

23. Ibid.

24. Kernfeld, *The New Grove Dictionary* (1988), 2:442.

25. Doug Long, "George Shearing: An Interview," *CODA Magazine*, no. 189 (1983): 5.

26. Kernfeld, *The New Grove Dictionary* (1988), 2:442.

27. Alyn Shipton, *A New History of Jazz* (London: Continuum, 2001), pp. 499–500.

28. Kernfeld, *The New Grove Dictionary* (1988), 2:442.

29. Long, "George Shearing," p. 6.

30. Shipton, *A New History of Jazz*, p. 500.

31. Paul Pelletier, liner notes to *George Shearing, George Meets the Lion: The Original Quintet & The Solos* (JASCD 363).

32. Collier, *The Making of Jazz*, p. 377.

33. Kernfeld, *The New Grove Dictionary* (1988), 2:519.

34. Collier, *The Making of Jazz*, p. 377.

35. Ibid., p. 378.

36. Quoted in "Tatum Time," *Bandleaders*, May 1944, p. 34.

37. Kernfeld, *The New Grove Dictionary* (1988), 2:519.

38. Collier, *The Making of Jazz*, p. 379.

39. Kernfeld, *The New Grove Dictionary* (1988), 2:519.

40. Scanlan, *The Joy of Jazz*, p. 109.

41. Schuller, *The Swing Era*, p. 489.

42. Kernfeld, *The New Grove Dictionary* (1988), 2:575.

43. George Simon, "A Style Is Born," *Metronome* 64, no. 10 (1948): 40.

44. Kernfeld, *The New Grove Dictionary* (1988), 2:575.

45. Simon, "A Style Is Born," pp. 17, 40.

46. Russ Chase, liner notes from *Charlie Ventura: Euphoria* (Savoy Records, SJL 2243).

47. Kernfeld, *The New Grove Dictionary* (1988), 2:575.

48. Kernfeld, *The New Grove Dictionary* (2002), 2:851.

49. Feather and Gitler, *Encyclopedia of Jazz*, p. 487.

50. Carr, *The Rough Guide*, p. 463.

51. Kernfeld, *The New Grove Dictionary* (2002), 2:851.

52. Ibid.

53. Kernfeld, *The New Grove Dictionary* (2002), 3:531.

54. Carr, *The Rough Guide*, p. 569.

55. Ibid.

56. S. I. Hayakawa, liner notes to *Bob Scobey's Frisco Band with Vocals by Clancy Hayes: Direct from San Francisco* (Good Time Jazz, L-12023).

57. Kernfeld, *The New Grove Dictionary* (2002), 2:419.

58. Quoted in Carr, *The Rough Guide*, p. 331.

59. Ibid.

60. Ibid.

61. Kernfeld, *The New Grove Dictionary* (2002), 2:419.

62. Carr, *The Rough Guide*, pp. 331–332.

63. Ibid., p. 332.

64. Kernfeld, *The New Grove Dictionary* (2002), 2:419.

65. Kernfeld, *The New Grove Dictionary* (2002), 1:603.

66. Carr, *The Rough Guide*, p. 168.

67. Kernfeld, *The New Grove Dictionary* (2002), 1:603.

68. Quoted in Carr, *The Rough Guide*, p. 168.

69. Ibid.

70. Kernfeld, *The New Grove Dictionary* (2002), 1:603.

71. Carr, *The Rough Guide*, p. 168.

72. Quoted in Whitney Balliett, liner notes to *Wilbur DeParis*, Collectables Jazz Classics (COL-CD-6816).

73. Kernfeld, *The New Grove Dictionary* (2002), 1:603.

74. Carr, *The Rough Guide*, p. 168.

75. Don Hill, "George Lewis: New Orleans Jazzman," *Cadence* 13, no. 1 (1987): 18.

76. Kernfeld, *The New Grove Dictionary* (2002), 2:582.

77. Hill, "George Lewis," p. 18.

78. Carr, *The Rough Guide*, p. 383.

79. Kernfeld, *The New Grove Dictionary* (2002), 2:582.

80. Ibid.

81. Lawrence McClellan, Jr., "Edward 'Kid' Ory," in *Dictionary of American Biography*, ed. Kenneth T. Jackson, Supplement 9, 1971–1975 (New York: Charles Scribner's Sons, 1994), p. 598.

82. Kernfeld, *The New Grove Dictionary* (2002), 3:204–205.

83. McClellan, "Edward 'Kid' Ory," p. 599.

84. Ibid.

85. Kernfeld, *The New Grove Dictionary* (2002), 1:333.

86. Carr, *The Rough Guide*, p. 84.

87. Kernfeld, *The New Grove Dictionary* (2002), 1:333.

88. Ibid.
89. Carr, *The Rough Guide*, p. 84.
90. Kernfeld, *The New Grove Dictionary* (2002), 1:582.
91. Carr, *The Rough Guide*, p. 163.
92. Kernfeld, *The New Grove Dictionary* (2002), 1:582.
93. Ibid.
94. Carr, *The Rough Guide*, p. 163.
95. Kernfeld, *The New Grove Dictionary* (2002), 1:582.
96. Kernfeld, *The New Grove Dictionary* (2002), 3:637.
97. Carr, *The Rough Guide*, p. 606.
98. Kernfeld, *The New Grove Dictionary* (2002), 3:637.
99. Carr, *The Rough Guide*, p. 606.
100. Ibid.
101. Ibid.
102. Quoted in Carr, *The Rough Guide*, p. 607.

Ella Fitzgerald (Institute of Jazz Studies, Rutgers University)

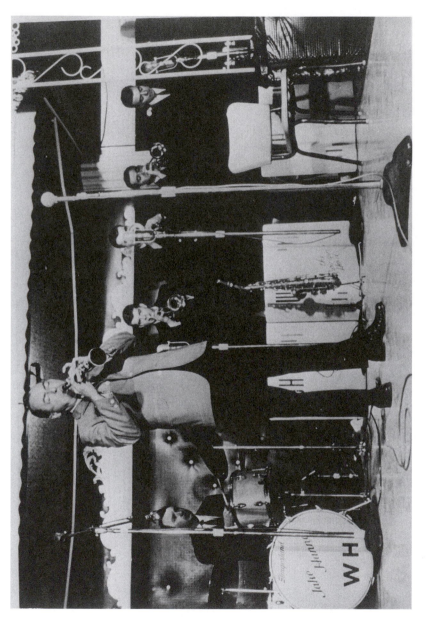

Woody Herman (Institute of Jazz Studies, Rutgers University)

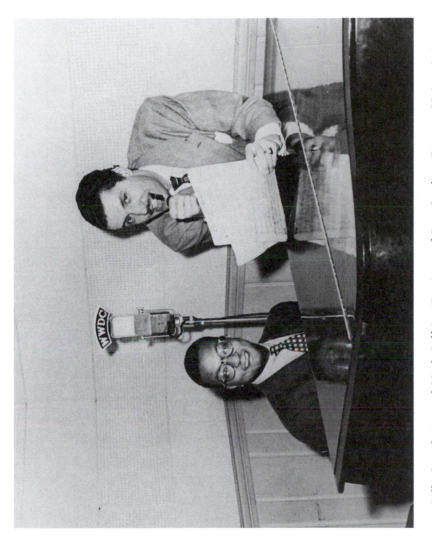

Billy Strayhorn and Herb Jeffries (Institute of Jazz Studies, Rutgers University)

Gerald Wilson Orchestra (Courtesy of Gerald Wilson)

Billie Holiday (Institute of Jazz Studies, Rutgers University)

Anita O'Day (Institute of Jazz Studies, Rutgers University)

Carmen McRae (Institute of Jazz Studies, Rutgers University)

Frank Sinatra (Institute of Jazz Studies, Rutgers University)

Sarah Vaughan (Institute of Jazz Studies, Rutgers University)

Art Tatum Trio (Institute of Jazz Studies, Rutgers University)

Kid Ory and His Creole Band (Institute of Jazz Studies, Rutgers University)

♪

A to Z

Adams Theater. A large Newark, New Jersey, venue that presented many Swing Era bands led by Woody Herman, Count Basie, Stan Kenton, Jimmie Lunceford, and Duke Ellingtton during the forties.

Albam, Emmanuel "Manny" (b. 1922). An arranger-composer who played woodwinds and arranged for the bands of Muggsy Spanier, Bob Chester, Georgie Auld, Boyd Raeburn, Herbie Fields, Bobby Sherwood, Sam Donahue, and Charlie Barnet. He later quit playing to focus on writing and, by 1955, had become one of the most successful arrangers in New York City. He has written charts for recording sessions by Coleman Hawkins, Stan Kenton, Woody Herman, Gerry Mulligan, Carmen McRae, Buddy Rich, Dizzy Gillespie, and many others.

Albany, Joseph "Joe" (1924–1988). A pianist who worked with Georgie Auld, Benny Carter, Stan Getz, and Boyd Raeburn in the forties. After more than a twenty-year hiatus from the music scene, Albany re-emerged as a solo artist for a 1970 recording as a leader, entitled *Bird Lives*, with sidemen Art Davis and Roy Haynes. Albany later led several recording dates for the Horo, Inner City, Interplay, Revelation, and Sea Breeze labels. His last album, entitled *Portrait of an Artist*, was recorded in 1982 by the Elektra label and revealed him as a sensitive and gifted pianist.

Allison, Mose (b. 1927). Allison, a pianist-vocalist-songwriter, began singing professionally in 1950. He later made his first recording session with Bob Brookmeyer and Al Cohn. Subsequently, Allison received his own recording contract with the Prestige label and worked with Cohn, Zoot Sims, and

Stan Getz while recording *Back Country Suite*, *Young Man Mose*, and *Seventh Son* as a leader in the fifties. Allison later recorded for the Atlantic, Epic, Columbia, Blue Note, and Elektra record labels. He is considered one of the best songwriters of twentieth-century blues.

Allyn, David (b. 1923). Allyn, a vocalist, worked in the forties with Jack Teagarden, Van Alexander, Henry Jerome, and Boyd Raeburn, and he later sang for Stan Kenton and Count Basie. Allyn excelled at singing ballads and recorded "I Only Have Eyes for You" and "Forgetful," in addition to songs by Rodgers and Hart and Jerome Kern. Allyn recorded with Boyd Raeburn during the earlier part of his career and continued performing into his later years.

Almeida, Laurindo (1917–1995). Almeida, a guitarist-arranger-composer, led his own orchestra and worked as a staff musician in Brazil. He later played with Stan Kenton's band from 1947 to 1950 and participated in the *Peanut Vendor* recording session. Almeida subsequently worked as a freelance studio musician, composed film scores, recorded a number of small group sessions with altoist Bud Shank, and recorded numerous bossa nova and classical albums. Almeida won five Grammys, an Oscar, and a *Downbeat* poll for his movie scores. He also wrote four books on guitar instruction and Brazilian popular music.

Alpert, Herman "Trigger" (b. 1916). A bassist who, during the forties, played in the bands of Alvino Rey, Glenn Miller, Tex Beneke, Woody Herman, Benny Goodman, and Frank Sinatra. Alpert later worked frequently in recording studios with such musicians as Ella Fitzgerald, Muggsy Spanier, Artie Shaw, Coleman Hawkins, Buddy Rich, Bud Freeman, Roy Eldridge, Ray McKinley, and Gene Krupa. Alpert also recorded "Trigger Happy" as a leader; sidemen included Urbie Green, Al Cohn, and Zoot Sims.

Alvarez, Alfred "Chico" (1920–1992). Alvarez, a trumpeter, played with Stan Kenton from 1941 to 1951 and was featured in Kenton's recordings of "Harlem Holiday" and "Machito." Kenton disbanded in the late forties, at which point Alvarez worked briefly with Benny Carter, Red Norvo, and Charlie Barnet. Alvarez later worked with Latin bands on the West Coast until 1958. Subsequently, he played in Las Vegas hotel-show bands into the early eighties.

Ammons, Gene "Jug" (1925–1974). A tenorist with a resonant and unique sound, Ammons was one of the most popular instrumentalists of his day. He played in the bands of Billy Eckstine and Woody Herman and co-led a two-tenor band with Sonny Stitt. Afterward, Ammons worked mostly as a soloist with small groups or in all-star jam sessions. His style, drawn from the work of Lester Young and Ben Webster, was highly melodic, though he had the flexibility of a bebop player. Ammons' playing appealed to both jazz buffs and popular audiences, and his later recordings for the Prestige label are particularly engaging. For example, *Blue Gene* features four of Ammons' originals that are played by a septet of top-level musicians and showcases his playing at its best.

Amy, Curtis (b. 1929). A tenorist from Houston, Texas, Amy moved to Los Angeles in 1955, played in Amos Milburn's band, led his own group, and worked with Gerald Wilson's orchestra through the sixties. After establishing himself on the West Coast, Amy toured extensively with Ray Charles. Amy has recorded with Wilson and has been a co-leader with Paul Bryant for the Pacific Jazz label.

Anderson, Chris (b. 1926). Anderson, a pianist, worked in the forties with Sonny Stitt, Howard McGhee, and Charlie Parker. He later played with Gene Ammons, Von Freeman, Stan Getz, Clifford Brown, and Sonny Rollins, and accompanied Dinah Washington. Anderson's recording with Charlie Parker for the Savoy label demonstrates his vast knowledge of harmony and keen sensitivity as an accompanist.

Anderson, Ernestine (b. 1922). Anderson sang with the rhythm-and-blues bands of Russell Jacquet and Johnny Otis in the forties. She changed to jazz in the fifties and worked with Lionel Hampton and Gigi Gryce. She recorded "Hot Cargo" in Sweden, which established her as a major artist. After returning to the United States, she signed a contract with Mercury Records and made several successful albums. More recently, she recorded for the Concord, Quest, and Koch labels, with the latter issuing "Isn't It Romantic?" which displays the depth of her rich contralto voice.

Anderson, William "Cat" (1916–1981). A trumpeter, Anderson began working professionally with Hartley Toots, Claude Hopkins, Erskine Hawkins, Lucky Millinder, and Lionel Hampton. Anderson joined Duke Ellington's orchestra in 1944 and remained in that organization throughout most of his life. As Ellington's lead trumpeter and soloist, Anderson had a five-octave range, the skill for playing half-valve effects, and excellent plunger mute technique. He also had a beautiful sound throughout the entire range of the instrument and could easily double a lead melody line two octaves higher. His trumpet playing is best heard with Ellington's recording of "El Gato," a trumpet feature, in *The English Concerts* from 1969 and 1971. Anderson's recordings as a leader in small-group settings were made in the late seventies. They are entitled *Cat Anderson Plays W.C. Handy* and *Old Folks*, and they display the full range of his trumpet playing.

Andrews, Ernest "Ernie" (b. 1927). A vocalist, Andrews recorded in the mid-forties for G and G and Aladdin Records while participating in the Central Avenue jazz scene in Los Angeles. He sang with the Harry James Orchestra for six years, beginning in the mid-fifties, and later recorded two albums as a leader for GHP Crescendo. He is one of the few surviving swing vocalists who can interpret blues, ballads, and swing standards in the tradition of Jimmy Rushing, Jimmy Witherspoon, and Joe Williams.

Anthony, Raymond "Ray" (b. 1922). Anthony, a trumpeter-bandleader, began his professional career at age fourteen with Al Donahue's band. He switched over to Glenn Miller's band in 1941 and later worked with Jimmy Dorsey until he entered the navy during World War II. While stationed in the Pacific, Anthony had one of the best military bands in that region. After discharge, he formed a civilian organization in 1946 that became one of the most popular postwar bands in the country. Anthony's Harry James–styled trumpet playing and the appealing style of his band made it possible for such tunes as "Harbor Lights" and "Bunny Hop" to become big hits. He also co-wrote the theme for the hit television show *Dragnet* in 1953, which brought him even greater popularity. He later appeared in over fifteen movies during the fifties. After Anthony disbanded in the late fifties, he formed a small group that featured female vocalists and performed in some of the top entertainment spots around the country.

Archway Lounge. A Chicago nightspot that opened in the late forties and became known as the Archway Supper Club. The venue hosted such Swing Era musicians as Carmen McRae, Ben Webster, and Jimmy Witherspoon.

Ashby, Harold (b. 1925). Ashby, a self-taught tenorist, played with Tommy Douglas, Walter Brown, and Jay McShann in Kansas City during the late forties. He also worked with blues musicians such as Willie Dixon, Otis Rush, Memphis Slim, Jimmy Witherspoon, and Chuck Berry in the fifties. Equally at home in both rhythm and blues and swing, Ashby later played in the bands of Mercer Ellington, Count Basie, and Duke Ellington.

Ashby, Irving (1920–1987). A guitarist, Ashby started working with several bands in the Boston area before playing in the bands of Lionel Hampton and Eddie Beal in Los Angeles. He replaced Oscar Moore in Nat "King" Cole's trio in 1947, joined Oscar Peterson in 1952, and toured Europe with Jazz at the Philharmonic. He recorded with Nat "King" Cole, Fats Waller, Lester Young, Wardell Gray, Erroll Garner, Louis Jordan, Charles Mingus, and Illinois Jacquet. Later, semi-retired, he wrote the *Guitar Work Book* and taught guitar.

Babasin, Harry (1921–1988). Babasin, a bassist-cellist, studied both instruments at North Texas State College before playing professionally in Midwestern territory bands in the early forties. He later played in the bands of Gene Krupa, Charlie Barnet, Boyd Raeburn, Benny Goodman, and Woody Herman. Babasin was the first to record the cello using a jazz pizzicato style, and played it in his own group called The Jazzpickers. He also played with Phil Moody, appeared in a movie, and recorded with Goodman, Raeburn, Harry James, Dodo Marmarosa, Chet Baker, and Barney Kessel.

Bagley, Donald "Don" (b. 1927). A bassist-arranger-composer, Bagley worked in the late forties with Wingy Manone and Shorty Sherock and in the fifties with Stan Kenton and Les Brown. Bagley later worked as a staff arranger for NBC and wrote film scores for several television shows. Bagley's skill as a solid and consistent bassist can be heard on recordings with Kenton, Zoot Sims, Shorty Rogers, and Lee Konitz.

Bailey, David "Dave" (b. 1926). Bailey, a drummer, began his professional career with Herbie Jones before playing with Johnny Hodges, Al Sears, Lou Donaldson, Charles Mingus, and others in the early fifties. Bailey gained prominence as a member of Gerry Mulligan's band in the late fifties, and subsequently worked with Ben Webster, Billy Taylor, the Clark Terry-Bob Brookmeyer Quintet, and Clark Terry's band. He has recorded with many notable musicians, including Mulligan, Taylor, Billy Strayhorn, Roger Kellaway, and Art Farmer.

Bailey, Ernest "Benny" (b. 1925). A trumpeter, Bailey began playing professionally with Bullmoose Jackson and played throughout the forties with Scatman Crothers, Jay McShann, Teddy Edwards, Dizzy Gillespie, and Lionel Hampton. After touring with Hampton for four years, Bailey settled in Europe where he played with the Harry Arnold Radio Band, Quincy Jones' big band, the Berlin Radio Band, Max Greger, the Radio Suisse Romande, the Clarke-Boland big band, George Gruntz, Eric Dolphy, and the Paris Reunion Band. Bailey is one of the few trumpeters who can play both lead in a section and solo with superb improvisational skill. He has recorded with Jones, Dolphy, Arnold, Dexter Gordon, Stan Getz, Benny Golson, and others.

Bailey, Pearl (1918–1990). Bailey, a vocalist, won her first amateur contest at Philadelphia's Pearl Theater in the early thirties and later won a singing contest at New York's Apollo Theater that led to work in the big bands of Edgar Hayes and Noble Sissle. She performed in USO tours and sang with Cootie Williams' big band in the early forties. Bailey made her solo debut at the Village Vanguard before touring with Cab Calloway after the war. She also signed a recording contract with Columbia Records and appeared on Broadway in *St. Louis Woman,*where she garnered national attention for her performances of "Legalize My Name" and "It's a Woman's Prerogative." Subsequently, she made nine films including *Carmen Jones* (1954) and *That Certain Feeling* (1956).

Bain, Robert "Bob" (b. 1924). A guitarist, Bain studied guitar and composition privately before making his debut as a professional musician with Freddie Slack in 1943. Bain continued working during the forties with Tommy Dorsey, Bob Crosby, Harry James, André Previn, and Phil Moore. From 1950 to 1972, he freelanced in Hollywood as a studio musician before playing in the *Tonight Show* band with Doc Severinsen until 1992. Bain has recorded with Dorsey, Nat "King" Cole, Frank Sinatra, Les Paul, Louis Bellson, Henry Mancini, and others.

Baker, Harold "Shorty" (1914–1966). A trumpeter, Baker gained invaluable experience during the thirties in bands led by Erskine Tate, Don Redman, and Teddy Wilson. Baker later played with Andy Kirk's band in the early forties, followed by several years with Duke Ellington's orchestra, where he was featured in tunes such as "Times A-Wastin'," "Blue Skies," and "Three Cent Stomp." He later worked with Ben Webster and Johnny Hodges until the mid-fifties, rejoined Ellington for another two years, and led his own group in New York City. His big sound and highly melodic style are prominently heard in *Giants of Small Band Swing, Volume 1,* on the Riverside label.

Baker's Keyboard Lounge. A long-standing Detroit nightclub that opened in the mid-thirties and presented a wide variety of Swing Era performers, such as Gene Krupa, Harry "Sweets" Edison, Herb Ellis, Eddie "Lockjaw" Davis, and the Modern Jazz Quartet.

Bales, Burton "Burt" (1916–1989). Bales, a pianist-vocalist, gained national exposure with Lu Watters, Bunk Johnson, and Dude Martin and worked as a soloist and leader of his own group. Bales later played in the bands of Turk Murphy, Bob Scobey, Marty Marsala, and again with Watters in the fifties while working off and on as a solo pianist. He left the music profession for more than a decade but later returned to music, mostly as a soloist in the San Francisco area. His recordings with Johnson, Murphy, and Scobey showcase his talent as a capable traditional jazz pianist.

Ballard, George "Butch"(1917–1950). Ballard, a drummer, began his professional career in 1942 with Fats Waller and Cootie Williams. After military service, Ballard worked with Louis Armstrong, Eddie "Lockjaw" Davis, Illinois Jacquet, Mercer Ellington, and Count Basie, as well as leading his own band in the late forties. In the early fifties, he toured with Duke Ellington and led his own group on the East Coast that accompanied such artists as Dinah Washington, Sonny Stitt, and Nina Simone. He later toured Europe with Clark Terry's Spacemen. His recordings with Ellington, Basie, Terry, and Eddie "Cleanhead" Vinson in *The 1940s Mercury Sessions* display his consistency as a big-band and small-group drummer.

Band Box. A dance hall in Chicago that featured bands such as Boyd Raeburn's in the early forties. The Band Box became an African-American establishment in the mid-forties and featured bands led by Andy Kirk, Stuff Smith, Louis Armstrong, and Red Saunders.

Bank, Daniel "Danny" (b. 1922). Bank, a woodwind specialist, began his professional career with Charlie Barnet in the early forties and continued throughout the decade with Benny Goodman, Paul Whiteman, Jimmy Dorsey, and Artie Shaw. In the fifties, Bank established himself as a dependable section player with Tommy Dorsey and several other studio big bands that recorded for Charlie Parker, Dizzy Gillespie, Cannonball Adderley, and Miles Davis–Gil Evans. Subsequently, Bank worked with Davis-Evans, Johnny Hodges, Louis Armstrong, Jimmy Heath, and many others, including a tour in Japan with Gunther Schuller. Bank's recordings with Art Farmer, Clifford Brown, Gene Krupa, Billie Holiday, Buddy Rich, Eddie "Lockjaw" Davis, and George Wallington demonstrate his versatility and consistency as a reed player.

Barber, William "Bill" (b. 1920). Barber is probably the first person to play modern jazz on tuba. A versatile tubist, he played with the Kansas City Philharmonic Orchestra, Claude Thornhill, and the Miles Davis' Nonet in the late forties, the Sauter-Finegan Orchestra in the early fifties, and the Miles Davis–Gil Evans band from 1957 to 1962. Barber also played with George Shearing and the Goldman Concert Band. He has worked on television and in Broadway shows and recorded with Davis-Evans, Gerry Mulligan, Kenny Burrell, and John Coltrane.

Barbour, David "Dave" (1912–1965). A guitarist-composer-arranger, Barbour worked as a studio musician and played with Wingy Manone, Red Norvo, Lenny Hayton, Hal Kemp, Artie Shaw, Raymond Scott, and Glenn Miller in the thirties. During the forties, he worked with Benny Goodman and served as Peggy Lee's music director until 1952. He and Lee co-wrote such hits as "It's a Good Day" and "Manana." He recorded with Charlie Barnet, Jack Teagarden, Boyd Raeburn, Jeri Southern, Nellie Lutcher, Benny Carter, Louis Armstrong, Bunny Berigan, and Nat "King" Cole.

Barcelona, Daniel "Danny" (b. 1929). Barcelona, a drummer, gained five years of valuable experience in Trummy Young's band before replacing the leader during his last two years with the organization. After leaving the band, Barcelona played with Louis Armstrong for over ten years and later freelanced in Hawaii and California. Barcelona made several recordings with Armstrong and appeared with him on television and in film.

Barksdale, Everett (1910–1986). A guitarist, Barksdale played with Erskine Tate, Eddie South, and Benny Carter in the thirties. During the forties, Barksdale worked with Herman Chittison, Leon Abbey, Buster Browne, Lester Boone, and Cliff Jackson and as a staff musician at CBS on the *Arthur Godfrey Show*. From 1949 to 1955, he worked with the famed Art Tatum trio and toured with the Ink Spots as their music director before rejoining the Tatum trio in 1956. Barksdale played both acoustic and electric bass with Buddy Tate in the late fifties and in the sixties returned as a staff musician for ABC. He recorded with Lena Horne, Al Hirt, Sammy Davis, Jr., Billie Holiday, Benny Carter, Dinah Washington, Sarah Vaughn, Red Allen, Tatum, Tate, and others.

Barnes, George (1921–1977). A guitarist who worked as a staff musician for NBC in Chicago, toured the Midwest with his own group, and played with Bud Freeman from 1935 to 1942. After military service, Barnes worked for ABC radio, performed in a duo with Carl Kress, played with Bucky Pizzarelli and Joe Venuti, and formed a quintet with Ruby Braff that made a number of excellent recordings.

Bartholomew, Dave (b. 1920). Bartholomew, a trumpeter-vocalist, garnered a reputation while playing with Fats Pichon's band around New Orleans in the late thirties. After military service, Bartholomew formed a band that played behind such singers as Roy Brown and in many of the New Orleans roadhouses. He wrote many hit songs and played a major role in the success of Fats Domino and other popular artists, with a rhythm-and-blues style crafted from swing, blues, and jazz. Bartholomew's swinging music kept people on the dance floor from the late forties to the early sixties. He wrote/directed many hit recordings that are collected in *The Genius of Dave Bartholomew* by EMI and *In the Alley* by Charly Records.

Bauer, William "Billy" (b. 1915). A guitarist, Bauer worked with Jerry Wald, Abe Lyman, Woody Herman, and Lennie Tristano in the forties and as a staff musician for NBC in the fifties before touring with Benny Goodman's band. He later played for a number of years in Broadway shows, led his own band, and worked with Lee Konitz. Over the past three decades, Bauer has taught guitar, written several guitar books, and freelanced. His solid Swing Era playing is clearly evident on recordings with the Metronome All-Stars.

Beckett, Frederick "Fred" (1917–1946). A trombonist who began playing professionally in the mid-thirties with Buster Smith, Andy Kirk, Nat Towles, and others before joining Harlan Leonard's band. After leaving Leonard, Beckett played with Lionel Hampton during the early forties. Beckett's solos on "Skee," "A La Bridges," and "My Gal Sal," recorded with Leonard in 1940, established him as the first modern trombonist in the Swing Era. He also recorded with Hampton before his premature death.

Bee Hive. One of Chicago's major jazz nightspots that hosted many high-profile musicians between the late forties and the mid-fifties. Some of the artists who appeared at the club include Lester Young, Louis Armstrong, Earl Hines, Slim Gaillard, Sonny Stitt, Pee Wee Russell, Miff Mole, Art Hodes, Coleman Hawkins, Lionel Hampton, and Dexter Gordon. Many of these featured artists played with resident rhythm sections during their engagements.

Bell, Aaron (b. 1922). A bassist who joined Andy Kirk in 1947 and later worked with Lucky Millinder, Ed Wilcox, Teddy Wilson, Herman Chittison, Lester Young, Dorothy Donegan, Eddie Heywood, Johnny Smith, and Mat Mathews. Bell led his own trio and worked with Billy Taylor in the fifties and played with Duke Ellington from 1960 to 1962. Bell later played in off-Broadway theater pit bands, served as director of the jazz program at Essex College in New Jersey, and chaired its Performing Arts Department until his retirement in 1994. During that thirty-year period, he continued to perform, tour, and serve as an artist-in-residence. Afterward, he continued to lead groups and perform in concerts. Bell has recorded with Ellington, Cat Anderson, Johnny Hodges, Jimmy Rushing, Harold Ashby, Lester Young, Billie Holiday, and John Coltrane.

Belletto, Alphonse "Al" (b. 1928). Clarinetist-saxophonist Belletto worked with Sharkey Bonano, Wingy Manone, Leon Prima, and the Dukes of Dixieland in the forties. He toured with his own group and played in Woody Herman's orchestra during the fifties. Since the 1960s, he has worked mostly in the New Orleans area. He has recorded with Herman and the Jazz Festival Masters.

Bellson, Louis (b. 1924). A drummer-composer-bandleader who began playing professionally with Ted Fio Rito and worked with Benny Goodman before and after two years of military service. After Goodman, Bellson played in Tommy Dorsey's orchestra in the late forties and worked with Harry James and Duke Ellington in the early fifties when he pioneered the use of two bass drums. Ellington featured Bellson on two of his own compositions entitled "Skin Deep" and "The Hawk Talks." Bellson also toured with Jazz at the Philharmonic, played in the Dorsey Brothers Orchestra, and recorded with Art Tatum and Oscar Peterson. Bellson later served as music director for Pearl Bailey (his wife) and led his own big bands for more than twenty years.

Beneke, Gordon "Tex" (1914–2000). A tenorist-bandleader, Beneke started out playing with Texas and Oklahoma territory bands before joining Glenn Miller's orchestra in 1938. After Miller disbanded in 1942, he toured with the Modernaires before serving in the navy as a dance bandleader. After discharge, Glen Miller's widow selected Beneke to reorganize and lead the Miller Band in 1946. Beneke led the Miller Band until 1950 and left to form his own band, "Tex Beneke and His Orchestra, Playing the Music Made Famous by Glenn Miller," that performed until the nineties. During Beneke's tenure with Miller, he was featured on "In the Mood," "Chattanooga Choo Choo," and "I've Got A Gal in Kalamazoo." He also appeared in two films, *Orchestra Wives* and *Sun Valley Serenade*, with the Miller Band.

Benjamin, Joseph "Joe" (1919–1974). Benjamin, a bassist, worked as a music copyist prior to joining Mercer Ellington's band in 1946. Benjamin worked with Billy Taylor, Artie Shaw, and Fletcher Henderson before performing with Duke Ellington in 1951. He played bass with Dizzy Gillespie, Sarah Vaughn, Gerry Mulligan, Ellis Larkins, Dave Brubeck, and others during the fifties while working as a studio musician. Benjamin later worked with Ben Webster, Harry Sweets Edison, and Tyree Glenn, before rejoining Duke Ellington in the seventies. He recorded as a sideman with Vaughn, Mulligan, Ellington, Brubeck, Billie Holiday, Johnny Hodges, Jerome Richardson, Barry Harris, and Kenny Burrell.

Bennett, Anthony "Tony" (b. 1926). A vocalist, Bennett recorded his first hit, "Boulevard of Broken Dreams," in 1951 with Columbia Records after being discovered by Pearl Bailey and Bob Hope. He later recorded over twenty Top 40 hits including "Stranger in Paradise," "Because of You," "Cold, Cold Heart," "Rags to Riches," and "I Left My Heart in San Francisco." Some of his albums include songs by Irving Berlin, George and Ira Gershwin, and Johnny Mercer. Bennett also worked with such jazz luminaries as Duke Ellington, Count Basie, Dizzy Gillespie, Al Cohn, and Zoot Sims. Bennett has toured many countries and performed at the North Sea and Mt. Hood jazz festivals. He has appeared on numerous television shows and in several movies, as well as receiving an award by *Life* magazine and an honorary doctorate from Berklee College of Music.

Bennett, Jean-Louis "Lou" (b. 1926). A pianist-organist-composer, Bennett began leading his own piano trio in Baltimore during the late forties before switching to organ in 1956 and touring with his trio. He later worked with Kenny Clarke, Jimmy Gourley, René Thomas, and Donald Byrd in Paris and Europe in the sixties. Bennett has continued to perform as a sideman and lead his own groups mostly in Europe. He has appeared in many movies and television shows, and recorded with Clarke in *Americans in Europe*.

Bennett, Max (b. 1928). Bennett, a bassist-composer, began playing professionally for Herbie Fields in 1949 and with Georgie Auld, Terry Gibbs, Charlie Ventura, and Stan Kenton in the early fifties. He later led his own group at the Lighthouse and played for Peggy Lee and Ella Fitzgerald while working as a studio musician. In the sixties, he worked as Peggy Lee's music director and as a member of Jimmy Rowles' Trio while freelancing with Pete Jolly, Shorty Rogers, Bud Brisbois, and Mike Barone. While playing with Quincy Jones off and on from 1968 to 1980, Bennett worked with Joni Mitchell, the Crusaders, Tom Scott's LA Express, Victor Feldman, and Aretha Franklin. Proficient on both acoustic and electric bass, Bennett is able to play in a variety of musical settings, which has greatly enhanced his stature as a modern musician.

Benskin, Samuel "Sammy" (1922–1992). A pianist-arranger-composer who worked with Stuff Smith, Don Redman, Freddie Green, Billie Holiday, and Al Cooper, and led his own group in the forties. Benskin later played with the Three Flames and accompanied Al Hibbler, Dinah Washington, and Diahann Carroll. He recorded with Holiday and trombonist Benny Morton in *The Blue Note Swingtets*.

Berklee College of Music. Musician, engineer, and visionary Lawrence Berk established the college as Schillinger House in Boston in 1945. The institution quickly gained a fine reputation for developing professional musicians with practical training in music performance and arranging/composition. As Schillinger House grew in the late forties and early fifties, major Swing Era bandleaders, such as Stan Kenton and Count Basie, often visited the institution whenever they were in Boston. Regarded as a top-notch institution for training musicians in jazz by *Downbeat* and *Metronome* magazines, Schillinger House changed its name to Berklee School of Music in 1954. Up to that point, the school had expanded its curriculum with majors in Arranging/Composition, Applied Music, and Music Education. Two established professional musicians, Joe Viola and Freddie Guerra, were faculty members, and the student body included vocalist Teddi King, trumpeter-arranger-composer Quincy Jones, and saxophonist Charlie Mariano. After the Later Swing Era, Berklee continued to grow with an innovative curriculum, expanding student enrollment, and a creative faculty. Consequently, the school changed its name again to Berklee College of Music in 1970 to reflect its educational mission and stature in higher education. After 1979, under the leadership of President Lee Eliot Berk, the college's curriculum was expanded to twelve different majors with over 3,800 students and more than 400 faculty members. Over the years, the college has recognized a number of Swing Era musicians such as Duke Ellington, Woody Herman, Teddy Wilson, Buddy Rich, and Billy Taylor for their accomplishments with honorary doctorate degrees.

Berman, Saul "Sonny" (1925–1947). A trumpeter who worked with Louis Prima, Tommy Dorsey, Georgie Auld, Harry James, Benny Goodman, and Woody Herman in the forties before his untimely death. Berman's solo on Herman's 1946 recording of "Sidewalks of Cuba" reveals that he was a remarkably talented musician. He played in both Herman's big band and small group.

Bernhart, Milt (b. 1926). A trombonist, Bernhart began playing professionally at age sixteen with Boyd Raeburn's band. He also worked in the bands of Teddy Powell, Stan Kenton, and Benny Goodman during the forties. Bernhart later played with Maynard Ferguson, Shorty Rogers, and The Lighthouse All-Stars, and worked as a staff musician in the film industry. He has recorded with Goodman, Kenton, Rogers, The Lighthouse All-Stars, and Anita O'Day.

Bernstein, Elmer (b. 1922). Bernstein, a pianist-composer, became known as one of the first film composers to incorporate jazz into his scores. After studying music in his youth, he continued with advanced training at the Juilliard School of Music before arranging for Glenn Miller's Army Air Force Band during World War II. He later worked as a pianist and then moved to California where he became a first-call film composer. Over the years, Bernstein has written scores for over one hundred movies and garnered thirteen Oscar nominations. His Swing Era–influenced film scores such as *The Sweet Smell of Success* and *The Man with the Golden Arm* have influenced numerous composers of movie soundtracks.

Berry, Emmett (1915–1993). Berry, a trumpeter, replaced Roy Eldridge in Fletcher Henderson's orchestra in the late thirties. After stints with Horace Henderson and Earl Hines, Berry played with Teddy Wilson's sextet at the Café Society for two years and left to join the CBS band under the direction of Raymond Scott. Berry worked with Count Basie from 1945 to 1950, and for a year with Jimmy Rushing's band at the Savoy. He later toured with Johnny Hodges' small group during the early fifties and worked with Sammy Price's Bluesicians in Europe in 1955. Throughout the remainder of the fifties, Berry played in numerous jazz and recording sessions on the East and West coasts with musicians ranging from Price to Miles Davis and Gil Evans. The sixties witnessed Berry's work as a busy freelancer before he retired in 1970. Berry's consistently high level of musicianship was captured in Sammy Price's 1955 and 1956 recordings entitled *Sammy Price and His Bluesicians* and *The Price Is Right*.

Bert, Eddie (b. 1922). A trombonist who played in the bands of Sam Donahue, Red Norvo, Woody Herman, Charlie Barnet, Stan Kenton, and Benny Goodman in the forties. The next decade found Bert with Herbie Fields, Ray McKinley, Les Elgart, Charles Mingus, and others. Since the fifties, Bert has played with numerous big bands, Broadway pit orchestras, and small groups. He has recorded with many high-profile artists including Benny Carter, Thelonious Monk, Phil Woods, and Clark Terry.

Best, Clifton "Skeeter" (1914–1985). Best, a guitarist, first worked with Abe Dunn and Slim Marshall in the thirties. Best later worked with Earl Hines and Erskine Hawkins before serving in World War II and playing with Bill Johnson's band in the forties. He later toured with Oscar Pettiford and freelanced with Sir Charles Thompson, Kenny Clarke, Jesse Powell, and Paul Quinichette during the fifties. He spent most of the sixties with Thompson and later taught guitar. Best recorded with Hines, Milt Jackson, Dizzy Gillespie, Ike Quebec, Lucky Thompson, Etta Jones, and Howard McGhee.

Best, Denzil (1917–1965). A drummer-composer, Best first started playing at age twenty-six and, in the mid-forties, worked and/or recorded with Ben Webster, Coleman Hawkins, Chubby Jackson, Illinois Jacquet, and Lee Konitz before becoming a founding member of George Shearing's quintet from 1949 to 1952. He played with Artie Shaw and Erroll Garner in the mid-fifties. Best later worked with Tyree Glenn and Nina Simone in addition to composing such tunes as "Dee Dee's Dance," "Allen's Alley," and "45 Degree Angle." He also wrote "Bemsha Swing" with Thelonious Monk.

Betts, William "Keeter" (b. 1928). After only one year of private lessons on bass, Betts began playing professionally with some local New York bands and became known while playing with Earl Bostic's band from 1949 to 1951. Betts worked with Dinah Washington in the mid-fifties and moved to Washington, D.C., in 1957, where he worked with Charlie Byrd at The Showboat until 1964. During that period, Betts toured overseas with Woody Herman and played with Bobby Timmons. Betts later worked with Tommy Flanagan and Ella Fitzgerald until the eighties, and he freelanced into the nineties.

Billy Berg's Swing Club. A popular Hollywood nightspot that presented a number of Swing Era musicians such as Erroll Garner, Louis Armstrong, and Coleman Hawkins in the mid-forties.

Black, David "Dave" (b. 1928). A drummer, Black started playing professionally with the house band at Philadelphia's Blue Note club where he gained invaluable experience backing up such musicians as Georgie Auld,

Charlie Parker, and Buddy DeFranco in the late forties. Black toured and recorded with Duke Ellington's orchestra between 1953 and 1955 and, after leaving Ellington, worked mostly with traditional jazz bands during the late fifties.

Blackburn, Lou (1922–1990). Blackburn, a trombonist, gained national visibility with Charlie Ventura in the mid-fifties and played in the bands of Lionel Hampton and Duke Ellington during the late fifties. Blackburn spent the sixties in Los Angeles working as a studio musician and relocated to Europe where he led his own bands. He recorded with Ellington and Charles Mingus.

Blue Note (club). A Chicago jazz club that presented numerous well-known Dixieland and swing musicians in the forties and fifties. Some of the musicians who appeared at the club include Miff Mole, Muggsy Spanier, Count Basie, Mildred Bailey, Joe Marsala, Billie Holiday, Sidney Bechet, and Duke Ellington.

Blue Note (records). A major jazz record company established in 1939 by Alfred Lion and co-managed with Francis Wolff. The label recorded a number of major swing and traditional jazz musicians such as Albert Ammons, Earl Hines, Edmond Hall, Sidney Bechet, Tiny Grimes, and Ike Quebec in the forties and early fifties. The company also recorded some early bebop sessions led by Thelonious Monk, Fats Navarro, and Bud Powell under the supervision of Artists & Repertoire (A&R) director and saxophonist Ike Quebec.

Bolden, Walter (b. 1925). Bolden, a drummer-composer-arranger, played with Gigi Gryce and Horace Silver in the late forties. He later worked with Stan Getz, Gerry Mulligan, Howard McGhee, George Wallington, Teddy Charles, Mat Mathews, Tony Scott, Carmen McRae, Sonny Rollins, Ray Bryant, Bennie Green, Abbey Lincoln, George Shearing, and Lambert, Hendricks, and Ross in the fifties. Bolden worked with Bobby Short, Johnny Hartman, Junior Mance, Art Farmer, Annie Ross, and others from the sixties through the nineties and played at major jazz festivals overseas. Some of his best-known compositions are "Harlem Mardi Gras," "Stressed Out," and "Mr. A.T."

Booker, Beryl (1928–1978). A pianist-vocalist, Booker played with local Philadelphia groups and led her own bands in the early forties. Around 1946, she began working in a trio with Slam Stewart and continued off and on with that group until 1951. She worked as Dinah Washington's accompanist from 1951 to 1953, and led her own trio with bassist Bonnie Wetzel and drummer Elaine Leighton that toured Europe in 1954. She later disbanded her trio and freelanced with different groups around New York City. Booker rejoined Stewart from 1955 to 1957 and Washington in 1959. She continued to perform in the sixties and seventies before her death. An underrated Erroll Garner–influenced pianist, Booker recorded as a leader for RCA and Emarcy with Stewart, Budd Johnson, Oscar Pettiford, and John Collins. She and her trio can be heard on Bluebird's *The Women: Classic Female Jazz Artists*.

Bostic, Earl (1913–1965). Bostic was an alto saxophonist-arranger who played with several bands in New Orleans before gaining a national reputation with the bands of Don Redman, Edgar Hayes, and Cab Calloway. Bostic made his recording debut with Lionel Hampton, led his own groups, and worked with Hot Lips Page in 1939. After a year with Lionel Hampton, Bostic freelanced with Artie Shaw, Paul Whiteman, and Louis Prima. In 1945, Bostic formed his own band and became a successful recording artist in the fifties with several hit recordings such as "Flamingo," "Moonglow," "Temptation," and "Cherokee" with the King label. He successfully fused jazz and rhythm and blues with a band that included such sidemen as Blue Mitchell, Johnny Coles, Benny Golson, Stanley Turrentine, John Coltrane, Jaki Byard, and Jimmy Cobb, who later became major jazz artists. Bostic's technical command of the instrument brought him admiration from his fellow saxophonists, as well as from his fans.

Bowman, Dave (1914–1964). Bowman was a pianist who toured England with Jack Hylton's band and worked at Nick's club in New York City with Bobby Hackett and Bud Freeman's Summa Cum Laude Orchestra. Bowman played with Jack Teagarden's band for about a year and worked briefly with Joe Marsala and Muggsy Spanier. Bowman later worked as a staff musician for ABC and NBC and often accompanied vocalist Perry Como. After 1954, he played with Bud Freeman and moved to Miami, Florida, where he worked in a hotel band until his death.

Braddy, Pauline (1922–1999). Braddy began studying drums at the Piney Woods School in Mississippi, where she became a member of the International Sweethearts of Rhythm in 1939. She toured with the band throughout the United States and overseas until the late forties. Braddy performed through the sixties with Vi Burnside's orchestra, the Edna Smith Trio, and the Two Plus One Trio (consisting of two females and one male on piano, bass, and drums). Afterward, she retired from music and worked in the business sector until the mid-nineties.

Bradshaw, Myron "Tiny" (1905–1958). A vocalist-drummer-bandleader, Bradshaw started out singing with the Wilberforce (Ohio) University Collegians under the direction of Horace Henderson. Bradshaw moved to

New York City in 1932 and played drums with Marion Hardy's Alabamians, the Savoy Bearcats, and the Mills Blue Rhythm Band before joining Luis Russell's band as a vocalist. He left Russell and formed his own band in 1934 that made its debut in New York's Renaissance Ballroom and toured the East Coast and Midwest while recording for the Decca label. During World War II, Bradshaw was commissioned as a major and led a military band that entertained the troops in the United States and overseas. Bradshaw resumed his career as a civilian bandleader in 1944 and recorded for the Blue Star, Manor, and Regis labels until 1945. He replaced the big band with a small group and entered the rhythm-and-blues field as a King recording artist in the late forties. Between 1949 and the early fifties, Bradshaw became very popular with such hits as "Gravy Train" and "Well, Oh Well."

Braff, Reuben "Ruby" (b. 1927). Braff is a self-taught cornetist-trumpeter who worked in the Boston area with such musicians as Bud Freeman, Pee Wee Russell, Edmond Hall, Urbie Green, Sam Margolis, George Wettling, and Joe Sullivan. Braff made some recordings with Vic Dickenson's septet in the early fifties that brought him national recognition. His swing-based style, however, made it difficult for him to work regularly in the fifties and sixties with modernists because his sound was not like that of Miles Davis or Dizzy Gillespie. Nevertheless, he worked with top musicians such as Benny Goodman and Tony Bennett and toured with the Newport All-Stars in the sixties. He freelanced in New York in the seventies and eighties and later experienced a marked rise in his popularity in the nineties.

Brass Rail. A Chicago nightspot that operated in the forties and fifties and sponsored appearances by Count Basie, Jack Teagarden, Joe Venuti, Art Hodes, and Wingy Manone.

Brown, Lester "Les" (1912–2001). Brown studied saxophone before organizing the Blue Devils while studying at Duke University in the thirties. Afterward, he started a twelve-piece orchestra in 1938 that made its debut at New York's Edison Hotel. After signing a contract with Bluebird Records and securing bookings by Joe Glaser, Brown's band played in top venues on the East Coast and in the Midwest. When vocalist Doris Day joined Brown in 1939, the band gained momentum, and in 1944 they recorded "Sentimental Journey," which became a big hit. A year later, their band, named Band of Renown, became a national success. The band later joined the Bob Hope radio and television shows and toured extensively. The fifties witnessed a highpoint for Brown when his band won *Downbeat*'s "best dance band" poll, *Billboard*'s "favorite band of 1958," and *Metronome*'s Number One rating. Brown and the band remained active and sustained their popularity into the nineties.

Brown, Roy (1925–1981). A New Orleans–born singer and songwriter, Brown became a highly popular Swing Era "jump blues" artist. During the early part of Brown's career, his recordings revealed influences by Billy Eckstine and Bing Crosby. By 1947, however, his style took on a high-strung and hard-swinging edge that resulted in the classic hit "Good Rockin' Tonight" on the Deluxe label. During Brown's tenure with Deluxe, he recorded several other hits including "Rockin' at Midnight," "Hard Luck Blues," and "Boogie at Midnight." After 1952, he recorded for King Records, and the relationship produced no hits or substantial record sales. He later switched to Imperial Records, however, and recorded "Let the Four Winds Blow," which became a Top 40 hit. He continued to record and tour during the sixties while working in the retail industry to supplement his income.

Brown, Ruth (b. 1928). Brown, a versatile vocalist, can sing blues, jazz, and pop music styles equally well. The decade of the fifties saw her record several hits for Atlantic Records and help bring rhythm and blues to the forefront during the Later Swing Era. Her early hits were in the jazz vein, including "I'll Wait for You," "So Long," and "Teardrops in My Eyes." When she crossed over into the jump blues style, however, songs such as "Wild Wild Young Men," "(Mama) He Treats Your Daughter Mean," "As Long As I'm Moving," and "Mambo Baby," reached a youthful and wider audience. In the late fifties, she topped the charts with "Lucky Lips" and "This Little Girl's Gone Rockin'." After the fifties, Brown's career with Atlantic ended, and she recorded three albums for Phillips/Mercury. From the mid-sixties to the mid-seventies, Brown survived by working outside of the music field but made a comeback in television and theater. She later recorded for Fantasy Records and became a member of the Rock-and-Roll Hall of Fame in 1991. To date, Brown still performs and records.

Brubeck, David "Dave" (b. 1920). A pianist-composer, Brubeck played with local California bands, studied music composition extensively, and toured with a military band in Europe during the mid-forties. After military service, he resumed his composition studies and played with a trio from 1949 to 1951. Brubeck organized his famed quartet in 1951 with altoist Paul Desmond, bassist Gene Wright, and drummer Joe Morello. The quartet became one of the most popular small groups in jazz history until it disbanded in 1968. *Time* magazine featured Brubeck in 1954, and his quartet recorded its first million-selling album, *Time Out*, in 1960. His quartet was the first jazz group to perform compositions in odd meters such as "Blue Rondo a la Turk" (9/8) and "Take Five" (5/4). He has received numerous awards including the BMI Jazz Pioneer Award and the National Music Council Award. Brubeck has toured Europe, Asia, Australia, South America, and the United States. He has worked with artists as diverse as Louis

Armstrong, Carmen McRae, Marian McPartland, and Jimmy Rushing. Brubeck continues to record and perform around the world.

Brunis, George (1902–1974). Brunis began his professional career as a trombonist on a Mississippi riverboat before playing in Chicago with Paul Mares' Friars Society Orchestra. Brunis worked with Ted Lewis from the mid-twenties to the mid-thirties and gained national prominence. He also worked with Louis Prima, Bobby Hackett, Chauncey Morehouse, Muggsy Spanier, and others in the late thirties. During the forties, Brunis worked with Art Hodes and Eddie Condon, rejoined Lewis and Spanier, and led his own groups. He rejoined Hodes for most of the fifties and spent the sixties with Spanier and Hodes. Brunis performed until the early seventies as a leader and sideman. He was one of the top tailgate trombonists, and his recordings showcase his talent as a soloist and ensemble player.

Bryant, Clora (b. 1927). Bryant, a trumpeter, grew up in Texas and attended Prairie View College to play with the Co-Eds, the school's all-girl orchestra, from 1943 to 1945. The band played at a number of military bases, at the Apollo Theater in New York City, and toured the East Coast. Bryant transferred to the University of California–Los Angeles briefly but postponed her education to work with the International Sweethearts of Rhythm and the Darlings of Rhythm during 1945 and 1946, the Four Vees in 1947, the Queens of Swing in 1948 and 1949, Jack McVea's all-girl orchestra in 1950, and with the Sepia Tones in 1951. She later completed her degree at UCLA and worked with Eric Dolphy, Damita Jo, Bill Berry's big band, Barry White, and Johnny Otis. She has taught music at both the high school and college levels.

Buckner, Milton "Milt" (1915–1977). A pianist-organist, Buckner started his professional career in the mid-thirties as a performer-arranger for McKinney's Cotton Pickers. During the forties, he established himself as a member of Lionel Hampton's orchestra when he wrote the classic "Hamp's Boogie Woogie." Buckner formed his own band and switched to the organ in the early fifties. He later became a popular Swing Era "jump blues" artist and recorded a hit entitled "Trapped." Buckner's name is closely associated with the "locked-hands" piano technique that was later popularized by George Shearing and Oscar Peterson. Buckner, who also worked with Illinois Jacquet and Clarence "Gatemouth" Brown, performed and recorded on piano and vibes in the sixties and seventies. Buckner is considered to be the pioneer of jazz organ playing.

Buckner, Theodore "Ted" (1913–1976). An altoist and the brother of Milt Buckner, Ted began playing professionally in the mid-thirties with J. Raschel's band and McKinney's Cotton Pickers. He became well known with Jimmie Lunceford's orchestra from 1939 to 1943 and led his own groups during the forties in Detroit before touring with Todd Rhodes in the early fifties. After returning to Detroit, he led his own bands, recorded with Johnny Ray, played in numerous Motown recording sessions, worked with the new McKinney's Cotton Pickers, and toured Europe with Sammy Price. Buckner's strong swing-style saxophone playing was showcased on Lunceford's recordings of "Ain't She Sweet," "Well, All Right Then," "Margie," and "Down by the Old Mill Stream."

Burke, Vinnie (b. 1921). Burke worked as a bassist with Joe Mooney, Tony Scott, and Cy Coleman's trio in the forties. During the fifties, he played with the Sauter-Finegan Orchestra, Marian MacPartland's trio, Gil Mellé, and Vic Dickenson, and served as the house bassist for Art Ford's television show in the fifties. Burke played with Mat Mathews, Bobby Hackett, and Bucky Pizzarelli in the sixties before working mostly in Newark for the next thirty years. He has recorded with Chris Connor, Tal Farlow, John Mehegan, Don Elliott, and others.

Burns, Ralph (b. 1922). Burns, a pianist-arranger-composer, studied at the New England Conservatory and began his professional career with Charlie Barnet's orchestra in the early forties. He later worked with Red Norvo and played and arranged for Woody Herman. In the forties, he wrote some of his best-known compositions for Herman such as "Apple Honey," "Bijou," "Lady McGowan's Dream," "Summer Sequence," and "Early Autumn." After leaving Herman, Burns became active as a freelance writer and/or music director for Harry Carney, Ben Webster, Ray Charles, and several Broadway shows. Since the seventies, Burns has been active writing charts for movies and vocal groups.

Bushkin, Joseph "Joe" (b. 1916). A pianist-composer-trumpeter, Bushkin worked with Bunny Berigan, Muggsy Spanier, Joe Marsala, and Eddie Condon from 1935 to 1940. Bushkin joined Tommy Dorsey's band in 1940 and wrote "Oh, Look at Me Now" for the band's vocalist Frank Sinatra. After Dorsey, Bushkin toured the Pacific as director of a GI show, worked with Benny Goodman, and appeared with Georgie Auld in a Broadway play. During the fifties, Bushkin worked frequently at The Embers in New York City, and recorded two solo albums, *Midnite Rhapsody* and *Listen to the Quiet*, that were big hits. He continued his solo career throughout the sixties with regular performances in New York and Las Vegas, retired from music in the seventies, and re-emerged in the eighties to resume his career. Bushkin is featured as a pianist, vocalist, and flugelhornist in a compilation of his recorded work entitled *The Road to Oslo/Play It Again, Joe*.

Butera, Samuel "Sam" (b. 1927). Butera, a tenorist-bandleader, learned to play from some of the great original jazz musicians. Immediately after high school, Butera started playing professionally with Ray McKinley's orchestra before working in the bands of Joe Reichman and Tommy Dorsey. Butera organized his own band in 1950 and landed a four-year engagement in New Orleans at the 500 Club. In 1953, he signed with RCA and made some solid recordings that featured his hard-edged style consisting of elements from swing, rhythm and blues, and bebop. Butera later became the leader of Louis Prima's band in Las Vegas called the Witnesses.

Butler, Billy (1928–1984). Butler, a guitarist, began working professionally with a Harlem-based vocal group from 1947 to 1949, led his own band between 1949 and 1952, and worked with organists Doc Bagby and Bill Doggett from 1953 to 1961. Butler co-wrote "Honky Tonk," which became Doggett's biggest hit. During the sixties, Butler worked and/or recorded with King Curtis, Dinah Washington, Panama Francis, Johnny Hodges, Jimmy Smith, David "Fathead" Newman, and as a leader for the Prestige label. He played for Broadway shows, Houston Person, and Norris Turney in the early seventies and later toured in Europe. Butler also recorded with Eddie "Lockjaw" Davis and Gene Ammons.

Butler, Frank (1928–1984). A drummer, Butler started out playing for USO shows before moving to San Francisco where he worked with Billie Holiday in 1949 and Dave Brubeck in 1950. He also played with Edgar Hayes, Duke Ellington, Curtis Counce, Prez Prado, Ben Webster, Helen Humes, Jimmy Witherspoon, and Harold Land in the fifties. He later worked with Curtis Amy, Miles Davis, John Coltrane, Terry Gibbs, Conte Condoli, Gerald Wilson, and Teddy Wilson in the sixties. After a hiatus from music, Butler resumed his career as a leader and sideman for Xanadu Records and toured with a Xanadu all-star band in 1980. Butler was a versatile drummer who played both swing and bop styles equally well and recorded with some of the top-ranked musicians in jazz.

Butterfield, Charles William "Billy" (1917–1988). A trumpeter, Butterfield worked in the orchestras of Andy Anderson and Austin Wylie before playing with Bob Crosby in the late thirties. Butterfield worked with Artie Shaw, Benny Goodman, and Les Brown in the early forties and as a studio musician before military service in the mid-forties. He subsequently led his own big band and returned to studio work while playing Dixieland at Nick's club in New York City. He also freelanced, played on numerous record dates, and worked off and on with Benny Goodman. Butterfield was considered an excellent swing player and lead trumpeter who can be heard with Ted Easton's Jazzband.

Butts, James "Jimmy" (1917–1998). A bassist who played piano until graduation from high school, switched to bass, and began playing professionally in the late thirties. He worked in the forties with Chris Columbus, Art Hodes, Les Hite, Don Redman, Sir Charles Thompson, Helen Humes, Trummy Young, Doc Wheeler's Sunset Royals, Leon Johnson, Buddy Tate, and others. Butts worked mostly in duos with Doles Dickens, Juanita Smith, and others in the fifties. Afterward, he formed his own group and worked mostly in the New York City area. Butts recorded with Thompson and Charlie Parker.

Byard, John "Jaki" (1922–1999). A pianist-composer, Byard began playing professionally in Worcester, Massachusetts, and in army bands from 1939 to 1946. After discharge, he played in the Boston area and toured with Earl Bostic between 1946 and 1950. Byard played with Jimmy Tyler and Herb Pomeroy and freelanced in Boston in the fifties before touring with Maynard Ferguson from 1959 to 1962. During the sixties, Byard gained recognition as a member of Charles Mingus' band and recorded with Don Ellis, Eric Dolphy, Charlie Mariano, Booker Ervin, Roland Kirk, and others. Byard later taught and presented clinics at a number of colleges and universities and at the Smithsonian Institution. Byard was one of the first to learn Duke Ellington's concept of "line writing" and to share it with many of his students and colleagues.

Byers, William "Billy" (1927–1996). Byers, a trombonist-composer-arranger, wrote film scores and played in the bands of Buddy Rich, Georgie Auld, Charlie Ventura, and Teddy Powell. Byers also worked as a staff musician and conductor for WMGM in New York, worked on film scores in Paris, and played in Johnny Richard's orchestra in New York during the fifties. In the sixties, he worked with Quincy Jones in Europe, New York City, and on the West Coast. Byers has written charts for Count Basie, Frank Sinatra, Duke Ellington, Peggy Lee, Billy Eckstine, Harry "Sweets" Edison, and Sammy Davis, Jr., and for television, movies, Broadway shows, and numerous recording sessions.

Byrd, Charlie (1925–1999). Byrd, a guitarist, toured with Joe Marsala from 1947 to 1949. In 1950, Byrd moved to Washington, D.C., and studied classical guitar while working in clubs and recording for a small record label. Throughout the fifties, he composed music for plays and films, led his own group in the Washington area, played with Woody Herman's sextet, and toured South America for the U.S. State Department. Byrd later appeared on the hit album *Jazz Samba* with Stan Getz, toured as a sideman, led his own groups, and recorded as a leader for several major record labels. Byrd won two *Downbeat* polls and wrote a method book for guitar.

Byrne, Robert "Bobby" (b. 1918). Byrne, a trombonist, joined the Dorsey Brothers' Orchestra at age sixteen and continued as a member of Jimmy

Dorsey's band until 1939. He led his own band and freelanced in New York City in the forties. He later led a Dixieland band for Steve Allen's television show and worked with Cootie Williams, Lionel Hampton, Urbie Green, Pearl Bailey, and Cannonball Adderley in the fifties. Afterward, Byrne became a record label executive and discontinued his performing career. He recorded with Barnet, the Dorsey Brothers, and Louis Armstrong.

Caceres, Ernesto "Ernie" (1911–1971). A clarinetist-baritone saxophonist, Caceres played in his brother's band before joining Bobby Hackett in the late thirties. In the forties, Caceres played in Dixieland groups, an army band, and with several swing organizations led by Glenn Miller, Tommy Dorsey, Benny Goodman, and Woody Herman. In the late forties, Caceres won a *Metronome* poll and recorded with the Metronome All-Stars. After 1950, he worked as a staff musician on Garry Moore's television show for six years while playing with many traditional groups at Nick's and other clubs in New York City that featured Dixieland. Caceres was equally at home playing bop, swing, and Dixieland styles.

Café de Society. A nightclub in Chicago that presented swing musicians such as Tab Smith in the mid-forties.

Café Society. One of downtown New York City's most important nightclubs that opened in the late thirties and hosted such jazz luminaries as Billie Holiday, Lena Horne, James P. Johnson, Teddy Wilson, Eddie Heywood, Art Tatum, Sarah Vaughn, and John Kirby during the forties. A second establishment of the same name was opened uptown in 1940 and presented many top-ranked swing musicians.

Café Tia Juana. A popular nightspot in Cleveland, Ohio, that presented both jazz and blues artists from the late forties through the Later Swing Era. Some of the venue's featured artists were Roy Eldridge, Dinah Washington, Erroll Garner, Ella Fitzgerald, Billie Holiday, Gene Ammons, Nat "King" Cole, Sarah Vaughn, and Sonny Stitt.

Cain, Jacqueline "Jackie" (b. 1928). A vocalist, Cain began working professionally with the Jay Burkhart Orchestra in Chicago in the late forties. She met Roy Kral in George Davis' group and worked with him as a vocal duo in the bands of Dave Garroway and Charlie Ventura. She and Kral married in 1949 and worked together as "Jackie and Roy" with their own groups, again for Ventura, and on their own television show in Chicago during the early fifties. In addition to recording numerous albums and commercials, the duo has co-written a number of songs and has received several Grammy nominations. Cain sings equally well as a soloist and with a duo. She and

Kral perfected the voice-horn unison ensemble approach with Charlie Ventura's band.

Calhoun, Eddie (1921–1994). A bassist, Calhoun began playing professionally in the mid-forties after serving in the military during World War II. From 1947 to 1955, he worked with Dick Davis, Ahmad Jamal, Horace Henderson, Johnny Griffin, Roy Eldridge, Miles Davis, and Billie Holiday. He later gained national visibility as a member of Erroll Garner's trio from 1955 to 1966. Afterward, he worked mostly in the Chicago area and toured Europe. He recorded with Garner and Jamal.

Callender, George "Red" (1916–1992). A bassist-tubaist-composer, Callender played and/or recorded with Buck Clayton, Louis Armstrong, and Nat "King" Cole in the late thirties. He later worked with Lester Young, Erroll Garner, Johnny Otis, Cee Pee Johnson, and led his own group on the West Coast and in Hawaii during the forties. Callender became active as a staff musician for NBC; played with Stan Kenton; recorded with Art Tatum, Charlie Parker, Dizzy Gillespie, and Lalo Schifrin; and became the first person to feature the tuba as a jazz solo instrument in his *Callender Speaks Low* album. He also played tuba during live performances and in recordings with such artists as Kenton, Frank Sinatra, Stevie Wonder, Charles Mingus, Thelonious Monk, and others. Callender toured Europe and remained active as a performer, composer, and teacher until his death. He recorded with many artists including Red Norvo, Billie Holiday, Dick Hyman, Art Pepper, Mel Tormé, Andre Previn, Wardell Gray, and Buddy Collette.

Calloway, Cabell "Cab" (1907–1994). Calloway, a vocalist-bandleader, began his professional career as a singer in the chorus of a theater troupe with his sister, Blanche, in Chicago during the mid-twenties while studying law at Crane College. He later worked at the Sunset Café and became the leader of the Alabamians, performing at the Savoy in New York City in the late twenties. After the Alabamians disbanded, Calloway performed as a vocalist in an all-black musical while working simultaneously with the Missourians (which became Cab Calloway and His Orchestra in 1930). Calloway recorded *Minnie the Moocher* a year later, and it brought him national recognition as the "Hi-De-Ho-Man." Subsequently, Calloway and his band became highly successful with tours in the United States and overseas, frequent recordings, and appearances in films such as *The Big Broadcast*, *The Swinging Kid*, and *Stormy Weather* during the thirties and forties. He later disbanded his orchestra and performed with small groups, as a single in nightclubs, and in musical theater. Calloway continued to perform in a variety of musical situations until the late eighties or early nineties, thus completing a legendary career in show business.

Capitol. A record company established in 1942 by Johnny Mercer and two of his business associates. Capitol recorded a large number of major Swing Era musicians such as Nat "King" Cole, Jonah Jones, George Shearing, Duke Ellington, Benny Goodman, and Marian McPartland during the forties and fifties. The company also recorded Miles Davis' landmark *Birth of the Cool* recording sessions in the late forties.

Capitol Lounge. A Chicago nightclub that operated in the forties and fifties and presented soloists and small groups. Some of the artists who appeared at the club were Roy Eldridge, Count Basie, and Dizzy Gillespie.

Carisi, John "Johnny" (1922–1992). A trumpeter-arranger-composer, Carisi played in the bands of George Handy, Herbie Fields, and Babe Russin during the late thirties and early forties. Carisi subsequently played in Glenn Miller's Army Air Force Band during World War II while stationed in New Haven, Connecticut, and worked with Ray McKinley, Lou Stein, Claude Thornhill, Skitch Henderson, and Charlie Barnet in the late forties. Carisi gained prominence after his composition "Israel" was recorded by Miles Davis in *Birth of the Cool* in 1948. Carisi also composed different styles of music ranging from ballet to chamber works. His charts for an Urbie Green big-band recording, Davis and Gil Evans' *Into the Hot* album represent only a small part of his overall output. Carisi continued to perform, write, and teach at the Manhattan School of Music and at Queens College.

Carlisle, Una Mae (1915–1956). A pianist-vocalist-composer, Carlisle started working as a musician for a Cincinnati, Ohio, radio station in the early thirties and was discovered by Fats Waller. She later worked with Waller before playing and recording in Europe in the late thirties. After a year overseas, she returned to the United States and recorded with Waller. In the early forties, Carlisle led her own all-star groups that included Benny Carter, Lester Young, and John Kirby and recorded such hits as "Walkin' by the River" and "I See a Million People." She toured, had her own radio shows, and played many club dates during the forties and early fifties. Unfortunately, she had to retire in the mid-fifties because of illness. She recorded with Don Redman and Bob Chester in 1950, and her Waller-influenced piano style can be heard on *The Women: Classic Female Jazz Artists*.

Carlson, Frank "Frankie" (b. 1914). A drummer, Carlson established himself professionally with Woody Herman's first band during a five-year period before playing with Benny Goodman and Stan Kenton. Carlson later worked as a studio musician in Los Angeles where he played for cartoons, films, and commercials while appearing regularly on television shows. He recorded with Herman, Kenton, Glenn Miller, Georgie Auld, June Christy, and Red Nichols.

Carnegie Hall. One of New York City's premier large performance halls, Carnegie Hall has hosted all styles of music since its inception in the late nineteenth century. Some of the country's most important jazz events were staged at this unusually large facility by such promoters as John Hammond and Norman Granz during the Later Swing Era. Two notable events held at the hall were Duke Ellington's *Black, Brown, and Beige* concert in 1943 and Woody Herman's performance of Stravinsky's *Ebony Concerto* in 1946.

Carr, Wynona (1924–1976). Carr, a versatile vocalist, could sing comfortably in a variety of music styles including gospel, rhythm and blues, and jazz. As a gospel singer, she garnered national attention with her recording of "The Ball Game." Carr was a unique artist who could infuse secular songs such as "St. James Infirmary" and "Good Rockin' Tonight" with religious music to create an original blend of jazz and blues. Carr originally worked as a soloist and choir director between 1949 and 1954 before she switched over to commercial music and recorded the ballad "Should I Ever Love Again," which brought out the beauty of her deep and dark alto voice. She also recorded some swing-type tunes such as "Ding Dong Daddy," "Nursery Rhyme Rock," and "Boppity Bop" that almost became hits before a two-year illness delayed her career. She recorded for Frank Sinatra's Reprise record label in 1960, but her career remained in her hometown of Cleveland, Ohio, where she sang in nightclubs and worked with church choirs up to the time of her death.

Carroll, Barbara (b. 1925). A pianist-vocalist, Carroll toured with a trio for the USO, led a trio at the Downbeat Club in New York City, and made her recording debut on the Discovery label in the forties. The next decade found her leading a trio at The Embers, appearing in the Broadway show *Me and Juliet*, performing with Benny Goodman, and accompanying Billie Holiday on a television show. Afterward, she left the music scene for over fifteen years and returned in the mid-seventies. Since her return, she has performed in New York City nightclubs, at Town Hall, and at several major jazz festivals. In addition to recording as a leader, Carroll has recorded with Serge Chaloff and Stan Hasselgard.

Carroll, Joseph "Joe" (1919–1981). Carroll became well known as a virtuoso scat vocalist during his tenure with Dizzy Gillespie between 1949 and 1953. Carroll and Gillespie recorded "Hey Pete! Let's Eat Mo' Meat," "In the Land of Oo-Bla-Dee," "Honeysuckle Rose," and "Oo-Shoo-Be-Do-Be" together, and Carroll recorded as a leader for several record labels.

After leaving Gillespie, Carroll worked as a soloist, toured with Woody Herman for one year, and began a solo career.

Carry, George "Scoops" (1915–1970). A clarinetist-altoist, Carry established his reputation in Lucky Millinder's orchestra during the early thirties and spent the rest of the decade working with Zutty Singleton, Fletcher Henderson, Roy Eldridge, Mildred Bailey, Art Tatum, and Horace Henderson. Throughout most of the forties, Carry played lead alto for Earl Hines before leaving the music profession to practice law in Chicago. Carry's smooth and fluid alto playing can be heard on sides by Eldridge and Hines.

Carter, Betty (1930–1998). Betty Carter, a vocalist, won an amateur contest in the mid-forties and toured with Lionel Hampton's band from 1948 to 1951 as Lorraine Carter. After leaving Hampton, she began her solo career and appeared in numerous nightclubs and theaters. She later worked with Miles Davis, Ray Charles, Sonny Rollins, and her own trio. Carter's trio, like Art Blakey's groups, has served as a touring music school for a number of young musicians through the years. She was also an ardent supporter of jazz education and made it possible for many young people to get started in music. Carter's stylistic roots from the Swing Era made it possible for her to develop her own style from the lyrical phrasing of Sarah Vaughn and Ella Fitzgerald's scat-singing. Carter's innovative and swinging vocal style made a major impact on younger singers who will keep her legacy as a major twentieth-century vocalist alive. During Carter's career, she performed at all of the world's major jazz festivals, founded her own record label, and recorded as a leader for the Verve, Impulse, Atlantic, and Roulette labels.

Carter, Robert "Bob" (b. 1922). A bassist, Carter started his professional career with bands in the Boston area during the late thirties. In the forties, he toured with territory bands on the East Coast, led his own band, served in the army, and worked with Ben Webster, Stuff Smith, Charlie Shavers, Charlie Ventura, and Benny Goodman. Carter also worked with Joe Mooney, Marian McPartland, Johnny Smith, Ventura, Lou Stein, Red Norvo, Shelly Manne, Bobby Hackett, and others. Carter has recorded with Goodman, Smith, Norvo, and Stan Getz.

Cary, Richard "Dick" (1916–1994). A pianist-trumpeter-composer, Cary began his career as a jazz pianist with Wild Bill Davison at Nick's club in New York City in 1941. He later played/recorded with Joe Marsala, Benny Goodman, Brad Gowans, Glen Gray, Muggsy Spanier, Billy Butterfield, Jean Goldkette, Louis Armstrong's All-Stars, and Jimmy Dorsey, and served as the house pianist at Nick's club. During the fifties, Cary played and arranged for Eddie Condon, Bobby Hackett, Pee Wee Russell, Jimmy McPartland, the

Dorsey Brothers, and Max Kaminksy. After the late fifties, Cary played with Bob Crosby, Ben Pollack, Red Nichols, and Matty Matlock. Cary also toured Australia, New Zealand, and Japan with Eddie Condon in the sixties. Throughout the seventies and eighties, Cary continued to perform, write, tour, and lead his own bands. Cary's recordings with Armstrong, Condon, Hackett, Bud Freeman, and Jack Teagarden showcase his unusual talents as a pianist and arranger.

Casey, Albert (b. 1915). Casey, a guitarist, became known as a member of Fats Waller's orchestra from 1934 to 1943. During that period, Casey also played with Buster Harding, Teddy Wilson, Billie Holiday, Mezz Mezzrow, Frankie Newton, James P. Johnson, and Sid Catlett. Afterward, Casey played in Clarence Profit's trio in 1944 and led his own trio before working with King Curtis from 1957 to 1961. Casey recorded with Waller, Newton, Holiday, Curtis, Wilson, Lionel Hampton, Louis Armstrong, Jay McShann, Milt Hinton, Chu Berry, the *Esquire* All-Stars, and the Satchmo Legacy Band.

Casey, Robert "Bob" (1909–1986). After playing banjo and guitar during his teens, Casey switched to the bass at age twenty and started playing professionally with dance bands in southern Illinois and Missouri in the late twenties. Casey worked with Wingy Manone, at NBC as a staff musician, and with Muggsy Spanier in the thirties. After Spanier's group disbanded, Casey played with Charlie Spivak and others in Chicago before joining Brad Gowans' group at Nick's in New York City during the early forties. Casey worked at Nick's and Condon's nightclubs for a number of years before playing with the Dukes of Dixieland and working intermittently along the East Coast until 1971.

Casino Gardens Ballroom. A venue located in Venice, California, that presented numerous big bands in the forties led by Woody Herman, the Dorsey Brothers, Harry James, and others.

Castle, Lee (1915–1990). Castle began working as a professional trumpeter with Joe Haymes and played in the bands of Artie Shaw, Tommy Dorsey, Jack Teagarden, Glenn Miller, and Will Bradley from 1936 to 1943. Castle later led his own group off and on throughout the forties. In 1953, Castle became a featured soloist with the Dorsey Brothers Orchestra, and he assumed the leadership of Jimmy Dorsey's orchestra after Dorsey's death in 1957 until the mid-eighties. Castle appeared in movies and on television.

Castro, Joseph "Joe" (b. 1927). A pianist-composer, Castro played in an army band from 1946 to 1947 and worked on the West Coast and Hawaii for a number of years with his own trio before accompanying June Christy and Anita O'Day in the fifties and early sixties. He also played and recorded with Teddy Edwards in 1960 and served as Tony Martin's music director from 1961 to 1963. Castro later worked in Las Vegas show bands, played occasionally in Hawaii, and freelanced in the Los Angeles area in the late sixties. Beginning in 1970, he wrote charts for Joe Williams, Al Hibbler, and Count Basie in addition to arranging and conducting for a number of Las Vegas shows and various film projects.

Cathcart, Richard "Dick" (1924–1993). A trumpeter-vocalist, Cathcart began playing professionally in the early forties with Ray McKinley and Alvino Rey. Cathcart played in the Army Air Force Band in the mid-forties and later worked as a studio musician for MGM before playing for a year with Ben Pollack. During the fifties, Cathcart led his own groups that were featured on radio and television and in movies. The sixties and seventies found him working mostly as a singer and leading his own group called Pete Kelly's Big Seven. In the eighties, Cathcart became busy again as a trumpeter with Dick Cary's band and with pianist Ray Sherman.

Cavanaugh, Page (b. 1922). A pianist-vocalist, Cavanaugh worked with Ernie Williamson's band in the late thirties and teamed up with guitarist Al Viola and bassist Lloyd Pratt during military service. After discharge, they settled in Los Angeles where they worked, appeared in several films, and recorded hits such as "All of Me," "The Three Little Bears," and "Walkin' My Baby Back Home." Cavanaugh's trio was patterned after the King Cole Trio, but Cavanaugh developed his own style with group vocals. Viola left the trio in 1950, and Cavanaugh continued to lead trios and quartets as well as the group Page 7 that consisted of a four-piece rhythm section, a baritone saxophone, and two trombones. Cavanaugh later recorded two CDs, *Page One* and *Page Two*, for the Star Line label.

Chaloff, Serge (1923–1957). A baritonist who worked in the big bands of Boyd Raeburn, Georgie Auld, and Jimmy Dorsey and participated in some small-group recordings in the mid-forties. Chaloff gained a national reputation with Woody Herman's Second Herd as a member of the Four Brothers saxophone section during the late forties. He worked with Count Basie in 1950 before returning to Boston, where he taught and recorded as a leader for the rest of his short life. Chaloff was one of the first baritone saxophonists to cross the bridge from swing to bop and capitalize on the instrument's deep, rich sound while playing modern musical phrases. Chaloff's innovative style and exciting solos have been captured in all of his recordings as a leader on the Mosaic label.

Chamblee, Edwin "Eddie" (b. 1920). A tenorist, Chamblee played in the Army Band and, after discharge, co-led a band with drummer Osie Johnson in the forties. From 1947 to 1954, Chamblee led his own bands before working in Lionel Hampton's band between 1954 and 1957. In the late fifties, Chamblee worked with Dinah Washington and Cozy Cole. Chamblee later played with Milt Buckner, Lionel Hampton (again), and Count Basie in the seventies and early eighties. From 1982 to 1992, he led his own group at Sweet Basil every Saturday in New York City until he retired.

Charles, Theodore "Teddy" (b. 1928). A drummer-vibist-composer, Charles worked with Bob Astor, Randy Brooks, Chubby Jackson, Benny Goodman, and Buddy DeFranco in the late forties. Charles played with Artie Shaw's orchestra and freelanced with Anita O'Day, Oscar Pettiford, Slim Gaillard, and Roy Eldridge in the early fifties. Later, Charles recorded for the Prestige label, led his own group, and served as music director for several record labels in the late fifties. For the next twenty years, he recorded for the Warwick, Motown, and Atlantic labels off and on, and spent the nineties performing, composing, and teaching four-mallet vibraphone technique to such vibists as Don Elliott, Warren Chiasson, Terry Gibbs, and Tito Puente. Charles has recorded with Bob Brookmeyer, Wardell Gray, Earl Bostic, and Aretha Franklin.

Cheatham, James "Jimmy" (b. 1924). A trombonist-arranger-composer, Cheatham first played in a community concert band before working in the late forties and early fifties with Buddy Collette, Wardell Gray, Gerald Wilson, and Benny Carter. Cheatham later toured with Maynard Ferguson and freelanced as an arranger for commercials and films in New York City from 1962 to 1972. Afterward, he toured with Duke Ellington, led his own group, and recorded for the Concord label. Cheatham has taught at two universities and performed at major jazz festivals in the United States, Europe, and New Zealand. He has won *Jazz Times* and *Downbeat* polls and appeared on television.

Childers, Marion "Buddy" (b. 1926). Childers, a trumpeter, played with Stan Kenton, Benny Carter, Les Brown, and Woody Herman in the forties. In the early fifties, he worked with Tommy Dorsey, Georgie Auld, and Charlie Barnet. Between 1943 and 1954, Childers played with Kenton for seven different brief periods. Known as a top-notch lead trumpeter, Childers later worked frequently with Frank Sinatra and the Akiyoshi-Tabackin big band. He recorded with Kenton, Carmen McRae, Anita O'Day, André Previn, Marty Paich, and Shorty Rogers, and as a leader on the Liberty label.

Christy, June [Shirley Luster] (1925–1990). Christy was a vocalist who began singing professionally as a teenager in a Springfield, Illinois, society band. She later worked with several bands in Chicago including Boyd Raeburn's orchestra in the early forties. Christy joined Stan Kenton in

1945 and remained until 1948. During that period, she recorded several hits with Kenton such as "I Been Down in Texas," "Ain't No Misery in Me," "How High the Moon," and the million-seller "Tampico," and played a major role in his success in the late forties. After Kenton disbanded, she embarked on a solo career and rejoined Kenton for special tours and concerts when he re-formed his band in 1950. As a soloist, she recorded "Everything Happens to Me" in 1949 and, in 1954, her first album, *Something Cool*, which garnered critical acclaim. As a result, she performed around the world in Europe, Australia, South Africa, and Japan until her semi-retirement in the mid-sixties. Afterward, she performed occasionally in West Coast nightclubs, the Newport Jazz Festival in New York, and at several international jazz festivals until the eighties.

Ciro's. A popular nightclub in West Hollywood that featured artists such as Nat "King" Cole, Duke Ellington, and Cab Calloway during the forties and fifties.

Civic Opera House. A large theater in Chicago that hosted numerous jazz concerts between the mid-forties and the sixties. Some of the concerts featured Duke Ellington, Coleman Hawkins, Jazz at the Philharmonic, Lester Young, Stan Getz, J. J. Johnson, Lionel Hampton, Nat "King" Cole, Gerry Mulligan, Ella Fitzgerald, Dave Brubeck, and many others.

Clark, Walter "Buddy" (1929–1999). A bassist-arranger, Clark played with Bud Freeman and Bill Russo before touring with Tex Beneke in the early fifties. Afterward, Clark worked with Red Norvo and Dave Pell and toured with Les Brown and Jimmy Giuffre until the end of the fifties. From the early sixties, Clark worked as a studio musician and worked with Med Flory as a co-founder of Supersax until 1975. Some of Clark's arrangements for that group include "Koko," "Lover Man," "A Night in Tunisia," and "Parker's Mood." He recorded with Terry Gibbs, Anita O'Day, Barney Kessel, Gerry Mulligan, and Supersax.

Clark, William "Bill" (1925–1986). Clark, a drummer, became known with Lester Young in 1950. Clark worked during the fifties with Duke Ellington, Mary Lou Williams, Lena Horne, Dizzy Gillespie, George Shearing, Toots Thielemans, Jackie Paris, and Rolf Kuhn. Clark recorded with Young, Williams, Gillespie, Shearing, and Kuhn before drifting away from the public's eye.

Cleveland, James "Jimmy" (b. 1926). A trombonist, Cleveland began developing his skill as a virtuoso in the army in the mid-forties and played in Lionel Hampton's band from 1949 to 1953. After leaving Hampton, he freelanced in New York City, won *Downbeat*'s New Star Award in 1955, and played/recorded with Johnny Richards, Dizzy Gillespie, and Gerry Mulligan before touring Europe with Quincy Jones in the late fifties. In the sixties, Cleveland worked in New York as a studio musician and toured Europe with Thelonious Monk. After the sixties, Cleveland continued working in studios, leading and recording with his own groups, and playing with Hampton and Gerald Wilson, as well as other West Coast big bands. He has recorded with Hampton, Benny Golson, Lucky Thompson, Art Farmer, Frank Wess, Eddie Jefferson, Gigi Gryce, Clifford Brown, Eddie "Lockjaw" Davis, and others.

Clooney, Rosemary (1928–2002). A vocalist, Clooney sang with Tony Pastor's band in the late forties, signed with Columbia Records in the early fifties, and became a solo artist with such hits as "Botcha Me," "Come On-A My House," "Hey There," and "This Old House." By 1954, she had appeared in films with Bing Crosby and Danny Kaye including the famous *White Christmas*. Clooney also recorded with Duke Ellington, Benny Goodman, Woody Herman, and the Hi-Los. After spending some time in retirement, she returned to performing and recording full time. She later became Concord Records' top artist and was featured in a number of commercials and PBS specials.

Club DeLisa. A Chicago nightclub that operated between the early thirties and the late fifties. A number of bands were in residence at the club under the leadership of Albert Ammons, Red Saunders, Jimmie Noone, Billy Eckstine, Fletcher Henderson, and Cab Calloway, to name a few.

Club Hangover. A San Francisco jazz venue that presented such Swing Era musicians as Earl Hines, Teddy Buckner, George Lewis, and Kid Ory in the forties and fifties.

Cobb, Arnett (1918–1989). A tenorist, Cobb worked professionally with Frank Davis and Chester Boone before playing in Milton Larkin's orchestra from 1936 to 1942. Cobb gained fame with Lionel Hampton's big band between 1942 and 1947 when he recorded *Flying Home #2*. After leaving Hampton, Cobb led his own popular band off and on for the next ten years in Texas. He retired in Houston, where he led his own big band while managing a nightclub. His highly emotional "Texas Tenor" style influenced a number of younger saxophonists such as David "Fathead" Newman and Wilton Felder.

Cohn, Alvin "Al" (1925–1988). A tenorist, Cohn began playing professionally with Joe Marsala's big band and later worked in the bands of Georgie Auld, Buddy Rich, Boyd Raeburn, Alvino Rey, and Artie Shaw during the forties. He established himself, however, in Woody Herman's big band in the late forties as one of the "Four Brothers" along with Stan Getz, Zoot Sims, and Serge Chaloff. After working with Artie Shaw, Cohn teamed up with Zoot Sims and formed a band that featured a two-tenor front line. Cohn retired from music for a while until 1952 and worked with Elliot Lawrence's band for the next six years. During that time, Cohn also worked as a staff musician for RCA Victor in 1955 and 1956 and recorded as a tenor saxophonist-arranger on numerous albums.

Cole, Helen Pauline (b. 1926). Cole, a drummer, began her professional career as a member of the Prairie View College Co-Eds in the forties. She later toured with Bert Etta Davis' sextet and Tiny Davis' Hell Divers. After leaving Tiny Davis, Cole organized the Helen Cole Quartet, led her own trio with bassist Margaret Blackstrom and trumpeter Toby Butler, and fronted a duo with Maurine Smith. Cole retired from music in the early seventies and worked as an accountant.

Coles, John "Johnny" (1926–1996). A trumpeter-flugelhornist, Coles played with Slappy and His Swingsters and Eddie Vinson from 1945 to 1951 before co-leading a group with Philly Joe Jones for a brief period. Coles played with Bullmoose Jackson, Earl Bostic, and James Moody in the fifties, and with the Gil Evans Orchestra during 1958 and 1964. Coles later played with Charles Mingus, Duke Pearson, George Coleman, Herbie Hancock's sextet, and Ray Charles. The seventies and eighties found Coles playing with Duke Ellington, Charles (again), Art Blakey, Philly Joe Jones' Dameronia, the Mingus Dynasty, and Count Basie. He recorded with Evans, Mingus, Buck Hill, Frank Morgan, Etta Jones, Gene Harris, and others. Coles' truly expressive sound is best heard, however, with Hancock on the soundtrack to Bill Cosby's *Fat Albert* television show.

Collette, William "Buddy" (b. 1921). Collette, a woodwind specialist, worked with several territory groups on the West Coast before leading a navy band during World War II. He played in the bands of Gerald Wilson, Les Hite, and Benny Carter in the late forties. After extensive freelance work, Collette became the first African-American to break into commercial radio and television, and he obtained a permanent studio job with the Groucho Marx show from 1951 to 1955. Collette took a leave of absence in 1955 and 1956 to tour with the Chico Hamilton Quintet but returned to studio work and arranging and composing for films and television.

Colosimo's. A Chicago café that opened in 1947 and featured many well-known musicians such as Billie Holiday, Louis Armstrong, Henry "Red" Allen, Una Mae Carlisle, John Kirby, and J. C. Higginbotham.

Commodore. A record company established by Milt Gabler in 1938. The label specialized in recording swing and "Chicago jazz" artists such as

Billie Holiday, Wild Bill Davison, George Brunis, Edmond Hall, Hot Lips Page, and Coleman Hawkins. At one point, many of the Chicago jazz recording sessions were supervised by A&R director and guitarist Eddie Condon.

Condoli, Secondo "Conte" (1927–2001). A trumpeter, Condoli played professionally with Woody Herman's band briefly in the mid-forties at age sixteen. After finishing high school, he rejoined Herman full time and played with other bands including Stan Kenton's orchestra. In 1954, Condoli left Kenton and formed his own band before relocating to the West Coast where he freelanced and played with Howard Rumsey's Lighthouse All-Stars. He later worked with Shelly Manne and became one of the top freelance trumpeters on the Los Angeles music scene. Condoli later gained a national reputation as the trumpet section leader and featured soloist in Doc Severinsen's *Tonight Show* band.

Conniff, Ray (1916–2002). Conniff, a trombonist-composer, played with Hank Biagini, Bunny Berigan, and Bob Crosby in the thirties before working with Artie Shaw, Bobby Hackett, Art Hodes, and Harry James' orchestra in the forties. In the mid-fifties, Conniff worked as a staff musician for NBC in New York City, arranged and conducted for Columbia records, and formed the Ray Conniff Singers. With the singers, Conniff arranged popular songs in unison or harmony for a men's choir against a women's choir plus a trumpet, trombone, or saxophone section, and a rhythm section. The Singers performed and recorded Conniff's arrangements for numerous popular albums and extensive tours in Europe, Japan, and Mexico. Although Conniff only played trombone occasionally, he would sometimes play with his singing group for live performances and on recordings. In addition to his popular vocal recordings, Conniff recorded as a jazz trombonist with Shaw, Berigan, Crosby, Hodes, and Billy Butterfield.

Connor, Chris (b. 1927). A vocalist, Connor first sang with a big band at the University of Missouri for a year and a half and worked for a while with a group in Kansas City. Connor sang with Claude Thornhill, Herbie Fields, and Jerry Wald from 1949 to 1952 when June Christy recommended her to Stan Kenton. Connor recorded her first hit, "All About Ronnie," with Kenton during their association in 1953 just before she started her solo career. She recorded three albums for Bethlehem Records before changing over to Atlantic in 1955 where she made twelve recordings. Connor's Anita O'Day–influenced vocal style has brought her a following of devoted fans for over fifty years.

Cook, John "Willie" (1923–2000). A trumpeter, Cook established himself as a professional in the bands of King Perry, Claude Trenier, Earl Hines, and

Dizzy Gillespie in the forties. He worked in the fifties with Gerald Wilson, Billie Holiday, and Duke Ellington. Cook later freelanced in New York City with Mercer Ellington, Jimmy Jones, and others before rejoining Duke Ellington from 1968 to 1973. A four-year retirement from music found Cook in Texas until he resumed playing in 1977 with Clark Terry and Count Basie, before settling in Sweden. Throughout the eighties and nineties, Cook played with a variety of bands in Europe and recorded numerous albums that established him as one of the best lead and solo trumpeters in jazz.

Cooper, Robert "Bob" (1925–1993). A tenorist, Cooper worked with Tommy Reynolds and Stan Kenton from 1944 to 1951 before freelancing in Los Angeles with Pete Rugolo, Shorty Rogers, and The Lighthouse All-Stars in the fifties. He also learned to play oboe and recorded with Bud Shank during this period. Cooper became active as a studio musician in the early sixties after touring Europe and Japan. He also composed many film and television scores while performing with Rogers, Bill Holman, Bob Florence, the Capp-Pierce Juggernaut, and other big bands. He recorded with a wide variety of artists including Rosemary Clooney, Marty Paich, Miles Davis, June Christy, Gene Harris, and Chet Baker.

Costanzo, James "Jack" (b. 1922). A percussionist, Costanzo taught dancing in Beverly Hills, played with a number of Latin bands, toured and recorded with Stan Kenton, and played with Nat "King" Cole until 1953. Since that time, Costanzo has worked with numerous singers and popular bands in addition to teaching percussion lessons to actors for their movie roles. He later performed with his own groups.

Crawford, Raymond "Ray" (1924–1997). A guitarist, Crawford played in the Four Strings with Ahmad Jamal during 1949 and 1950 before working with Jamal's trio from 1951 to 1956. Crawford later played with Jimmy Smith, Tony Scott, and recorded "Old Wine, New Bottles" and "Out of the Cool" with Gil Evans in 1959 and 1960. Subsequently, Crawford free-lanced in Hollywood studios, performed in concerts, and formed his own sextet. After reuniting with Jimmy Smith in the mid-sixties, the two played together from about 1971 to the 1980s until Crawford started teaching and playing occasionally. He recorded with Jamal, Evans, Sonny Criss, and Sonny Stitt.

Criss, William "Sonny" (1927–1977). Criss, an altoist, worked with Johnny Otis, Howard McGhee, Billy Eckstine, and Gerald Wilson in the late forties. During the fifties, he freelanced in Los Angeles; toured with Billy Eckstine, Stan Kenton, and Buddy Rich; played with Howard Rumsey's Lighthouse All-Stars; and led his own group. He worked in Paris from 1962 to 1965 and led his own groups in clubs, concert performances, and appearances on radio and television. Criss returned to Los Angeles in 1965 where he freelanced and recorded some notable albums for Prestige Records. He toured Europe in the seventies and performed at the Monterey Jazz Festival in 1977 with Dizzy Gillespie.

Crotty, Ron (b. 1929). A bassist, Crotty established himself professionally as a member of Dave Brubeck's trio, quartet, and octet from 1948 to 1953. He later worked in the San Francisco Bay area with Brew Moore and Earl Hines and recorded as a leader of his own trio in 1955.

Crow, William "Bill" (b. 1927). A bassist, Crow played trumpet, valve trombone, and drums while in the army during the forties. After military service, he freelanced on drums and trombone before switching to bass in 1950 but worked with various bands on drums, trombone, and bass for a year or so. After 1952, he played bass exclusively with Stan Getz, Teddy Charles, Claude Thornhill, Terry Gibbs, Marian McPartland, Al Cohn, Jerry Wald, and Gerry Mulligan into the mid-fifties. Crow later worked with Mulligan's big band, McPartland, Al Cohn, Mose Allison, Quincy Jones, Benny Goodman, Lee Konitz, the Clark Terry-Bob Brookmeyer Quintet, and others. He has toured Europe and Japan, played in several Broadway shows, and written numerous articles and record reviews.

Daley, Joseph "Joe" (1918–1994). A multi-reed instrumentalist, Daley worked with a number of bands in the forties and fifties including Woody Herman. Daley also worked with such vocalists as Tony Bennett and Judy Garland. He led his own groups in the Midwest and worked on the West Coast until the end of the eighties. Daley also appeared at the Newport Jazz Festival and recorded for RCA.

Dameron, Tadley "Tadd" (1917–1965). Known primarily as a bop musician, Tadd combined swing with modern jazz and was one of the first musicians to apply elements from both styles in big-band writing. After playing piano in the bands of Freddie Webster, Blanche Calloway, and Zach Whyte, Dameron established himself as an arranger by 1940. He played with Vido Musso before joining Harlan Leonard and writing a number of arrangements for Leonard's recordings. Dameron also worked as an arranger for Jimmie Lunceford, Billy Eckstine, Georgie Auld, Sarah Vaughn, Dizzy Gillespie, and Coleman Hawkins during the forties. At the same time, he played with Babs Gonzales and led his own groups that featured Allen Eager and Fats Navarro. Dameron appeared at the Paris Jazz Festival with Miles Davis in 1949 and played in "Bullmoose" Jackson's band from 1951 to 1952. The following year, he organized his own band and worked in Atlantic City, New Jersey. Throughout most of the fifties, Dameron worked off and on but later resumed his career full time as a bandleader and arranger for Sonny Stitt and Milt Jackson. Dameron also wrote some arrangements for Benny Goodman in the early sixties. His compositions such as "Good Bait," "If You Could See Me Now," "Lady Bird," and "Cool Breeze" have become jazz classics.

D'Amico, Henry "Hank" (1915–1965). A clarinetist, D'Amico worked with Red Norvo and Paul Specht before leading his own groups in the late thirties. In the early forties, he played with Bob Crosby, Les Brown, Benny Goodman, Tommy Dorsey, and Raymond Scott. From 1944 to 1955, D'Amico worked as a staff musician for ABC and, during that time, played with Jack Teagarden's band. Afterward, D'Amico either led his own groups or worked as a sideman. He recorded with Norvo, Crosby, Lester Young, Charlie Shavers, and Wingy Manone.

Dance Orchestra Leaders of America (DOLA). An organization formed in 1955 by bandleaders and ballroom operators to revive the big-band industry. DOLA held its first meeting on September 26–27 at the LaSalle Hotel in Chicago where officers were elected and committees were formed to deal with such issues as industry-wide promotion, musicians and the AFM, and problems that occur between leaders and ballroom owners. Popular leaders such as Les Brown, Tommy Dorsey, Freddie Martin, and Lawrence Welk supported the organization's efforts. In fact, one prominent leader offered an annual contribution of $5,000 to DOLA for its efforts in giving support to an industry that had helped countless numbers of musicians make a good living for many years. Although the goals of this organization were noteworthy, its challenge to jump-start the big-band business proved unattainable in the end.

Davenport, Wallace (b. 1925). A trumpeter, Davenport played with the Young Tuxedo Brass Band in New Orleans at age thirteen. He worked with Papa Celestin, local swing and bebop bands, and served in the military during the forties. He toured the United States and Europe off and on with Lionel Hampton from 1953 to 1964, worked with Count Basie during 1964 to 1966, and returned to Hampton's band between 1966 and 1969. Davenport also worked at various times with Lloyd Price and Ray Charles during the sixties. After 1969, he returned to New Orleans where he worked with traditional jazz groups, led his own groups, and played with gospel singers. He also toured Europe with the Newport Jazz Festival All-Stars in the mid-seventies. He has recorded with Basie, Hampton, Bob Wilber, and Arnett Cobb.

Davis, Bert Etta (1923–1982). An altoist, Davis gained professional experience with the Prairie View College Co-Eds in the forties along with trumpeter

Clora Bryant. The band toured the East Coast and played at all of the major theaters including the Apollo in New York City. She played in a small group later that worked in the Southwest and the Midwest. Afterward, she joined Tiny Davis' Hell Divers and toured with the group for three years. From 1951 to 1970, Bert Etta settled in Chicago where she led an all-male band, performed with Memphis Slim's group, and toured with Dinah Washington as a featured soloist. Davis played with an all-female group in Sweden in the early sixties for about a year and then returned to Chicago where she led an organ combo until 1970. Subsequently, she returned to her home in San Antonio, Texas, and changed professions but continued in music as a sideline.

Davis, Eddie "Lockjaw" (1921–1986). Davis, a tenorist, taught himself to play in eight months and began freelancing in New York City before working with Cootie Williams, Lucky Millinder, Andy Kirk, and Louis Armstrong from 1942 to 1946. Davis led his own groups and recorded under his own name from 1946 to 1952, worked in Count Basie's band in 1952–1953, and continued with Basie as saxophonist-road manager off and on from 1957 to 1973. He led one of the first tenor and organ trios between 1955 and 1960 and co-led a two-tenor quintet with Johnny Griffin. Davis also worked as a booking agent and played with trumpeters Roy Eldridge and Harry "Sweets" Edison. Although Davis was a New Yorker, his "Texas tenor" style can be heard on several Prestige recordings.

Davis, Ernestine "Tiny" (1907–1994). A trumpeter, Davis established herself as a professional with the popular Harlem Playgirls in the mid-thirties. She gained international prominence in the forties as a featured trumpeter with the International Sweethearts of Rhythm. After the mid-forties, Davis organized her own sextet called the Hell Divers that toured the United States and the Caribbean until the early fifties. She later moved to Chicago, where she performed with her own small group and co-owned a nightclub.

Davis, Kay (b. 1920). Davis was a vocalist who joined Duke Ellington in 1944. She was featured in a wordless vocal style on Ellington's recordings of "Creole Love Call," "Mood Indigo," and "On a Turquoise Cloud." She toured Europe with Ellington's band in 1948 and 1950. After leaving Ellington in 1950, she retired from music and settled in Chicago.

Davis, Lemuel "Lem" (1914–1970). Altoist Davis began playing with Charlie Brantley's band in the late thirties. Around 1940, he worked with Coleman Hawkins and Eddie Heywood in New York City before leading his own recording dates for the Savoy label in the mid-forties. He played with John Kirby in 1946 before rejoining Heywood and leading his own groups in the late forties. Throughout the fifties, he played and recorded with Buck Clayton. Davis recorded with Joe Thomas' Big Six in *Giants of Small Band Swing, Vol. 2* for Riverside and is featured on his own album entitled *Changing Face of Harlem, Vol. 2.*

Davis, Sammy Jr. (1925–1990). This New York City–born entertainer was a superb dancer and intense interpreter of Broadway show tunes. He worked as a member of the Will Mastin Trio before signing with Decca Records in 1954 and recording such hits as "Love Me or Leave Me," "That Old Black Magic," "New York Is My Home," "Something's Gotta Give," "I'll Know," and "Earthbound." Though continuing to record, his success in films, Broadway musicals, television shows, and nightclubs eventually overshadowed his career in the studio. In fact, Davis' rendition of "What Kind of Fool Am I?" from the musical *Stop the World I Want to Get Off* actually became his first million-selling record in 1962. Another hit, "I've Gotta Be Me" from the musical *Golden Rainbow*, followed in 1968; however, his interpretation of "Candy Man" actually became his first Number-One hit.

Davis, William "Wild Bill" (1918–1995). A pianist-organist-arranger, Davis first played guitar with Milt Larkin and arranged for Earl Hines between 1939 and 1943. He played piano and arranged for Louis Jordan in the mid-forties and concentrated on the Hammond organ in 1949. During the fifties, Davis doubled on piano and organ while leading his own trio, which was a major attraction. He later arranged "April in Paris" for Count Basie's orchestra, recorded with Johnny Hodges, and played in Duke Ellington's orchestra for two years. Davis also worked with Al Grey, Buddy Tate, Illinois Jacquet, and Lionel Hampton.

Davis, William "Will" (1926–1984). Davis, a pianist, played with Snookum Russell, Paul Bascomb, Milt Jackson, Howard McGhee, Wardell Gray, and Sonny Stitt in the forties. As the house pianist at Detroit's Crystal Bar, Davis later played for Lester Young, Coleman Hawkins, and Charlie Parker. He freelanced in New York City during the fifties and recorded with Jackson, Stitt, and Kenny Burrell.

Davison, William "Wild Bill" (1906–1989). Davison started playing cornet professionally as a teenager and worked with several Chicago bands from 1927 to 1932. He worked as a leader in Milwaukee, Wisconsin, in the thirties and became a popular sideman in some of New York City's Dixieland nightclubs in the early forties. After military service between 1943 and 1945, he returned to New York where he led his own bands and worked at Eddie Condon's club for the next twelve years. Davison was the first to bring African-American musicians into the band at Condon's. After 1957, he continued to record and tour in the United States and abroad. Davison had a big sound on his instrument and was equally proficient as a soloist and ensemble player. His playing is heard at its best on *Wild Bill Davison and His Commodores,* recorded on the Commodore label in 1943.

Dawn Club. A nightspot in San Francisco that featured traditional jazz in the forties. Some of the notable artists to perform at the club were Kid Ory and Lu Watters with his Yerba Buena Jazz Band.

Dawson, Alan (1929–1996). A drummer-vibist, Dawson worked with Tasker Crosson, Hopeton Johnson, Jimmy Martin, Ike Roberts, Frankie Newton, and others in the forties. Dawson later played with Sabby Lewis' band and Serge Chaloff in Boston during the early fifties. After fulfilling his military duties in an army band, Dawson toured briefly with Lionel Hampton's band and rejoined Sabby Lewis from 1953 to 1956. After Lewis, he taught at Boston's Berklee College of Music and moonlighted with Al Vega, John and Paul Neves, Herb Pomeroy, and the house band at Lennie's on the Turnpike for eight years. Dawson played in Dave Brubeck's group from 1968 to 1975 and freelanced with such artists as Charlie Shavers, Buck Clayton, Roy Eldridge, Al Cohn, Zoot Sims, Sonny Stitt, Budd Johnson, Red Allen, Coleman Hawkins, Jaki Byard, and Phil Woods. Dawson's most notable recordings were with tenor saxophonist Booker Ervin's quartet that included pianists Jaki Byard or Gildo Mahones, and bassist Richard Davis, for the Prestige label in the early sixties. Although Dawson learned his craft during the latter part of the Swing Era, he was a versatile drummer who could play all jazz styles and had masterful technical facility. He recorded with Illinois Jacquet, Dexter Gordon, Ruby Braff, Tal Farlow, Roland Hanna, Hank Jones, Brubeck, Hampton, and others.

Day, Doris (b. 1924). Known mostly as a high-profile actress, Day was one of the best big-band vocalists in the forties. At age fifteen, she began singing professionally with Barney Rapp's orchestra in the Cincinnati area. Afterward, she sang briefly with Bob Crosby's band but established herself with the orchestra of Les Brown with major hits such as "Sentimental Journey" and "My Dreams Keep Getting Better All the Time." In fact, Day played a major role in the success of Brown's band. Early in her career, Day became a movie actress and scored a success with *It's Magic.* She continued acting and singing in other movies that produced two of her biggest hit songs: "Que Sera Sera" and "Secret Love." Day's singing style consists of precise phrasing and a solid sense of swing in both jazz and popular songs.

DeArango, William "Bill" (b. 1921). A guitarist, DeArango served in the army before working in New York City with Ben Webster, Eddie "Lockjaw" Davis, Ike Quebec, Ray Nance, Charlie Parker, Dizzy Gillespie, and leading his own groups in the late forties. DeArango returned to his hometown in Cleveland, Ohio, in the late forties and performed part-time while teaching private students and managing a music store. He was a modern guitarist who measured up to the best players in the forties before changing his career path. Fortunately, his playing is available on recordings by Gillespie and Red Norvo.

Dearie, Blossom (b. 1926). A vocalist-pianist-composer, Dearie sang with Woody Herman's Blue Flames and Alvino Rey's Blue Reys in the forties. In the early fifties, she worked with Annie Ross in Paris and formed a vocal group called the Blue Stars that featured some of her own arrangements. Dearie returned to the United States in 1956 and gained popularity singing and playing piano with her own trio in nightclubs on the East and West coasts. In the seventies through the nineties, she performed regularly at New York's Russian Tea Room, Danny's Skylight Room, and at Ronnie Scott's in London. She has recorded with King Pleasure, Stan Getz, and as a leader with Herb Ellis, Ray Brown, and Jo Jones. Her songs include "Sweet Georgie Fame," "Hey John," and "I'm Shadowing You" with lyrics by Johnny Mercer.

Decca. A record company originally established in England. Jack Kapp founded an American branch in the mid-thirties. Under Kapp's leadership, the label recorded many Swing Era artists including Art Tatum, Jimmie Lunceford, Chick Webb, Ella Fitzgerald, Louis Armstrong, Louis Jordan, the Mills Brothers, Woody Herman, Lionel Hampton, and Andy Kirk. Kapp instituted a policy of joint collaborations among Decca's artists that resulted in some classic recordings.

Dedrick, Lyle "Rusty" (b. 1918). A trumpeter-composer, Dedrick played professionally with Dick Stabile and Red Norvo before working in Claude Thornhill's band, serving in the military, and playing with Ray McKinley in the forties. From the late forties through the sixties, he arranged and composed for Maxine Sullivan, Don Elliott, and Lee Wiley while working as a studio musician. Dedrick served as the music director of Free Design and played with Lionel Hampton from 1969 to 1971. After leaving Hampton, he taught at the Manhattan School of Music and continued writing music. He recorded with Elliott and Sullivan.

Deems, Barrett (1913–1998). Deems, a drummer-bandleader, led his own groups before working in Joe Venuti's band from 1938 to 1944. He later played with Red Norvo in the late forties and worked in the fifties with Charlie Barnet, Muggsy Spanier, and Louis Armstrong. After leading his own groups at Chicago's Brass Rail, Deems worked with Jack Teagarden, the Dukes of Dixieland, and Bill Reinhardt in the sixties. He worked with Benny Goodman in the seventies and with Wild Bill Davison and Keith Smith in the early eighties. Deems freelanced in Chicago during most of the nineties to round out his seventy-year career as one of the world's most-respected Swing Era drummers. He appeared in movies and on television and recorded with Armstrong and the *Chicago Jazz Summit*. He is author of the *Drummer's Practice Routine*.

DeFranco, Bonaface "Buddy" (b. 1923). Clarinetist DeFranco won the Tommy Dorsey National Swing contest at age fourteen and began his big-band career with Johnny "Scat" Davis in 1939. DeFranco's career shifted into high gear with Gene Krupa, Charlie Barnet, and at various times with Tommy Dorsey during the forties. After a year with Count Basie's septet in 1950, DeFranco led a big band for a while and some small groups for the next several years until the clarinet lost its popularity as a jazz instrument at the end of the Swing Era. He continued his career as leader of the Glenn Miller Band from 1966 to 1974, co-leader of a quintet with vibist Terry Gibbs, and as a clinician at a number of colleges and universities. DeFranco has won numerous polls and is considered one of the top clarinetists in the history of modern jazz.

DeLuxe. A record company established in the mid-forties that recorded such Swing Era musicians as Billy Eckstine, Benny Carter, and Dud Bascomb.

DeNicola, Antonio "Tony" (b. 1927). A drummer-educator, DeNicola played in the Air Force Band and worked with bands in the Midwest and on the West Coast in the late forties. He later worked with Freddie Martin and played at various times with Charlie Ventura in the fifties. DeNicola played with Harry James during 1958 and 1962 and Billy Butterfield in 1963. DeNicola later taught in the Trenton public school system and at Trenton State College until his retirement in 1992. He has recorded with James, Flip Phillips, and Kenny Davern.

Dennis, William "Willie" (1926–1965). Mainly a self-taught trombonist, Dennis began playing professionally with Elliot Lawrence and continued with Sam Donahue and Claude Thornhill in the late forties. He worked during the fifties with Charles Mingus, Woody Herman, Benny Goodman, and Buddy Rich. Dennis became active in television and recording studios while touring with Gerry Mulligan's Concert Jazz Band, and with Benny Goodman in the Soviet Union during the early sixties. Dennis had a fluid and unconventional jazz trombone style that demonstrated his knowledge of the instrument's limitations, which he avoided with his lip and slide flexibility. He recorded with Goodman, Herman, Mingus, Mulligan, J. J. Johnson, Bennie Green, Kai Winding, and Phil Woods.

DeParis, Wilbur (1900–1973). DeParis, a trombonist-bandleader and major contributor to the Dixieland Revival, worked as sideman for Noble Sissle,

Louis Armstrong, Teddy Hill, Roy Eldridge, Duke Ellington, and others before forming his "New" New Orleans Band in the late forties. DeParis' band had a unique style that combined Dixieland and swing while including elements from other styles such as Afro-Cuban music. By the early fifties, he began recording for Atlantic Records and several of his albums received critical acclaim. His band also began an eleven-year residency at Jimmy Ryan's nightclub in New York City. His band also toured for the U.S. State Department, appeared on television, and performed at the Antibes Jazz Festival in France. In addition to DeParis' excellent performance and band-leading skills, his compositions such as "Madagascar," "Mardi Gras," and "March of the Charcoal Grays" gave his band a stylistic edge over most of the other Dixieland bands in the fifties and sixties.

DeRosa, Clement "Clem" (b. 1925). DeRosa, a drummer-arranger-composer-educator, began playing professionally with Harry Altman and John LaPorta on Long Island, New York. DeRosa gained national attention playing with Jimmy Dorsey, Boyd Raeburn, Vaughn Monroe, Georgie Auld, Bobby Hackett, Coleman Hawkins, Teddy Wilson, Bill Harris, Chubby Jackson, and others from 1945 to 1955. Afterward, DeRosa became an educator and ultimately the president of the International Association for Jazz Education. He directed the McDonald's Tri-State High School Jazz Ensemble and the Glenn Miller Orchestra. DeRosa has appeared on television, in film, and recorded with the Glenn Miller Orchestra and Charles Mingus.

Desmond, Paul (1924–1977). An altoist, Desmond gained worldwide recognition as a member of Dave Brubeck's quartet. Desmond started out with Jack Fina in 1950 and played with Alvino Rey in 1951. After a brief period with Rey, Desmond joined Brubeck in 1951 and remained in the quartet until it disbanded in 1967. Desmond composed Brubeck's biggest hit, "Take Five," which is one of the first jazz compositions written in 5/4 time. After leaving Brubeck, Desmond led his own groups in such venues as New York's Half Note and Bourbon Street in Toronto, Canada. He recorded with Jim Hall, Gerry Mulligan, and Chet Baker.

Dew Drop Inn. A popular uptown venue for African Americans in New Orleans that featured many top performers including the International Sweethearts of Rhythm, Joe Turner, and Dave Bartholomew between the mid-forties and the mid-sixties.

Dixon, Eric "Big Daddy" (1930–1989). A tenorist-flutist-composer, Dixon started playing saxophone at age twelve and gained national visibility in the mid-fifties with Cootie Williams, Bennie Green, and Johnny Hodges. Dixon went on to establish himself further with Quincy Jones and Count Basie with whom he played for almost twenty years. His tenor saxophone and flute playing is available on recordings by Basie, Green, and Oliver Nelson. Dixon also wrote arrangements for Basie's band including "Frankie and Johnny" and "It's Only a Paper Moon."

Dixon, Lucille (b. 1923). Dixon, a bassist, studied with Fred Zimmerman (principal bassist for the New York Philharmonic Orchestra) and attended Brooklyn College. In the early forties, she toured with Earl Hines and the International Sweethearts of Rhythm. She organized her own band in the mid-forties and later performed in New York City's Greenwich Village for a number of years. In addition to her work in jazz, Dixon has been affiliated with several symphonic organizations including the Symphony of Panama in the mid-fifties and the Symphony of the New World.

Doggett, William "Bill" (1916–1996). Doggett, a pianist-organist-arranger, began playing professionally in the late thirties with Jimmy Gorman, Lucky Millinder, and Jimmy Mundy. Throughout the forties, Doggett rejoined Millinder; played and arranged for the Ink Spots; freelanced with Louis Armstrong, Lionel Hampton, Jimmy Rushing, Lucky Thompson, and Illinois Jacquet; and arranged Monk's "Round Midnight" for Cootie Williams' orchestra. Doggett replaced Wild Bill Davis in Louis Jordan's band from 1948 to 1951. Influenced by Davis, Doggett started playing organ in 1951 and recorded with Eddie Davis and Ella Fitzgerald. Beginning in the mid-fifties, he led his own bands and became highly successful as a rhythm-and-blues artist after recording his biggest hit, "Honky Tonk," in 1956. Doggett later arranged and conducted for an Ella Fitzgerald recording session, toured extensively with his combo, played reunion dates with the Ink Spots, and recorded with Della Reese.

Donahue, Sam (1918–1974). A tenorist-arranger-bandleader, Donahue played with Gene Krupa, Harry James, and Benny Goodman, and led his own civilian band before serving as a bandleader in the navy during World War II. After discharge, he taught at Hartnett Studios in New York City until 1951. He played with Tommy Dorsey, fronted Billy May's orchestra, and led his own band in the fifties. Donahue later worked with Stan Kenton and fronted Tommy Dorsey's orchestra in the early sixties. A few years later, Donahue retired as one of the best organizers and big-band leaders in the music industry. As a saxophonist, he played in the Coleman Hawkins tradition, and his swinging tenor can be heard in some of Kenton's Capitol recordings.

Donaldson, Robert "Bobby" (1922–1971). A drummer, Donaldson performed with Boston-area bands including those of Sabby Lewis, Tasker Crosson, Joe Nevils, and the Jones Brothers from 1939 to 1941. After military service in the early forties, Donaldson toured with Cat Anderson in 1946 and worked with Paul Bascomb, Willis Jackson, and Edmond Hall at the Café Society from 1950 to 1952. Throughout the fifties, he worked with Sy Oliver, Lucky Millinder, Andy Kirk, Buck Clayton, Benny Goodman, Eddie Condon, Budd Freeman, Charlie Shavers, Coleman Hawkins, Dorothy Donegan, Teddy Wilson, Rex Stewart, Eddie Heywood, Frankie Laine, and others. Donaldson also appeared on a number of television shows as well as in radio and TV commercials. He recorded his own *Dixieland Jazz Party* for Savoy Records and *Jazz Unlimited* for the Crest label.

Donegan, Dorothy (1924–1998). A pianist, Donegan first worked in Los Angeles cocktail lounges before appearing in the film *Sensations of 1945* and later touring with the play *Star Time*. Most of her performing career was spent in nightclubs where she displayed a swinging style, superb piano technique, and imitations of other pianists and vocalists. The later years of her career finally witnessed the recognition she deserved with numerous club dates, concerts, jazz cruises, and international festivals. She lectured at several colleges and universities and received an American Jazz Masters award from the National Endowment for the Arts. She was forced to retire during the last year of her life because of illness. Her recordings are on the Timeless and Chiaroscuro labels.

Downbeat. A landmark in New York City clubs that presented many Swing Era artists from the mid-forties to the mid-fifties. Some of the musicians who performed there were Jay McShann, Ella Fitzgerald, Eddie Heywood, Sarah Vaughn, Art Tatum, and Tiny Grimes.

Downbeat. A popular jazz club in Philadelphia that featured such artists as Charlie Ventura, Roy Eldridge, Dizzy Gillespie, Buddy DeFranco, Red Garland, and Fats Navarro in the forties.

Down Beat Room Café. An important nightclub located on famous South Central Avenue in Los Angeles. The venue presented a number of swing and bop musicians such as Buddy Collette, Charles Mingus, and Lucky Thompson in the forties.

Downtown. A Chicago establishment that sponsored a number of swing bands for week-long engagements in the mid-forties. Charlie Barnet, Billy Eckstine, Andy Kirk, Jimmie Lunceford, Eddie Heywood, Nat "King" Cole, Noble Sissle, and the International Sweethearts of Rhythm performed at the venue.

Drome. A popular Detroit club that opened in the late forties and presented noted performers such as Terry Pollard, Yusef Lateef, and Frank Rosolino.

Dukes of Dixieland. A New Orleans–based group formed in 1948 by brothers Frank and Fred Assunto and managed by their father, "Papa Jac" Assunto. Before settling in the Crescent City, the Dukes won a Horace Heidt talent contest and toured with Heidt before turning professional. The group gained fame after signing a contract with Audio Fidelity Records, which helped the Dukes become one of the most successful traditional jazz groups in the South. The group became best known for its residency at the Famous Door in New Orleans during the fifties. After the death of trumpeter-singer Fred Assunto in 1966 and that of his brother Frank in 1974, however, Papa Jac retired from the group to teach until his death in 1985. The group continued after 1985 as an interracial band and has made appearances in Hollywood, California.

Duran, Edward "Eddie" (b. 1925). A guitarist, Duran started playing professionally at age fifteen. After serving in the navy, he worked in San Francisco with Flip Phillips, Stan Getz, Cal Tjader, Freddie Slack, Earl Hines, Red Norvo, George Shearing, and others during the mid-forties and fifties. He later led his own groups, played with Benny Goodman, and freelanced in New York City. Duran has recorded with Getz, Tjader, Ron Crotty, Jerry Coker, and his own group.

Duvivier, George (1920–1985). Duvivier, a bassist, played with the Royal Baron Orchestra around 1937 before working professionally with Coleman Hawkins' band in 1941. Duvivier wrote charts for Jimmie Lunceford, served in the army in the mid-forties, and arranged full time for Lunceford during the late forties. In the fifties, Duvivier played bass for vocalists Nellie Lutcher, Billy Eckstine, Pearl Bailey, and Lena Horne. He also played and recorded with Terry Gibbs, Bud Powell, and Eric Dolphy along with frequent non-jazz work as a studio musician. He played on such soundtracks as *Serpico*, *The Godfather*, and *Requiem for a Heavyweight*. Duvivier was a highly accomplished bassist who could play in a variety of musical situations and create some of the most interesting bass lines ever played in jazz.

Eager, Allen (b. 1927). A tenor and alto saxophonist, Eager toured with Bobby Sherwood in 1943 before working with Sonny Dunham, Hal McIntyre, Shorty Sherock, Herman, Tommy Dorsey, Johnny Bothwell, Tadd Dameron, and Buddy Rich during the forties and early fifties. From 1953 to 1960, Eager worked off and on with his own group and played with Howard McGhee and Oscar Pettiford. In the sixties, he appeared on Frank Zappa's first album during a long hiatus from jazz before a return in the early eighties to tour Europe with Chet Baker and work occasionally on the U.S. mainland in the early eighties. Eager has recorded with Bothwell, Coleman Hawkins, Gerry Mulligan, Serge Chaloff, Kai Winding, and under his own name.

Eckstine, William "Billy" (1914–1993). After winning several talent shows during his youth, Eckstine began singing professionally in the thirties and established himself when he joined Earl Hines' band in 1939 in Chicago. Eckstine recorded several hits with Hines such as "The Jitney Man," "Jelly, Jelly," and "Stormy Monday." By 1943, he formed his own big band that was probably the most innovative of its kind with a number of modern musicians such as Dizzy Gillespie, Sarah Vaughn, and Art Blakey. Although the band was a modern bebop organization, Eckstine recorded several hits such as "Prisoner of Love" and "A Cottage for Sale" in the mid-forties. Eckstine disbanded in 1947 and continued to perform as a solo act, record, and work with small groups. After the forties, he recorded a number of hits and million-sellers and, despite racial barriers, became the first African-American male vocalist to reach international prominence by appealing to both black and white audiences. In fact, Eckstine became a national sex symbol. He continued to perform until the early nineties and influenced numerous male singers.

Eddie Condon's. A famous New York City traditional jazz nightclub opened by the guitarist in 1945. The venue presented "Chicago Jazz" regularly until Condon's death in 1975. The club usually featured a resident band that included such sidemen as Wild Bill Davison, Pee Wee Russell, George Brunis, Edmond Hall, and Bud Freeman.

Edwards, Theodore "Teddy" (b. 1924). A clarinetist-tenor saxophonist, Edwards toured with Ernie Fields before moving to Los Angeles in 1945 where he worked with Roy Milton, Howard McGhee, Benny Carter, and The Lighthouse All-Stars until the early fifties. He played with Max Roach–Clifford Brown in 1954 and in Gerald Wilson's band from 1954 to 1964. In the meantime, he worked with Leroy Vinnegar, Terry Gibbs, Benny Goodman, McGhee, Count Basie, Dizzy Gillespie, and the Milt Jackson–Ray Brown Quintet through the sixties. Since the seventies, Edwards has worked with Bill Berry, the Jackson-Brown Quintet, and the Capp-Pierce Juggernaut, and composed for the Belgian Radio Orchestra and a movie soundtrack. Edwards is heard at his best in his own recordings for the Pacific Jazz, Prestige, Xanadu, Muse, Steeplechase, and Timeless labels.

Eldorado Ballroom. The centerpiece in Houston, Texas, for jazz and rhythm and blues throughout the Swing Era. Some of the artists who performed there include Lionel Hampton, Bullmoose Jackson, Count Basie, and Arnett Cobb.

Elgart, Les (1918–1995). A trumpeter-bandleader, Elgart spent his early career with Bunny Berigan, Hal McIntyre, Woody Herman, and New York's CBS studios prior to serving in the military. After discharge, Les and his brother Larry formed a big band in 1947 that played charts by such arrangers as Nelson Riddle and Ralph Flanagan. The band performed at some of the top venues on the East Coast, in army camps, and numerous one-nighters. Despite the activity, the band folded in 1949, and Les and his brother freelanced until a second band was organized in 1952 by Larry and saxophonist-arranger Charlie Albertine. Although Larry and Charlie were co-directors, Les basically fronted the band. The second band became highly popular with a danceable style that appealed to the masses. The Elgart band recorded several hit albums such as *Sophisticated Swing*, *College Prom Favorite*, and *Barefoot Ballerina*. The Elgart band also recorded "Bandstand Boogie" (theme song) for *American Bandstand*, which endured after Dick Clark became the show's host.

El Grotto. A nightclub in Chicago's Pershing Hotel that hosted numerous Swing Era artists such as Earl Hines, Tiny Bradshaw, Johnny Otis, T-Bone Walker, Eddie "Lockjaw" Davis, and Roy Eldridge.

Elk's Ballroom. A dance hall located in Cambridge, Massachusetts, that presented big bands led by artists such as Cab Calloway in the forties. The venue also sponsored "battles of the bands" between regional bands like Sabby Lewis' and visiting bands led by players such as Hot Lips Page.

Elk's Hall. Located on Los Angeles' South Central Avenue, the venue presented such artists as Dexter Gordon, Lucky Thompson, Howard McGhee, and Wardell Gray in the forties.

Ellington, Mercer (1919–1996). The son of Duke Ellington, Mercer was a trumpeter-bandleader from Washington, D.C., who moved to New York City in the late thirties and tried his hand at leading his own bands. Needless to say, he found it difficult to follow in his father's footsteps. He contributed some noteworthy tunes to his father's repertoire, however, such as "Blue Serge" and "Things Ain't What They Used to Be." He later worked in several music-related jobs such as management, retail, and disc jockeying. He also played trumpet in the bands of his father and Cootie Williams. Mercer took over Duke's band in 1974 after his death and kept the legacy of his father's music alive. Some of the albums Mercer recorded with the band include *Music Is My Mistress*, *Only God Can Make a Tree*, and *Take the Holiday Train*. Mercer's most notable contribution to swing is his *Black and Tan Fantasy* album recorded by Coral Records in the late fifties that included Clark Terry, Johnny Hodges, Ben Webster, and Billy Strayhorn.

Ellis, Mitchell "Herb" (b. 1921). A guitarist, Ellis played with the Casa Loma Orchestra, toured with Jimmy Dorsey from 1944 to 1948, and played with the Soft Winds trio between 1948 and 1953. Ellis played in Oscar Peterson's trio from 1953 to 1958 and accompanied Ella Fitzgerald between

1958 and 1962. He played in the house band for Steve Allen's television show and worked in studios on the West Coast in the sixties. Since that time, he has remained active in studio work, played numerous concerts, and toured Europe and Japan with Joe Pass, Charlie Byrd, Barney Kessel, Ray Brown, and occasionally with Oscar Peterson.

Embassy Auditorium. This large Los Angeles hall featured Count Basie, a *Jazz at the Philharmonic* concert, and a jazz series named *Jazz à La Carte*. Jazz concerts were presented at the auditorium from the mid-forties to the eighties.

Embers. A New York City club that hosted soloists and small groups from the late forties to the sixties. Some of the venue's featured performers were Jonah Jones, Art Tatum, Erskine Hawkins, Buck Clayton, Roy Eldridge, Earl Hines, Mary Lou Williams, and Tyree Glenn.

English, Bill (b. 1925). A drummer, English began playing with rhythm-and-blues bands in the early fifties, worked with Amos Milburn on the West Coast in 1954, and played in New York City with Erskine Hawkins and Bennie Green in 1956. In the late fifties, English led his own group and played in the Apollo Theater's house band. He played and/or recorded in the sixties with Earl Hines, Joe Newman, Quincy Jones, Gene Ammons, Stanley Turrentine, Kenny Burrell, and Eddie Jefferson before recording with Eric Dixon in the early seventies. English also recorded with Coleman Hawkins.

Evans, Ernest "Gil" (1912–1988). Evans, a composer-arranger-pianist-bandleader, played solo piano in local establishments in Stockton, California, while in high school. He led his own band for five years in the mid-thirties and, after Skinnay Ennis assumed leadership, remained as its arranger until 1941. Evans worked as Claude Thornhill's arranger in the forties except for military service. During Evans' tenure with Thornhill, he added French horns, flutes, and tuba to the big band and incorporated interweaving tonal textures from Western orchestral works. Evans' originality attracted the attention of such modern musicians as Miles Davis, Gerry Mulligan, and John Lewis. These musicians collaborated and concluded that they wanted a full orchestral sound with the smallest number of instruments, which resulted in the *Birth of the Cool* sessions under Davis' leadership. The sessions made use of a nonet or nine-piece band that was a smaller version of Thornhill's orchestra for which Evans arranged such charts as "Moondreams" and "Boplicity." Evans' creative use of the nonet as an orchestral palette for the soloist laid a solid foundation for the "cool" school of jazz that emerged in the early fifties. While Evans' status as an arranger-composer began to rise among musicians and jazz buffs after the release of the album, he mostly freelanced and wrote charts for vocalists such as Helen Merrill, Johnny Mathis, and Tony Bennett throughout most of the fifties. Evans and Davis collaborated again between 1957 and 1960 and recorded *Miles Ahead*, *Porgy and Bess*, and *Sketches of Spain*. Here, Evans used a nineteen-piece band to provide Davis (on trumpet/flugelhorn) with an accompaniment or backdrop of orchestral textures that revolutionized jazz writing for large ensembles. Needless to say, these three albums were the springboard that established Evans as one of the best arrangers-composers in the history of jazz.

Ewing, John "Steamline" (b. 1917). A trombonist, Ewing began playing professionally with Gene Coy. Ewing worked with Horace Henderson and Earl Hines in the late thirties and played in the forties with Louis Armstrong, Lionel Hampton, Jimmie Lunceford, Cab Calloway, Jay McShann, and again with Hines. After working with Cootie Williams in 1950, Ewing played with Gerald Wilson, George Jenkins, and Teddy Buckner in the fifties and beyond. Ewing freelanced in Los Angeles and toured Europe and Japan. Ewing is mostly known as a consistent and solid big-band trombonist who established himself on Earl Hines' recordings of "Windy City Jive," "Yellow Fire," "Swingin' On C," "XYZ," and "Grand Terrace Shuffle."

Famous Door. Established in the mid-thirties, this club hosted numerous Swing Era musicians until 1950. Some of the jazz giants who performed there were John Kirby, Woody Herman, Benny Carter, Red Nichols, Andy Kirk, and Red Norvo.

Farlow, Talmadge "Tal" (1921–1998). A guitarist, Farlow started playing the instrument at age twenty-one. Largely self-taught, Farlow began playing professionally in 1947 with Dardanelle Breckenbridge's trio at the Copa Lounge in New York City. He worked with vibist Marjorie Hyams and clarinetist Buddy DeFranco in the late forties, played with Red Norvo and Artie Shaw's Gramercy Five in the early fifties, and led his own trio from 1956 to 1958. Afterward, he retired from music for ten years but re-emerged in 1969 to tour with George Wein's group and appear at the Newport Jazz Festival. After the early seventies, Farlow mostly performed and toured part-time while recording and teaching guitar privately until his death. He recorded with DeFranco, Shaw, Norvo, and Oscar Pettiford, and wrote the *Tal Farlow Guitar Method*.

Fatool, Nicholas "Nick" (1915–2000). A drummer, Fatool started out by working in Providence, Rhode Island, with local groups before playing with Joe Haymes, George Hall, and Benny Goodman in the late thirties. Fatool spent the forties with Artie Shaw, Claude Thornhill, Jan Savitt, Alvino Rey, and Harry James, as well as in Los Angeles recording studios with such artists as Billy Butterfield, Louis Armstrong, Glen Gray, and Erroll Garner. The fifties saw Fatool with *The Bing Crosby Show*, Bob Crosby's orchestra, and in annual Dixieland Jubilees sponsored by Frank Bull and Gene Norman. He later worked and/or toured with Pete Fountain, Bob Crosby (again), Louis Armstrong, Phil Harris, Matty Matlock, Peanuts Hucko, Dick Cary, and others. Fatool recorded with Shaw, Goodman, Lionel Hampton, Billie Holiday, Stan Hasselgard, Nat "King" Cole, and Yank Lawson.

Feather, Leonard (1914–1994). A pianist-composer-journalist, Feather composed and produced recordings for Benny Carter, George Chisholm, Duke Ellington, Louis Armstrong, and Dizzy Gillespie. He also organized jazz concerts and produced recording sessions for George Shearing, Sarah Vaughn, and Dinah Washington. It was in fact his "Salty Papa Blues," "Evil Gal Blues," and "Blowtop Blues" that provided the foundation for Washington's career. His publications *Inside Bebop* (1949) and the first *Encyclopedia of Jazz* (1955) established him as one of the most important journalists in jazz.

Feld, Morey (1915–1971). Feld, a drummer, acquired experience in the bands of Joe Haymes and Ben Pollack before gaining national recognition with Benny Goodman in the early forties. Feld later worked with Buddy Morrow in the late forties before playing with Billy Butterfield, Bobby Hackett, and Peanuts Hucko in the early fifties. While leading his own group in 1955, Feld joined ABC as a staff musician until the end of the decade and played later in the World's Greatest Jazz Band. Feld recorded with Teddy Wilson, Wild Bill Davison, Red Norvo, and others.

Ferguson, Maynard (b. 1928). A trumpeter and valve trombonist, Ferguson first appeared with Boyd Raeburn, worked briefly as a solo act, and played with Jimmy Dorsey in the late forties. After a stint with Charlie Barnet, he gained international recognition as a member of Stan Kenton's band from 1950 to 1953. After leaving Kenton, Ferguson freelanced in Los Angeles in the mid-fifties and led his own big bands from 1957 to 1965 before downsizing to smaller groups. Since that time, Ferguson has led bands featuring programs of pop and jazz-rock hits that led him to commercial success. His upper-range trumpet playing has made him an icon in certain jazz circles. However, recent years have witnessed him playing with a more melodic style. He has continued to lead his own band, tour, and conduct clinics/workshops. In addition to his own albums as a leader, Ferguson has recorded with Kenton, Dinah Washington, and Clifford Brown.

Fields, Herbert "Herbie" (1919–1958). A clarinetist-saxophonist, Fields led his own band, played with Lionel Hampton, and recorded for two labels (Savoy and RCA) in the forties. He also won *Esquire*'s New Star on alto poll in 1945. During Fields' short life and career, he recorded with Hampton, Miles Davis, Helen Humes, and Oscar Pettiford.

Fishkin, Arnold (1919–1999). Fishkin began his professional career as a bassist in Bunny Berigan's band in the late thirties and played in the early forties with Jack Teagarden and Les Brown before military service. After discharge, he played with Lennie Tristano, Charlie Barnet, Stan Getz, and Shorty Rogers in the late forties. After playing with Lee Konitz from 1949 to 1951, Fishkin freelanced, worked as a staff musician for ABC and CBS, and participated in numerous recording sessions in the fifties and sixties. He has recorded with Howard McGhee, Hank Jones, Coleman Hawkins, Chubby Jackson, Maynard Ferguson, and Charlie Parker.

Fitzgerald, Ella (1917–1996). Fitzgerald, one of the most innovative vocalists in jazz history, began singing professionally after winning a number of amateur contests. She worked with Chick Webb's band from 1935 until his death in 1939. They recorded their million-seller, "A-Tisket, A-Tasket," in 1938 that established Fitzgerald as a solid Swing Era vocalist. After 1939, she took over the Webb band, but World War II practically destroyed its membership. Afterward, she started a solo career and continued as a Decca recording artist a connection that was established earlier with Webb. She recorded with the label from 1942 to 1955 and collaborated with artists such as Louis Armstrong, Louis Jordan, the Ink Spots, and the Mills Brothers. While with Decca, Fitzgerald toured with Norman Granz's Jazz at the Philharmonic and developed her famous scat vocal style from imitating the instrumentalists. Granz became her manager in 1955, and she switched over to his new Verve label and recorded the memorable *Song Book* albums that featured the music of Cole Porter, Jerome Kern, Johnny Mercer, and the Gershwins. These albums helped expose Fitzgerald to a larger audience, which made it possible for her to become the "First Lady of Song."

Flame Show Bar. A nightspot that opened in Detroit during the late forties and featured such artists as Erroll Garner, Sarah Vaughn, Savannah Churchill, Dinah Washington, and Billie Holiday.

Flax, Martin "Marty" (1924–1972). A baritonist, Flax made his professional debut with Chubby Jackson in 1949. He worked with Woody Herman, Louis Jordan, Pete Rugolo, Lucky Millinder, Prez Prado, and Les Elgart; toured overseas with Dizzy Gillespie and Herman; led his own group; and played tenor saxophone with Claude Thornhill in the fifties. Flax later played in Buddy Rich's band and in Las Vegas nightclubs in the sixties. He recorded with Jackson, Gillespie, and Sam Most.

Flory, Meredith "Med" (b. 1926). Flory, an altoist-vocalist-composer, served in the air corps, performed on clarinet with Claude Thornhill and

Art Mooney, played lead tenor saxophone with Woody Herman, and led his own group in the forties. The late fifties found Flory singing on the West Coast on Ray Anthony's television series, leading his own band, and acting in films and on television. He later worked with Buddy Clark and organized Supersax, which performed at major jazz festivals in Canada, Japan, and on the West Coast. Flory has recorded with Thornhill and Supersax.

Fontana, Carl (b. 1928). A trombonist, Fontana first played in his father's band during the early forties and gained national visibility in the bands of Woody Herman, Al Belletto, Lionel Hampton, Hal McIntyre, Stan Kenton, Kai Winding, and in Las Vegas shows in the fifties. Fontana also toured at various times with Herman and Benny Goodman, and he played with Louis Bellson, Supersax, the World's Greatest Jazz Band, Georgie Auld, and Jake Hanna. Although most of Fontana's work has been as a section player, he is a notable trombone soloist whose work bridges the gap between Swing Era and bebop music styles. He has recorded with Herman, Kenton, Hanna, Martial Solal, and others.

Ford, James "Jimmy" (1927–1994). Ford, a clarinetist-altoist-vocalist, began playing professionally in the late forties with Johnny "Scat" Davis, Milt Larkin, Kai Winding, Tad Dameron, and others. Ford worked in the sixties with Red Rodney, Bud Powell, and in Maynard Ferguson's band as a lead altoist and vocalist. Afterward, Ford worked with his Texas friends such as Arnett Cobb, Eddie Vinson, and Stephen Fulton with whom he co-led a group. He also toured Europe with Cobb and recorded with Rodney and Ferguson.

Forest Club. Opened during the early forties in Detroit, the Forest Club was part of a multipurpose building. The club featured top-name musicians such as Nat "King" Cole, Earl Hines, Lionel Hampton, and Louis Jordan.

Forrest, James "Jimmy" (1920–1980). A tenorist who started out playing in his mother's band, the Eva Dowd Orchestra, prior to working as a teenager in the bands of Eddie Johnson, Fate Marable, and the Jeter-Pillars Orchestra. He later toured with Don Albert in 1938 before playing with Jay McShann, Andy Kirk, and Duke Ellington in the forties. Forrest later formed his own group and recorded "Night Train," which became a big hit while he was working in the rhythm-and-blues field for about eight years. He subsequently returned to jazz and worked in Harry "Sweets" Edison's group, recorded as a leader, played in the Count Basie Orchestra as a featured soloist, and formed a quintet with trombonist Al Grey.

Foster, Frank (b. 1928). A saxophonist-arranger-composer who played with several territory bands in Ohio and the Wilberforce University Collegians in the late forties. Foster moved to Detroit in 1949 and worked with Snooky Young, Wardell Gray, Phil Hill, and Elvin Jones before military service in the early fifties. He joined Count Basie's band in 1953 where he played and wrote such charts as "Shiny Stockings," "Blues Backstage," and "Down for the Count" that brought him international attention. After leaving Basie in 1964, Foster played and arranged for the bands of Woody Herman, Lloyd Price, Duke Pearson, Thad Jones, Mel Lewis, Elvin Jones, and many others. He also led his own bands including the Loud Minority and Living Color. He later led the Count Basie Orchestra from 1986 to 1995. Although well known as a writer and bandleader, Foster is a highly competent saxophonist who is comfortable in both small-group and big-band settings.

Fournier, Vernel (1928–2000). A drummer, Fournier played with the Alabama State Collegians in the mid-forties and moved to Chicago where he worked with King Kolax, Paul Bascomb, Teddy Wilson, and others until 1953. Fournier played in the house band at the Bee Hive club in the mid-fifties and toured with Ahmad Jamal from 1957 to 1962, when he played on Jamal's landmark recording of "Poinciana." Fournier also worked with George Shearing, Larry Novack, Jamal, Nancy Wilson, and his own trio in the sixties and seventies. After 1980, he worked with such artists as Joe Williams, Billy Eckstine, and John Lewis while teaching in the jazz program at the New School in New York City. Fournier was the first drummer out of the Later Swing Era to adapt the New Orleans second-line beat to modern jazz on "Poinciana" with Jamal.

Fowler, William (b. 1917). An educator/guitarist/composer, Fowler directed army bands in Europe during World War II. After military service, he studied at the University of Utah from 1946 to 1954 and taught there until 1973. From 1973 to 1988, he served as a professor at the University of Colorado. Fowler established himself as an outstanding educator and author. He wrote articles for *Downbeat* and *Keyboard* magazines; wrote twenty-three instruction books for guitar, bass, and keyboard; and directed a number of jazz clinics. He also formed his own record label.

Fowlkes, Charles "Charlie" (1916–1980). Fowlkes, a baritonist, gained prominence during the forties playing in the bands of Tiny Bradshaw, Lionel Hampton, and Arnett Cobb until 1951. Fowlkes played in Count Basie's orchestra from 1951 to 1969 until a knee injury forced him to leave the band and play mostly in New York City. Except for rejoining Basie in 1975, Fowlkes' career was mostly dormant. He was best known as a solid and consistent section player as heard in some of Basie's recordings.

Francis, David "Panama" (1918–2001). A drummer who played professionally in the bands of Tab Smith, Billy Hicks, and Roy Eldridge during the late thirties before playing in Lucky Millinder's orchestra from 1940 to 1946. Francis led his own group briefly and worked with Willie Bryant in the mid-forties prior to playing in Cab Calloway's band between 1947 and 1952. In 1952–1953, he worked with Duke Ellington, Charlie Shavers, Slim Gaillard, and Conrad Janis' Dixieland Five. Throughout the rest of the fifties, he worked with rhythm-and-blues musicians such as the Platters, Brook Benton, Little Willie John, Frankie Avalon, and Jackie Wilson along with other artists such as Illinois Jacquet, Tony Bennett, Carmen McRae, Ray Charles, Buddy Holly, and Jimmy Witherspoon. Francis later worked as a studio musician and freelanced with many other first-rate musicians.

Freeman, Earl "Von" (b. 1922). A tenorist-composer, Earl Freeman worked with Horace Henderson, served in the navy, played in the house band at Chicago's Pershing Hotel with his brothers, and worked with Sun Ra in the forties. Freeman later performed mostly with blues musicians such as Jimmy Reed and Otis Rush but returned to jazz around 1969. Since the early seventies, Freeman has performed in numerous small clubs, mostly in the Chicago area, and recorded as a leader and sideman. He is one of the few surviving tenor saxophonists who developed his craft during the Swing Era and absorbed the bebop language. He continues to play his own unique brand of modern swing.

Freeman, Russell "Russ" (b. 1926). A pianist-composer, Freeman became well known in the late forties with groups led by Howard McGhee, Dexter Gordon, and Charlie Parker. Freeman later played in the bands of Charlie Barnet, Chet Baker, Benny Goodman, and Shelly Manne in the fifties. More recently, Freeman has worked primarily in the commercial music field. He recorded four albums, however, with Art Pepper, Bill Watrous, Sonny Stitt, and Manne. Annie Ross wrote lyrics to his composition "Music Is Forever," and Mariah Carey wrote lyrics to his "The Wind." Both vocalists recorded his music. Freeman also recorded with The Lighthouse All-Stars, Miles Davis, Clifford Brown, Lee Konitz, Serge Chaloff, and Shorty Rogers.

Fuller, Walter "Gil" (1920–1994). An arranger-composer, Fuller wrote charts for Floyd Ray and Tiny Bradshaw while in his teens. He later fulfilled his military obligation, wrote for Les Hite, and arranged music for Jimmie Lunceford, Charlie Barnet, Benny Carter, Count Basie, Woody Herman, Artie Shaw, Tito Puente, and Machito. Fuller was one of the first to write bebop arrangements for big bands and scored groundbreaking charts for Dizzy Gillespie, Billy Eckstine, and James Moody in the forties. The next decade found Fuller working mostly in professions other than music, but the sixties witnessed a revival of his career with charts for Ray Charles and Stan Kenton's Neophonic Orchestra, along with a directorship of the house band at the Monterey Jazz Festival. Fuller is best known for his arrangements of "Ray's Idea," "One Bass Hit," "Things to Come," "Swedish Suite," and "Oop-Bop-Sh-Bam" for Gillespie's big band in the mid-forties. Fuller fused jazz with Afro-Cuban music successfully in arrangements for Tito Puente and Machito as well as for several vocalists. Fuller was undoubtedly one of the most versatile and talented writers to emerge from the Later Swing Era, and some of his most exciting arrangements were recorded in 1946–1948 by Dizzy Gillespie's orchestra.

Gaillard, Bulee "Slim" (1915–1991). Gaillard, a pianist-guitarist-drummer, started performing at age fifteen as a guitarist and tap dancer. He and bassist Slam Stewart formed a duo in 1937 called Slim and Slam that recorded a big hit entitled "Flat Fleet Floogie." Gaillard served in the army during World War II and moved to the West Coast in 1944, where he worked regularly on a variety of radio shows. In the mid-forties, Gaillard toured with Dizzy Gillespie and Charlie Parker, and he continued performing until the end of the fifties when his career reached its peak. Although Gaillard did not record frequently after 1945, his recordings from 1937 to 1945 captured the breadth of his talent and are available on *Jazz Chronological Classics, 1994–1997.*

Galbraith, Barry (1919–1983). A guitarist, Galbraith gained prominence in the bands of Red Norvo, Teddy Powell, Claude Thornhill, and Hal McIntyre in the forties. Galbraith also worked as a staff musician for CBS and NBC from 1947 to 1970. In the meantime, he toured with Stan Kenton, played as part of a USO tour in Iceland, and took part in numerous popular and jazz recording sessions. He also taught in the jazz department at the City College of New York from 1970 to 1975. Galbraith's clean and precise playing was captured in the recordings of Coleman Hawkins, Sheila Jordan, Helen Merrill, Dinah Washington, Gil Evans, George Russell, Clifford Brown, and others.

Garcia, Russell "Russ" (b. 1916). A trumpeter-arranger-composer, Garcia worked with Horace Heidt, Al Donahue, and as a staff musician for NBC in Hollywood in the forties. He later worked with Buddy DeFranco, Charlie Barnet, Roy Eldridge, and Johnny Hodges, and recorded as a leader in the fifties. Garcia played with Ray Brown and arranged for Stan Kenton's orchestra in the sixties while writing numerous film scores. Garcia also wrote a method book on arranging and composed "Variations for Flugelhorn, String Quartet, Bass, and Drums."

Gardner, Julie (b. 1925). Gardner, who played accordion and sang, worked with Earl Hines briefly in the early forties before playing in the bands of Sabby Lewis, Louis Jordan, and Charlie Barnet. She later performed as a soloist or with her own small group and toured Alaska, the Caribbean, and the Pacific.

Garland, William "Red" (1923–1984). A pianist, Garland played with swing musicians such as Hot Lips Page, Ben Webster, Roy Eldridge, and Coleman Hawkins from 1945 to 1955. Afterward, he played in Miles Davis' famous quintet with John Coltrane, Paul Chambers, and Philly Joe Jones from 1955 to 1957. Garland also freelanced with Donald Byrd, Coltrane, and Art Taylor; formed his own trio; and rejoined Davis in the late fifties. Garland and his trio with Byrd and Coltrane recorded several albums for Prestige in the early sixties. He worked through the late sixties before fading from the jazz scene and making a comeback for a while in the late seventies. Garland's unique melodic style contained all of the essential elements of swing, bebop, and the blues and influenced a generation of pianists such as Mulgrew Miller, Donald Brown, and James Williams. Garland recorded with Jackie McLean, Sonny Rollins, Arnett Cobb, and Art Pepper.

Garner, Erroll (1921–1977). A pianist and younger brother of Linton Garner, Erroll began working professionally in Pittsburgh with Leroy Brown's band, vocalists, and in piano duets. He later played in Slam Stewart's trio in the mid-forties. Except for participating in some all-star jam sessions, Erroll Garner either worked as a soloist or leader of his own trio. He had a unique style based on a complete independence of his hands. For example, he played with a flexible and steady left hand while playing octaves with his right hand in a rhythmically free manner. He also had an orchestral approach to playing the piano that incorporated Swing Era musical language and some elements from bebop while maintaining massive audience appeal. Garner's *Body and Soul* and *Concert by the Sea* albums recorded by Columbia Records document his brilliance as a pianist and showcase his most popular composition, "Misty."

Garner, Linton (1916–2003). A pianist and older brother of Erroll Garner, Linton led his own band in Pittsburgh and served in the army in the early forties. After discharge, he worked in Billy Eckstine's big band as a pianist and arranger in 1946 and 1947. The sides he recorded with the Eckstine band are on *Billy Eckstine 1946–1947* (Classics). Linton wrote charts for Dizzy Gillespie's big band that recorded his "Minor Walk" in 1947 and his "Duff Capers" in 1948. These sides are included in Gillespie's *The Complete RCA Victor Recordings*. Garner also played in recording sessions that included such artists as Fats Navarro, Max Roach, Sonny Rollins, J. J. Johnson, Bennie Green, and Julius Watkins in the late forties. Garner also served as the accompanist for comedian Timmy Rogers and toured with dancer Teddy Hale from 1947 to 1955.

Garrick's Stage Bar. A multi-purpose venue in Chicago that showcased many Swing Era musicians in the forties. The establishment hosted artists such as Billie Holiday, Ben Webster, Lil Armstrong, Louis Jordan, Ethel Waters, Eddie South, Alberta Hunter, Stuff Smith, and Henry "Red" Allen.

Garrison, Arvin "Arv" (1922–1960). A guitarist, Garrison formed his own trio in 1941 that performed across the United States until 1948. In 1946, he named the trio after his wife, Vivien Garry, the group's bassist. He returned to his home in Toledo, Ohio, in the fifties and performed locally until his untimely death. Garrison's composition "Five Guitars in Flight" featured himself, Tony Rizzi, Irving Ashby, Barney Kessel, and Gene Sargent on guitars, with the Earl Spencer Orchestra, in a 1947 recording on the Black and White label. He recorded with Howard McGhee, Charlie Parker, and Dizzy Gillespie.

Gaskin, Leonard (b, 1920). Gaskin, a bassist, played with Duke Jordan and Max Roach in a house band at a Harlem nightclub and with Dizzy Gillespie in the early forties. He freelanced later with Eddie South, Charlie Shavers, Erroll Garner, Don Byas, and Charlie Parker, and toured England with Eddie Condon until the late fifties. Gaskin worked in the studios during the sixties. Since that time, he has performed with Sy Oliver, Panama Francis, Oliver Jackson's trio, and Big Nick Nicholas, and has led his own trio. His round and clear sound can be heard in recordings with King Pleasure, Jack Teagarden, Stan Getz, J. J. Johnson, and the Swingville All-Stars.

Gee, Matthew (1925–1979). A trombonist, Gee played with Coleman Hawkins, served in the army, and worked with Dizzy Gillespie and Joe Morris in the forties. The next decade saw Gee with Gene Ammons–Sonny Stitt, Count Basie, Illinois Jacquet, Sarah Vaughn, the Apollo's house band, and at Birdland on Monday nights. From 1959 to 1963, Gee worked intermittently with Duke Ellington's orchestra and later played mostly with small groups. Some of Gee's compositions are "Wow," "The Swingers," "Get the Blues, Too," and "Gee!" He recorded with Gillespie, Basie, Ellington, Jacquet, Ammons, Stitt, King Pleasure, Lou Donaldson, and Johnny Griffin.

Geller, Herbert "Herb" (b. 1928). An altoist, Geller worked with Joe Venuti and Claude Thornhill in the late forties. He spent the fifties as a major player on the West Coast jazz scene with Billy May, Maynard Ferguson, Shorty Rogers, Bill Holman, Benny Goodman, Louis Bellson, and his own group. Geller later moved to Germany where he has performed with Kenny Clarke, Benny Bailey, Friedrich Gulda, and the West Berlin Radio Orchestra. He has also taught at conservatories in Hamburg and Bremen. Geller won *Downbeat*'s New Star poll in 1955 and has recorded with

Chet Baker, Dinah Washington, Barney Kessel, Shelly Manne, Marty Paich, and others.

Geller, Lorraine (1928–1958). Lorraine, a pianist, toured with the International Sweethearts of Rhythm from 1949 to 1952. She married Herb Geller and moved with him to Los Angeles where she worked with Shorty Rogers, Maynard Ferguson, Zoot Sims, Stan Getz, Charlie Parker, Dizzy Gillespie, Kay Starr, and Herb Geller's group. She recorded in 1956 as a leader with Red Mitchell.

Getz, Stanley "Stan" (1927–1991). A tenorist, Getz made his professional debut with Dick "Stinky" Rogers in 1942 and worked with Jack Teagarden, Bob Chester, Stan Kenton, Benny Goodman, and Tommy Dorsey before playing in Woody Herman's Second Herd from 1947 to 1949. Getz rose to prominence with Herman's Four Brothers saxophone section (including Zoot Sims, Al Cohn, and Serge Chaloff). After Herman, Getz led his own groups, toured Scandinavia as a soloist, worked in NBC's studios in New York City, played with Kenton, and toured with Jazz at the Philharmonic in the fifties. After a hiatus from music, Getz resumed his career as a bandleader and became a dominant jazz figure with the album *Jazz Samba*, which featured guitarist Charlie Byrd and the music of Antonio Carlos Jobim. After the album became a big hit, Getz recorded *Jazz Samba Encore* with Luis Bonfa and *The Girl from Ipanema* with Astrud Gilberto. The latter album became one of the most popular crossover albums in the history of jazz. Getz's unique way of blending jazz and bossa nova made a major impact on American popular music, and it established him as one of the most successful artists in jazz.

Gibbs, Terry (b. 1924). Gibbs, a vibist-percussionist-composer, worked with Aaron Sachs, Tommy Dorsey, Chubby Jackson, Buddy Rich, and Woody Herman in the forties. Gibbs led his own groups, worked as music director for Mel Tormé's television show, played with Benny Goodman's sextet, and led his own big band on the West Coast during the fifties. From the sixties through the eighties, Gibbs worked as music director for Steve Allen and Regis Philbin, won *Downbeat*'s New Star Award in 1962, and co-led a group with Buddy DeFranco. Gibbs' adaptable style bridged the gap between swing and bop and can be heard on recordings by Herman, Goodman, Rich, and Stan Getz.

Gillespie, John "Dizzy" (1917–1993). Gillespie, a famous bebop trumpeter-bandleader-composer, started his professional career with Frank Fairfax's band in Philadelphia before moving to New York City, where he joined Teddy Hill's band in the late thirties. He also toured with Hill, played with the Savoy Sultans, rejoined Hill, and worked with Mercer Ellington. In

1939, Gillespie joined Cab Calloway's orchestra and remained with the group until 1941. Subsequently, he worked with Benny Carter, Earl Hines, Charlie Barnet, Duke Ellington, and Lucky Millinder before joining Billy Eckstine's innovative big band as trumpeter and music director. Gillespie formed his first big band in 1945 and toured for a few months but disbanded to participate in the bebop movement with small groups. A year later, Gillespie re-formed his big band, then won *Metronome*'s Band of the Year award in 1947. During that two-year period, Gillespie's band recorded tunes such as "Ray's Idea," "Our Delight," and "Things to Come" for the Musicraft label in 1946. He switched to RCA Victor Records in 1947 and recorded "Two Bass Hit," "Cool Breeze," "Oop-Pop-A-Da," and "Cubana Be, Cubana Bop," which revolutionized the sound of big-band music in the Later Swing Era.

Giuffre, James "Jimmy" (b. 1921). Giuffre, a woodwind instrumentalist-composer, gained national recognition as a composer after writing the famous "Four Brothers" chart for Woody Herman's band in 1950. Giuffre, an accomplished clarinetist, flutist, and saxophonist, worked with Boyd Raeburn and Jimmy Dorsey in the late forties and with Buddy Rich in 1950. After playing and writing for Herman in 1950, he played with Shorty Rogers and The Lighthouse All-Stars and toured with Jazz at the Philharmonic throughout the fifties. Giuffre continued to lead his own groups and write in different musical styles from small groups to string orchestras. He taught for a number of years at the New England Conservatory.

Gleason's Musical Bar. Established in Cleveland, Ohio, in 1944, the club presented both jazz and blues artists for about twenty years. The early fifties witnessed artists such as Johnny Hodges, Illinois Jacquet, Snooky Young, James Moody, Bennie Green, and Dizzy Gillespie in performance at the venue.

Glenn, Tyree (1912–1974). Glenn was probably the only trombonist to double on the vibraphone. He gained professional experience with Tommy Mills, Charlie Echols, Eddie Barefield, Eddie Mallory, and Benny Carter before playing in Cab Calloway's band from 1940 to 1946. Glenn toured Europe with Don Redman in 1946 and played in Duke Ellington's orchestra from 1947 to 1950, doubling on trombone and vibes. After Ellington, Glenn replaced Tiny Kahn on the vibraphone with Jack Sterling's CBS daily radio show from 1953 to 1963. Glenn also led his own group and recorded six albums for the Roulette label while working as a studio musician. He later played with Louis Armstrong for six years and appeared at the 1972 Newport Jazz Festival.

Glow, Bernie (b. 1926). A trumpeter, Glow began working professionally as a teenager with Louis Prima before playing with Raymond Scott's CBS band, Artie Shaw, Boyd Raeburn, and Woody Herman in the forties. Glow worked as a staff musician from 1950 to 1955 and established himself as an excellent lead trumpeter. He played in many recording sessions with such musicians as Herman, Miles Davis and Gil Evans, Dizzy Gillespie, Gunther Schuller, J. J. Johnson, George Benson, and Gato Barbieri.

Gonsalves, Paul (1920–1974). Gonsalves, a long-standing featured tenor soloist with Duke Ellington for almost twenty-five years, played with Sabby Lewis' Boston-based band in the early forties until military service. After the war, he rejoined Lewis briefly before working in Count Basie's orchestra and Dizzy Gillespie's big band in the late forties. Gonsalves had an in-depth knowledge of the styles of Ben Webster and Don Byas but developed himself as a unique soloist as can be heard in such ballads as "Chelsea Bridge" and "Happy Reunion." He is best identified, however, with his legendary twenty-seven-chorus solo on "Dimenuendo and Cresendo in Blue" with Ellington at the Newport Jazz Festival in 1956, as well as on a similar version of "Take the 'A' Train." Gonsalves was undoubtedly one of the top swing-styled tenorists of his day.

Gonzales, Lee "Babs" (1919–1980). Gonzales began working as a professional vocalist with Charlie Barnet and Benny Carter in the early forties. He formed a vocal trio in the mid-forties and worked on 52nd Street at the time of his first recording for Blue Note in 1947. From the late forties through the seventies, he recorded with a number of bop musicians, worked as a disc jockey and promoter, managed James Moody, and toured throughout Europe. Gonzales' composition "Oop-Pop-a-Da" became popular with Dizzy Gillespie. Gonzales later wrote a book entitled *I Paid My Dues: Movin' on Down de Line.*

Gordon, Dexter (1923–1990). Gordon, a tenorist, landed his first important job with Lionel Hampton in 1940 and stayed with him until 1943. Gordon spent six months with Louis Armstrong in 1944 before joining Billy Eckstine's big band and recording his first solo on "Blowin' the Blues Away." Gordon recorded "Blue 'n' Boogie" with Dizzy Gillespie, led his own sessions for Savoy Records, and played on recordings by Benny Carter, Sir Charles Thompson, and Red Norvo. Although Gordon recorded two albums in 1955, he was mostly inactive musically during much of the fifties. He made a remarkable comeback, however, in the early sixties and went on to have a highly successful career.

Gordon, Joseph "Joe" (1928–1963). A trumpeter, Gordon led his own small group at the Savoy in Boston around 1947. He later played in the bands of Georgie Auld and Lionel Hampton before working with Charlie Parker sporadically between 1952 and 1955. He also worked with Dizzy Gillespie and Horace Silver in the mid-fifties and moved to Los Angeles where he worked with Harold Land, Benny Carter, Shelly Manne, Barney Kessel, and Dexter Gordon.

Gordon, Robert "Bob" (1928–1955). Gordon, a baritone saxophonist, began playing professionally at age eighteen. He worked in the bands of Alvino Rey, Billy May, and Horace Heidt between 1948 and 1952. From 1952 until the end of his life, Gordon participated in a number of recording sessions with Chet Baker, Clifford Brown, Stan Kenton, Maynard Ferguson, Shelly Manne, Lennie Niehaus, and others.

Gozzo, Conrad (1922–1964). A trumpeter, Gozzo made his professional debut in Isham Jones' band in 1938. From 1939 to 1942, Gozzo worked with Tommy Reynolds, Red Norvo, Johnny "Scat" Davis, Bob Chester, Claude Thornhill, and Benny Goodman prior to playing in Artie Shaw's navy band until 1945. After military service, Gozzo rejoined Goodman briefly and worked with Woody Herman, Boyd Raeburn, and Tex Beneke before moving to Los Angeles in 1947. He played on Bob Crosby's radio show for the next four years and established himself as a first-call lead trumpeter. He recorded with Goodman, Herman, Harry James, Ray Anthony, Stan Kenton, Shorty Rogers, Billy May, Buddy Rich, and others. Gozzo was best known for his feature on Herman's recording of "Stars Fell on Alabama."

Graas, John (1924–1962). A French hornist-composer, Graas began playing professionally with the Indianapolis Symphony Orchestra in 1941 and left a year later to work with Claude Thornhill. Afterward, Graas led an army band from 1942 to 1945. Following military service, he played in the Cleveland Symphony for a year and worked with Tex Beneke and Stan Kenton until 1950. Graas moved to Hollywood in the early fifties and freelanced in the studios. He also wrote many television and film scores and toured with Liberace. He was considered a first-rate French horn player and composer who passed away at an early age. He recorded as a leader and with Kenton, Shorty Rogers, Gerry Mulligan, Bob Cooper, and Pete Rugolo.

Graettinger, Robert "Bob" (1923–1957). A Canadian-born saxophonist-composer-arranger, Graettinger made his professional debut with Bobby Sherwood at age sixteen. For a number of years, Graettinger worked in the bands of Benny Carter, Jan Savitt, Johnny Richards, and Alvino Rey before concentrating full time on arranging and composing. He joined Stan Kenton and wrote arrangements such as "Autumn in New York" and "Laura" as well as his own pieces such as "Incident in Jazz," "City of Glass," and "House of Strings." His jazz writing style leaned more in the direction of American and European avant-garde composers. His modern jazz compositions are featured in Kenton's Capitol Records CD titled *Stan Kenton Plays Bob Graettinger*.

Gramercy Five. A small group Artie Shaw organized in 1940. He led three different groups with the same name during his career that included such musicians as Roy Eldridge, Billy Butterfield, Barney Kessel, John Guarnieri, Dodo Marmarosa, Hank Jones, Joe Roland, Tal Farlow, Joe Puma, Al Hendrickson, Morris Rayman, Nick Fatool, and Lou Fromm.

Granz, Norman (1918–2001). An entrepreneur and founder of Verve Records, Granz discovered jazz on the radio during the Swing Era. After listening to Coleman Hawkins' 1939 recording of "Body and Soul," he realized that swing was more than just dance music. Granz began organizing jam sessions in Los Angeles in 1942 and produced his first recording session with Lester Young, Nat "King" Cole, and Red Callender. In 1944, Granz took his jam sessions to the concert hall, which became the first Jazz at the Philharmonic concert. After hearing a transcription of the concert over an Armed Forces Radio broadcast, he concluded that a live recording could document a level of excitement from a performance that is not possible in a studio. In 1945, he formed his own record company and issued *Jazz at the Philharmonic, Volume 1* on Asch Records. By the early fifties, he was organizing concerts, managing talent, and producing records on his own record label (Clef). Jazz at the Philharmonic concerts featured practically all of the top musicians such as Lionel Hampton, Dizzy Gillespie, Lester Young, Ella Fitzgerald, Stan Getz, Roy Eldridge, Buddy Rich, Charlie Parker, Ray Brown, Flip Phillips, and Illinois Jacquet, to name a few. In 1956, with Ella Fitzgerald's career in his hands, he consolidated his three jazz labels (Clef, Down Home, and Norgram) under the Verve banner and produced Fitzgerald's popular songbook series. Granz later discontinued the semi-annual national Jazz at the Philharmonic tours and concentrated on building his record catalog, which by the end of the fifties numbered over one thousand albums. Some of his classic albums include Art Tatum's famous solo recordings that are now in the Grammy Hall of Fame. Granz produced other albums that featured such artists as Oscar Peterson, Flip Phillips, Count Basie, and Fred Astaire. Granz continued the Jazz at the Philharmonic tours in Europe throughout the sixties with artists as diverse as Marlene Dietrich and John Coltrane. Granz produced his last session on Verve entitled *Ella Fitzgerald: All That Jazz* in 1989.

Gray, Wardell (1921–1955). A tenorist, Gray worked with local bands in Detroit as a teenager. He later played with Earl Hines, Benny Carter, Billy Eckstine, and recorded "The Chase" with Dexter Gordon. Gray also recorded "Relaxin' at Camarillo" with Charlie Parker and performed in a series of concerts produced by Gene Norman. Benny Goodman heard Gray in one of Norman's concerts and invited him to join his sextet in New York in 1948. Gray played with Count Basie briefly and rejoined Goodman as a member of his big band in 1948 and 1949. Gray's style, influenced by Lester Young and Charlie Parker, is heard at its best on his own recording of "Sweet Georgia Brown."

Greco, Buddy (b. 1926). Greco, a pianist-vocalist, began performing in public at age sixteen. Shortly thereafter, Benny Goodman hired him for a job that lasted four years. With the experience gained from Goodman, Greco began a solo career that led to his most successful hit, "The Lady Is a Tramp." Greco later became one of the top-ranking entertainers in Las Vegas and a frequent hit-making recording artist. The nineties found Greco still selling out concerts in the Emerald City and recording hit-making albums. As a Las Vegas entertainer, it is ironic that he is an average singer—but an excellent pianist.

Green, Bennie (1923–1977). A trombonist, Green began playing professionally with local Chicago groups. He joined Earl Hines in 1942, served in World War II, and rejoined Hines from 1946 to 1948. Green worked with Gene Ammons before playing with Charlie Ventura's group from 1948 to 1950 where he gained national attention. Green returned to Hines' group and toured the country between 1951 and 1953. His resonant and warm sound, clean articulation, and smooth legato style can be heard on Charlie Ventura's recordings of "Eupohoria," "Sweet Georgia Brown," and "I'm Forever Blowing Bubbles."

Green, Urban "Urbie" (b. 1926). Green, a trombonist, began playing professionally at age sixteen with the bands of Bob Strong and Tommy Reynolds before working on the West Coast with Frankie Carle and Jan Savitt between 1945 and 1947. He played with Gene Krupa from 1947 to 1950 and achieved national recognition with Woody Herman's band from 1950 to 1953. After Herman, Green became a studio musician and worked with Buck Clayton, Benny Goodman, Count Basie, and Elliot Lawrence. Green also led the Tommy Dorsey Orchestra and his own bands that played for concerts and dances in a variety of venues. He has a big, dark sound on the instrument and plays with exceptional precision and control. He won the *Downbeat* Critics New Star award in 1954.

Greenlee, Charles (1927–1993). A trombonist, Greenlee first played with Floyd Ray in 1944. In 1945, Greenlee worked with Benny Carter, Buddy Johnson, and Lucky Millinder before playing in the bands of Dizzy Gillespie and Lucky Thompson between 1946 and 1948. He rejoined Gillespie during 1949 and 1950 and played with Gene Ammons in 1950. A year later, Greenlee retired from music for a while but returned with Yusef Lateef's group in 1957 and joined Maynard Ferguson in 1959 on a full-time basis. He later taught at the University of Massachusetts–Amherst and recorded for the Baystate record label.

Grey, Albert "Al" (1925–2000). Trombonist Al Grey played bugle, served as a drum master for the navy, and played in a navy dance band during World War II. After discharge in 1945, he joined Benny Carter's Chocolate Dandies. He also played in Carter's big band before working with Jimmie Lunceford and Lucky Millinder in the late forties and with Lionel Hampton from 1948 to 1952, when he started playing with a plunger mute. He worked for Decca Records as a studio musician in 1952 and 1953 and played with Gatemouth Brown, Arnett Cobb, Oscar Pettiford, and Dizzy Gillespie from 1954 to 1957. Grey reached international prominence as a member of Count Basie's orchestra between 1957 and 1961, where he was featured on "Blues in Hoss Flat" and other jazz classics. He performed and recorded in a variety of jazz settings and established himself as the world's foremost plunger mute player on the trombone.

Grimes, Lloyd "Tiny" (1916–1989). A guitarist, Grimes first played piano and danced at the Rhythm Club in New York City. He later switched to the four-string electric guitar and played with the Cats and a Fiddle from 1939 to 1941. He established himself professionally as a member of the famed Art Tatum trio with Slam Stewart in the early forties. Grimes also recorded as a sideman with Charlie Parker and led a rhythm-and-blues band called the Rocking Highlanders that featured tenor saxophonist Red Prysock in the mid-forties. After disbanding, Grimes toured the Midwest with his new band in the early fifties and worked in New York City where he performed regularly in Harlem and Greenwich Village. He toured Europe and performed regularly throughout the remainder of his life.

Gryce, George "Gigi" (1925–1983). Gryce, an altoist-flutist-composer, studied composition extensively at the Boston Conservatory and in Paris on a Fulbright Fellowship with Nadia Boulanger and Arthur Honegger. Gryce played with Lionel Hampton, Art Farmer, and Tadd Dameron, and led his own groups in the fifties. Gryce spent most of the sixties and seventies teaching in Ghana and New York. His jazz compositions include "Hymn to the Orient," "Minority," and "Nica's Tempo." He recorded with Art Farmer, Dizzy Gillespie, Benny Golson, Duke Jordan, and Oscar Pettiford, and as a leader.

Guarnieri, John "Johnny" (1917–1985). A pianist-composer, Guarnieri first played professionally with George Hall and Benny Goodman in the late thirties. He played with Artie Shaw, Jimmy Dorsey, Raymond Scotts' CBS radio orchestra, and Cozy Cole and recorded with Lester Young, Slam

Stewart, Ben Webster, Roy Eldridge, Louis Armstrong, and Don Byas in the forties. Guarnieri later worked as a staff musician for NBC in New York City before moving to the West Coast, where he played at the Hollywood Plaza hotel as a solo pianist and recorded as a leader in the sixties. During the next decade, he performed as a solo pianist and toured Europe with Slam Stewart. He specialized in stride piano playing, composed over 3,500 tunes, and wrote a book entitled *From Ragtime to Tatum*. Guarnieri recorded with Goodman, Dorsey, Armstrong, Stewart, Ruby Braff, Buddy Tate, Jack Teagarden, and Vic Dickenson.

Gwaltney, Thomas "Tommy" (b. 1921). A clarinetist-altoist-vibist, Gwaltney studied privately, played with college bands, and served in an army band in the early forties. As a result of health problems sustained in the war, he switched to vibes for a while and then played with Charlie Byrd and Sol Yaged in the late forties. Gwaltney worked with Bobby Hackett, Billy Butterfield, and again with Byrd from the late forties through the early sixties. Since 1965, he has spent most of his time promoting the Virginia Beach Jazz Festival, managing the Blues Alley jazz club in Washington, D.C., and playing with his own group. He has recorded as a leader and with Bobby Hackett.

Hagood, Kenneth "Kenny" (1926–1989). A vocalist, Hagood began singing professionally at age seventeen and worked with Benny Carter, Dizzy Gillespie, and Tadd Dameron in the forties. Hagood later lived in Paris for a number of years before returning to his hometown of Detroit where he worked in the late eighties. He recorded with Thelonious Monk, Miles Davis, Gillespie, and Charlie Parker.

The Haig. A small Los Angeles nightclub that presented numerous solo pianists in the forties and featured many West Coast jazz groups led by such musicians as Lee Konitz, Gerry Mulligan, Wardell Gray, Warne Marsh, and Curtis Counce.

Hall, Alfred "Al" (1915–1988). Hall, a bassist, worked with Billy Hicks, Skeets Tolbert, and Teddy Wilson's orchestra in the thirties. Hall later played with Wilson's sextet, Ellis Larkins, Mary Lou Williams, Kenny Clarke, Erroll Garner, and on *The Mildred Bailey Show* as a CBS staff musician in the forties. In the fifties, Hall worked again with Garner, played briefly with Count Basie, freelanced, played in Broadway show bands, and worked with Harry Belafonte. Hall worked on Broadway and as a freelancer in the sixties and seventies with Yves Montand, Phil Moore, Benny Goodman, Hazel Scott, Tiny Grimes, Alberta Hunter, Doc Cheatham, and others. Hall's versatility is evident in the recordings he made with Wilson, Garner, Clarke,

Goodman, Paul Gonsalves, Duke Ellington, Johnny Hodges, Helen Merrill, Jack Teagarden, Sonny Stitt, and others.

Hambone Kelly's. A venue in El Cerrito, California, that featured Dixieland musicians such as Kid Ory, Lou Watters, James P. Johnson, and Mutt Carey in the late forties.

Hamilton, Chico (b. 1928). Hamilton started his professional career as a drummer with Floyd Ray and Lionel Hampton in 1940, and he worked with Slim Gaillard, Lester Young, and Duke Ellington before serving in the military for four years. After discharge in 1946, he played with Jimmy Mundy and Count Basie for two years and joined Lena Horne from 1948 to 1955. During that time, he worked with other vocalists such as Billy Eckstine, Sarah Vaughn, Nat "King" Cole, Ella Fitzgerald, Billie Holiday, and Sammy Davis, Jr. After the Swing Era, Hamilton has mostly led his own groups with sidemen such as Buddy Colette, Jim Hall, Eric Dolphy, Charles Lloyd, Gabor Szabo, Arnie Lawrence, Richard Davis, George Bohanan, Arthur Blythe, Larry Coryell, and Steve Turre. Hamilton currently performs, records, and teaches in the jazz program at the New School in New York City.

Hamilton, James "Jimmy" (1917–1994). A clarinetist-saxophonist-composer, Hamilton learned several instruments including trumpet, trombone, piano, and saxophone before playing in Frank Fairfax's trumpet section with Dizzy Gillespie and Charlie Shavers in 1935. After switching to clarinet and saxophone, Hamilton played in the bands of Lucky Millinder and Jimmy Mundy before working in Teddy Wilson's big band from 1939 to 1941. Hamilton played in Benny Carter's sextet from 1941 to 1942, with subsequent work in the bands of Eddie Heywood and Yank Porter. Hamilton joined the Duke Ellington Orchestra in 1943 as one of its featured clarinet and/or tenor saxophone soloists and remained until 1968. Afterward, he relocated to St. Croix, Virgin Islands, where he led his own quartet and taught high school.

Handy, George (1920–1997). Handy, a pianist-composer-arranger, began his career at age eighteen with Michael Loring while still a student at the Juilliard School of Music. He later played with Raymond Scott and started writing music in 1941. Handy's most significant charts were written for Boyd Raeburn from 1944 to 1945, and again in 1946. Some of his charts for Raeburn include "There's No You," "Out of This World," "Tonsillectomy," "Yerxa," "Dalvatore Sally," and "Hey Look—I'm Dancing." Handy also arranged for the Armed Forces Radio Service, Alvino Rey, Ina Ray Hutton, and Herbie Fields. Handy played piano, arranged and composed, and recorded with Dizzy Gillespie and Charlie Parker, the Vivien Garry Trio, and Zoot Sims. As a leader, Handy recorded two albums for RCA.

Hangover Club. An important club that presented Dixieland jazz in the forties and fifties on Vine Street in Hollywood. Some of the musicians who played long residencies there include Earl Hines, Peter Dailey, and Bob Zurke.

Harden, Wilbur (1925–1969). A trumpeter-flugelhornist from Birmingham, Alabama, Harden played professionally in the blues bands of Roy Brown and Ivory Joe Hunter in the late forties and early fifties followed by membership in a navy band. Afterward, he joined Yusef Lateef's quintet in 1957 and led four recording dates for the Savoy label in 1958. He also appeared with John Coltrane and Curtis Fuller on subsequent Savoy recording sessions. Harden's historical significance rests in the fact that he was one of the first jazz trumpeters to double on flugelhorn. Furthermore, he was a fiery player with a uniquely dark and resonant sound on both instruments. Unfortunately, Harden was forced to retire from playing because of illness. It is important to note here that he recorded "Hard Luck and Good Rocking" with Roy Brown in 1947 at the height of the Later Swing Era.

Harding, Lavere "Buster" (1917–1965). Harding, a pianist-arranger, taught himself before studying formally with Schillinger in New York City. Harding led his own band in Cleveland, Ohio, and worked as an arranger-second pianist in Teddy Wilson's big band during the thirties. He led his own quartet in New York City, worked as Cab Calloway's staff arranger, accompanied Billie Holiday, played in Roy Eldridge's big band, and freelanced as an arranger in the forties. He continued as a freelance arranger-composer for the next fifteen years, and some of his clients included Holiday, Jonah Jones, and Dizzy Gillespie. Harding was best known as an excellent swing-styled arranger who also played in Jonah Jones' famous quartet in the early sixties. Some of Harding's well-known charts are "Jonah Joins the Cab," "A Smooth One," "Little Jazz," "Rockin' the Blues," "Hobnail Boogie," "Nails," and "Paradise Squat." He recorded with Holiday and Eldridge.

Harper, Herbert "Herbie" (b. 1920). Harper started his professional career as a trombonist with a Texas territory band. He later played in the bands of Johnny "Scat" Davis, Gene Krupa, Charlie Spivak, Benny Goodman, Charlie Barnet, and Teddy Edwards in the forties. Harper worked with Stan Kenton, Jerry Gray, Ray Brown, June Christy, and Maynard Ferguson in the fifties before playing in the NBC studio orchestra on the West Coast. He worked with Bob Florence off and on into the eighties. Harper recorded with Billie Holiday, Steve White, Roger Newman, Marty Paich, and Bill Perkins.

Harris, Benjamin "Little Benny" (1919–1975). A trumpeter, Harris shined shoes and studied aviation before entering the music profession. His music career began when he joined Tiny Bradshaw's band in 1939 and remained for six months. He joined Earl Hines in 1941 and later worked with Pete Brown, John Kirby, Don Redman, Benny Carter, Herbie Fields, Boyd Raeburn, Don Byas, and many others. Although Harris worked with many swing bands, he became a key figure in the bop movement through his association with Dizzy Gillespie and Charlie Parker. Harris' most enduring musical contributions are his compositions such as "Ornithology," "Reets and I," "Crazeology," "Wahoo," and "Bud's Bubble."

Harris, Charles "Charlie" (b. 1916). A bassist, Harris toured with Mac Crockette from 1939 to 1943 and worked with Lionel Hampton, Herbie Fields, Milt Buckner, and Arnett Cobb throughout the forties. He toured with Nat "King" Cole and played with Stuff Smith in the fifties before working with Stan Kenton in 1960. Harris recorded with Hampton, Cole, and Wynonie Harris.

Harris, Willard "Bill" (1916–1973). Harris was a trombonist who worked with Gene Krupa and Ray McKinley briefly before playing in the bands of Bob Chester and Benny Goodman during the early forties. Harris led his own sextet with Zoot Sims, Ernie Figueroa, Clyde Hart, Specs Powell, and Sid Weiss at the Café Society Uptown in 1944 and recorded for the Commodore label. Harris joined Woody Herman in 1944 and remained until the band broke up in 1946. He also worked with Charlie Ventura and toured with Jazz at the Philharmonic before rejoining Herman in 1948. His exciting style is heard at its best on Herman's recordings of "Apple Honey" and "Bijou."

Harris, Wynonie (1915–1969). A hard-swinging vocalist-drummer, Harris began his career as a comedian and dancer. He later taught himself to play drums and formed his own band but established himself as a vocalist with Lucky Millinder's orchestra. Harris' work with Millinder resulted in two big hits called "Hurry Hurry" and "Who Threw the Whiskey in the Well." Afterward, Harris recorded as a leader and became a major attraction in 1948 with his big hit of "Good Rockin' Tonight." Other hits such as "I Like My Baby's Puddin'" and "Drinkin' Wine Spo-Dee-Oh-Dee" followed until 1952 when he changed his style and recorded less-suggestive songs that ultimately ended his career.

Hartman, John "Johnny" (1923–1983). Hartman, a vocalist-pianist, served in the military during World War II and worked with Earl Hines in 1947 before singing with Dizzy Gillespie's big band from 1947 to 1949. After leaving Gillespie, he worked with Erroll Garner in 1949 and began a solo career that included frequent club dates, international tours, and television appearances. Hartman performed and recorded with John Coltrane, Roland Hanna, George Mraz, and others from the sixties to the early eighties. Hartman's smooth baritone voice can also be heard on his own 1955 Bethlehem recording.

Hawes, Hampton (1928–1977). Hawes, a pianist, taught himself how to play and worked professionally while attending high school. During the forties, he worked with Big Jay McNeely, Wardell Gray, Sonny Criss, and Dexter Gordon. Hawes performed with Charlie Parker, Shorty Rogers, and Howard Rumsey before spending three years in military service and leading his own trio from 1950 to 1958. Between 1958 and 1963, he was inactive musically but resumed his career and worked with Jon Hendricks, Jackie McLean, Harold Land, Red Mitchell, and Jimmy Garrison in the mid-sixties. Hawes toured internationally during the late sixties and played in duos with Leroy Vinnegar, Carole Kaye, and Mario Suraci in the seventies. He also performed at a number of European jazz festivals and recorded with Joan Baez and Charlie Haden. Hawes also recorded with Art Farmer, Barney Kessel, Art Pepper, Sonny Rollins, and Freddie Redd.

Haymer, Herbert "Herbie" (1915–1949). A tenorist, Haymer started out playing alto saxophone with local New Jersey bands in the early thirties. He later switched to tenor and played in the Carl Sears–Johnny Watson Orchestra. He played stints with Charlie Barnet and Rudy Vallee before gaining national recognition with Red Norvo and Jimmy Dorsey between 1935 and 1941. Haymer also worked with Benny Goodman, Dave Hudkins, Woody Herman, and Kay Kyser before army service in the mid-forties. He later settled in California and played with Red Nichols, freelanced, and worked in the studios. Haymer recorded with Norvo, Dorsey, Herman, Charlie Shavers, Nat "King" Cole, and Buddy Rich.

Haynes, Roy (b. 1925). Haynes, a drummer-bandleader, began playing professionally in Boston with Sabby Lewis, Frankie Newton, and Pete Brown in the early forties. From 1945 to 1949, he worked with Luis Russell, Lester Young, Kai Winding, Bud Powell, and Miles Davis. Haynes played with Charlie Parker from 1949 to 1953 and worked throughout the fifties with Stan Getz, Sarah Vaughn, Phineas Newborn, Lee Konitz, Thelonious Monk, Kenny Burrell, Lennie Tristano, George Shearing, and Lambert, Hendricks, and Ross. Haynes led his own group, substituted for Elvin Jones with John Coltrane's quartet, and worked with Stan Getz in the sixties. The seventies saw him in groups led by Billy Taylor, Dizzy Gillespie, and Chick Corea. Since the eighties, Haynes has mostly led and recorded with his own groups. He has won several awards including an honorary doctorate from Berklee

College of Music in 1992. Although Haynes developed his inventive style in the Later Swing Era, he combined both swing and bop languages effectively as heard in recordings by Young, Vaughn, Parker, Davis, Monk, Wardell Gray, Dave Brubeck, Oliver Nelson, Milt Jackson, and many others.

Heard, Eugene "Fats" (1923–1987). A drummer, Heard studied at the Cleveland Institute of Music and served in the navy during World War II. From the late forties to the early fifties, he played with Lionel Hampton and Erroll Garner. After leaving Garner in 1955, he returned to Cleveland, Ohio, and toured off and on with Sarah Vaughn, Teddy Wilson, and Carmen McRae until retiring from music in 1959. During his career, he recorded with Garner.

Heard, James "J. C." (1917–1988). Heard, a drummer-bandleader, joined Teddy Wilson's orchestra in 1939 and worked in the forties with Benny Carter, Cab Calloway, and Erroll Garner before leading his own group, freelancing, and touring overseas. He co-led a band with Toshiko Akiyoshi in Japan and freelanced in China, the Philippines, and Australia in the mid-fifties. Afterward, he returned to New York City where he worked with Roy Eldridge, Coleman Hawkins, and Lester Lanin, while leading his own bands and touring Europe with Sammy Price in the late fifties. In the early sixties, Heard led his own groups on the West Coast and played with Dorothy Donegan in New York City. He later appeared as a single with all-star bands in Europe and the United States. He recorded with numerous artists who admired his refined style ranging from swing to bop.

Heath, James "Jimmy" (b. 1926). A saxophonist, Heath worked with Nat Towles, Howard McGhee, Gil Fuller, Dizzy Gillespie, Percy, and his own band during the forties. In the fifties, he played with Kenny Dorham, Miles Davis, and the Gil Evans Orchestra. He later played with Donald Byrd and Art Farmer, led his own group, became active as a composer-arranger, and started teaching for Jazzmobile in New York City. As a composer-arranger, he wrote for Chet Baker, Blue Mitchell, Yusef Lateef, Milt Jackson, Billy Taylor, Clark Terry, and for European radio bands. Heath spent a considerable amount of time teaching at several colleges in New York and Connecticut between 1973 and his retirement in 1998. Some of his compositions include "Gingerbread Boy," "CTA," and "Three Ears." He has recorded with the Heath Brothers, Miles Davis, J. J. Johnson, Nat Adderley, Sam Jones, Elmo Hope, and others. Although much of Heath's career has been spent performing and recording in bop-style groups, he is actually a swing musician who expresses himself well in a bop setting.

Heath, Percy (b. 1923). A bassist, Heath served in the military as a fighter pilot and studied at the Granoff School of Music in Philadelphia before playing his first professional job with pianist Red Garland in 1946. After serving as the house bassist at Philadelphia's Downbeat club, Heath moved to New York City and worked with Howard McGhee, J. J. Johnson, Miles Davis, and others in the late forties. He joined Milt Jackson's quartet in 1951 and later spent most of his career with the Modern Jazz Quartet.

Hefti, Neal (b. 1922). Hefti, a trumpeter-arranger, wrote his first arrangements for Nat Towles' band while in high school. Hefti worked in the bands of Bob Astor, Charlie Barnet, Horace Heidt, and Charlie Spivak in the early forties and toured with Woody Herman's band between 1944 and 1946. Hefti first established himself as an arranger for Herman with such charts as "Woodchopper's Ball," "The Good Earth," and "Blowin' Up a Storm." He later contributed such arrangements as "Li'l Darling," "Cute," "Little Pony," and "Whirlybird" to the Count Basie Orchestra after writing for Charlie Ventura and Harry James in the late forties. After the Swing Era, Hefti focused mostly on writing for television and movies, yet his level of success as an arranger-composer of big-band swing music is practically unparalleled.

Henderson, Luther (b. 1919). Henderson, a pianist-arranger-composer, studied at Juilliard, the Navy School of Music, and New York University prior to working with Mercer Ellington and as Lena Horne's pianist-music director in the forties. Afterward, Henderson worked as a music director for many Broadway and off-Broadway shows including *Ain't Misbehavin'*, *Purlie*, *Doctor Jazz*, *Jelly's Last Jam*, *Funny Girl*, and *That's Entertainment*. He has served as a vocal coach, music director, and/or accompanist for Nancy Wilson, Dinah Shore, Eartha Kitt, Liza Minnelli, Florence Henderson, Diahann Carroll, Polly Bergen, and others. Henderson has composed for films and worked on television shows for Bergen, Dean Martin, Ed Sullivan, Carol Burnett, Victor Borge, and the Miss Teen USA Pageant. He recorded as an arranger for Ellington and the Canadian Brass.

Hendricks, Jon (b. 1921). A vocalist-songwriter-drummer from Newark, Ohio, Hendricks grew up singing in church as well as at parties and banquets in his youth. During the thirties, Hendricks sang on radio with occasional accompaniment by Art Tatum after his family moved to Toledo. When his family moved to Detroit in the early forties, he sang with a local band before military duty in Europe from 1942 to 1946. After discharge, he studied at the University of Toledo, taught himself to play drums, and worked as a singer-drummer until 1951. He moved to New York City in 1952 and worked as an office clerk while moonlighting as a songwriter for King Pleasure, Louis Jordan, and others until 1957. After some freelance recording with Dave Lambert and Annie Ross, the Lambert, Hendricks, and Ross vocal trio was formed. The trio recorded and toured with Count Basie in

1958, and by 1959 Hendricks had become an in-demand lyricist. By 1962, Yolande Bavan had replaced Ross, and the vocal trio finally broke up in 1964. Hendricks then worked as a solo artist in the United States, Europe, and Africa until 1972. He finally moved back to the United States and took up residence in California where he worked as a jazz critic, staged a jazz revue at the Broadway Theater in San Francisco, and taught at three universities in northern California. Hendricks has written lyrics to such jazz classics as "High Fly," "Little Niles," "Moanin'," "Along Came Betty," "Now's the Time," "Desafinado," and "Four," to name a few. In addition to his albums with Lambert, Hendricks, and Ross/Bavan, he has recorded with Art Blakey, Al Grey, Manhattan Transfer, King Pleasure, and Jimmy Rowles.

Henry, Ernest "Ernie" (1926–1957). An altoist, Henry started out on violin at age eight and switched to alto at twelve. He began playing with Tadd Dameron's band at the Famous Door on New York City's 52nd Street in 1947 and worked with Charlie Ventura, Fats Navarro, Max Roach, Georgie Auld, and Kenny Dorham in the same year. Henry worked during the fifties in the bands of Dizzy Gillespie, Illinois Jacquet, and Thelonious Monk. Henry was deeply influenced by Charlie Parker but developed his own blues-based style that captured the attention of his peers with his first Riverside recording date as a leader. As a sideman, he recorded with Gillespie, Monk, Dorham, Navarro, and Matthew Gee.

Herbert, Morton "Mort" (1925–1983). Herbert, a bassist, started out on trumpet and later taught himself to play bass. While working with a number of different swing bands in the forties and fifties, he served in the navy from 1943 to 1946, attended Rutgers University between 1949 and 1952, and worked with Sol Yaged, Marian McPartland, Don Elliott, and the Sauter-Finegan Orchestra between 1955 and 1958. He toured with Louis Armstrong in the United States and abroad from 1958 to 1961. After 1962, he worked as a district attorney and a practicing attorney but continued to freelance as a musician with artists such as Herb Ellis. Herbert recorded with Armstrong, Elliott, and as a leader.

Herman, Woodrow "Woody" (1913–1987). Herman, a woodwind instrumentalist-vocalist-bandleader, began his professional career while a teenager with Tom Gerun's band from 1929 to 1933. Herman worked with Harry Sosnik and Gus Arnheim in 1934 and joined the famous Isham Jones Orchestra in 1935. After Jones retired a year later, Herman became the orchestra's leader, but the band struggled during the late thirties despite a hit recording with the "Woodchopper's Ball" in 1939. By the forties, Woody Herman's orchestra was working in some of the country's top venues such as the Glen Island Casino, Chicago's Hotel Sherman, and the Hollywood Palladium. The war completely changed the band's personnel, however, and, by 1945, it was practically a new organization. The band won both *Downbeat* and *Metronome* polls, and its recordings for Columbia yielded favorable sales. Herman disbanded and formed the Second Herd in 1947 that featured the famous Four Brothers saxophone section. Herman later formed several other "Herds" and gained worldwide recognition as a band-leader. He also participated in the country's jazz education movement, and his bands provided professional training for numerous musicians for more than thirty years.

Heywood, Eddie (1915–1989). A pianist-bandleader, Heywood studied piano with his father, Eddie Sr., at the age of eight. Eddie Jr. began playing professionally at age fourteen in his hometown of Atlanta, Georgia, in a theater band. He also worked with Wayman Carver and Clarence Love in the thirties and moved to New York City around 1938. From 1938 to 1941, he freelanced in Harlem nightclubs and played with Benny Carter's orchestra, Zutty Singleton's trio, and Don Redman. Heywood formed his own sextet in 1941 that included Doc Cheatham and Vic Dickenson. After recording with Billie Holiday and performing in such venues as the Village Vanguard, Heywood's group made a hit with its rendition of "Begin The Beguine" in 1944, which established him as a major swing artist. As a result, Heywood's group worked frequently on New York City's 52nd Street and on the West Coast until 1947. Between 1947 and 1950, partial paralysis in his hands forced him to stop performing. He made a successful comeback in 1951, however, and formed a trio that became very popular for its easy listening style and resulted in a major hit with his own composition entitled "Canadian Sunset" in 1956. He continued to perform intermittently and focused much of his attention on composing and arranging.

Hibbler, Albert "Al" (1915–2001). A vocalist, Hibbler was born blind and studied music formally before singing with local Arkansas bands. He worked with Dub Jenkins' band in Memphis, Tennessee, before leading his own band in San Antonio, Texas, in the early forties. He toured with Jay McShann in 1942 and worked with Duke Ellington's band from 1943 to 1951. Hibbler sang in a style some considered controversial but referred to as "tonal pantomime" by Duke Ellington. While with Ellington, Hibbler won *Esquire*'s New Star award in 1947 and *Downbeat*'s Band Vocalist awards in 1948 and 1949. Hibbler's most popular hit was "Unchained Melody." He later recorded with Jimmy Mundy, Mercer Ellington, Billy Taylor, Gerald Wilson, and Count Basie.

Hickory House. Located on New York City's famous 52nd Street, this nightclub opened in the early thirties and hosted numerous Dixieland and swing musicians for over thirty years. The club sponsored many residencies that included musicians such as Joe Marsala, Eddie South, John Kirby and his sextet, Red Norvo, Mary Lou Williams, Hot Lips Page, and Billy Taylor.

Hi Hat. A Boston nightclub that presented musicians such as Charlie Parker and Sonny Stitt with local rhythm sections in the late forties as well as the fifties.

Hill, Roger "Buck" (b. 1927). A tenorist from Washington, D.C., Hill started out playing soprano saxophone before changing to alto and later to tenor. After high school, he played his first professional engagement at the Republic Gardens in 1943. He served in the military during the mid-forties and, after discharge, returned to Washington and worked with Billy White's big band and John Malachi, as well as at the Howard Theater and nightclubs such as the Showboat Lounge. After 1950, Hill alternated between performing and working as either a mail carrier or a cab driver. As a performer, he worked with such jazz luminaries as Sonny Stitt, Max Roach, Milt Jackson, and Shirley Horn in the Washington area. Hill led recording sessions for the Steeplechase label from 1978 to 1981 and for Muse during the eighties.

Hi Note. A Chicago venue at which Coleman Hawkins, Red Norvo, Billie Holiday, Anita O'Day, and Mary Lou Williams appeared in the late forties and early fifties.

Hirt, Alois "Al" (1922–1999). A well-known Dixieland trumpeter, Hirt started playing at age six and studied at the Cincinnati Conservatory in the early forties. After military service in 1946, he toured with the Dorsey Brothers, Ray McKinley, and Horace Heidt. Hirt left the road to work at a radio station in New Orleans for several years before forming a band that gained a strong local following in the mid-fifties. Once the band started recording albums around 1958, it drew national attention, and Hirt eventually became a high-profile artist on the RCA label. He later ran his own Bourbon Street nightclub, appeared on a number of television shows, worked off and on as a single, and led a big band at Carnegie Hall in New York City.

Hodeir, André (b. 1921). A critic-composer from Paris, Hodeir studied at the conservatory from 1942 to 1947, and he played violin with Django Reinhardt from 1947 to 1950. In 1951, Hodeir conducted a recording session for James Moody with strings and became the editor of *Jazz Hot* magazine. He later co-led a group with saxophonist-flutist Bobby Jasper from 1954 to 1969 before teaching in Paris and at Harvard University in the seventies. Hodeir became known as a controversial jazz critic. His books include *Jazz: Its Evolution and Essence*, *Since Debussy*, *Toward Jazz*, and *Worlds of Jazz*. He has composed scores for television and over thirty films.

Holiday, Billie [Elenora Fagan] (1915–1959). Holiday began her professional career as a vocalist at age fifteen in a small Brooklyn, New York, nightclub. She later worked in several other clubs around the city in the early thirties. Producer John Hammond discovered Holiday in 1933, at which point she began making her legendary small-group recordings led by Teddy Wilson, with other top musicians such as Lester Young, Roy Eldridge, Benny Goodman, and Ben Webster for the Columbia label until 1942. During that period, she worked with Count Basie and Artie Shaw. After her Columbia years, Holiday recorded the hit "Travelin' Light" with Paul Whiteman and made history when Decca Records recorded her with strings. The Decca sessions yielded such hits as "Lover Man," "Don't Explain," "Ain't Nobody's Business," and "God Bless the Child." From 1952 to 1959, Holiday recorded for Verve and returned to the small-group recordings that originally made her famous. With later sides like "These Foolish Things," she continued her legacy as one of the most influential vocalists in the history of American popular music.

Holley, Major "Mule" (1924–1990). Holley, a bassist, started out on violin and tuba. He began playing bass in the navy band and, after discharge, continued studying at the Groth School of Music. He later worked with Charlie Parker, Ella Fitzgerald, Dexter Gordon, and Wardell Gray. In 1950, Holley recorded with Oscar Peterson, worked as a staff musician for BBC-TV in London from 1954 to 1956, played with Woody Herman in 1958, and toured with the Al Cohn–Zoot Sims Quintet in 1959 and 1960 in South America for the U.S. State Department. During the sixties, Holley worked with Coleman Hawkins, Roy Eldridge, Kenny Burrell, Quincy Jones, Duke Ellington, and others before teaching at Boston's Berklee College of Music from 1967 to 1970. He later worked at a number of nightclubs in New York City with Jaki Byard and Donald Byrd–Pepper Adams and toured Europe with Helen Humes and the Kings of Jazz. Holley was one of the principal descendants of Slam Stewart, who sang and bowed his solos simultaneously in unison/octaves. Holley's energetic playing lifted the spirits of numerous players and listeners during his life and career. He recorded with countless numbers of musicians including Hawkins, Humes, Sims, Jay McShann, and Harry "Sweets" Edison.

Holloway, James "Red" (b. 1927). Holloway, a saxophonist, studied clarinet and saxophone in high school and served as a leader of the U.S. Fifth Army Band. After discharge in 1946, he attended the Chicago Conservatory and worked with Yusef Lateef and Dexter Gordon until 1948. Afterward, Holloway played for Roosevelt Sykes, several blues artists, Billie Holiday,

Lionel Hampton, Sonny Rollins, and others until the early sixties. From 1963 to 1966, he toured with Jack McDuff and moved to Los Angeles, where he worked in the house band at the Parisian Room between 1969 and 1984, including some European tours. Since the eighties, Holloway has reached a wide audience as a swinging big-toned tenorist who can excite his audiences as well as his peers such as Clark Terry and Horace Silver with whom he has recorded.

Hollywood Canteen. A popular hangout for military personnel during World War II that was located on West Sunset Boulevard in Los Angeles. Some of the musicians who performed there include Lucky Millinder, Lena Horne, Count Basie, and Gerald Wilson.

Hollywood Palladium. In 1940, this legendary dance hall began presenting numerous swing bands that were broadcast live on radio in the forties and on television during the fifties.

Hood, William "Bill" (1924–1992). A baritone saxophonist-composer, Hood originally studied piano but taught himself to play saxophones and compose. After conducting a show in the Pacific at the end of World War II, he played with Freddie Slack in the late forties. In the early fifties, Hood moved to California where he worked with Shorty Rogers, Bill Holman, Chet Baker, Benny Goodman, Terry Gibbs, Benny Carter, Quincy Jones, Jack Nimitz, and others until the early eighties, when he worked as a studio musician. He became inactive in the late eighties because of illness.

Hope, Elmo (1923–1967). Hope, a pianist-composer, studied piano during his youth and won several awards for playing solo recitals during his teens. From 1948 to 1951, he toured with Joe Morris' rhythm-and-blues band and freelanced with Clifford Brown, Sonny Rollins, and others between 1951 and 1956. Hope toured with Chet Baker in 1957 and moved to Los Angeles, where he played with artists such as Lionel Hampton and Harold Land. Hope returned to New York City in 1961 and only played occasionally because of illness during his final years. He was a unique and original composer who used a wide spectrum of harmonic colors in his writing. During his short life and career, he recorded with Brown, Rollins, Jackie McLean, Lou Donaldson, and as a leader.

Horne, Lena (b. 1917). Horne started out as a dancer at the Cotton Club in the mid-thirties and later gained singing experience with Noble Sissle's orchestra. She then sang with Teddy Wilson and Charlie Barnet's orchestra. She became popular as a vocalist at the Café Society and subsequently signed a Hollywood contract to appear in such movies as *Cabin in the Sky*, *Boogie Woogie Dream*, and *Stormy Weather*. Horne was primarily a popular singer who worked mostly with jazz artists such as Horace Henderson, Phil Moore, and Lennie Hayton, who served as her music directors. She published her autobiography, *In Person, Lena Horne* in 1950 and appeared in the Broadway musical *Jamaica* in the late fifties. She remained active in music into the late nineties.

Hucko, Michael "Peanuts" (1918–2003). A clarinetist-tenorist, Hucko worked with Jack Jenney, Will Bradley, Bob Chester, and Joe Marsala before playing in Glenn Miller's Army Air Force Band during World War II. After discharge, he played in the orchestras of Benny Goodman and Ray McKinley. From 1947 to 1950, Hucko played with Eddie Condon and worked in the fifties with Bobby Hackett, Jack Teagarden, ABC and CBS, and Louis Armstrong. During the sixties, he led his own band, played on Lawrence Welk's television show, and led the Glenn Miller Orchestra before forming his own group. Hucko recorded with Bradley, Teagarden, Hackett, Buck Clayton, Chris Connor, and Sidney Bechet.

Humes, Helen (1913–1981). Humes, a strong Swing Era vocalist, could sing in practically any genre ranging from big band swing to rhythm and blues. She developed her big-band singing skills in the orchestras of Victor Andrade, Stuff Smith, and Al Sears. She later recorded with Harry James' band in 1937 and gained prominence after replacing Billie Holiday in Count Basie's orchestra. Humes recorded a number of ballads and blues tunes for several different record labels during the forties. As a solo act, she recorded two hits, "Million Dollar Secret" and "E-Baba-Le-Ba," which combined blues with jazz. She concentrated solely on jazz, however, after the late fifties and recorded two critically acclaimed albums, *Songs I Like to Sing* in 1960 and *Swingin' with Humes* in 1961, for the Contemporary label. She toured with Red Norvo for a while before retiring from music during 1967–1973 and making a comeback at the 1973 Newport Jazz Festival. Afterward, she toured with Basie and recorded for various record labels until the end of her singing career.

Hutton, Betty (b. 1921). A vocalist, Hutton started out singing in a variety of musical genres. She became known, however, as a movie star in such films as *Annie Get Your Gun* in 1950 and *The Greatest Show on Earth* in 1952. Suffice it to say, most of her hits in the forties and fifties resulted from her movies. Her wide-ranging interpretation of songs during the early part of her career can be heard in *Betty Hutton: Best of the RCA Years*.

Hyams, Margie (b. 1923). Hyams, a vibist, was discovered by Woody Herman who hired her to play in his band in 1944. She led her own trio from 1945 to 1948 while playing off and on in some all-female groups that recorded and performed under the leadership of Mary Lou Williams at Carnegie Hall. Hyams later played in George Shearing's quintet in 1949 and 1950. Her solo style effectively combines languages from swing and bop and can be heard on recordings by Herman and Shearing. After Hyams' eighteen-month stint with Shearing's band, she married and retired from music.

Hyman, Richard "Dick" (b. 1927). A pianist-arranger, Hyman studied with Teddy Wilson before working with Dizzy Gillespie, Benny Goodman, Charlie Parker, and as a studio musician in the fifties. He is well known for his work as a solo pianist and composer of musical scores for a number of Woody Allen films. As a pianist, Hyman has re-created the work of historic pianists on *Dick Hyman Plays Duke Ellington*, *The Music of Jelly Roll Morton*, and *Dick Hyman Plays Fats Waller*.

Institute of Jazz Studies. The institute was established in 1952 by noted jazz author Marshall Stearns. It has been housed at Rutgers University in Newark, New Jersey, since the mid-sixties, and its jazz collection now consists of numerous files on individuals and selected topics, over five thousand books, and more than five thousand photographs, band arrangements, and musical scores. The institute's current director is world-renowned jazz author Dan Morgenstern.

International Sweethearts of Rhythm. The most popular all-female big band in the Later Swing Era, the International Sweethearts of Rhythm was organized in 1937 at the Piney Woods School in Mississippi by its principal, Dr. Lawrence C. Jones. The band was originally formed as a fundraising effort to help the school meet its financial goal of educating orphaned African-American and other minority children. After performing around Piney Woods initially, the band eventually toured frequently around the United States and entertained troops overseas during the war years. The band performed at venues such as the Rhumboogie in Chicago, the Apollo in New York City, Washington's Howard Theater, and other establishments in Kansas City, Des Moines (Iowa), the South, and throughout the East Coast. Newspapers and magazines such as the *Pittsburgh Courier* and *Billboard* gave the band excellent reviews. The Sweethearts disbanded in the late forties, and the young women who were members then pursued a variety of professions that ranged from music to medicine.

Isaacs, Charles "Ike" (1923–1981). A bassist, Isaacs played in the army and studied with Wendell Marshall around 1941. He later played with Tiny Grimes and an air force band in 1949 and 1950 prior to working with Earl Bostic, Mat Mathews, Paul Quinichette, and Bennie Green in the early fifties. He formed his own group, the Four Maestros, toured with Carmen McRae as her music director (and husband), and worked as

Lambert, Hendricks, and Ross' music director until the end of the fifties. He later played with Count Basie, Gloria Lynne, and Erroll Garner and led his own trio. Isaacs recorded with Bostic, Green, McRae, Basie, Garner, Ray Bryant, Joe Williams, and others.

Jackson, Benjamin "Bullmoose" (1919–1989). Jackson, a vocalist-tenor saxophonist, became known as a ballad singer with successful recordings of "I Love You" and "Yes I Do" for the King label. He later switched over to a swinging boogie-woogie style with such tunes as "I Want a Bowlegged Woman" and "Ten Inch" that appealed mostly to adult listeners. After the mid-fifties, Jackson ended up working outside of the music profession for the rest of his life except for a brief tour in the seventies with a rhythm-and-blues band.

Jackson, Grieg "Chubby" (b. 1918). Jackson, a bassist, worked in the bands of Mike Riley, Johnny Messner, Raymond Scott, Jan Savitt, Henry Busse, and Charlie Barnet before playing with Woody Herman in the mid-forties and fifties. Jackson was an important member of Herman's band because of his energetic bass playing and the spirit he instilled among the band's members. He also performed with Charlie Ventura's group and led his own quintet on a tour in Sweden. Jackson won *Esquire*'s New Star and Gold Star awards in the mid-forties, and he recorded with the *Esquire* All-Stars on both of their albums for the RCA Victor label.

Jackson, Milton "Milt" (1923-1999). Jackson started out singing and playing the piano before switching to the vibraphone during his teens. He moved to New York City in the mid-forties to play with Dizzy Gillespie's big band and sextet. Jackson worked with Charlie Parker, Woody Herman, Tadd Dameron, and others before leading his own quartet in the early fifties. Jackson's quartet became the Modern Jazz Quartet, and he remained with the group throughout its entire history.

Jackson, Willis "Gator" (1928–1987). Jackson was a tenor and soprano saxophonist who studied music at Florida A&M University and played in Cootie Williams' bands from 1948 to 1955. From that point on, he toured the country with his own group and rhythm-and-blues stars such as Dinah Washington, Jackie Wilson, and the Ravens. Although Jackson's career was closely connected to R&B, he was a strong jazz player with a style and sound influenced by Illinois Jacquet and Gene Ammons. Largely unknown as a composer, some of Jackson's compositions included "Miss Ann," "Brother Elijah," "West Africa," and "Cookin' Sherry," which won the French Grand Prix du Disque in 1959.

Jacquet, Jean-Baptiste "Illinois" (b. 1922). Jacquet, a tenorist, first worked with Milt Larkin's territory band and Floyd Ray in 1940 before playing in

Lionel Hampton's band in 1941 and 1942, when he recorded his famous sixty-four-bar tenor solo on "Flying Home." He later worked in Cab Calloway's band during 1943 and 1944 and enjoyed success as a featured soloist with Count Basie in 1945 and 1946. Jacquet's romping solo in "Blues" at the first Jazz at the Philharmonic concert in 1944 excited the audience and helped establish the event. He continued performing on Jazz at the Philharmonic's national tours from 1947 to 1955, led his own groups, and worked as a guest soloist. Jacquet currently performs in a variety of musical settings and is still considered one of the most swinging tenor saxophonists in jazz.

Jarvis, Jane (b. 1915). A pianist-pipe organist, Jarvis first worked for several Indiana radio stations and later accompanied Ethel Waters, Sophie Tucker, Paul Whiteman's band, and others. She was also active as a performer in the Midwest and played with such artists as Maxine Sullivan and Billy Butterfield. She worked with Milt Hinton, Osie Johnson, and Eddie Getz in the late forties, and with Eddie South in the mid-fifties. Jarvis played pipe organ for the Milwaukee Braves' home games in the fifties and for the New York Mets at Shea Stadium during the sixties and seventies. While working for the Mets, she played piano in New York City with such artists as Ruby Braff, Helen Humes, and Roy Eldridge. She also worked at the Muzak Corporation for eighteen years and eventually became its vice president. Once Jarvis retired as a baseball organist, she became a full-time jazz pianist and recorded an album for the Arbors label and two more for Audiophile. She has performed many times with bassist Milt Hinton as a duo and toured Japan as a member of the Statesmen of Jazz. Jarvis received honorary doctorates from Vincennes and Harvard universities.

Jazz at 76. A venue that opened in Boston around 1950 and hosted groups such as Vic Dickenson's Dixieland Stompers, Bobby Hackett's band, and Jimmy McPartland's Chicago Five.

Jazz at the Philharmonic (JATP). A name for concerts initiated by Norman Granz in Los Angeles at the Philharmonic Auditorium in 1944. The concerts evolved into tours that were scheduled for several months a year in the United States and abroad until 1957. Granz recorded many of the concerts and captured the excitement of live performances on twelve-inch 78-rpm records. Artists such as Dizzy Gillespie, Roy Eldridge, Charlie Shavers, Charlie Parker, Flip Phillips, Benny Carter, Charlie Ventura, Illinois Jacquet, Ben Webster, Bill Harris, J. J. Johnson, Nat "King" Cole, Oscar Peterson, Herb Ellis, Gene Krupa, Buddy Rich, Lionel Hampton, Ella Fitzgerald, Billie Holiday, Count Basie, and Duke Ellington were featured in many JATP concerts.

Jefferson, Edgar "Eddie" (1918–1979). A vocalist-lyricist who, in the early forties, began to create lyrics to fit improvised solos. This technique was later adopted by noted imitator King Pleasure and popularized by Lambert, Hendricks, and Ross in the late fifties. Jefferson's pioneering technique, known as "vocalese," can be heard in his recording for Hi-Lo Records in 1951 along with his versions of "Parker's Mood" and "Moody's Mood for Love." He became James Moody's vocalist and road manager from 1953 to 1957 and, after a ten-year period of obscurity and re-emergence as a dancer, rejoined Moody from 1968 to 1973. Jefferson co-led a band with drummer Roy Brooks and worked with altoist Richie Cole until his death.

Jeffries, Herb [Umberto Balentino] (b. 1916). Jeffries began his career as a professional vocalist at age fourteen with Erskine Tate's band in Chicago. He worked with Earl Hines and Blanche Calloway in the early thirties prior to appearing in several all-black western films as a singing cowboy. Jeffries worked with Duke Ellington's orchestra in the early forties and established himself as a jazz vocalist with recordings of songs such as "Jump for Joy," "The Brownskin Gal," and "Flamingo." After leaving Ellington, Jeffries recorded as a single for Exclusive Records and performed in Hollywood nightclubs from the mid-forties to the mid-fifties. The sixties and seventies found him active as both a vocalist and an actor who formed his own record company in 1978. From that point on, Jeffries continued to perform in nightclubs and on jazz cruises until the nineties. His rich baritone voice can be heard on such songs as "Body and Soul," "Jungle Rose," and "My Blue Heaven" that were recorded on the Exclusive label.

Jimmy Ryan's. A world-famous nightclub on 52nd Street in New York City that opened in 1940 and presented numerous Dixieland and swing musicians until it closed in the early eighties. Wilber DeParis, Max Kaminsky, Sidney Bechet, Zutty Singleton, J. C. Higginbotham, Henry "Red" Allen, and Roy Eldridge were a few musicians of note to perform at the club.

Joe Segal's Jazz Showcase. One of Chicago's most popular nightspots that was established in the late forties and located in the Blackstone Hotel. Numerous Swing Era artists appeared there through the fifties.

Johnson, Harold "Money" (1918–1978). A trumpeter-flugelhornist-vocalist, Johnson started out playing in territory bands in the mid-thirties. From 1937 to 1944, Johnson played in Nat Towles' band and briefly worked with Count Basie. After two years with Bob Dorsey, Johnson played with Lucky Millinder and Cootie Williams in the late forties. He worked later with Reuben Phillips, Herbie Fields, and Lucky Thompson and toured South America with Panama Francis during the fifties. Johnson worked as a studio musician and played with Mercer Ellington, Buddy Johnson, Earl Hines, and Duke Ellington from the early sixties until 1971. He recorded with Ellington, Phillips, Buck Clayton, Horace Henderson, and Clarence Williams.

Johnson, James "J. J." (1924–2001). Johnson, a trombonist-composer-arranger, is known as the world's most innovative and modern player on his instrument. Johnson made his professional debut in Snookum Russell's territory band in 1942. He worked with Benny Carter from 1942 to 1945 and played in Count Basie's orchestra in 1945 and 1946. Johnson worked in the late forties with Dizzy Gillespie, Woody Herman, and several small bebop groups before touring with Oscar Pettiford in the early fifties. After a two-year hiatus, Johnson returned to music in 1954 and co-led a two-trombone quintet with Kai Winding until 1956. Afterward, Johnson led his own quintets/sextets with such noted musicians as Bobby Jasper, Wilbur Little, Elvin Jones, Nat Adderley, Albert "Tootie" Heath, Tommy Flanagan, Freddie Hubbard, Cedar Walton, and Clifford Jordan throughout the sixties. He spent the seventies and most of the eighties on the West Coast as a composer-arranger in the film industry. Johnson returned to performing in the late eighties and formed a quintet with tenor saxophonist Ralph Moore, pianist Stanley Cowell, bassist Rufus Reid, and drummer Victor Lewis. The quintet recorded two notable albums live at New York City's Village Vanguard in July 1988 entitled *Quintergy* and *Standards*. These two CDs clearly document Johnson's bop trombone style that was firmly rooted in sophisticated swing. Johnson's ultra-high degree of control and technical command of the trombone was nothing less than astonishing. As a sideman, he recorded with Miles Davis, Charlie Parker, and the Metronome All-Stars. Some of Johnson's most enduring compositions are "Lament," "Tea Pot," "Coppin' the Bop," and "Commutation."

Johnson, John "Plas" (b. 1931). A tenorist, Johnson first played with the Johnson Brothers Band. During the fifties, he played with Johnny Otis, Charles Brown, and several rock-and-roll bands on the West Coast. Johnson gained international recognition, however, as the featured soloist on Henry Mancini's soundtrack for *The Pink Panther* in 1963 and on the soundtrack of *Lady Sings the Blues* in 1972. From 1970 to the 1990s, he worked as a staff musician for the Merv Griffin television show and played with such musicians as Bill Berry and Herb Ellis. The big-toned tenorist has recorded with Ellis, Jake Hanna, Milt Jackson, Oliver Nelson, and Gerald Wilson.

Johnson, Osie (1923–1966). Johnson, a drummer-arranger-vocalist, began playing professionally with the Harlem Dictators in 1941. He played with Sabby Lewis in Boston, the navy band, Willie Smith, Clark Terry, and in several Chicago nightclubs during the forties. During that period, Johnson also wrote two arrangements, "It's Too Soon to Know" and "Fool That I

Am," for a Dinah Washington recording session. In the early fifties, he toured with Earl Hines and played for Illinois Jacquet, Dorothy Donegan, and Tony Scott. After 1954, Johnson became a first-call studio musician and freelance jazz artist in New York City. He also worked as a staff musician for CBS and NBC and appeared with Erroll Garner and the Cleveland Symphony Orchestra. Johnson participated in numerous recording sessions with such artists as Ben Webster, Al Cohn, Joe Williams, George Russell, Maynard Ferguson, Quincy Jones, Helen Merrill, Clifford Brown, Lucky Thompson, Zoot Sims, and Joe Newman.

Johnson, Richard "Dick" (b. 1925). A clarinetist-alto saxophonist, Johnson played in many bands during World War II and studied at the New England Conservatory in the late forties. He worked with Neal Hefti, Charlie Spivak, Buddy Morrow, and Benny Goodman in the fifties. Johnson has also led his own groups and played with the bands of Xavier Cugat, Buddy Rich, and Woody Herman. Johnson was later selected by Artie Shaw to lead the new Artie Shaw Orchestra. He has recorded with Eddie Costa, Woody Herman, and George Masso.

Johnson, William "Bunk" (1889–1949). Johnson, a trumpeter-bandleader, became active as a professional musician at the beginning of the twentieth century in the bands of Buddy Bolden, Frankie Dusen, Bob Russell, and Adam Olivier. Johnson later worked with Ma Rainey, Louis Fritz, Julia Lee, and Sammy Price before retiring from music by the mid-thirties. He was rediscovered in the early forties by two jazz historians who supervised a series of his recordings that helped stimulate the Dixieland Revival Movement. After performing intermittently as a sideman and recording as a leader, Johnson led his own band in New York City in the mid-forties and worked as a soloist in New York, Chicago, and Louisiana before settling in New Iberia, Louisiana, in 1948. His trumpet style was relaxed, and he recorded a number of sides such as "Down by the Riverside," "Panama," "Ballin' the Jack," and "Bunk's Blues" that displayed his effectiveness as a bandleader. Johnson's return to the music profession in the forties made a major impact on traditional jazz.

Johnson, Woodrow "Buddy" (1915–1977). Johnson, a pianist-vocalist-composer-bandleader, led one of the most popular big bands in the Later Swing Era. Johnson popularized the walking rhythm, and his band featured vocalists Ella Johnson (his sister) and Arthur Prysock along with saxophonist Purvis Henson. The key to Johnson's popularity was his unique ability to arrange/compose for large ensembles and write popular songs. His arrangements/compositions for big bands appealed to dancers, jazz buffs, and musicians alike. Johnson's songs such as "Walk 'Em," "Satisfy My Soul," and "Since I Fell for You" became major hits and helped lay the foundation for rhythm and blues. He recorded for the Decca label from 1939 to 1952 before switching to Mercury Records. Johnson had a successful career as a Swing Era bandleader, and some of his songs are still being performed today.

Jones, Burgher "Buddy" (b. 1924). Jones, a bassist, gained prominence with Charlie Ventura in the late forties. He later played with Stan Getz, Lennie Tristano, and Elliot Lawrence's small group that performed on Jack Sterling's radio show during the fifties and early sixties. Jones later worked in Hollywood studios and with such artists as Al Cohn and Bobby Hackett. He recorded with a number of musicians including Andy Kirk, Joe Newman, Sam Most, and Phil Woods.

Jones, Edward "Eddie" (1929–1977). A bassist, Eddie Jones played with Frank Wess, Benny Golson, and Sarah Vaughn before joining Count Basie in 1952 for ten years. After leaving Basie, Jones played on Broadway, worked with the Newport All-Stars, toured overseas, and performed with a symphony orchestra. He recorded with Basie, the Newport All-Stars, Wess, Joe Newman, Frank Foster, Thad Jones, Coleman Hawkins, and others.

Jones, Etta (1928–2001). A vocalist, Jones made her professional debut with Buddy Johnson's band in the mid-forties. She worked with J. C. Heard in the late forties, and with Earl Hines in the early fifties. She became highly successful after her hit recording of "Don't Go to Strangers." She toured frequently overseas and recorded as a leader for the Prestige label.

Jones, Henry "Hank" (b. 1918). Jones, a pianist, worked with Hot Lips Page, Andy Kirk, Billy Eckstine, Coleman Hawkins, Howard McGhee, and John Kirby in the mid-forties. He toured with Jazz at the Philharmonic in 1947 and accompanied Ella Fitzgerald from 1948 to 1953. He freelanced as a studio musician, worked with Benny Goodman, and recorded with Charlie Parker in the fifties. From 1959 to 1975, Jones worked for CBS as a staff musician on the *Ed Sullivan Show* and with Ray Bloch's orchestra while touring and recording with many jazz artists, including Goodman and Stan Getz. After 1975, Jones led several different trios, served as the pianist-conductor of the Broadway musical *Ain't Misbehavin'*, and recorded in solo or duo settings as well as a sideman with other leaders' bands. Jones has appeared in film and on numerous television shows. Jones' highly sophisticated piano work as a soloist, accompanist, and ensemble musician is on thousands of recordings by artists ranging from Artie Shaw to Gene Ammons.

Jones, James "Jimmy" (1918–1982). A pianist, Jimmy Jones grew up in Chicago where he played locally before working with Stuff Smith and J. C. Heard in the forties. Jones toured with Sarah Vaughn in the late forties and early fifties before freelancing in New York City and rejoining Vaughn in the mid-fifties. After leaving Vaughn in the late fifties, he became a noted arranger-conductor for such vocalists as Harry Belafonte, Lena Horne, and Ella Fitzgerald. Jones also arranged music for a number of recordings and television shows. Although he was most respected as a composer-arranger, Jones' skills as a pianist are noteworthy on his own group's recording in *Giants of Small Band Swing, Volumes 1 and 2* on the Riverside label.

Jones, Renauld (1910–1989). A trumpeter, Jones gained national exposure in the bands of Chick Webb and Don Redman during the thirties. He worked in the forties with the orchestras of Jimmie Lunceford, Erskine Hawkins, and, most notably, Duke Ellington. The fifties found Jones in the big bands of Count Basie, George Shearing, and Woody Herman. His consistent trumpet playing was recorded with Webb and Basie.

Jones, Robert "Jonah" (1909–2000). A trumpeter-bandleader, Jones worked in the thirties with Jimmie Lunceford, Stuff Smith, and McKinney's Cotton Pickers before playing in the bands of Benny Carter and Fletcher Henderson in 1940 and 1941. Jones worked in Cab Calloway's big band and small group, the Cab Jivers, from 1941 to 1952. Between 1952 and 1955, he played with Joe Bushkin, Earl Hines' all-star band, the pit band for *Porgy and Bess* on Broadway, Urbie Green, and Big Chief Moore, and toured in France and Belgium. Jones formed his own quartet in 1955 and held a long residency at New York City's Embers nightclub from 1955 to 1964. He toured in Europe, Asia, and Australia and made several hit recordings during the sixties and seventies. Afterward, Jones worked occasionally until the nineties as one of the most successful Swing Era trumpeters in the history of jazz.

Jones, Samuel "Sam" (1924–1981). A bassist-composer, Jones made his professional debut with Tiny Bradshaw's band in the early fifties. He later worked with Kenny Dorham and Les Jazz Modes co-led by Charlie Rouse and Julius Watkins in the mid-fifties. Jones later gained international prominence with Cannonball Adderley's quintet/sextet. Two of his best-known compositions are "Unit 7" and "Del Sasser" recorded by Adderley. Jones had a big sound and propulsive walking-bass style that can be heard on albums by Adderley, Bill Evans, Oscar Peterson, and many others.

Jones, Thaddeus "Thad" (1923–1986). Jones, a trumpeter-flugelhornist-composer-arranger-bandleader, played in a group with his brothers (Elvin and Hank) in Pontiac, Michigan, and in Saginaw with Sonny Stitt during the late thirties. Thad played with army bands, including a tour overseas from 1943 to 1946. After military service, he led his own group in the late forties and worked with Billy Mitchell and Charles Mingus' Jazz

Workshop in the early fifties. He became well known with Count Basie's orchestra from 1954 to 1963 and later played/arranged for Harry James, Basie, Thelonious Monk, Gerry Mulligan, and George Russell. Jones later worked as a staff musician for CBS, organized a quintet with baritonist Pepper Adams, and formed the Thad Jones–Mel Lewis Orchestra with Lewis that became one of the world's leading jazz organizations. While leading the orchestra, Jones often played melodious flugelhorn solos over his own arrangements with modern voicings that featured muted brass, flutes, and reeds to create rich and subtle sounds within a large ensemble. Some of Jones' best-known compositions are "A Child Is Born," "Big Dipper," "Consummation," "Mean What You Say," and "Central Park North."

Jones, William "Willie" (1929–1991). A drummer, Jones worked with Lester Young, Cecil Payne, Joe Holiday, Thelonious Monk, Kenny Dorham, J. J. Johnson, and Charlie Parker. He also recorded with Monk, Young, Charles Mingus, Elmo Hope, and Randy Weston in the mid-fifties. Jones later became a community activist and established jazz programs in several New York public schools. Although Jones worked with several bop musicians, his drumming style evolved from the Later Swing Era.

Jones, Wilmore "Slick" (1907–1969). Jones, a drummer, made his professional debut with Fletcher Henderson's orchestra in the mid-thirties and worked in the forties with Fats Waller, Una Mae Carlisle, and Louis Jordan. Subsequently, he worked with Wilbur DeParis and Doc Cheatham until the mid-fifties. His reputation as a swinging drummer is duly confirmed on the recordings of Waller, Sidney Bechet, and Lionel Hampton.

Jordan, Irving "Duke" (b. 1922). A pianist who became associated with the early bebop movement, Jordan established himself during the Later Swing Era with Al Cooper's Savoy Sultans, Roy Eldridge, and Teddy Walters in the forties. After working with Charlie Parker, Jordan played for Sonny Stitt, Oscar Pettiford, Stan Getz, and Gene Ammons in the fifties before touring Europe where he later took up residence. As a notable composer, Jordan's classic, "Jordu," has been performed by countless numbers of jazz musicians over the years. His skill as a consummate pianist is well documented in recordings by Stan Getz, Cecil Payne, Chet Baker, Coleman Hawkins, and others.

Jordan, Louis (1908–1975). Jordan, a saxophonist-vocalist-bandleader, began playing professionally at age fifteen, and he worked in the thirties with Kaiser Marshall, Leroy Smith, and Chick Webb. Jordan formed his own band in 1938 that later became known as the Tympani Five. He rose to national prominence in the forties and recorded a number of million-sellers such as "Caldonia," "Beware," "Is You Is or Is You Ain't My Baby," "Saturday

Night Fish Fry," and "Choo Choo Ch' Boogie." Jones established himself as a "jump blues" artist and was known as one of the most popular Swing Era musicians in jazz history. He effectively combined excellent musicianship with showmanship and helped lay the foundation for rhythm and blues. Jordan recorded with such artists as Ella Fitzgerald, Bing Crosby, and Louis Armstrong and worked until the early seventies during his highly successful career.

Jordan, Stephen "Steve" (1919–1993). Jordan, a guitarist, began playing with Will Bradley in the late thirties, and he worked with Artie Shaw, Saxie Dowell's navy band, Bob Chester, Freddie Slack, Glen Gray, Johnny Bothwell, Boyd Raeburn, Stan Kenton, and Jimmy Dorsey in the forties. Jordan changed careers and worked in NBC's production department in the early fifties before returning to music and working with Benny Goodman and Ruby Braff from 1953 to 1958. Afterward, Jordan left the jazz scene again until 1965 when he resurfaced and performed off and on until the early nineties. He recorded with Bradley, Raeburn, Gene Krupa, Pee Wee Russell, Vic Dickenson, Buck Clayton, and Jimmy Rushing.

Jordan, Taft (1915–1981). A trumpeter, Taft Jordan became known as a member of the Chick Webb Band during the thirties and early forties. He continued working in the forties and early fifties with his own group, Duke Ellington, Lucille Dixon's big band, and Don Redman. Jordan later worked on Broadway, in New York City studios, and toured overseas. He recorded with Ellington, Webb, Benny Goodman, and others.

Kahn, Norman "Tiny" (1923–1953). Kahn started on harmonica, switched over to drums at age fifteen, and worked with Boyd Raeburn, Georgie Auld, Chubby Jackson, and Charlie Barnet in the late forties. He played in Stan Getz's quintet in 1951 and worked with Elliot Lawrence's band on Jack Sterling's CBS daily radio show, during which he doubled on vibes in the early fifties. He also worked with Serge Chaloff, Lester Young, Al Cohn, and Red Rodney. Kahn was a solid timekeeper from the Jo Jones' school of drumming and a talented composer-arranger whose charts include "Father Knickerbopper," "Tiny's Blues," "Godchild," "Flyin' the Coop," "Over the Rainbow," and "Leo the Lion." Kahn, a self-taught writer, influenced several noted arrangers such as Al Cohn and Johnny Mandel. Unfortunately, Kahn's short life did not allow him the opportunity to make musical contributions beyond the Later Swing Era.

Katz, Richard "Dick" (b. 1924). A pianist, Katz studied music extensively before playing professionally in the early fifties with Al Casey, Tony Scott, and the J. J. Johnson–Kai Winding Quintet. After the Swing Era, Katz became well known as a versatile performer who worked as a record producer and became an authority of Nat "King" Cole's piano style.

Kay, Connie (1927–1994). Kay made his debut as a professional drummer in 1939 with Fats Noel. Kay played with Miles Davis and Sir Charles Thompson in the mid-forties and Lester Young in the late forties. He later worked with Charlie Parker and Coleman Hawkins before playing with Stan Getz and rejoining Lester Young from 1950 to 1955. Kay joined the Modern Jazz Quartet and spent most of his career with that group.

Kelly's Stable. A club that opened in the thirties in New York City and presented numerous Swing Era musicians in the forties. The long list of artists who performed at Kelly's includes Lester Young, Nat "King" Cole, Art Tatum, Billie Holiday, Benny Carter, Dinah Washington, Roy Eldridge, Una Mae Carlisle, and Dizzy Gillespie.

Kelson, John (b. 1922). A multi-reed instrumentalist, Kelson began playing professionally at age fifteen. He worked with Barney Bigard, Lucky Thompson, Kid Ory, Benny Carter, Benny Goodman, Lionel Hampton, Roy Milton, and a navy band in the forties. Kelson also worked off and on with Johnny Otis, Billy Vaughn, Nelson Riddle, Ray Anthony, Bill Berry, Duke Ellington, and Bob Crosby during the fifties. He later toured internationally with Hampton, Vaughn, and Mercer Ellington while working as a studio musician from the mid-sixties to the mid-eighties. After a ten-year hiatus from the music profession, Kelson played in Count Basie's band during the late nineties.

Ken Club. A venue that opened in Boston in the early forties and presented Swing Era musicians such as Henry "Red" Allen and Sidney Bechet.

Kenton, Stanley "Stan" (1911–1979). Kenton's career as a pianist-arranger began in the thirties with the bands of Everett Hoagland, Gus Arnheim, Vido Musso, and Johnny Davis. Kenton organized his Artistry in Rhythm orchestra in 1941 and premiered it at the Rendezvous Ballroom in Balboa, California. He signed with the Decca label in the same year and recorded popular charts such as "Taboo" and "Gambler's Blues." He switched over to Capitol Records the following year and gained popularity on the Pepsodent radio show. Anita O'Day joined the band in 1943 and recorded the hit "And Her Tears Flowed Like Wine." A year later, June Christy replaced O'Day and recorded such commercial hits as "Tampico" and "Willow Weep for Me." Kenton employed arrangers Dave Matthews and Pete Rugolo along with instrumentalists such as Stan Getz, Vido Musso, Ed Safransky, Kai Winding, and Shelly Manne who contributed much to the band's quality and identifiable sound throughout the forties. Kenton disbanded in 1947, took a break, and returned with his Innovations in Modern Music orchestra in the early fifties.

He continued to lead bands and promote his concept of concert jazz around the world from the fifties until 1977.

Killian, Albert "Al" (1916–1950). Killian began playing trumpet professionally at age eighteen and worked with Charlie Turner, Barron Lee, and Teddy Hill in New York City in the late thirties. Killian later worked with Don Redman, Claude Hopkins, Count Basie, Charlie Barnet, and Lionel Hampton from 1940 to 1945. Subsequently, he worked with Earle Spencer, Boyd Raeburn, led his own group, and performed with Jazz at the Philharmonic on the West Coast before joining Duke Ellington in 1947. He remained with Ellington until his death. Killian was among the few big-band trumpeters who could play lead and solo equally well. He recorded with Barnet, Hampton, Basie, Ellington, Lester Young, T-Bone Walker, and Slim Gaillard.

King. A record company established in 1944 by Syd Nathan. After trumpeter Henry Glover became the A&R director, the label recorded Swing Era bandleaders such as Lucky Millinder, Earl Bostic, and Bill Doggett during the late forties and in the fifties.

King, Teddi (1929–1977). King won a vocal contest after high school and sang for the USO and American Theatre Wing in the forties. She later worked with George Graham and Jack Edwards and recorded with Nat Pierce in the early fifties. King gained wide recognition while touring with George Shearing's quintet in 1952 and 1953. After 1953, she embarked on a solo career and recorded for the Coral and Victor labels. She appeared with Shearing in the film *Cool Canaries*.

Kohlman, Freddie (1918–1990). A drummer-vocalist-bandleader, Kohlman started playing professionally in the bands of Papa Celestin, A. J. Piron, Joe Robichaux, and Sam Morgan in New Orleans. Kohlman played in Chicago with Stuff Smith, Albert Ammons, Earl Hines, and Lee Collins in the thirties. He returned to New Orleans in 1941 and led his own band in the forties. Kohlman played with Louis Armstrong and worked at a Chicago nightclub as its house drummer in the fifties before returning again to New Orleans in the sixties. He then worked with the Dukes of Dixieland, the Onward Brass Band, and Louis Cottrell, Jr. Kohlman played at several European jazz festivals with his own group and recorded with Bob Wilber, the Excelsior Brass Band, the Heritage Hall Jazz Band, and as leader of the Mardi Gras Loungers.

Kotick, Theodore "Teddy" (1928–1986). A bassist, Kotick started on guitar and switched to bass in high school. After playing in the Boston area, he moved to New York City in 1948 and worked with Buddy Rich, Johnny

Bothwell, Tony Pastor, and Artie Shaw until 1950. In the fifties, he worked with Stan Getz, Charlie Parker, George Wallington, Horace Silver, and the Al Cohn–Zoot Sims Quintet. Kotick toured with Claude Thornhill and worked with Martial Solal in the sixties before returning to Massachusetts in the early seventies and working mostly in the New England area. He recorded with Parker, Getz, Silver, Wallington, George Russell, Phil Woods, Al Haig, Herbie Nichols, and others. Kotick was best known for his ability to anchor rhythm sections with a strong and steady pulse.

Kral, Roy (b. 1921). Kral, a vocalist-pianist-arranger, worked with Charlie Agnew, played in army bands, worked as a staff arranger for a Detroit radio station, and performed with Georgie Auld, George Davis, Dave Garroway, and Charlie Ventura during the forties. While working with Davis in 1947, Kral met Jackie Cain, and the two of them worked together for Garroway and Ventura. They married in 1949 and worked as a vocal duo known as Jackie and Roy. After the Swing Era, they recorded many jazz albums, jingles, and commercials. Kral is best known as a fine pianist and arranger.

Krueger's Auditorium. A large venue in Newark, New Jersey, that presented many big bands in the Later Swing Era led by Les Hite, Lucky Millinder, Jay McShann, and others.

Kyle, William "Billy" (1914–1966). A pianist, Kyle worked with Tiny Bradshaw and the Mills Blue Rhythm Band before playing in John Kirby's band from 1938 to 1942. Kyle served in the army between 1942 and 1945 and rejoined Kirby in 1946. From 1946 to 1952, Kyle worked off and on with Sy Oliver, performed in Broadway pit orchestras, and toured internationally with Louis Armstrong's band. Kyle's melodic, single-line solo style can be heard on recordings with Kirby, Armstrong, Maxine Sullivan, Lionel Hampton, Benny Carter, Dave Brubeck, and others.

Lambert, David "Dave" (1917–1966). Lambert, a vocalist, studied drums for only one year and played in Hugh McGuiness' trio in the late thirties. After military service in the early forties, Lambert sang in Gene Krupa's band in 1944 and 1945 and led a vocal group in the Broadway show *Are You with It*. In the early fifties, he organized the Dave Lambert Singers, wrote arrangements for Carmen McRae, and served as a vocal group contractor. He formed Lambert, Hendricks, and Ross with John and Annie in 1957 and freelanced later in New York City.

Lamond, Donald "Don" (b. 1921). Lamond began his professional career as a drummer with Sonny Dunham in 1943 and worked in the forties with Boyd Raeburn and Woody Herman. Lamond freelanced in New York City on a number of television shows including those of Steve Allen, Garry Moore, and Ed Sullivan during the fifties. In addition, he performed and recorded with Lester Young, Stan Getz, Dick Hyman, Roy Eldridge, Bud Powell, Coleman Hawkins, and Charlie Parker. Lamond later performed with the Newport Jazz Festival All-Stars and recorded with Bucky Pizzarelli and Maxine Sullivan. He later led his own big band and played with Harry West's band at Disney World in Florida. Lamond recorded with Herman, Serge Chaloff, Billie Holiday, Ruby Braff, Bud Freeman, Benny Goodman, Zoot Sims, and others.

Larkins, Ellis (b. 1923). A pianist who first played professionally in a trio led by guitarist Billy Moore in 1942. Larkins led his own trio from 1943 to 1952 while working in Edmond Hall's sextet and recording with Coleman Hawkins, Mildred Bailey, and Dickie Wells. He also accompanied Ella Fitzgerald, Helen Humes, and Joe Williams. Larkins is considered a sensitive and lyrical pianist, especially on ballads, and has demonstrated his ability as an expert accompanist for a number of vocalists and cornetist Ruby Braff.

Lawrence [Broza], Elliot (b. 1925). Lawrence, a pianist-arranger-bandleader, started out as music director at Philadelphia's radio station, WCAU, in 1945. CBS's network broadcasts of the WCAU band around the country cast it in the spotlight, and it eventually became a popular band with bookings at top venues and college proms. The band also received a recording contract from Columbia Records. Lawrence, an excellent arranger-composer, contributed "Brown Betty," "Sugar Town Row," "Heart to Heart," and the popular "Elevation" to the band's library. The band also played charts by other writers such as Johnny Mandel, Nelson Riddle, Gerry Mulligan, Tiny Kahn, and Al Cohn. Lawrence and his band enjoyed a great deal of success until he disbanded around 1955 and became a Broadway theater conductor. Although most jazz histories hardly mention Lawrence's contributions to the Later Swing Era, he experimented with various instrumental combinations that utilized curved soprano saxophones and bass trumpets. His experiments with these combinations, well-crafted arrangements, and a high-quality ensemble had a positive influence on modern jazz.

Lee, Peggy [Norma Delores Egstrom] (1920–2002). Lee began singing professionally at age fourteen and worked in the Midwest and on the West Coast after graduating from high school. She joined Benny Goodman's band in 1941 and recorded the hit song "Why Don't You Do Right" a year later. After leaving Goodman in 1943, she took a break from the profession and emerged as a solo artist with Capitol Records in 1944. A noted songwriter, Lee co-wrote a number of hits with guitarist Dave Barbour such as "I Don't Know Enough About You" and penned other hits such as "Mariana," "You Was Right Baby," and "It's a Good Day." Throughout the fifties, Lee performed in nightclubs and acted in such films as *Pete Kelly's Blues* and

The Jazz Singer. From the early sixties to the nineties, she worked on a limited schedule and collaborated with major jazz artists such as Quincy Jones, Benny Carter, and Lou Levy.

Leighton, Bernard "Bernie" (1921–1994). Leighton made his professional debut as a pianist in New York City with Bud Freeman during the late thirties and worked for Raymond Scott, Benny Goodman, and CBS as a studio musician in the early forties. After military service, Leighton studied at Yale University and worked mostly as a studio musician while recording with such artists as Artie Shaw, James Moody, Billie Holiday, Bob Wilber, and Charlie Parker. He also accompanied many vocalists such as Rosemary Clooney, Frank Sinatra, Maxine Sullivan, Peggy Lee, and Tony Bennett. Leighton toured in England and Belgium.

Levy, John (b. 1912). Levy, a bassist, began playing at age seventeen while in high school. He started working professionally in Chicago with Earl Hines, Red Saunders, and Tiny Parham before playing in Stuff Smith's trio in 1943. Levy played with Erroll Garner, Phil Moore, Charlie Ventura, and Ben Webster in New York City during the mid-forties, and recorded with Billy Taylor, Lennie Tristano, and Rex Stewart in 1947. Levy played with George Shearing in 1948 and led his own group from 1949 to 1951 before changing his career to manage a number of jazz artists such as George Shearing, Nancy Wilson, Joe Williams, and Cannonball Adderley.

Levy, Louis "Lou" (1928–2001). Levy, a pianist, first played professionally in his hometown of Chicago with the bands of Jimmy Dale, Jay Burkhart, and Georgie Auld while in his late teens. During the forties, Levy worked with Sarah Vaughn, Chubby Jackson's group, and Woody Herman's band. He played with Tommy Dorsey, Flip Phillips, and an all-star sextet in the early fifties before a hiatus from 1951 to 1954. Afterward, he returned to music and spent the next eighteen to twenty years accompanying Peggy Lee, Ella Fitzgerald, and Nancy Wilson. He later moved to the West Coast where he worked with Supersax, Lena Horne, Tony Bennett, and Frank Sinatra in the seventies before relocating to freelance in New York City.

Lewis, George (1900–1968). Clarinetist-bandleader Lewis became a major figure in the Dixieland Revival after Bunk Johnson's death in 1949. Like many other revivalists, Lewis worked with some of the top traditional jazz bands in the twenties and, less frequently, during the Depression in the thirties. After working as a longshoreman during that time, he returned to music in the early forties and, by the early fifties, had formed his own band that performed at major venues and festivals around the country and abroad until the late sixties. Lewis was regarded as a highly competent clarinetist, and his band received similar recognition. Some of the band's sides such as "Panama Rag," "Gettysburg March," and "Down by The Riverside" reveal why it is considered one of the polished Dixieland ensembles in the Later Swing Era.

Lewis, James "Jimmy" (1918–2000). Lewis, a bassist, played guitar and sang in the Nashville area from 1939 to 1942, switched to bass in 1942, and played with the Tennessee State University band until 1944. He worked with Leo Hines in 1945 through 1947 and with John Hinsley during 1948 and 1949. Lewis played in the bands of Count Basie, Duke Ellington, Cootie Williams, and King Curtis in the fifties. Afterward, he freelanced extensively, played for the Broadway musical *Hair*, accompanied Alberta Hunter, and led his own trio. He recorded with Basie, Curtis, Lou Donaldson, Grant Green, and Reuben Wilson.

Lewis, John (1920–2001). Lewis, a pianist-composer, began his professional career in 1946 as a member of Dizzy Gillespie's big band after spending three years in the army. Lewis worked with Charlie Parker, Ella Fitzgerald, Illinois Jacquet, and Miles Davis before playing in the Milt Jackson Quartet. Jackson's quartet subsequently became the Modern Jazz Quartet, and Lewis assumed the position of music director for the group's long history.

Lewis, Melvin "Mel" (1929–1990). Lewis, a drummer and bandleader, started playing professionally with Boyd Raeburn in 1948. After Raeburn, he played in the orchestras of Alvino Rey, Ray Anthony, and Tex Beneke from 1948 to 1954. Lewis co-led a band with Bill Holman and worked in Terry Gibbs' big band during 1961 and 1962. He also played with Benny Goodman, Dizzy Gillespie, and Friedrich Gulda before co-leading the famous Thad Jones–Mel Lewis Orchestra that played on Monday nights at New York City's Village Vanguard. The orchestra also toured the United States and abroad. Lewis recorded with numerous artists and was one of the few top-ranked big-band drummers who continued to swing long after the Later Swing Era.

Lewis, William "Sabby" (1914–1994). A pianist-arranger-bandleader, Lewis entered the jazz field after moving to Boston in the early thirties. He gained experience with Tasker Crosson's Ten Statesmen in the mid-thirties and formed his own septet in 1936. Lewis led small groups and big bands in Boston and New York City through the late seventies. Some of his sidemen have included Paul Gonsalves, Sonny Stitt, Cat Anderson, Alan Dawson, Roy Haynes, Idrees Sulieman, and Freddie Webster. Although Lewis seldom played outside of the Northeast corridor, he influenced generations of musicians with the high quality of his performance organizations.

The Lighthouse. Located in Hermosa Beach, California, this club began presenting jazz in the late forties when bassist Howard Rumsey started leading Sunday afternoon jazz sessions. Rumsey organized The Lighthouse All-Stars in the early fifties as the venue's house band, and by 1955 the club had become a nationally known jazz spot.

Linn, Raymond "Ray" (1920–1996). Linn, a trumpeter, joined Tommy Dorsey at age eighteen. He worked with Woody Herman, Artie Shaw, and Boyd Raeburn in the forties and played with Bob Crosby, Shorty Rogers, Buddy DeFranco, Maynard Ferguson, and Les Brown in the fifties. Linn became active as a studio musician and recorded with Ella Fitzgerald, Frank Sinatra, and Sarah Vaughn. He also recorded with Anita O'Day and Barney Kessel. Two of Linn's compositions, "The Way It Was in LA" and "Where's Prez," were recorded by Mark Murphy and Les Brown.

Liston, Melba (1926–1999). A trombonist-arranger-composer, Liston started her career in a pit band in 1942. She worked in Gerald Wilson's orchestra, arranged and played on Dexter Gordon's small-group recording, and toured with Count Basie during the forties. After a brief hiatus from music, she worked with Dizzy Gillespie in 1950, freelanced in the early fifties, and rejoined Gillespie in the mid-fifties for several international tours. Her warm and robust trombone sound is featured in "One O'Clock Jump" and in her own arrangement of "Warm Mood," recorded by Gerald Wilson's Orchestra in 1945–1946 for the Black & White record label.

Lloyd's Manor. A venue with a lounge and ballroom in Newark, New Jersey, that presented the big bands of Billy Eckstine, Lionel Hampton, and Luis Russell in the forties.

Love, Preston (b. 1921). An altoist, Love made his professional debut on drums at age fifteen but switched to alto saxophone and played in the bands of Lloyd Hunter, Nat Towles, Count Basie, Lucky Millinder, and Harlan Leonard in the forties. Love later formed his own rhythm-and-blues band and recorded for Federal Records in the fifties. Afterward, he toured frequently with his band, led a West Coast Motown band, and toured Europe with the Countsmen. Love later returned to his hometown in Omaha, Nebraska, where he taught, worked as a disc jockey, and wrote his autobiography entitled *A Thousand Honey Creeks Later.* He recorded with Basie's big band.

Lowe, Curtis (b. 1919). Lowe, a tenor and baritone saxophonist, began playing professionally in 1940 before serving in a navy band during World War II. After discharge, he worked in the fifties with Lionel Hampton, Dave Brubeck's octet, Johnny Otis, Johnny Hodges, and Earl Hines. Lowe later worked for the musicians' union in Chicago for more than twenty years until his retirement in 1984. He recorded with Hampton and Hines.

Lowe, Mundell (b. 1922). Lowe, a guitarist-arranger-composer, first played with local bands on New Orleans' famed Bourbon Street. He later worked with Pee Wee King and Jan Savitt before military service in the early forties. After discharge, Lowe played in Ray McKinley's band, worked in off-Broadway plays, and worked in a quartet that included Dick Hyman, George Duvivier, and Ed Shaughnessy for an NBC television show from 1945 to 1958. Lowe also worked with the Sauter-Finegan Orchestra, Billy Taylor, and his own quartet at the Embers in New York City. Lowe composed for films and television shows in Los Angeles during the mid-sixties. He also freelanced, toured Europe, and served as music director for the Monterey Jazz Festival. He has recorded with Sarah Vaughn, Billie Holiday, Carmen McRae, Ruby Braff, Benny Carter, Joe Williams, Mel Powell, Charlie Parker, Spike Robinson, and others.

Lucie, Lawrence "Larry" (b. 1914). A guitarist-banjoist, Lucie worked in the thirties with June Clark, Duke Ellington, Benny Carter, Fletcher Henderson, and the Mills Blue Rhythm Band. He later worked with Coleman Hawkins' big band and with Louis Armstrong, and he co-led a combo with vocalist Nora Lee King in the forties. He played in bands led by Luis Russell, Cozy Cole, and Louis Bellson in the fifties before spending the following two decades as a freelance studio musician. Lucie also worked with Count Basie, Lucky Millinder, the Armstrong tribute band, and the New York Jazz Repertory Company. He taught at Manhattan Community College, co-hosted a television show with Nora Lee King (his wife), and authored *Lucie's Special Guitar Lessons*. He recorded with numerous artists including Carter, Henderson, Teddy Wilson, Billie Holiday, Ella Fitzgerald, Roy Eldridge, and others.

Lyon, James "Jimmy" (1921–1984). Lyon made his professional debut at age seventeen and, after military service, served as the solo pianist at Fred Waring's estate in the late forties. Afterward, Lyon worked in New York City with Tal Farlow, Buddy DeFranco, and Gene Williams. From 1950 to 1952, Lyon toured with June Christy and Stan Kenton, and he freelanced with Sam Donahue, Connie Haines, Bobby Byrne, and Benny Goodman. He led his own trio from 1953 to 1962 and played solo piano at numerous New York City establishments beginning in the early sixties. He also accompanied many vocalists including Mabel Mercer. Lyon always played in a simple swing style that was captured in some of Mercer's recordings.

Macero, Ted (b. 1925). A composer-saxophonist-producer, Macero served in the navy and studied at the Navy School of Music. He freelanced and taught in Glens Falls, New York, for a year after military service and moved to New York City in 1948 to study at Juilliard where he earned both bachelor's and master's degrees. He organized his own band, taught in New Jersey, and played with Larry Clinton in the early fifties. Macero was a founding member of the Charles Mingus Jazz Workshop and performed and recorded with Mingus from 1953 to 1955. Macero later became a noted producer for Columbia Records and supervised Miles Davis' famous recording, *Kind of Blue*, as well as other major albums by Davis, Dave Brubeck, Ramsey Lewis, and Thelonious Monk.

Machito (1912–1984). Machito, a percussionist-vocalist-bandleader, was born as Frank Raul Grillo and raised in Cuba. Machito played with bands in Cuba in the thirties before working with Xavier Cugat and Noro Morales in the United States. Afterward, he formed his own band and played jazz-influenced arrangements that resulted in a unique Afro-Cuban sound that featured guest artists such as Dizzy Gillespie, Flip Phillips, Charlie Parker, and Howard McGhee. Machito played throughout the United States and abroad until the early eighties and was a major influence on numerous jazz musicians over a period of four decades.

Malachi, John (1919–1987). A pianist-arranger, Malachi began playing professionally with Trummy Young in 1943 and worked throughout the forties with Billy Eckstine's orchestra and as his accompanist. Malachi later accompanied numerous vocalists such as Pearl Bailey, Dinah Washington, Sarah Vaughn, Al Hibbler, Dakota Staton, Gloria Lynne, and Joe Williams. Afterward, Malachi freelanced in Washington, D.C., until the end of his career. He recorded with Eckstine, Vaughn, and composer T. J. Anderson.

Mancini, Enrico "Henry" (1924–1994). Mancini, a pianist-arranger-composer, became one of the top film scorers in the movie industry, and his movie scores were heavily influenced by swing music. After military duty overseas, Mancini joined Tex Beneke's band as a pianist and arranger. After his work with Beneke, he began writing for films such as *Ma and Pa Kettle at Home* and *The Creature from the Black Lagoon* at Universal Studios in California. Mancini later established himself as an innovative film composer with his score for Orson Welles' *Touch of Evil* in 1958. In this particular score, Mancini incorporated swing music and set the stage for a new era in film scoring. He further demonstrated his enthusiasm for jazz with his score of *Peter Gunn* that combined big-band swing with pop, which elevated his career to a record high. Along with his work in film, Mancini recorded a number of albums, and his *The Blues and the Beat* is considered his best swing recording.

Mandel, John "Johnny" (b. 1925). Mandel, a trombonist and bass trumpeter, worked professionally with Georgie Auld, Boyd Raeburn, Buddy Rich, Jimmy Dorsey, Woody Herman, and others during the forties, but he was best known as a composer-arranger. In 1949, he wrote for Artie Shaw, and for network television in the early fifties. After some tours with Count Basie in 1953, he focused primarily on writing for motion pictures, television, and various recording projects. He wrote film scores for *I Want to Live* in 1958, *The Sandpiper*, and *The Americanization of Emily and Harper*. His television scores include *M.A.S.H*, *Mr. Roberts*, and *Ben Casey*. Mandel has arranged/conducted for Frank Sinatra, Anita O'Day, Tony Bennett, Nancy Wilson, Barbra Streisand, and others. He won an Academy Award for "The Shadow of Your Smile" from *The Sandpiper*.

Manne, Shelly (1920–1984). Manne, a drummer, made his recording debut with Joe Marsala in 1941 and worked briefly in the big bands of Raymond Scott, Les Brown, Will Bradley, and Bobby Byrne. In the early forties, Manne played in a large number of small-group recordings with such artists as Flip Phillips, Barney Bigard, Dizzy Gillespie, Oscar Pettiford, Eddie Heywood, and Kai Winding. Manne also played in the classic Coleman Hawkins' *The Man I Love* session. Manne worked with Stan Kenton at various times between 1946 and 1952, toured with Jazz at the Philharmonic during 1948 and 1949, and worked with Woody Herman in 1949. After playing with Kenton, Manne became one of the most popular jazz drummers on the West Coast. He formed his first quintet, Shelly Manne and His Men, in 1953 and began recording regularly as a leader.

Marcane Ballroom. A Cleveland, Ohio, venue that featured big bands led by Elliott Lawrence, Charlie Barnet, Claude Thornhill, Artie Shaw, Stan Kenton, Woody Herman, and others.

Margolis, Samuel "Sam" (1923–1996). Margolis, a clarinetist-tenorist, began playing professionally in Boston-area bands that backed up artists such as Vic Dickenson, Bobby Hackett, and Rex Stewart in the forties and early fifties. Margolis recorded with Ruby Braff in 1954 and played with him between 1957 and 1958 at the Newport Jazz Festival and in New York City. Afterward, Margolis worked mostly in Boston from 1958 to the mid-eighties and moved to Florida where he worked locally for the following ten years.

Markham, John (b. 1926). A drummer, Markham began his professional career with Charlie Barnet from 1950 to 1952. Markham worked throughout the fifties with Billy May, a television orchestra, Ella Fitzgerald, Peggy Lee, Red Norvo, and Benny Goodman. Markham later worked with Dick Stabile, Frank Sinatra, Tennessee Ernie Ford, and at the Playboy Club in Los Angeles in the sixties. After the early seventies, Markham worked mostly in the San Francisco area. He has recorded with Norvo, Goodman, Vince Guaraldi, Eddie Duran, Cal Tjader, and Brew Moore.

Markowitz, Irving "Marky" (1923–1986). Markowitz, a trumpeter, began his professional career as a member of Charlie Spivak's orchestra in the early forties and worked later with Jimmy Dorsey, Boyd Raeburn, Woody Herman, and Buddy Rich. In the fifties, Markowitz performed and recorded with Art Farmer, Gene Krupa, and Dizzy Gillespie. During the rest of Markowitz's career, he worked with Al Cohn, George Russell, Herbie Mann, Maynard Ferguson, and others. He recorded with Herman, Krupa, and Rich.

Marmarosa, Michael "Dodo" (1925–2002). Marmarosa played piano with local bands in Pittsburgh before working with Gene Krupa, Tommy Dorsey, and Artie Shaw's Gramercy Five in the early forties. Marmarosa relocated to Los Angeles in 1946, where he recorded with Lester Young and Boyd Raeburn, worked regularly with Barney Kessel, and became the house pianist for Atomic Records. He also recorded with Charlie Parker on "Relaxin' at Camarillo," and with Lucky Thompson on his Lucky Seven session for RCA. In 1947, he won *Esquire*'s New Star Award and rejoined Artie Shaw from 1949 to 1950. After recording with the International All-Stars in 1950, he gradually slipped into obscurity for most of the decade and then resurfaced briefly to record *Dodo's Back* for Argo Records in 1961. Although he spent most of his career working in swing bands, Marmarosa was a fine bop pianist.

Marsh, Warne (1927–1987). A tenorist, Marsh began performing with the Hollywood Canteen Kids in 1944 and worked later with Hoagy Carmichael's Teenagers. Marsh served in the military during the mid-forties and freelanced in Los Angeles after discharge from the army. He toured briefly with Buddy Rich, led his own group intermittently, and played with Lennie Tristano and Lee Konitz during the fifties and early sixties. After the mid-sixties, Marsh's career consisted of teaching, recording, leading his own group, and touring Europe as a soloist. Marsh recorded with Konitz, Rich, Chet Baker, Bill Evans, Art Pepper, and others.

Marshall, Wendell (b. 1920). Marshall, a bassist, played briefly with Lionel Hampton and served in the military before working with Stuff Smith, leading his own group, and playing with Mercer Ellington in 1947. In 1948, he joined Duke Ellington's orchestra and remained in that organization until 1955. After leaving Ellington, Marshall played in numerous recording sessions with Art Blakey, Kenny Clarke, Milt Jackson, Hank Jones, Gigi Gryce, Donald Byrd, and many others. Influenced by Blanton and Oscar Pettiford, Marshall's occasional solo work is highly effective, but he concentrated more on sturdy rhythm-section playing. He later worked exclusively in pit orchestras on Broadway.

Masso, George (b. 1926). Masso, a trombonist-composer-pianist, worked professionally with Jimmie Palmer's orchestra, an army band, Jimmy Dorsey, and the Latin Quarter Orchestra in the forties. Masso earned two degrees, taught from 1955 to 1974, and returned to performing and arranging at the encouragement of Bobby Hackett. Masso played with Benny Goodman's sextet and Bobby Hackett's quintet and freelanced with Buck Clayton, Bobby Rosengarden, and Woody Herman. As a composer-arranger, Masso wrote extensively for solo instruments, trios and quintets, and big-band charts. His swing-styled trombone playing has been recorded on the Arbors label.

Matthews, David "Dave" (b. 1911). A saxophonist-arranger, Matthews played with Ben Pollack, Jimmy Dorsey, Benny Goodman, and Harry James in the thirties when he wrote an arrangement of "Two O'Clock Jump." In the early forties, he played in the bands of James (again), Hal McIntyre, Woody Herman, Stan Kenton, and Charlie Barnet. Matthews worked as an arranger on the West Coast from the late forties until the early seventies. He is well known for his Ellington-styled arrangements of tunes such as "Perdido." As a saxophonist, Matthews' style was influenced by Coleman Hawkins and Ben Webster, and it is documented in recordings by Jack Teagarden and the Capitol Jazzmen.

Maxwell, James "Jimmy" (b. 1917). A trumpeter, Maxwell played with Jimmy Dorsey, Gil Evans, Maxine Sullivan, and Skinnay Ennis in the thirties. Between 1939 and 1943, Maxwell worked in the bands of Benny Goodman, Raymond Scott, and Paul Whiteman. Maxwell was a staff musician for CBS from 1943 to 1945 and a member of Whiteman's orchestra in 1946. Maxwell played with the NBC Symphony Orchestra in the late forties, the Great Neck Symphony in the early fifties, and in the big bands of Quincy Jones, Oliver Nelson, and Gerry Mulligan from 1958 to 1966. Maxwell also played in the *Perry Como Show* orchestra from 1945 to 1965. Maxwell substituted for Cat Anderson in Duke Ellington's orchestra and toured the Soviet Union with Benny Goodman. Maxwell is proficient on bagpipes and has performed in New York City's St. Patrick's Day Parade.

May, Earl (b. 1927). A bassist, May is self-taught except for one year of study with Charles Mingus. May played with Gene Ammons, Miles Davis, Sonny Stitt, and Mercer Ellington in 1951, and he spent most of the fifties as a member of Billy Taylor's trio. He served as Gloria Lynne's music director from 1959 to 1963 and worked with Carmen McRae and Sarah Vaughn in the mid-sixties before playing with Herbie Mann's group from 1965 to 1967. After leaving Mann, May worked in the bands of Dizzy Gillespie, Joe Newman, Johnny Hartman, Frank Foster, Archie Shepp, and George Benson during the seventies. He spent part of the eighties playing in pit orchestras for Broadway shows. He continues to freelance in a variety of musical settings, and he has recorded with Taylor, Stitt, Irvin Stokes, and John Coltrane.

May, William "Billy" (b. 1916). May, a trumpeter-arranger-composer, arranged and played for Charlie Barnet from 1938 to 1940 and Glenn Miller in the early forties. He also played with the NBC radio band, worked with Les Brown and Woody Herman, and arranged for Alvino Rey. In 1944, May moved to California and participated in numerous commercial recording sessions. He made his own big-band recording for Capitol Records in 1951, which became a hit and made it possible for him to tour with the band until 1954. He then turned the band over to Sam Donahue and returned to freelancing in Hollywood, where he arranged charts for many vocalists such as Frank Sinatra. May is well known for his arrangements of "Lament for May," Sposin'," "In a Mizz," and Charlie Barnet's famous hit recording of "Cherokee."

McCall, Mary Ann (b. 1919). A vocalist, McCall sang with Buddy Morrow and Tommy Dorsey in the late thirties, Woody Herman from 1939 to 1941, Charlie Barnet from 1941 to 1943, and with Herman again from 1946 to 1950. She worked as a solo artist in the early sixties and played briefly with Charlie Ventura in 1954 and 1955 before retiring from music. She also worked with Ralph Burns, Phil Moore, Al Cohn, and Ernie Wilkins. McCall won a *Downbeat* poll as the best band vocalist in 1949 and recorded as a leader on the Columbia label. She also recorded with Herman, Barnet, and Ventura.

McDuff, Eugene "Brother Jack" (1926–2001). A pianist-organist-composer, McDuff started out on bass and switched to piano. He began playing professionally with his own group in the Midwest during the early fifties and continued working in Chicago with Porter Kilbert, Eddie Chamblee, Willis Jackson, Johnny Griffin, and Max Roach. McDuff switched to organ in the late fifties and subsequently led his own groups. He recorded on the Prestige label from 1960 to 1966 and recorded for Concord Records in the nineties. McDuff performed at all of the major jazz festivals and toured throughout Japan, Europe, and the United States. He recorded with Joe Henderson, George Benson, Pat Martino, Sonny Stitt, Gene Ammons, Roland Kirk, Joe Williams, and others.

McGarity, Robert "Lou" (1917–1971). McGarity started out on the violin and switched to trombone in high school. He worked with Kirk Devore in Atlanta, Nye Mahew at the Glen Island Casino in New York in 1936 and 1937, and Ben Bernie from 1938 to 1940. McGarity attracted national attention as a member of Benny Goodman's band from 1940 to 1942 and from 1946 to 1947. McGarity also spent a year in 1942–1943 with Raymond Scott's band. After some studio work in Los Angeles around 1947, McGarity moved to New York City and worked in radio, television, and recording studios for the next fifteen years. He toured Japan with Bob

Crosby in the mid-sixties and worked off and on until the end of his life. His swinging trombone style is on recordings by Goodman, Eddie Condon, Louis Armstrong, and the World's Greatest Jazz Band.

McGhee, Andrew "Andy" (b. 1927). McGhee, a multi-reed instrumentalist, studied at the New England Conservatory of Music and began his professional career in the late forties on alto sax with Hank Mason's band. The early fifties saw McGhee in the army, and after discharge he played with Fat Man Robison in 1953 and 1954. McGhee later toured with Lionel Hampton from 1957 to 1963 and in Woody Herman's band between 1963 and 1966. After leaving Herman, he joined the faculty at Berklee College of Music, where he taught full time for over thirty years. During that time, McGhee toured Europe with Lionel Hampton's Golden Men of Jazz, the Big Five, and as a soloist. McGhee has also performed at the Umbria Jazz Festival, in Korea, and on international jazz cruises. He has written three method books for saxophone and flute and recorded with Hampton, Herman, and Alan Dawson. McGhee currently performs in a variety of musical settings, and his swing-styled tenor playing can be heard on his own 1993 CD entitled *Could It Be* with pianist Ray Santisi, bassist Marshall Wood, and drummer John Ramsay.

McGhee, Howard (1918–1987). A trumpeter, McGhee played with Lionel Hampton briefly in 1941 and worked in Andy Kirk's band during 1941 and 1942, where he recorded his own *McGhee Special* and his arrangement of "Hip Hip Hooray." McGhee played briefly with Billy Eckstine, Count Basie, and Georgie Auld after working with Charlie Barnet in 1942 and 1943. McGhee played with Coleman Hawkins and Jazz at the Philharmonic and recorded with Charlie Parker in the mid-forties. He recorded for the Bethlehem label in 1955 and 1956, but he was inactive during the rest of the fifties. McGhee, who influenced many bebop trumpeters, resumed his career in the sixties and seventies.

McIntyre, Harold "Hal" (1914–1959). McIntyre, an altoist-saxophonist-clarinetist, led his first band in the mid-thirties for a year before working in Glenn Miller's orchestra for four years. McIntyre started his professional big band in 1941, and he played a successful engagement at the Glen Island Casino that established him as a bandleader. *Metronome* voted the organization as "the most promising new orchestra" in the early forties. Afterward, McIntyre's band performed in some of the nation's top venues such as the Meadowbrook in New Jersey and the Hollywood Palladium. The band also performed for President Roosevelt's Birthday Ball at the Statler Hotel in Washington, D.C., in 1945 and toured overseas to entertain GIs during World War II. After the overseas tour, McIntyre's band appeared in two films and performed around the country an average of fifty-two weeks a year from 1945 to 1952. The band enjoyed success in spite of the fact that it was not a commercial organization. It was generally considered a swinging jazz band that played high-quality music.

McKenna, David "Dave" (b. 1930). McKenna, a pianist, worked in the Boston area and played in Charlie Ventura's group before spending 1950 and 1951 as a member of Woody Herman's band. After serving in the army from 1951 to 1953, he rejoined Ventura during 1953 and 1954 and worked later with such top-name artists as Gene Krupa, Al Cohn, Zoot Sims, Stan Getz, Eddie Condon, Bobby Hackett, and Bob Wilber. McKenna is considered to be a major swing pianist, and he currently performs in a variety of settings.

McKibbon, Albert "Al" (b. 1919). A bassist, McKibbon began playing with Lucky Millinder in the early forties and worked with Tab Smith, J. C. Heard, and Coleman Hawkins from 1945 to 1947. He became known as a swinging and steady working bassist who played comfortably in swing, bebop, and Latin jazz styles. McKibbon replaced Ray Brown in Dizzy Gillespie's big band in 1947 and worked with Dizzy off and on until 1950. Throughout the fifties, McKibbon was featured on the cool sessions with the Miles Davis Nonet, recorded with Earl Hines, Johnny Hodges, Count Basie, and Thelonious Monk, and played with George Shearing. McKibbon later toured with the Giants of Jazz, worked as a studio musician, and accompanied notable singers such as Sammy Davis, Jr.

McKinley, Raymond "Ray" (1910–1985). A drummer-vocalist, McKinley began his career at age nine in Fort Worth, Texas, bands before touring at age fifteen with Texas territory bands. He spent the thirties in the bands of Tommy and Jimmy Dorsey prior to co-founding a band with trombonist Will Bradley in 1939. The band achieved commercial success with a boogie-woogie style and with McKinley's vocals on such hits as "Beat Me Daddy," "Eight to the Bar," and "Scrub Me Mama with a Boogie Beat." McKinley and Bradley parted company in 1942, however, and McKinley formed his own band briefly until he entered military service, where he played in Glenn Miller's Army Air Force Band. After discharge in 1946, McKinley collaborated with arrangers Eddie Sauter and Dean Kincaide and led one of the most progressive big bands in the Later Swing Era until 1951. After taking a break, he worked as a disc jockey, freelance musician, and studio drummer before replacing Tex Beneke as leader of the Glenn Miller band from 1956 to 1966. McKinley later worked in a variety of musical settings until his death.

McKusick, Harold "Hal" (b. 1924). A saxophonist-clarinetist-flutist, McKusick played with Les Brown, Woody Herman, Boyd Raeburn, Johnny Otis, Al Donahue, Buddy Rich, Alvino Rey, and Claude Thornhill in the forties. He worked with Terry Gibbs, Elliott Lawrence, and Don Elliott from 1950 to 1956. McKusick later worked with Urbie Green and George Williams and made a number of recordings on the West Coast. He formed his own group consisting of four saxophones and a rhythm section and worked a lot of commercial gigs in the late fifties. McKusick worked as a staff musician for CBS in New York City from 1958 to 1972. He led his own groups, taught privately, and recorded with Raeburn, George Russell, Jimmy Giuffre, Charlie Parker, and Lee Konitz.

McNeely, Cecil "Big Jay" (b. 1927). McNeely, a tenorist-vocalist, started out playing in Los Angeles' Central Avenue nightclubs during the forties. Influenced by Illinois Jacquet and Arnett Cobb, McNeely became a hard-swinging saxophonist with an uncanny ability to get people on the dance floor. McNeely's first big hit, "Deacon's Hop," established him as a major artist, and he took advantage of his success by becoming a featured artist on the country's Chitlin' Circuit. By the end of the fifties, McNeely topped the charts again with his vocal rendition of a ballad entitled "There Is Something on Your Mind" that helped lay the foundation for the Soul Music Era. Except for a lighter touring schedule in the sixties, he has continued to perform, record, and appear on television. McNeely recorded with the Aladdin, Atlantic, Exclusive, and Federal labels.

McPartland, Marian (b. 1918). A pianist from England, Marian met cornetist Jimmy McPartland while performing for military personnel in Europe and moved to the United States in 1946 following their marriage. She played with McPartland's group in the late forties and formed her own trio in 1950 that performed in New York City clubs during the fifties. Since that time, she has continued to perform, teach, and promote jazz via radio and television. McPartland has performed in many national and international jazz festivals, received several awards, and written a book, *All in Good Time*, published by Oxford University Press.

McRae, Carmen (1920–1994). McRae began singing as a teenager and worked on a chorus line in Atlantic City, New Jersey, before working as a full-time secretary and a part-time pianist-vocalist. She worked professionally in the mid-forties with Count Basie, Benny Carter, and Mercer Ellington before moving to Chicago, where she worked again as a pianist-vocalist. She performed in several nightclubs and developed her vocal skills before returning to New York to embark on a recording career. After recording with accordionist Mat Mathews and as a solo artist for a small label, McRae landed a contract with Decca Records. She recorded four successful sides for Decca in 1954 and received a *Downbeat* Best Female Singer award. McRae subsequently rose to international prominence and enjoyed a fifty-year career as one of the top vocalists in jazz.

McShann, James "Jay" (b. 1916). McShann, a pianist-vocalist, began performing professionally in Tulsa, Oklahoma, in 1933 and worked as a sideman until he formed his first band in 1938. His band made a number of recordings in the early forties that included altoist Charlie Parker. After spending two years in the army, McShann reorganized his band in New York City and moved to the West Coast in the late forties, where he led and recorded with small groups. Since the fifties, he has been based in Kansas City while touring the United States, England, Belgium, France, and Japan. McShann's swinging style is a combination of boogie-woogie and blues elements. He has recorded with Ben Webster, Marian McPartland, and Eddie "Cleanhead" Vinson, as well as on his own albums.

Meadowbrook Inn. A famous ballroom owned by Frank Dailey in Cedar Grove, New Jersey, that hosted numerous swing bands between the mid-thirties and fifties. Some of the featured bands were led by Charlie Barnet, Count Basie, Fats Waller, and others.

Merrill, Helen (b. 1930). Merrill, a vocalist, began singing in amateur contests at age fourteen and was later encouraged to pursue a professional music career by Dizzy Gillespie, Miles Davis, Stan Getz, and Don Byas. She toured with Reggie Childs' orchestra in the mid-forties and worked club dates in the late forties. Merrill joined Earl Hines in the early fifties and recorded under her own name for the Emarcy label from 1954 to 1958. She has also recorded with Quincy Jones, Gil Evans, Clifford Brown, Stephane Grappelli, Roger Kellaway, Red Mitchell, and many others.

Metropolitan Theatre. A large venue in Cleveland, Ohio, that featured the International Sweethearts of Rhythm and other bands led by Billy Eckstine, Lucky Millinder, and Earl Hines in the forties.

Middleton, Velma (1917–1961). A vocalist, Middleton worked professionally as a solo act in nightclubs during the thirties. She joined Louis Armstrong in 1942 as a vocalist with his big band and remained with him until the end of her life. She worked with Armstrong in various large and small ensemble settings where she sang, danced, and performed duets with him. She recorded with Armstrong and led two of her own sessions that included Cozy Cole and Earl Hines as sidemen.

Milburn, Amos (1927–1980). Milburn, a pianist-vocalist, was one of the early rhythm-and-blues musicians. After spending a few years in the navy overseas during World War II, he worked in Houston and San Antonio before moving to Los Angeles where he signed with Aladdin Records. From 1947 to 1954, he recorded a number of major hits including "After Midnight," "Hold Me Baby," and "Chicken Shack Boogie" that brought him national recognition. Milburn toured the country with a small group and enjoyed a number of Top 10 rhythm-and-blues hits. He was a lyrical blues singer and exciting pianist who was a major influence on Fats Domino.

Miller, Clarence "Big" (1922–1992). A vocalist-bassist, Miller led his own band in the mid-forties before working in Jay McShann's band from 1949 to 1954. Miller sang with Duke Ellington in 1955 and then started a solo career. He became a big hit at the South Bay Jazz Festival in 1957 and at the Monterey Jazz Festival in 1960. Afterward, Miller performed, taught, and appeared in a number of Canadian films. He toured Europe and Japan in the eighties.

Millinder, Lucius "Lucky" (1900–1966). Millinder, a singer and dancer, began his career in the thirties when he assumed leadership of the Mills Blue Rhythm Band from 1934 to 1938. Afterward, he worked with Bill Doggett before forming his own band in 1940. Millinder's repertoire included blues, jazz, rhythm and blues, and accompaniment for vocal soloists, vocal groups, and dancers. He had a reputation as a fine conductor with a retentive musical ear and the ability to spot talent. One of the band's most talented vocal soloists was Sister Rosetta Tharpe who recorded such songs as "Rock Me," "That's All," and "Trouble in the Mud." Millinder's band also played charts arranged by Tab Smith and Chappie Willett. Most of the band's instrumentalists were excellent section players and soloists such as Dizzy Gillespie, Freddie Webster, Tab Smith, Sam "The Man" Taylor, Bullmoose Jackson, and Bill Doggett. Millinder's music was highly popular among audiences at the Savoy and the Apollo in New York City. He recorded such instrumentals as "Mason Flyer," "Little John Special," and "Ride Red Ride." Millinder recorded for Decca Records between 1941 and 1947 and signed with RCA Victor until he changed over to the King label in 1950. He enjoyed commercial success in the rhythm-and-blues field until he disbanded in 1952.

Minerve, Harold "Geezil" (1922–1992). A multi-reed instrumentalist, Minerve worked with Ida Cox, Joe Robichaux, Clarence Love, and Ernie Fields in the early forties. Following military service, Minerve rejoined Fields from 1946 to 1950 and left to play in Buddy Johnson's band in the fifties. Minerve later played with Mercer Ellington, Ray Charles, Arthur Prysock (music director), and Duke Ellington, and freelanced in New York City. He also recorded with Duke Ellington.

Minton's Playhouse. A famous nightclub in New York City that featured weekly jam sessions on Monday nights. Minton's played a major role in the development of bebop by providing musicians such as Dizzy Gillespie, Charlie Christian, Charlie Parker, Little Benny Harris, Kenny Clarke, and

Roy Eldridge with the opportunity to work on a new and innovative musical language.

Miramar Ballroom. A Gary, Indiana, establishment that presented a number of swing performers in the late forties such as Lucky Millinder, Charlie Ventura, and Roy Milton.

Mitchell, Keith "Red" (1927–1992). Mitchell played piano in the army and later switched to bass. He worked with Jackie Paris, Mundell Lowe, and Charlie Ventura in the late forties before playing for Woody Herman from 1949 to 1951. Between 1952 and 1956, Mitchell worked with Red Norvo, Gerry Mulligan, and Hampton Hawes. He later played with Andre Previn and Dizzy Gillespie before working in Europe until the early nineties. In addition to being an outstanding bassist, Mitchell was a competent vocalist, pianist, and songwriter. He recorded with numerous artists including Helen Merrill, Billie Holiday, Roger Kellaway, Chet Baker, Benny Carter, Mel Tormé, Jimmy Rowles, Barney Kessel, Hank Jones, Stan Getz, and Jimmy Raney.

Mitchell, William "Billy" (b. 1926). Mitchell, a tenorist, worked with Nat Towles and joined Lucky Millinder's band in 1948. Mitchell played with Jimmie Lunceford, Gil Fuller, and Milt Buckner in the forties, and he replaced Gene Ammons in Woody Herman's orchestra in 1949. During the early fifties, Mitchell led his own group in Detroit and left to tour with Dizzy Gillespie in 1956 and 1957. Afterward, he played with Count Basie from 1957 to 1961 and left to form a group with Al Grey between 1962 and 1964. After returning to Basie in 1966 and 1967, he served as the music director for Stevie Wonder and Dizzy Gillespie. Mitchell subsequently became quite active as a performer-educator. He has recorded with Basie, Gillespie, Sarah Vaughn, Frank Wess, Milt Jackson, and others.

The Mocambo. A famous supper club located on Hollywood's West Sunset Boulevard that featured such performers as Sarah Vaughn, Eddie South, and Dinah Washington.

Modern Jazz Quartet. The Modern Jazz Quartet (MJQ) is generally considered as one of the most innovative small groups in jazz. The group was formed in 1951 with pianist John Lewis, bassist Ray Brown, and drummer Kenny Clarke. Percy Heath later replaced Brown as the group's bassist, and John Lewis became its music director. In 1955, drummer Connie Kay replaced Kenny Clarke and established the MJQ's long-standing membership. The group's style consisted of elements from European concert music, bebop, and swing. The MJQ toured and recorded extensively until it disbanded in 1974. The group reunited a number of times during the next two decades and finally disbanded in 1997. It was one of the most sophisticated bands in the history of jazz.

Moncur, Grachan Jr. (1915–1996). A Miami-born bassist, Moncur began his professional career with George Kelly's band in the thirties and moved to Newark, New Jersey, where producer John Hammond discovered him. With Hammond's support, Moncur recorded with Bunny Berigan, Bud Freeman, and Mildred Bailey. He worked with Teddy Wilson in the mid-thirties and became a founding member of the Savoy Sultans from 1937 to 1945. Moncur freelanced in Miami, Florida, during the fifties and sixties, and he recorded with Ace Thomas, Ike Quebec, and saxophonist Joe Thomas.

Mondragon, Joseph "Joe" (b. 1920). Mondragon, a self-taught bassist, started his professional career with local bands in Los Angeles and rose to prominence as a member of Woody Herman's orchestra in 1946. After Herman, he worked during the next ten years with June Christy, Alvino Rey, Shorty Rogers, Buddy Rich, Shelly Manne, and Buddy DeFranco. Mondragon later worked regularly with Ella Fitzgerald in the early sixties and played on numerous movie soundtracks. He recorded with Billie Holiday, Chet Baker, Art Pepper, Shorty Rogers, Benny Carter, and Gerry Mulligan. Mondragon had a big sound and was a first-call jazz bassist on the West Coast.

Monroe, Vaughn (1911–1973). A vocalist-trumpeter, Monroe started out as the leader of a Boston-area society band before forming his own band in Wayland, Massachusetts, around 1940. His band attracted national attention during the early forties while touring the country playing one-nighters, ballrooms, and theaters. He signed with RCA Victor, and his recording entitled "There I've Said It Again" sold over a million copies and topped the charts. Other hits included "Let It Snow, Let It Snow, Let It Snow," "Someday," and "Cool Water." Monroe made it on the *Camel Caravan* radio show, became a popular star of television commercials, and appeared in several movies. In fact, he was a big box-office attraction like Benny Goodman, Tommy Dorsey, and Harry James. Monroe disbanded in 1953 and became a solo artist, with frequent appearances throughout the United States and abroad until the mid-sixties. Afterward, he semi-retired in Florida until his death.

Monterose, Frank "J. R." (1927–1993). A Detroit-born tenorist, Monterose played in several territory bands from 1948 to 1950 and moved to New York City in 1951. A year later, he played with Buddy Rich and worked with local bands in Syracuse, New York, from 1952 to 1954. He joined Claude Thornhill and worked with Ralph Sharon, Teddy Charles, and Eddie Bert in 1955. Monterose later played with Kenny Dorham, Charles Mingus,

Terry Gibbs, and George Wallington in the late fifties. He also led his own groups and recorded with Charles, Dorham, Bert, and René Thomas.

Montgomery, William "Monk" (1921–1982). The brother of Wes and Buddy Montgomery, Monk taught himself how to play the bass and toured the United States and Europe with Lionel Hampton's band from 1950 to 1953. He became recognized as the first jazz musician to play the electric bass. Monk later worked with Georgie Auld, Art Farmer, and the Montgomery Brothers. After the fifties, he doubled on acoustic bass and worked with vibists Cal Tjader and Red Norvo. Monk also worked as a disc jockey and led the first African-American jazz group to tour South Africa.

Moody, James (b. 1925). A saxophonist-flutist, Moody received his first formal music training in the air force band. He played in Dizzy Gillespie's big band form 1946 to 1948, relocated to Europe where he performed in a group co-led by Miles Davis and Tadd Dameron, performed at the Paris Jazz Festival, and recorded his famous solo of "I'm in the Mood for Love" on alto saxophone for Metronome in 1949 in Sweden. During most of the fifties, he led his own small groups, worked with Gene Ammons in the early sixties, and played in Dizzy Gillespie's quintet from 1963 to 1971. He worked in a Las Vegas hotel band that accompanied such performers as Tony Bennett, Lou Rawls, and Bill Cosby in the seventies. Afterward, Moody led his own quartet for a decade. He continues to perform and conduct clinics at numerous colleges and universities throughout the United States and abroad. Although Moody has worked mostly in bebop bands, his style contains bop and swing musical elements. In fact, he is one of the few saxophonists playing today who can really swing.

Mooney, Joe (1911–1975). Mooney, an accordionist-pianist-vocalist, started playing the accordion in 1935 and doubled on piano in Frank Dailey's orchestra during the late thirties. He later freelanced and contributed arrangements to the bands of Les Brown, Larry Clinton, and Paul Whiteman (with whom Mooney recorded). Mooney formed a quartet consisting of accordion, guitar, bass, and a reed player in 1941 called the Music Masters. By 1946, the group became known as the Joe Mooney Quartet; it consisted of Andy Fitzgerald on clarinet, Jack Hotop on guitar, and John Frega on bass. The group, which featured Mooney's vocals, had a quiet sound that resembled the King Cole Trio. For about three years, the group had a popular following on New York City's 52nd Street and recorded such tunes as "Do You Long for Oolong," "Tea for Two," "September Song," and "Little Orphan Annie" that display the group's musical sophistication. Mooney switched to organ around 1950 and worked in Florida. He recorded with the Sauter-Finegan Orchestra in 1952 and later played occasional return engagements in New York City. In 1954, Mooney won a *Downbeat* poll as an organist.

Moonglow. A popular Buffalo, New York, venue that operated throughout the Swing Era and presented numerous well-known African-American bands.

Moore, Milton "Brew" (1924–1973). A tenorist, Moore played his first professional job with Fred Ford's band in New Orleans in 1942. He played with several bands in Memphis, New Orleans, and New York City before working with Claude Thornhill, Kai Winding, and Machito in the forties. The fifties found Moore playing with Lennie Tristano, Warne Marsh, Bob Milke, Cal Tjader, and his own group. He worked with Kenny Clarke in Paris during the early sixties and lived in Denmark in the mid-sixties before working in New York City from 1967 to 1970. Moore's Lester Young–influenced style of tenor playing can be heard in his own recordings and as a sideman with Winding, Charlie Parker, George Wallington, Stan Getz, and Chuck Wayne.

Moore, Oscar (1916–1981). Moore made his professional debut at age eighteen and earned national recognition as the first modern small-group guitarist with Nat "King" Cole's trio. His Charlie Christian–style solos and chordal work complemented Cole's piano in a supportive role. The Cole Trio (with Wesley Prince or Johnny Miller on bass) influenced such pianists as Art Tatum, Oscar Peterson, and Page Cavanaugh who formed similar trios in the forties and fifties. Moore's playing earned him the number-one guitar slots in both *Downbeat* and *Metronome* polls every year between 1945 and 1948. He also won the *Esquire* Silver Award in 1944 and 1945 as well as the Gold Award in 1946 and 1947. During Moore's ten-year tenure with Cole (1937–1947), he became one the most influential guitarists in the Swing Era. After he left Cole, he worked with Johnny Moore's Three Blazers in the Los Angeles area and recorded two albums as a leader in 1954. In 1955, Moore retired from music and worked in a different profession.

Moore, Phil (1918–1937). A pianist-vocalist-composer, Moore actually pioneered the "block chord" piano style that was mostly credited to Milt Buckner. Moore was one of the first African Americans to work as a staff arranger and conductor in the film industry for MGM in Hollywood during the late forties. He served as an accompanist for Lena Horne and Dorothy Dandridge, and he coached a number of vocalists including Marilyn Monroe, Frank Sinatra, and Ava Gardner. His success as a vocal coach reached a point where he ran his own studio in Hollywood during the latter part of his career. He recorded with such artists as Dizzy Gillespie, Laverne Baker, Bobby Short, and Ernestine Anderson.

Moore, William "Billy" (1917–1989). A pianist-composer, Billy Moore replaced Sy Oliver as Jimmie Lunceford's chief arranger in 1939 and 1940. Influenced by Oliver, some of Moore's best-known arrangements for Lunceford are "Battle Axe," "Monotony in Four Flats," "What's Your Story, Morning Glory," "Bugs Parade," and "Belgium Stomp." During the forties, he arranged for Charlie Barnet, Jan Savitt, and Tommy Dorsey. Moore moved to Europe around 1950 and arranged for French bands, served as music director for the Peters Sisters, worked as a staff arranger for Berlin Radio, and toured Europe with the Delta Rhythm Boys.

Moorehead, Consuela (b. 1926). Moorehead, a pianist and sister of bassist Bill Lee, studied music at Fisk and Northwestern universities where she earned bachelor's and master's degrees. She has performed with the New York Bass Choir led by Lee, the Richard Davis Trio, and a family quartet called The Descendants of Mike and Phoebe. Moorehead has also performed as a single and served as an artist-in-residence in the Virginia public school system.

Morrison, John "Peck" (1919–1988). A bassist, Morrison served in an army band in Italy in 1946. After military duty, he toured with Lucky Thompson in the early fifties and played with Horace Silver, Gigi Gryce, and Zoot Sims before working with the J. J. Johnson–Kai Winding Quintet in the mid-fifties. Morrison also played with Duke Ellington, Gerry Mulligan, Lou Donaldson, and Johnny Smith. During the late fifties, Morrison served as the house bassist at New York City's Five Spot. He later toured with Carmen McRae and recorded with Johnny Coles, Duke Ellington, Shirley Scott, and Red Garland. Morrison also played with Sy Oliver in Paris and freelanced in New York City during the mid-eighties.

Morrow, Buddy (b. 1919). Morrow, a trombonist, studied at Juilliard before playing in the orchestras of Eddie Duchin, Artie Shaw, Vincent Lopez, Bunny Berigan, Tommy Dorsey, and others during the thirties. Morrow worked with Bob Crosby in the early forties before military service during World War II and returned to civilian life as a member of Jimmy Dorsey's orchestra in the mid-forties. Morrow led his own band for a year and worked as a studio musician before forming a commercial swing band in 1950. The band made a hit recording of "Night Train" and enjoyed over ten years of success. Morrow is a highly skilled trombonist and capable big-band leader.

Morrow, George (1925–1992). A bassist, George Morrow served in the military during World War II and freelanced on the West Coast from 1946 to 1953 with such artists as Teddy Edwards, Sonny Criss, Billie Holiday, Wardell Gray, Dexter Gordon, and Charlie Parker. Morrow became well known with the Clifford Brown–Max Roach Quintet in the mid-fifties. He worked with Anita O'Day, Chet Baker, and Sonny Rollins and performed in Europe between 1956 and 1976. Afterward, Morrow played in the house band at Disney World in Orlando, Florida, where he played with numerous high-profile visiting artists. He recorded with several of the aforementioned musicians along with Dinah Washington and Curtis Amy.

Morse, Ella Mae (b. 1924). Morse, a vocalist, worked with Jimmy Dorsey's band at age fifteen, and she recorded her first major hit, "Cow Cow Boogie," at eighteen with Freddie Slack's orchestra for Capitol Records. Morse also recorded other hits in the forties such as "House of Blue Lights" and "Mr. Five by Five." She recorded another hit, "Blacksmith Blues," with Nelson Riddle's orchestra in 1951 and worked as a single artist until she retired from music in 1957. Morse was considered a fine Swing Era big-band vocalist but became best known as a pop singer in the last few years of her career.

Mosca, Salvatore "Sal" (b. 1927). Mosca, a pianist, played with an army band from 1945 to 1947, Saxie Dowell in 1947, and Lee Konitz from 1949 to 1965. Mosca rejoined Konitz in the seventies and later led his own groups. He recorded with Konitz, Warne Marsh, and Miles Davis. Mosca has devoted a considerable amount of time studying and teaching.

Most, Abe (b. 1920). A clarinetist, Most began playing professionally at age sixteen. He played clarinet and saxophone with Les Brown's band for four years before military duty from 1942 to 1945. After discharge, he played with Tommy Dorsey in 1946 and rejoined Les Brown. Most worked as a studio musician in the Los Angeles area and played jazz in nightclubs in the fifties. He has performed in many jazz festivals and concerts, as well as recording occasionally in the swing clarinet tradition. He has performed and given impressions of Artie Shaw and Benny Goodman.

Mulligan, Gerald "Gerry" (1927–1996). Mulligan, a baritonist, became an accomplished writer after selling some of his arrangements to a radio station. Mulligan played briefly in the bands of Gene Krupa and Claude Thornhill, and he became established as a writer after Krupa and Thornhill recorded some of his charts in the late forties. At Thornhill's recommendation, Gil Evans hired Mulligan as the baritone saxist-arranger for the famous Miles Davis Nonet sessions from 1948 to 1950. Some of Mulligan's arrangements for these sessions include "Boplicity," "Jeru," "Venus de Milo," and "Godchild." He later recorded with his own groups, wrote for Stan Kenton, performed with Howard Rumsey's The Lighthouse All-Stars, and formed his first piano-less quartet with Chet Baker, Bob Whitlock, and Chico Hamilton in the early fifties. Mulligan also toured Europe and achieved international visibility after receiving critical acclaim for a 1954 performance in Paris.

Murphy, Melvin "Turk" (1915–1987). A trombonist-bandleader, Murphy established himself in the San Francisco traditional jazz movement during the late thirties with Lu Watters' Yerba Buena Jazz Band. After military service in the forties, he returned to Watters' band until the end of the decade. Murphy formed his own band and garnered a national reputation in the fifties with performances in San Francisco, New York, and New Orleans. He signed with Columbia Records in the mid-fifties and recorded frequently for the next thirty years. In addition to touring and recording, Murphy served as an effective advocate for the Dixieland Revival. His big trombone sound and thoughtful musical phrasing are best heard in his band's recordings of "Canal Street Blues" and "Big Butter and Egg Man."

Music Inn. An establishment that replaced the historic Storyville club in Boston's Copley Square Hotel in 1951. Traditional jazz musicians such as Bobby Hackett performed there and were often broadcast live over the radio.

Mussulli, Henry "Boots" (1917–1967). An alto/baritone saxophonist, Mussulli worked in Boston before joining Teddy Powell's band in 1942. He also played with Stan Kenton, Vido Musso's All-Stars, Gene Krupa, and Charlie Ventura in the forties. He rejoined Kenton in the early fifties before returning to Boston, where he taught and played with Herb Pomeroy, Toshiko Akiyoshi, and Serge Chaloff. Mussulli later managed his own nightclub in Milford, Massachusetts, where he also led his own band in the late fifties. Mussulli's band was well known for its ability to swing and excite dancers.

Nash, Richard "Dick" (b. 1928). Nash made his professional debut as a trombonist with Sam Donahue in 1947 and, subsequently, played with Glen Gray, Tex Beneke, and an army band overseas. After military service, Nash worked with Billy May, freelanced in Los Angeles, and joined CBS as a staff musician in the fifties. Since that time, Nash has remained active as a freelance musician and teacher. He has recorded with Erroll Garner, Ella Fitzgerald, Natalie Cole, and others.

Nash, Theodore M. "Ted" (b. 1922). A tenorist and the older brother of trombonist Dick Nash, Ted began playing professionally with Les Brown in the mid-forties and worked with Jerry Gray from 1947 to 1952. He later worked with Mort Lindsay's band on Merv Griffin's television show and freelanced extensively in Los Angeles. Nash's skillful use of the saxophone's upper register can be heard in Joe Thomas' *Giants of Small Band Swing* on the Riverside label. He has also recorded with Fitzgerald, Bob Crosby, Pete Rugolo, Billy May, Dave Barbour, and Barney Kessel.

Navarro, Theodore "Fats" (1923–1950). Navarro, a trumpeter, worked in Walter Johnson's band in Miami, Florida, during high school and joined

Sol Allbright after graduation. Navarro played with Snookum Russell and Andy Kirk during the early forties and joined Billy Eckstine's band in 1945 to replace Dizzy Gillespie. Navarro played with Illinois Jacquet and worked briefly with Lionel Hampton, Coleman Hawkins, and Tommy Reynolds before playing in Tadd Dameron's band at the Royal Roost club in New York City in the late forties. Navarro also recorded with Benny Goodman's sextet and for the Blue Note label with Dameron and Bud Powell. Like many bop musicians, Navarro played mostly in swing bands and developed one of the most unique trumpet styles in jazz during the forties. He influenced a generation of trumpeters, including Clifford Brown.

Newman, Joseph "Joe" (1922–1992). A trumpeter-composer, Newman studied at Alabama State Teachers College. He played with Lionel Hampton and Count Basie, and he toured with Illinois Jacquet in the forties. After a period of freelancing, Newman rejoined Count Basie from 1952 to 1961, performed with Benny Goodman and Benny Carter, and recorded several albums as a leader. Newman later freelanced as a notable swing trumpeter until health problems forced him to retire one year before his death.

Newsom, Thomas "Tommy"(b. 1929). Newsom, a multireed instrumentalist and composer, studied at the Peabody Conservatory from 1948 to 1952 and toured overseas with an air force band in 1955. He later toured Latin America and the Soviet Union with Benny Goodman in the early sixties. Following the tour, Newsom joined NBC as a staff musician and played with the *Tonight Show* band under Skitch Henderson and Doc Severinsen until 1992. Newsom played alto and tenor saxophones, served as an assistant director, and contributed many excellent charts to the band's library. During Newsom's thirty-year tenure with NBC, he appeared regularly as a sideman or leader of small groups in Los Angeles and won two Emmy awards for his contributions as an arranger. Newsom has recorded with Jack Lemmon, Rosemary Clooney, Boots Randolph, J. J. Johnson's big band, Louie Bellson, and Jake Hanna. He holds an honorary doctorate.

Nicholas, George "Big Nick" (b. 1921). A tenorist-vocalist, Nicholas began working in the Detroit area and played with Earl Hines and Tiny Bradshaw in the early forties. He studied at the Boston Conservatory and played in Sabby Lewis' band in the mid-forties. Nicholas later worked with J. C. Heard, Dizzy Gillespie, Lucky Millinder, Claude Hopkins, Hot Lips Page, and Cozy Cole. Nicholas played with Jonah Jones, Shorty Allen, and Buck Clayton, and he led his own band in the fifties. During that time, he began scat-singing and leading jam sessions at a Harlem nightclub. Afterward, he taught in Virginia from 1977 to 1979. Nicholas has recorded with Bennie Green and Dizzy Gillespie and as a leader.

Nichols, Herbert "Herbie" (1919–1963). Nichols, a pianist-composer, played with a number of bands led by Rex Stewart, Snub Mosley, and Milt Larkin during the forties and fifties, along with some rhythm-and-blues bands. His unique compositional style became known after a 1955 recording for the Blue Note label. Billie Holiday and Mary Lou Williams recorded some of Nichols' most notable compositions such as "Lady Sings the Blues" and "Mary's Waltz." Unfortunately, he died after a short and unstable music career. Nichols' music has been resurrected over the past ten years, however, by several younger jazz musicians and is now receiving some of its due credit.

Nick's. An important nightclub in New York City that featured Dixieland music throughout the forties and fifties. Some of the club's resident and guest musicians were Pee Wee Russell, Meade "Lux" Lewis, Wild Bill Davison, George Brunis, Miff Mole, Bob Casey, Muggsy Spanier, and Brad Gowans.

Niehaus, Leonard "Lennie" (b. 1929). An altoist-arranger-composer, Niehaus studied at California State University in Los Angeles from 1946 to 1951 before joining Stan Kenton in 1952. After military service, he rejoined Kenton from 1954 to 1959. Between the early sixties and the mid-eighties, he co-led a quintet with Bill Perkins and served as a clinician for many colleges, bands, and orchestras. Niehaus won *Downbeat*'s New Star alto saxophone award in 1955, composed movie scores for some of Clint Eastwood's films, and wrote music for Billy Crystal's television show. Niehaus has won a Grammy Award, two BMI film awards, and was nominated for a British Academy award.

Nottingham, James "Jimmy" (1925–1978). Nottingham, a trumpeter-flugelhornist, played in Willie Smith's navy band in the mid-forties and worked in the orchestras of Lionel Hampton, Charlie Barnet, Lucky Millinder, and Count Basie until 1950. During the fifties, Nottingham worked with Herbie Fields and played in Latin bands before organizing a group with Budd Johnson in 1962. For the next eleven years, he worked as a staff musician for CBS while playing jazz with such luminaries as Dizzy Gillespie, Benny Goodman, Quincy Jones, Clark Terry, Thad Jones–Mel Lewis, and Ray Charles. Nottingham was known as a superior lead trumpeter and plunger mute soloist. He recorded with Coleman Hawkins, Joe Williams, King Curtis, Ruth Brown, and Chuck Willis.

O'Connell, Helen (1918–1993). A vocalist, O'Connell worked on St. Louis Radio and sang with Larry Funk's band before she established herself nationally as a member of Jimmy Dorsey's orchestra from 1938 to 1943 with such hits as "All of Me," "Amapola," "Green Eyes," "Tangerine," and "Star Eyes." She left Dorsey and became musically inactive for a while but returned as a solo act in the fifties along with working on the *Today* show. She later toured with the Four Girls Four, a vocal quartet that featured Kay Starr, Rosemary Clooney, and Rose Marie.

O'Day, Anita [Anita Belle Colton] (b. 1919). O'Day began singing while dancing in a Chicago marathon contest as a teenager. After singing with Erskine Tate's orchestra in one marathon, she decided to become a professional vocalist. O'Day worked in several Chicago nightclubs during her late teens, and Gene Krupa hired her a few years later. She worked with Krupa from 1941 to 1943 and helped make his band a big hit when she and Roy Eldridge recorded the duet, "Let Me Off Uptown." O'Day went on to work with Stan Kenton's band in 1944 and 1945 and recorded the hit, "And Her Tears Flowed Like Wine." During her tenure with Kenton, she won the *Equire* Silver Award in 1945 and two *Downbeat* awards in 1944 and 1945. O'Day began a solo career after leaving Kenton and eventually landed a record contract with Verve and recorded several successful albums in the mid-fifties. Subsequently, she appeared at the Newport Jazz Festival in 1958, toured Europe and Japan in the sixties and seventies, appeared in three films and a documentary on *60 Minutes*, and received a National Endowment for the Arts Jazz Masters Award in 1997. She has influenced a number of singers including June Christy, Helen Merrill, and Chris Connor.

O'Farrill, Arturo "Chico" (1921–2001). O'Farrill, an arranger-composer-conductor, studied trumpet for four years at a Georgia military school. He played and worked with several Cuban bands, studied arranging, and arranged "Undercurrent Blues" for Benny Goodman in the forties. O'Farrill arranged for Machito, Stan Kenton, and Dizzy Gillespie and toured with his own group in the fifties. Since the late fifties, O'Farrill has presented jazz concerts in Mexico City, worked in Las Vegas, arranged for Count Basie, Buddy DeFranco, and Cal Tjader, and written extensively for radio and television. He also composed a symphony and conducted a number of concerts in Europe and the United States at Carnegie Hall and Lincoln Center. His best-known charts are the "Afro-Cuban Jazz Suite" and "Manteca Suite" written for Dizzy Gillespie in the fifties.

On the Levee. Kid Ory opened this club in San Francisco near the end of the Later Swing Era. Ory's band was in residence at the club for a number of years during the fifties.

Onyx. A popular New York City nightspot that presented Dixieland, swing, and bebop at various times during the thirties and forties. Some of the musicians who appeared at the club include John Kirby and his sextet, Lester Young, Dizzy Gillespie, Hot Lips Page, Sarah Vaughn, Roy Eldridge, Barney Bigard, Billie Holiday, and Cozy Cole.

Ory, Edward "Kid" (1886–1973). A trombonist-composer-bandleader, Ory played with early jazz artists such as Johnny Dodds, King Oliver, Sidney Bechet, and Louis Armstrong in the twenties. Ory retired from music during the thirties and returned to the profession as one of the key figures of the Dixieland Revival in the early forties as a member of Barney Bigard's band. After appearing on Orson Welles' radio program in 1944, Ory formed his Creole Jazz Band, toured extensively, and made the famous Cresent recordings. After nearly twenty years of performing in the United States and overseas, Ory composed his famous "Muskrat Ramble," appeared in films such as *New Orleans* and *The Benny Goodman Story*, and completed the soundtrack for *Crossfire*. He was an influential "tailgate" trombonist and made a major impact on early jazz and the revival movement. Ory was also one of the most eloquent bandleaders in jazz.

Osborne, Mary (1921–1992). A guitarist, Osborne toured with Dick Stabile, Russ Morgan, Buddy Rogers, and Joe Venuti before recording with Mary Lou Williams, Coleman Hawkins, Wynonie Harris, Ethel Waters, Mercer Ellington, and the Beryl Booker Trio in the early forties. Osborne led her own trio in 1946 and played on Jack Sterling's daily CBS radio show from 1952 to 1963. Afterward, she freelanced and taught before relocating to Bakersfield, California, where she continued to perform occasionally up to the nineties. Her inventive and swinging playing can be heard on Bluebird's *The Women: Classic Female Jazz Artists*.

Otis, Johnny [John Veliotes] (b. 1921). Otis, a pianist-vibist-drummer, started out as a jazz drummer and played in the bands of Harlan Leonard, George Morrison, and Lloyd Hunter before leading his own band in Los Angeles in the mid-forties. Afterward, he led another band that included Hampton Hawes and Big Jay McNeely before moving over to rhythm and blues and featuring such vocalists as Big Mama Thornton and Little Esther Phillips. Otis became highly successful in this musical genre and recorded with Dinah Washington, using his own band, and special guest Ben Webster in 1951. Otis later became a radio disc jockey and hosted a weekly rhythm-and-blues television show.

Ousley, Harold (b. 1929). An alto and tenor saxophonist, Ousley began playing professionally with circus bands from 1949 to 1955; also during that period he played with King Kolax and Miles Davis. In the mid-fifties, Ousley played with Howard McGhee, Billie Holiday, and Joe Williams before working with Dinah Washington, Clark Terry, and Bud Powell in the late fifties. Ousley went on to work with such artists as Machito, Joe Newman, Jack McDuff, Lionel Hampton, Count Basie, Duke Ellington, Percy Mayfield, Ruth Brown, Jimmy Witherspoon, and Bill Doggett. Although Ousley's career began near the end of the Later Swing Era, his style has strong roots in the work of Lester Young and Ben Webster. Ousley has won a BMI Jazz Pioneers award, appeared in the film *Cotton Comes to Harlem*, and hosted his own cable television show *Harold Ousley Presents*. He has recorded with Washington and George Benson.

Paich, Martin "Marty" (b. 1925). A pianist-arranger-composer, Paich began working professionally with Gary Nottingham in 1941 and, after military service, graduated from the Los Angeles Conservatory. Paich worked in the fifties with Shelly Manne, Jerry Gray, Shorty Rogers, Peggy Lee, and Dorothy Dandridge, and he arranged the score for *Lady and the Tramp*. After the early sixties, he became an active Hollywood studio arranger-composer and worked with such singers as Lena Horne, Mel Tormé, Sammy Davis, Jr., Astrud Gilberto, and Ray Charles.

Palmier, Remo (b. 1923). Palmier, a guitarist, started playing professionally with Nat Jaffe in 1942. Palmier worked with Coleman Hawkins, Red Norvo, Billie Holiday, Mildred Bailey, and Phil Moore in the early forties. Palmier joined CBS as a staff musician in 1945, where he worked until 1972 on the *Arthur Godfrey Show*. During that period, Palmier also performed with Teddy Wilson, Sarah Vaughn, and Hank Jones. Other work followed with Bobby Hackett, Benny Goodman, Dick Hyman, Louis Bellson, and others. He won two *Esquire* polls in 1945 and 1946 and recorded with *Esquire*'s All-American Poll Winners, Dizzy Gillespie, Charlie Parker, Lena Horne, Benny Carter, and others.

Paradise Theater. Located in the heart of downtown Detroit, the venue presented many top-ranked Swing Era musicians from the early forties to the early fifties. The theater presented big bands led by Lionel Hampton, Dizzy Gillespie, and Duke Ellington.

Paramount Theater. A popular and long-standing venue in downtown Los Angeles that presented top-name swing musicians from the thirties to the mid-fifties.

Parker, John "Knocky" (1918–1986). A pianist, Parker worked with several Texas swing bands, recorded with the Wanderers, and played with the Light Crust Doughboys during the thirties. After military service, he played with the Zutty Singleton–Albert Nicholas trio on the West Coast. Parker later received a Ph.D. in American Studies and taught at Columbia University while playing jazz in New York City. He later expanded his career to include English teaching and lecturing on jazz, with demonstrations of different jazz styles. He performed and/or recorded with Doc Evans, Tony Parenti, Omer Simeon, Inez Cavanaugh, and Joe Turner.

Parker, Leo (1925–1962). A baritonist, Parker made his recording debut on alto sax with Coleman Hawkins' band in 1944. Parker played in Billy Eckstine's big band during 1944 and 1945 and switched to baritone saxophone in 1946. He worked subsequently with Dizzy Gillespie and in Illinois Jacquet's band. After recording "Mad Lad" with Sir Charles Thompson, Parker became known as an exciting baritone saxophonist via recordings with Dexter Gordon, Charlie Parker, J. J. Johnson, and Fats Navarro in the forties. Parker performed and recorded intermittently in the fifties but returned to music full time in the early sixties and recorded two albums for Blue Note and Prestige Records. His big bluesy sound and style, which successfully combined jazz and blues, set him apart from his peers.

Parkway Ballroom. A famous venue that catered mostly to Chicago's African-American population from the early forties to the mid-fifties. It hosted such Swing Era artists as King Kolax, Horace Henderson, and Gene Ammons.

Pasadena Civic Auditorium. A major California performance venue that presented jazz concerts by such swing artists as Lionel Hampton, Stan Kenton, and Charlie Ventura. A number of performances were also recorded at the auditorium.

Paschal's La Carousel. An Atlanta, Georgia, nightclub that originally opened in 1947 as a restaurant and became a nightclub in the fifties. The club hosted such legendary Swing Era artists as Count Basie and Dizzy Gillespie. Paschal's later alternated sets between visiting artists and local groups, which attracted record audiences on weeknights as well as on weekends.

Pate, John "Johnny" (b. 1923). Pate, a bassist-composer-arranger, learned how to play and write while serving as a member of the 218th Army Band in the mid-forties. After discharge, he worked with the Red Allen–J. C. Higginbotham band and with Stuff Smith from 1947 to 1951. Pate worked with Eddie South, Dorothy Donegan, and Ahmad Jamal in the fifties. Between 1957 and 1960, Pate led his own group and made his recording debut as a leader in 1957 for Federal Records. He worked as the house bassist at Chicago's Blue Note club, where he accompanied such artists as Sarah Vaughn and Ella Fitzgerald. He later played and/or arranged for Duke Ellington, James Moody, Wes Montgomery, Shirley Horn, Stan Getz, Kenny Burrell, Phil Woods, and others. During the seventies, Pate arranged, composed, and conducted for a number of movies and television shows.

Payne, Cecil (b. 1922). Payne is a composer and performer who plays baritone and alto saxophones, flute, and clarinet. He started playing alto saxophone in 1937 and worked in Pete Brown's band from 1938 to 1941.

He played clarinet in the army band in the mid-forties, and baritone sax with Roy Eldridge's big band for a brief period. Payne played alto, however, on his first recording date with J. J. Johnson and Bud Powell. He later played baritone in Dizzy Gillespie's big band in the late forties, where his fine technical facility and throaty sound can be heard on "Ow!" and "Stay on It." Payne worked in New York City with Coleman Hawkins, James Moody, Tadd Dameron, and others between 1949 and 1952 before playing in Illinois Jacquet's band from 1952 to 1954. Payne later worked with bop musicians such as Kenny Dorham and Duke Jordan, as well as with swing organizations such as the Count Basie Orchestra. He still performs in spite of his failing eyesight.

Payne, Percival "Sonny" (1926–1979). Payne started out as a professional drummer with Hot Lips Page, worked with Earl Bostic, and played in Tiny Grimes' band in the forties. He later played in Erskine Hawkins' orchestra and led his own band in the early fifties. Payne played with Count Basie from 1955 to 1965, Frank Sinatra between 1965 and 1967, Harry James from 1967 to 1973, and Basie again in 1973 and 1974. In 1976, Payne toured Europe with Illinois Jacquet and rejoined Sinatra. Count Basie's orchestra was known for its ability to swing and, naturally, Sonny Payne played a major role. This fact is also evident in Payne's recordings with Buckner; Ella Fitzgerald; Mel Tormé; Paul Quinichette; Stan Getz; and Lambert, Hendricks, and Ross.

Pell, David "Dave" (b. 1925). Pell played tenor saxophone with Bob Astor, Tony Pastor, Bob Crosby, and Les Brown during the late forties and early fifties. He led his own group off and on during the late fifties and worked as a studio musician in the sixties and seventies. Pell subsequently worked mostly as a record producer for various labels. He recorded with Chet Baker and Benny Goodman.

Pemberton, William "Bill" (1918–1984). Pemberton, a bassist, played with Frankie Newton from 1941 to 1945 and worked in the bands of Herman Chittison, Mercer Ellington, and Eddie Barefield in the late forties and the fifties, including a stint with Art Tatum in 1956. From 1960 to 1966, Pemberton worked as a studio musician before playing with Earl Hines between 1966 and 1969. From 1969 to 1975, he worked with Oliver Jackson, Budd Johnson, and Dill Jones in addition to Max Kaminsky, Vic Dickenson, and Ruby Braff. During the late seventies and early eighties, Pemberton worked with Panama Francis' Savoy Sultans and recorded with Doc Cheatham and Ivory Joe Hunter.

Pepper, Arthur "Art" (1925–1982). Pepper, an altoist, worked with Benny Carter, Gus Anaheim, and several bands on Central Avenue in Los Angeles and played with Stan Kenton briefly before serving in the military for two years. After discharge, he rejoined Kenton in 1947 and remained with him until 1952. During the fifties, Pepper recorded frequently as a sideman and as a leader. He produced two particularly important albums during this time: *Art Pepper Plays Modern Jazz Classics* and *Art Pepper Meets the Rhythm Section*. He worked sporadically during the sixties but made a comeback in 1975 and recorded some excellent albums for the Contemporary and Galaxy labels. He also demonstrated a high level of musicianship on the clarinet and tenor sax. The years between 1975 and 1982 were among his most productive and established him as one of the most important altoists in jazz.

Perkins, Carl (1928–1958). Perkins, a pianist, began working professionally with Tiny Bradshaw and Big Jay McNeely in the late forties. Perkins worked as a single and with Miles Davis before two years of military service. After discharge, he worked with Oscar Moore, Chet Baker, Harold Land, Art Pepper, Dexter, Curtis Counce, Buddy DeFranco, and Max Roach–Clifford Brown in the fifties. He recorded with Baker, Counce, Land, Pepper, and Leroy Vinnegar.

Perkins, William "Bill" (b. 1924). A multi-reed instrumentalist and composer, Perkins studied music and electrical engineering extensively before starting his professional music career in 1950 with Jerry Wald. During the fifties, Perkins played with Woody Herman, Stan Kenton, and Terry Gibbs before working as an engineer, mixer, and/or tape editor in the sixties. He later played with Marty Paich, Doc Severinsen's *Tonight Show* band, Lennie Niehaus, Johnny Mandel, and the Akiyoshi-Tabackin big band. He also played with The Lighthouse All-Stars, Bud Shank, and Shorty Rogers. Perkins invented the Saxophone-Synthesizer Interface and co-invented the Trumpet-to-Synthesizer Interface. He recorded with Gibbs, Herman, Kenton, Chet Baker, John Lewis, The Lighthouse All-Stars, and others.

Peterson, Oscar (b. 1925). Peterson, a pianist-composer-bandleader, was born in Montreal, Canada, and established himself as a boogie-woogie style pianist before relocating to the United States to join Jazz at the Philharmonic around 1950. Afterward, Peterson formed his own trio with bassist Ray Brown and guitarist Irving Ashby. After two changes of guitarists to Herb Ellis, Peterson's trio became one of the most popular small groups in jazz history. When Ellis left the trio in 1958, drummer Ed Thigpen became the group's third member. Peterson's style was influenced by Nat "King" Cole, Teddy Wilson, Art Tatum, and Erroll Garner. He has superior technique and an incredible ear for music. Peterson has performed in a duo setting and recorded with such artists as Joe Pass, Dizzy Gillespie, and Clark Terry.

Pettiford, Oscar (1922–1960). Pettiford taught himself to play the bass at age fourteen, toured the South and Midwest with a family band, performed around Minneapolis, and joined Charlie Barnet in early 1943 as part of a two-bass team with Chubby Jackson. Pettiford left Barnet and worked on New York City's 52nd Street with Dizzy Gillespie, Roy Eldridge, and his own group. He first recorded with Leonard Feather's All Stars on the Commodore label and became widely known after playing in the famous *The Man I Love* sessions with Coleman Hawkins. After winning *Esquire*'s Gold Award, Pettiford worked with Boyd Raeburn, Duke Ellington, and Woody Herman in the forties. He recorded frequently as a leader and sideman and led his own group doubling on bass and cello during the fifties.

Philharmonic Hall. An important Los Angeles auditorium where Norman Granz started his historic Jazz at the Philharmonic concert series in 1944. Other concerts later featured such Swing Era artists as Count Basie, Billie Holiday, Duke Ellington, and Stan Kenton.

Phillips, Joseph "Flip" (1915–2001). Phillips began his career by playing clarinet in a local New York restaurant in the late thirties. He worked with Frankie Newton and switched to tenor while playing with Larry Bennett in the early forties. Phillips garnered national acclaim as a featured soloist in Woody Herman's First Herd in the mid-forties. Influenced by Ben Webster's warm sound and Illinois Jacquet's romping swing style, Phillips became even more popular during his tours with Jazz at the Philharmonic from 1946 to 1957 by honking solos on such songs as "Perdido." He co-led a small group with trombonist Bill Harris and worked with Benny Goodman before a fifteen-year retirement. Phillips returned to music full time in 1975 and performed until the end of his life.

Pierce, Nathaniel "Nat" (1925–1992). Pierce, a pianist-arranger, studied at the New England Conservatory. He worked professionally in the Boston area between 1943 and 1951, including a tour with Larry Clinton in 1948 and his own big band in 1950. His first significant job was as Woody Herman's pianist-arranger from 1951 to 1955. He freelanced in New York with musicians such as Pee Wee Russell, Lester Young, Ruby Braff, and Emmett Berry, and led an all-star big band that included such players as Buck Clayton, Gus Johnson, and Paul Quinichette. He rejoined Herman from 1961 to 1966, often serving as the band's pianist, arranger, and road manager. After 1966, he worked frequently in Los Angeles and toured with Erroll Garner as his road manager.

Pioneer Club. A Boston venue that operated in the early fifties and presented many Swing Era artists along with regular after-hours jam sessions.

Pizzarelli, John "Bucky" (b. 1926). A self-taught guitarist, Pizzarelli played with Vaughn Monroe's orchestra, served in the military during the early forties, and rejoined Monroe from 1946 to 1952. After 1952, Pizzarelli worked as a studio musician for NBC for twelve years. He later toured with the Three Suns, worked on the *Dick Cavett Show* for ABC, toured with Benny Goodman, and recorded with Bud Freeman, Zoot Sims, Joe Venuti, Stephane Grappelli, and others. Pizzarelli plays a seven-string guitar and has continued to perform in the swing tradition as a well-respected artist up to the present day.

Plater, Robert "Bobby" (1914–1982). Plater, a clarinetist-flutist-saxophonist, became known as a top-notch section player. He began his professional debut with the Savoy Dictators in the late thirties and played in Tiny Bradshaw's band in the early forties. Plater led his own band while serving in the army and, after discharge, played in Lionel Hampton for eighteen years. After Hampton, Plater joined Count Basie and played in his band for eighteen years, where he later served as Basie's music director. He recorded with Hampton, Basie, and Teresa Brewer.

Pleasure, King [Clarence Beeks] (1922–1981). A vocalist-lyricist, Pleasure gained a foothold in the music industry after winning an amateur contest at New York's Apollo Theater. He became popular after singing the words to James Moody's "I'm in the Mood for Love." He also recorded "Parker's Mood" and "Jumpin' with Symphony Sid" for the Prestige label. The technique of creating lyrics to fit improvised jazz solos became known as "vocalese" and is actually credited to Eddie Jefferson, but Pleasure was recognized as its founder. He moved to the West Coast in 1956 and lived in obscurity until the end of his life.

Poindexter, Norwood "Pony" (1926–1988). Poindexter, an alto and soprano saxophonist, began his professional career in 1940 with Sidney Desvigne's band at the Cave Club in New Orleans. Poindexter gained fame with Billy Eckstine in the late forties and Lionel Hampton in the early fifties. Poindexter later worked as a leader and sideman on the West Coast in nightclubs such as San Francisco's Jazz Cellar and Bop City. In the early sixties, he played in the backup band for Lambert, Hendricks, and Ross before moving to Europe. He recorded with the aforementioned vocal trio and Wes Montgomery.

Pollard, Terry Jean (b. 1931). A pianist-vibist, Pollard made her professional debut with Johnny Hill in 1948 and worked with Emmet Slay and Billy Mitchell in the early fifties. She gained national recognition as pianist and co-vibist in Terry Gibbs' quartet in the mid-fifties. During that period, she appeared with Gibbs on Steve Allen's television show and on tour with the Birdland All-Stars. After working with Gibbs, she returned to her hometown in Detroit where she played with Yusef Lateef and led her own trio until illness forced her to quit playing in the early eighties. Although retaining her Swing Era roots, Pollard was a contemporary jazz soloist.

Pomeroy, Irving "Herb" (b. 1930). Pomeroy, a trumpeter-composer-educator, worked in Boston with Charlie Parker and Charlie Mariano before touring with Lionel Hampton from 1953 to 1954. Pomeroy led his own big band and played briefly with Stan Kenton before joining the Berklee College of Music faculty in 1955. While teaching full time, Pomeroy remained active as a performer, composer, arranger, and bandleader. The personnel in his big bands have included such players as Joe Gordon, Boots Mussulli, Bill Berry, Sam Rivers, Michael Gibbs, Alan Dawson, Hal Galper, Dusko Goykovich, Ernie Watts, Pat and Joe LaBarbera, Phil Wilson, Harvey Mason, and Miroslav Vitous. Pomeroy has recorded with Charlie Parker, Serge Chaloff, Mariano, John Lewis, and others. As a recognized clinician, Pomeroy currently conducts workshops and serves as a guest conductor. He still performs on trumpet and flugelhorn.

Porcino, Al (b. 1925). A trumpeter, Porcino joined Louis Prima in 1943 and worked in the bands of Tommy Dorsey, Georgie Auld, Gene Krupa, Woody Herman, Stan Kenton, and Chubby Jackson during the forties. The decade of the fifties saw Porcino work with Pete Rugolo, Charlie Barnet, Count Basie, Herman, and Kenton before co-leading a big band with Med Flory on the West Coast. It was his tenure with Terry Gibbs' orchestra, however, that established him as a top-notch lead trumpeter during 1959 and 1962. He continued playing with such singers as Judy Garland, Frank Sinatra, and Peggy Lee along with the bands of Buddy Rich and Thad Jones–Mel Lewis in the sixties. Porcino performed and/or recorded with Chuck Mangione and Mel Tormé before moving to Germany in 1977, where he worked in radio bands and led his own big band. He has toured Europe, Japan, and the United States as a performer and/or clinician and has recorded with Auld, Krupa, Rich, Kenton, Al Cohn, Dizzy Gillespie, Charlie Parker, Ella Fitzgerald, and Oliver Nelson.

Porter, Roy (b. 1923). Porter, a self-taught drummer and composer, began playing professionally with Milt Larkin and worked with Howard McGhee, Benny Carter, and Dexter Gordon, along with his own big band on the West Coast, during the forties. The fifties found him in the bands of Earl Bostic, Louis Jordan, and Prez Prado. Afterward, Porter was largely inactive in jazz except for leading his own group in 1970. He wrote his autobiography, *There and Back: The Roy Porter Story*, in 1991.

Potter, Charles "Tommy" (1918–1988). A bassist, Potter worked professionally in the forties with Trummy Young, Billy Eckstine, Max Roach, and

Charlie Parker. The following decade found Potter performing with Stan Getz, Count Basie, Earl Hines, the trios of Eddie Heywood and Bud Powell, Tyree Glenn, and his own trio. Potter worked with Harry "Sweets" Edison, Buck Clayton, and Al Cohn–Zoot Sims in the early sixties. He performed only part time in the seventies while holding a full-time job as a civil service employee. Potter was best known as a first-rate rhythm section player, and the quality of his work is well documented on the recordings of Getz, Powell, Miles Davis, Eddie Condon, Wardell Gray, Jimmy Forrest, and others.

Potts, William "Bill" (b. 1928). A pianist-arranger-composer, Potts toured Florida and Massachusetts with his own group before working with Bob Astor and Marvin Scott in the late forties. Potts served in the military from 1949 to 1956 and toured Canada and Iceland frequently in an army band. After military duty, he played/toured with Woody Herman, Ralph Marterie, Bobby Vinton, Paul Anka, Clark Terry, Stan Getz, Phil Woods, Al Cohn, Zoot Sims, Ella Fitzgerald, Eddie Fisher, and others. Potts also served as arranger-conductor-pianist for singers such as Vinton and Anka. Potts later led his own big band, worked as an audio engineer, wrote numerous arrangements for recording dates, and taught at Montgomery College in Maryland for over fifteen years. He is best known for his composition "The Jazz Soul of Porgy and Bess."

Powell, Earl "Bud" (1924–1966). A pianist-composer and brother of pianist Richie Powell, Bud began playing professionally at age fifteen with Valaida Snow's Sunset Royals. He became associated with Thelonious Monk and the legendary musical activity on 52nd Street in the early forties. Powell played and recorded with Cootie Williams' band in 1943 and 1944, and he worked with John Kirby, Sid Catlett, Allen Eager, Don Byas, and Dizzy Gillespie in the late forties. Throughout the fifties, Powell led his own trio at Birdland in New York City. In 1959, he worked in a trio with Kenny Clarke and Pierre Michelot in Paris but later worked sporadically because of ill health. He moved back to New York City in 1964 after his health improved and returned to Birdland with a trio. He appeared at Carnegie Hall in 1965 and worked infrequently until his death. Powell recorded with Parker, Gillespie, Williams, Dexter Gordon, J. J. Johnson, Fats Navarro, Johnny Griffin, Charles Mingus, and as a leader on the Blue Note label.

Powell, Gordon "Specs" (b. 1922). Powell, a drummer, began playing professionally with Edgar Hayes and Eddie South in the late thirties before working with John Kirby, Benny Carter, Benny Goodman, and Red Norvo, and as a staff musician for CBS in the forties. Powell won *Esquire*'s New Star Award in 1945 and recorded with Kirby, Coleman Hawkins, Billie Holiday, Charlie Ventura, Erroll Garner, Mary Lou Williams, Leonard Feather, Mildred Bailey, Dizzy Gillespie, Charlie Parker, Teddy Wilson, Slam Stewart, and Red Norvo. After a fruitful career in music, Powell left the profession and moved to the West Coast.

Powell, Jesse (1924–1982). A tenorist, Jesse Powell studied music at Hampton University in Virginia from 1939 to 1942. After leaving school, he played with Hot Lips Page, Luis Russell, Count Basie, Howard McGhee's sextet, and Dizzy Gillespie's big band in the forties. After 1950, Powell freelanced in New York City and played a variety of musical styles including rhythm and blues. His big-toned "Texas tenor" style can be heard on sides by McGhee and Gillespie.

Powell (Epstein), Melvin "Mel" (1923–1998). Powell, a pianist, became a professional at age eighteen as a member of Benny Goodman's orchestra. Prior to Goodman, Powell had already worked in the bands of Bobby Hackett, George Brunis, Muggsy Spanier, and Wingy Manone. While with Goodman in 1941 and 1942, Powell was featured on his own charts such as "The Earl," "Mission to Moscow," "Clarinade," and the hit "Jersey Bounce." He played in Raymond Scott's CBS orchestra in early 1942 before entering military service and touring with Glenn Miller's Army Air Force Band. After Powell's discharge from the military, he rejoined Goodman and worked with him intermittently in the mid-forties. He also worked in the studios and led some recording dates in the early fifties while studying composition with Paul Hindemith at Yale University. Powell focused his attention on serial composition for a number of years and later became the dean of the California Institute of the Arts' School of Music in Valencia, California.

Powell, Richard "Richie" (1931–1956). A pianist and brother of Bud Powell, Richie worked around New York City and Philadelphia from 1949 to 1951 before playing in Paul Williams' band and Johnny Hodges' orchestra during the early fifties. He joined the Max Roach–Clifford Brown Quintet as its pianist-arranger in 1954 but died in an automobile accident with Clifford Brown two years later. Although associated mostly with bop, Powell was also experienced in swing and rhythm and blues. The Roach-Brown Quintet's classic album *Live at Basin Street* displays the breadth and depth of Richie Powell's talent as a pianist and writer. He also recorded with Dinah Washington and Sonny Rollins.

Powell, Seldon (1928–1997). Seldon Powell, a multi-reed instrumentalist, studied in New York City in the late forties and graduated later from Julliard. From 1949 to 1951, he played with Tab Smith and Lucky Millinder before playing in military bands in Europe during the early fifties. After returning to New York City, Powell performed and/or recorded with such artists as Erskine Hawkins, Sy Oliver, Don Redman, Louis Bellson, Neal Hefti, and Eddie Jefferson. Powell also worked as a staff musician for ABC, played in

Broadway pit bands, and toured Europe. Powell's warm and resonant sound has been recorded with artists ranging from Benny Goodman to Richard "Groove" Holmes.

Pozo, Francisco "Chino" (1915–1980). A percussionist, Pozo taught himself to play piano and bass before moving to the United States from Cuba in 1937. He performed with Machito, the Jack Cole Dancers, and several Latin groups led by Tito Puente, Prez Prado, Jose Curbelo, Noro Morales, and Tito Rodrigues during the forties. Pozo also worked with Charlie Parker, Tadd Dameron, Peggy Lee, Stan Kenton, Herbie Mann, Xavier Cugat, and others through the fifties. Pozo later performed with guitarist Gabor Szabo and singer Paul Anka, and recorded with Lee, Louis Jordan, Billy Taylor, and Fats Navarro. Pozos is a cousin of Chano Pozo.

Pozo, Luciano "Chano" (1915–1948). Chano, a drummer-percussionist-vocalist-dancer, gained fame in Cuba as a performer-composer in the forties and performed with Dizzy Gillespie's big band at Carnegie Hall in 1947. Pozo co-wrote "Manteca" and "Cubana Be-Cubana Bop" with Gillespie, which established both individuals as the original founders of "Afro-Cuban Jazz." Pozo toured the United States and Europe with Gillespie in 1948 until his untimely death. Pozo made a major contribution to jazz in just one year and left his legacy as a great Cuban drummer in recordings by Gillespie, Chico O'Farrill, James Moody, Charlie Parker, and Milt Jackson.

Pratt, Bobby (1926–1994). Pratt studied trombone and began working professionally at age fifteen. In the forties, he worked with Charlie Barnet, Georgie Auld, Johnny Richards, Stan Kenton, Raymond Scott, Sam Donahue, and others. Pratt also learned to play piano and participated in jam sessions with Ben Webster, Coleman Hawkins, Trummy Young, Slam Stewart, and Big Sid Catlett while substituting for Vic Dickenson on trombone in Eddie Heywood's sextet in the fifties. Pratt played trombone and/or piano with Roy Eldridge, Max Kaminksy, Zutty Singleton, Herman Autrey, and solo piano in the sixties and seventies. In the eighties and nineties, Pratt continued playing trombone as a sideman and piano in a solo, duo, trio, or accompaniment setting. He also performed on a movie soundtrack and on television with Eldridge and Bobby Hackett.

Prestige. A record company established in 1949 that recorded many famous musicians, mostly in small-group settings. Some of the Swing Era artists recorded by the label include Stan Getz, Wardell Gray, Gene Ammons, Sonny Rollins, and Thelonious Monk.

Prysock, Arthur (b. 1924). A vocalist, Prysock sang with local bands in Hartford, Connecticut, while working during the day as a laborer in the early forties. He then joined Buddy Johnson's orchestra in 1944 and remained until 1952. During that time, Prysock and Johnson's band made fifteen hit recordings including "I Worry About You," which became one of their most popular songs. Prysock embarked on a solo career after leaving Johnson and became highly popular in the sixties, with several appearances on the *Tonight Show* and a recording with the Count Basie Orchestra. Prysock later served as a guest lecturer at a college on Long Island in the eighties. Prysock's deep and clear baritone voice is heard at its best on many of Buddy Johnson's recordings from the forties.

Prysock, Wilbert "Red" (1926–1993). The brother of Arthur Prysock, tenorist Wilbert Prysock started out on piano before switching to saxophone. Red joined Tiny Grimes' band for two years after discharge from military service in 1947. Afterward, Prysock recorded with Grimes occasionally; worked in the bands of Roy Milton, Tiny Bradshaw, and Cootie Williams; played in rock-and-roll shows; and led his own group from 1950 to 1961. Throughout the sixties, he led organ trios and served as the music director of bands that accompanied his brother Arthur. Red recorded as a leader for the Mercury label and as a sideman with his brother.

Puente, Ernesto "Tito" (1925–2000). Puente, a percussionist-bandleader, started playing professionally during his youth with Latin bands before studying at Juilliard in New York City. After he collaborated with such artists as Cal Tjader, Doc Severinsen, and Woody Herman, he mostly led his own bands throughout the rest of his career. Puente has been one of America's most successful bandleaders with five Grammy awards, over 100 albums, frequent appearances on television, and numerous international tours. Puente has made a major contribution to American music by successfully mixing jazz with Latin rhythms. In addition to his own albums, he has recorded with Ray Barretto, Benny Golson, Pancho Sanchez, and others.

Quebec, Ike (1918–1963). A fine swing-styled tenorist, Quebec played in the bands of Coleman Hawkins, Roy Eldridge, and Benny Carter before working with Cab Calloway's big band and small group from 1944 to 1951. Influenced by Coleman Hawkins and Ben Webster, Quebec had a distinctive sound that was resonant and breathy. His bluesy and highly melodic style shines through on ballads and swings on up-tempo tunes. Most of the fifties saw a lull in Quebec's music career, but he made a miraculous comeback as a recording artist and A&R person for Blue Note records. His career reached an all-time high in the early sixties, culminating with his *Blue & Sentimental* album. It included a stellar rhythm section with guitarist Grant Green, bassist Paul Chambers, and Philly Joe Jones on drums.

Quinichette, Paul (1916–1983). Quinichette, a tenorist, majored in music at Tennessee State University. He played with a number of territory bands in Denver and Omaha before touring with Jay McShann in the early forties. Quinichette worked with Johnny Otis on the West Coast in the mid-forties and went to New York City with Louis Jordan's group before playing in Lucky Millinder's band during the late forties. Other work followed with the bands of Hot Lips Page and Henry "Red" Allen prior to a tour with Count Basie's band in the early fifties. Quinichette patterned his style after that of Lester Young, which earned him the title of "Vice Pres" during his tour with Basie. Quinichette worked with Benny Goodman, Billie Holiday, and Nat Pierce while leading his own groups in the mid-fifties. After a long hiatus from music, he returned to the scene in 1973 to work with Buddy Tate and Sammy Price before his health declined. Quinichette's warm sound is heard at its best on *Six Classic Tenors*, recorded in 1952, which features him on four tracks with Count Basie's rhythm section and pianist Kenny Drew.

Raeburn, Boyd (1913–1966). Raeburn, a saxophonist, began his career as a bandleader in 1933 and led a commercial dance band in the Midwest for almost a decade. Around 1940, he changed his style to swing and established himself in Chicago with engagements at the Chez Parie and the Bandbox. He switched to "progressive jazz" in the mid-forties and impressed jazz fans in New York City during an extended engagement at the Lincoln Hotel. The keys to Raeburn's progressive or modern sound was the work of his chief arrangers: Ed Finckel, George Handy, and Johnny Richards. Finckel contributed charts such as "Bernie's Tune" and "Whispering" to the band's library, while Handy arranged ballads such as "Out of This World" and "There's No You." Richards, a "romanticist," wrote "Prelude to the Dawn" and "Man with a Horn" for the band. Throughout most of the forties, Raeburn's band enjoyed a respectable following with its modern and advanced sounds. The band did not appeal to the public-at-large, however, and Raeburn disbanded in 1948. He freelanced around New York with pickup bands until 1952 when he left the music profession.

Ramey, Eugene "Gene" (1913–1984). A bassist, Ramey worked with Countless Johnson in 1936, with Jay McShann's band from 1938 to 1944, and with Luis Russell in the mid-forties. Ramey worked on New York City's 52nd Street in the late forties with Charlie Parker, Hot Lips Page, Ben Webster, and Coleman Hawkins. The early fifties found Ramey with Count Basie and with Art Blakey and on tour with Dorothy Donegan. From the mid-fifties to the mid-seventies, he freelanced with McShann, Buck Clayton, Eddie Vinson, Teddy Wilson, and Muggsy Spanier and also toured Europe. Ramey returned to his home in Texas in 1976 and worked with local bands over the next several years. At the height of his career, Ramey was a first-call bassist who could play Dixieland, swing, and bebop styles equally well.

He recorded with McShann, Parker, Clayton, Dexter Gordon, Stan Getz, Jimmy Forrest, J. J. Johnson, and Fats Navarro.

Ramirez, Roger "Ram" (1913–1994). Ramirez, a pianist-organist-composer, turned professional at thirteen and worked with the Louisiana Stompers, Rex Stewart, the Spirits of Rhythm, Willie Bryant, and Bobby Martin in the thirties. Ramirez worked in the forties with Ella Fitzgerald, Charlie Barnet, Frankie Newton, John Kirby, Hot Lips Page, and Sid Catlett as a solo pianist, and in trios. After hearing Wild Bill Davis, he switched to organ in 1953 and worked in New York City, toured Europe with T-Bone Walker, and played at a number of jazz festivals. He composed "Mad About You" and is best known for composing "Lover Man." He recorded with Stewart, Ella Fitzgerald, Duke Ellington, Ike Quebec, King Pleasure, and Annie Ross.

Ray, Caroline (b. 1925). A multi-instrumentalist and vocalist, Ray studied at Juilliard and performed with local bands in New York City as a college student. She joined the International Sweethearts of Rhythm after her graduation from Juilliard in 1946 and spent two years as a vocalist-rhythm guitarist with the Sweethearts. Ray joined Erskine Hawkin's band in 1948 as its vocalist for a year and worked with local bands on piano and bass for several years before entering the Manhattan School of Music in 1954 and receiving a master's degree in 1956. She continued to perform as a vocalist and electric/acoustic bassist.

Rehak, Frank (1926–1987). Rehak, a trombonist, began playing during World War II while serving in the navy. After discharge, he played in the orchestras of Jimmy Dorsey, Gene Krupa, Benny Goodman, and Claude Thornhill. Rehak also played in the Sauter-Finnegan band and toured with Dizzy Gillespie by 1957. From 1957 to 1962, Rehak played and recorded with Miles Davis–Gil Evans and went on to play in Woody Herman's band until 1969 when he left the music profession. He recorded with Gillespie, Sonny Rollins, Johnny Hartman, Ivory Joe Hunter, George Russell, and others.

Rhumboogie. A nightclub that operated in St. Louis, Missouri, during the forties and presented a number of major Swing Era artists.

Rhumboogie Club. A popular Chicago venue that hosted many swing artists in the forties such as Sarah Vaughn, Fletcher and Horace Henderson, the International Sweethearts of Rhythm, and Milt Larkin.

Rich, Bernard "Buddy" (1917–1987). Rich began playing drums professionally in the late thirties in Joe Marsala's band. He later worked with the bands of Bunny Berigan, Artie Shaw, and Tommy Dorsey before two years of military service. After discharge, he joined Dorsey for two more years and then formed his own band in 1946. Rich's band had some excellent sidemen such as Stan Fishelson, Earl Swope, Johnny Mandel, Allen Eager, and Tubby Phillips, and its library contained charts by such arrangers as Tadd Dameron, Ed Finckel, and Billy Moore, Jr. Although Rich's band was a high-quality organization, it had difficulty gaining a foothold in the big-band business. Rich disbanded after a couple of years and toured with Norman Granz's Jazz at the Philharmonic. Throughout the fifties and most of the sixties, Rich worked as a sideman with Tommy Dorsey and Harry James. Rich formed another big band in the mid-sixties, however, and became one of the country's most successful bandleaders during the next two decades.

Richards, Charles "Red" (1917–1998). A pianist, Richards played and recorded with Skeets Tolbert from 1938 to 1941, served in the army from 1942 to 1944, and played with Tab Smith's band in the late forties. Richards worked with Sidney Bechet, Bob Wilber, the DeParis Brothers, and Sid Catlett before freelancing with Bobby Hackett, Jimmy McPartland, Roy Eldridge, Rex Stewart, Buster Bailey, and Mezz Mezzrow in the early fifties. Richards toured with Frank Sinatra and Muggsy Spanier between 1953 and 1957, and he worked as a single for a year before freelancing with Fletcher Henderson's alumni bands and Wild Bill Davison. Richards later formed the Saints and Sinners with Vic Dickenson in 1960, which received national acclaim. From 1970 until his death, he played solo piano, worked with Panama Francis' Savoy Sultans, and recorded with Doc Cheatham.

Richards, Johnny (1911–1968). Richards, a composer-arranger-bandleader, started out as a saxophonist and orchestrator at the Mastbaum Theatre in Philadelphia. During the forties, he composed film scores in London and Hollywood and also received a master's degree from UCLA. During the early forties, he played clarinet, tenor saxophone, and trumpet as leader of his own band and wrote arrangements for Boyd Raeburn in the mid-forties. Richards also arranged charts for Charlie Barnet, Stan Kenton, and Dizzy Gillespie. After writing film scores in Mexico during the late forties, Richard moved to New York City and arranged charts for recording dates by Helen Merrill, Sonny Stitt, and Sarah Vaughn in the early fifties. Richards led his own big band off and on during the late fifties and mid-sixties. He is widely known for composing "Young at Heart," which became a popular hit by Frank Sinatra. Richards was a highly skilled arranger who wrote colorful orchestrations that are heard to great effect in the recordings of Kenton and Merrill.

Richardson, Jerome (1920–2000). A woodwind specialist, Richardson started out playing with local Texas bands from 1934 to 1941. He worked briefly in Jimmie Lunceford's orchestra before navy service during World War II and played with Marshall Royal and Lionel Hampton in the late forties. Richardson then played in Earl Hines' band in the early fifties. Afterward, Richardson freelanced with Cootie Williams, Lucky Millinder, Chico Hamilton, Oscar Pettiford, Johnny Richards, Gerry Mulligan, Quincy Jones, Peggy Lee, Billy Eckstine, Gerald Wilson, Kenny Burrell, Brook Benton, Julie London, Oliver Nelson, and the Thad Jones–Mel Lewis Orchestra while working as a studio musician. Regarded as a first-rate section player, Richardson was also a fine jazz soloist and ballad singer. He appeared on numerous television shows and recorded with Dizzy Gillespie, Milt Jackson, J. J. Johnson, Joe Williams, Oliver Nelson, and many others.

Richman, Abraham "Boomie" (b. 1921). Richman, a tenorist, began playing in the Boston area before moving to New York City in 1942. He worked with Muggsy Spanier and Jerry Wald before playing in Tommy Dorsey's orchestra from 1946 to 1952 and with Benny Goodman in 1953 and 1954. Throughout the fifties and sixties, Richman freelanced as a studio musician and recorded with Neal Hefti, Al Cohn, Peanuts Hucko, Ruby Braff, Red Allen, Urbie Green, and the Sauter-Finegan Orchestra.

Riddle, Nelson (1921–1985). Riddle, a trombonist-arranger-composer, played and wrote for Tommy Dorsey, Bob Crosby, and Charlie Spivak during the early part of his career. Riddle later became a first-call arranger-composer for numerous recording sessions and television shows. He arranged for Nat "King" Cole, Peggy Lee, Ella Fitzgerald, and Frank Sinatra. During the eighties, Riddle arranged and conducted for pop singer Linda Ronstadt, resulting in a number of highly successful albums. He recorded with Sinatra, Fitzgerald, Dorsey, Antonio Carlos Jobim, and many others.

Rivers, Samuel "Sam" (b. 1923). A saxophonist-composer, Rivers studied at the Boston Conservatory from 1947 to 1952 while playing with Herb Pomeroy, Joe Gordon, Jaki Byard, and Gigi Gryce in the fifties. Rivers later toured Japan with Miles Davis and recorded with his own group for Blue Note records. Rivers worked with Cecil Taylor, McCoy Tyner, Dewey Redman, Clifford Jordan, and others in New York City while teaching in his own studio. Rivers has served as an artist-in-residence/lecturer at Wesleyan University and Connecticut College, and he worked with Dizzy Gillespie and Dave Holland. Rivers has won a *Downbeat* Critics Poll, played at all of the major jazz festivals, and recorded with several artists including James Blood Ulmer.

Roche, Mary "Betty" (1918–1999). Roche, a vocalist, won an amateur contest at the Apollo Theater before performing and recording with the Savoy Sultans in the early forties. She became well known for singing the blues section in Duke Ellington's "Black, Brown, and Beige" at his 1943 Carnegie Hall concert. She also performed briefly with Hot Lips Page and Lester Young before working and recording with Earl Hines in 1944. After a hiatus from music, Roche rejoined Ellington in 1952–1953 and regained her popularity with a humorous bebop version of "Take the 'A' Train." After her only recording with Ellington, she recorded three albums for Bethlehem and Prestige in the late fifties and early sixties before leaving music permanently.

Rodney, Robert "Red" (1927–1994). A trumpeter, Rodney began working professionally in the forties with the swing orchestras of Jerry Wald, Jimmy Dorsey, Elliot Lawrence, Gene Krupa, Buddy Rich, and Claude Thornhill. Rodney also worked with Oscar Pettiford, Charlie Parker, and Charlie Ventura from 1949 to 1952. He worked with local Philadelphia bands, spent five years as a booking agent, and worked with Ira Sullivan and Sammy Davis, Jr., in the fifties. After the Swing Era, Rodney took a hiatus from jazz for about fifteen years and worked in Las Vegas show bands for five years before returning to his first love. He toured Europe, teamed up again with Ira Sullivan, and led his own quintet. Rodney's awards include an honorary doctorate from Harvard University and induction into *Downbeat*'s Hall of Fame.

Rogers, Milton "Shorty" (1924–1994). Rogers, a trumpeter-arranger, gained his early professional experience with Will Bradley and Red Norvo. After military service, Rogers garnered national recognition as a member of Woody Herman's bands in the late forties. He later worked in Stan Kenton's orchestra in the early fifties before leading his own big band and small groups on the West Coast that recorded a number of albums. Throughout the fifties and beyond, he composed extensively for movies and television with such scores as *The Wild One* and *The Man with the Golden Arm*. Rogers gave up the trumpet and concentrated exclusively on arranging and composing, but he made a comeback in jazz in the early eighties. A middle-register trumpeter with a distinctive sound, Rogers was more influential as a writer.

Roland, Gene (1921–1982). A brass and reed instrumentalist-arranger-composer, Roland played in an air force band and later worked with Stan Kenton, Lionel Hampton, and Lucky Millinder as a player-arranger in the forties. During that time, Roland also worked in the bands of Count Basie, Artie Shaw, and Claude Thornhill. Roland arranged for Woody Herman and Stan Kenton, led his own bands, and served as a conductor-composer for the Radiohaus Orchestra in Denmark. He later toured with Kenton, led his own bands, and worked as a singer. Roland was the first to write for four saxophones and rhythm section, which laid the foundation for Herman's Four Brothers sound and introduced four mellophoniums to Kenton's band. Roland, in fact, made a major impact on the sound of big bands in the Later Swing Era. In addition to Kenton, Roland also recorded with Paul Quinichette and Oscar Pettiford.

Roseland State Ballroom. A Boston dance hall that hosted many swing musicians such as Cab Calloway and Duke Ellington in the early forties.

Rosengarden, Robert "Bobby" (b. 1924). Rosengarden, a drummer, played in military bands from 1943 to 1945 and worked with Teddy Phillips and Henry Busse before moving to New York City in 1946. Rosengarden later played with Charlie Spivak, Raymond Scott, Skitch Henderson, and others until 1948. A year later, he joined NBC as a staff musician and worked regularly in New York studios. In addition, he has worked with Benny Goodman, Gerry Mulligan, the World's Greatest Jazz Band, and the New York Jazz Repertory Company. He also served as the bandleader for Dick Cavett's television show and music director at the Empire Room in New York's Waldorf-Astoria Hotel. Rosengarden has recorded with Billie Holiday, Lena Horne, Frank Sinatra, Joe Williams, Ella Fitzgerald, Benny Goodman, Duke Ellington, and Dave Brubeck.

Rosolino, Frank (1926–1978). Rosolino, a trombonist, played in the army band during World War II and worked professionally with Bob Chester, Glen Gray, Gene Krupa, Tony Pastor, Herbie Fields, and Georgie Auld from 1946 to 1951. Rosolino played in Stan Kenton's orchestra in the mid-fifties before moving to the West Coast, where he worked with The Lighthouse All-Stars, Benny Carter, Conte Condoli, and others. He recorded with Kenton, Carter, Condoli, Howard Rumsey, Buddy Collette, Helen Humes, Chet Baker, and Dexter Gordon and on numerous movie soundtracks. Rosolino was a fine jazz trombonist and a competent scat singer.

Ross, Arnold (1921–2000). A pianist-organist, Ross first worked with Frank Dailey and Jack Jenney in the late thirties. Ross played in the forties with Vaughn Monroe, Harry James, Jazz at the Philharmonic, Charlie Parker, and an army band before freelancing in California during the early fifties. He later worked with Lena Horne, Bob Crosby's television show, Spike Jones' television show, Dave Pell, and Billy Eckstine and led his own groups. After a hiatus from the music scene in the early sixties, Ross worked in studios, accompanied several vocalists, and led his own trios until recently. He recorded with James, Dizzy Gillespie, and Willie Smith.

Rouse, Charles "Charlie" (1924–1988). Rouse, a tenorist, studied clarinet at Howard University before switching to saxophone and working in the bands of Billy Eckstine, Dizzy Gillespie, and Duke Ellington in the forties.

Rouse also recorded with Tadd Dameron and Fats Navarro at that time. The fifties saw Rouse with Count Basie's small group, Bennie Green's quintet, the Oscar Pettiford Sextet, Buddy Rich, and as co-leader of Les Jazz Modes with Julius Watkins. From 1959 to 1970, Charlie Rouse gained prominence in the Thelonious Monk Quartet and freelanced regularly. After a hiatus from music, he joined Sphere, a cooperative group that included pianist Kenny Barron, bassist Buster Williams, and drummer Ben Riley. Rouse's recordings with Monk, Les Jazz Modes, Clifford Brown, Gerry Mulligan, and Sphere more than show off his swinging bop style.

Rowles, James "Jimmy" (1918–1996). Rowles started playing piano during his freshman year at Gonzaga University, Spokane, Washington. He later worked in the bands of Garwood Van and Muzzy Marcellino and played with Slim Gaillard, Lee and Lester Young, Billie Holiday, and Benny Goodman in the early forties. Rowles also played in Woody Herman's orchestra and, later, in Skinnay Ennis' army band. After discharge, he rejoined Herman in 1946 and worked later in the bands of Les Brown, Tommy Dorsey, and Bob Crosby. Rowles freelanced with Peggy Lee, Betty Hutton, Stan Getz, Charlie Parker, Benny Carter, Chet Baker, and Zoot Sims, while leading his own trios in Los Angeles in the fifties and sixties. Rowles' style included a mixture of swing and bebop.

Royal, Ernest "Ernie" (1921–1983). Ernie, a trumpeter and brother of altoist Marshall Royal, began his professional career playing in the bands of Les Hite and Cee Pee Johnson in the late thirties. Royal later played with Lionel Hampton, Phil Moore, Count Basie, Woody Herman's Second Herd, and a navy band in the forties. He spent the early fifties playing with Jacques Helian, Wardell Gray, and Stan Kenton along with tours in Europe and North Africa. From 1957 to 1972, Royal worked for ABC in New York City as a staff musician, played in Broadway shows, and participated in numerous recording dates with Gil Evans, Oliver Nelson, Quincy Jones, and others. Royal was known as an exceptional lead trumpeter and Swing Era–styled soloist who understood the bebop language. Royal also recorded with Coleman Hawkins and Billy Taylor.

Royal Peacock. A nightclub and theater that opened in the late forties in Atlanta, Georgia, and presented a variety of Swing Era musicians such as Nat "King" Cole, Lucky Millinder, Ivory Joe Hunter, Cab Calloway, and B. B. King.

Royal Roost. A jazz establishment that operated in New York City during the mid-forties and fifties. The club hosted Jimmie Lunceford, Charlie Parker, Lester Young, Lennie Tristano, and other artists who played swing, bop, and cool jazz styles.

Rugolo, Pete (b. 1915). Rugolo, an arranger-composer, studied with Darius Milhaud at Mills College in Oakland, California, and later became Stan Kenton's chief arranger in the late forties. In 1949 and 1950, he served as a record producer for Capitol Records, where he supervised Miles Davis' famous *Birth of the Cool* sessions. He also led his own big band that recorded for Columbia Records in 1954. Rugolo arranged and conducted for Billy Eckstine, Peggy Lee, Nat "King" Cole, Dinah Washington, Mel Tormé, and Woody Herman. Various *Downbeat* polls selected him as Best Arranger four times in the late forties and early fifties. Afterward, Rugolo wrote mostly for movies and television. His jazz charts effectively capture the influence of Milhaud and other composers of European music.

Rumsey, Howard (b. 1917). A bassist, Rumsey studied in Los Angeles and Chicago before making his professional debut with Vido Musso in 1938. From 1939 to 1945, Rumsey played in the bands of Johnny "Scat" Davis, Stan Kenton, Freddie Slack, and Charlie Barnet, but he is best known for organizing and leading The Lighthouse All-Stars from 1950 to 1960. He later managed The Lighthouse in Hermosa Beach for the next decade and quit playing bass before running his own club, known as Concerts by the Sea, from 1972 until he retired in 1985. Rumsey is one of the few accomplished musicians from the Swing Era who became a successful entrepreneur. He recorded with Barnet, Kenton, and The Lighthouse All-Stars.

Rushing, James "Jimmy" (1903–1972). Rushing, a vocalist, made his professional debut in a Hollywood nightclub at age twenty after attending college in Ohio. He also performed at private parties, traveled as an itinerant musician, and toured with Walter Page's Blue Devils in the late twenties. Rushing made his first record with Page in 1928, and he joined Bennie Moten's band after the Blue Devils disbanded a year later. Rushing's tenure with Moten lasted from 1929 until the leader's death in 1935. Shortly afterward, Rushing joined Count Basie's band and became an internationally recognized vocalist with recordings such as "Goin' to Chicago," "Good Mornin' Blues," and "Baby, Don't Tell on Me." Rushing remained with Basie until he disbanded in 1950 and then led his own small group for the next two years. He began working as a single in 1952 and toured around the world with major artists such as Benny Goodman, Buck Clayton, Harry James, and Thelonious Monk. Rushing recorded for the Vanguard and Columbia labels, and he won both the British and *Downbeat* critics polls in 1957, 1958, and 1959. He also appeared in films and on major television shows during his long and successful career.

Russell, Curley (1920–1986). Russell, a bassist, began his career in the swing bands of Don Redman and Benny Carter in the early forties. After the mid-forties, Russell worked and/or recorded with Dizzy Gillespie, Art

Blakey, Coleman Hawkins, Charlie Parker, Stan Getz, Charlie Parker, and Bud Powell and toured with Buddy DeFranco in the fifties. Although Russell established himself in the Later Swing Era, he became known as a premier bebop bassist through his work and recordings with Gillespie, Blakey, Powell, Clifford Brown, Fats Navarro, Tadd Dameron, and Sonny Stitt.

Russell, George (b. 1923). A pianist-composer, Russell played with the Collegians at Wilberforce University in Ohio. He arranged for Benny Carter, Earl Hines, Dizzy Gillespie ("Cubano Be-Cubano Bop"), Charlie Ventura, Claude Thornhill, Artie Shaw, and Buddy DeFranco in the forties. During the fifties, Russell wrote *The Lydian Chromatic Concept of Tonal Organization*, recorded with his own groups, and taught at the Lenox School of Jazz in Massachusetts. The sixties found Russell touring with his own sextet, studying and teaching in Scandinavia, and beginning his long tenure as a faculty member at Boston's New England Conservatory. He has received numerous awards including MacArthur and Guggenheim fellowships, six National Endowment of the Arts (NEA) grants, and recognition as a NEA Jazz Master. Since the seventies, Russell has continued to perform, write, conduct, and teach.

Russo, Santo "Sonny" (b. 1929). A trombonist, Russo began playing professionally in the late forties with Buddy Morrow, Lee Castle, Sam Donahue, and Artie Shaw. In the fifties, Russo worked with Art Mooney, Tito Puente, Jerry Wald, Tommy Tucker, Buddy Rich, the Sauter-Finegan Orchestra, Neal Hefti, the Dorsey Brothers, Maynard Ferguson, Louis Bellson, and Broadway show bands. He later played with Machito, Benny Goodman, and Doc Severinsen's *Tonight Show* band in New York City. Russo also worked with Frank Sinatra and recorded with many vocalists. Russo's rock-solid section playing can be heard in recordings by Ferguson and the Sauter-Finegan Orchestra.

Russo, William "Bill" (1928–2003). Russo, a trombonist-composer-bandleader, studied with Lennie Tristano, played in local Chicago bands, and led an experimental jazz orchestra in the forties. During the next decade, he played and wrote for Stan Kenton, led his own quintet, and taught at the School of Jazz in Lenox, Massachusetts. He spent the early sixties in Europe working for the BBC and British Jazz Orchestra, then returned home to Chicago and worked as a faculty member at Columbia College in 1965. He also directed the Chicago Jazz Ensemble until his recent death. Russo was best known as an experimental composer, and the depth of his work is documented in recordings by Kenton and the Chicago Jazz Ensemble.

Rutherford, Elman "Rudy" (1924–1995). A clarinetist-saxophonist, Rutherford played in the bands of Lionel Hampton, Count Basie, and Ted Buckner in the forties. Rutherford rejoined Basie and worked with Wilbur DeParis and Ram Ramirez in the fifties. After the Swing Era, Rutherford worked with Buddy Tate, Earl Hines, and Illinois Jacquet, led his own groups in New York City, and served as vocalist Marion Williams' music director. He recorded with Basie, DeParis, Hines, Jacquet, and Lester Young.

Sachs, Aaron (b. 1923). Sachs, a clarinetist-tenorist, began working professionally in his late teens with Van Alexander and played with Red Norvo and Benny Goodman in the early forties. Sachs recorded with Sarah Vaughn and Eddie Heywood, won *Esquire*'s New Star Award (1945), and recorded with his own group in the forties. He toured with Earl Hines, freelanced in New York City, and worked with Louis Bellson in the fifties. Afterward, Sachs taught and freelanced. His playing on recordings by Norvo and Shelly Manne demonstrate that he had a thorough knowledge of modern music and could express himself freely in different musical settings.

Safransky, Edward "Eddie" (1918–1979). A bassist, Safransky played with Hal McIntyre, Miff Mole, Stan Kenton, and Charlie Barnet in the forties before working in New York's radio and television studios and playing with Benny Goodman in the early fifties. Safransky later worked as a staff musician for NBC. His big sound and clean articulation can be heard on Kenton's "Painted Rhythm," "Artistry in Bolero," and Pete Rugolo's "Safransky (Artistry in Bass)."

Salvador, Sal (b. 1925). Salvador, a self-taught guitarist, played professionally around Springfield, Massachusetts, with Joe Morello and Phil Woods before working with Mundell Lowe, Terry Gibbs, and for Columbia Records as a staff musician between 1940 and 1951. Throughout the fifties, Salvador played with Stan Kenton and led his own quintet. The sixties saw him lead his own big band and accompany a number of singers such as Eydie Gormé, Johnny Mathis, Paul Anka, and Tony Bennett. Salvador dedicated a lot of his time to lecturing and teaching in the seventies and spent the eighties playing in his own bands. Salvador has written several guitar method books and owns a record label. He has recorded with Kenton, Nick Brignola, Merv Griffin, and Joe Franklin.

Santamaria, Ramon "Mongo" (1922–2003). A percussionist, Santamaria first worked professionally in Havana, Cuba, during the forties before settling in the United States and playing with Tito Puente, George Shearing, and others in the early fifties. Santamaria became quite popular as a bandleader after the Swing Era and made several Latin-jazz hit recordings.

Savoy Ballroom. One of Chicago's key jazz centers, the ballroom presented most of the great swing musicians during the forties. Some of the top musicians to appear at the venue were Louis Jordan, Stan Kenton, Count Basie,

Ella Fitzgerald, Gene Krupa, Woody Herman, Duke Ellington, the International Sweethearts of Rhythm, and Dizzy Gillespie.

Savoy Ballroom. Like several other large cities, Los Angeles had its own ballroom with the same name as New York City's famous dance venue. A number of swing musicians such as Earl Bostic, Les Hite, and Benny Carter performed there between 1930 and the mid-fifties.

Savoy Ballroom. Pittsburgh, Pennsylvania's own Savoy featured high-profile swing musicians such as Erroll Garner, Duke Ellington, Woody Herman, Cab Calloway, and Billy Eckstine during the Swing Era.

Schaefer, Harold "Hal" (b. 1925). A pianist-composer, Schaefer began performing at age thirteen in the Catskills before working with Lee Castle, Ina Ray Hutton, Benny Carter, Harry James, Boyd Raeburn, Billy Eckstine, and Peggy Lee and leading his own groups during the forties. He also arranged charts for recordings and shows and composed film scores. Since the fifties, he has performed in New York City nightclubs and worked as a vocal coach. He won *Downbeat*'s New Star Award in 1945, recorded with Boyd Raeburn, and toured Cuba, South America, and Europe.

Schildkraut, David "Davey" (1925–1998). An altoist, Schildkraut made his professional debut in 1941 with Louis Prima and spent the forties working with Anita O'Day and Buddy Rich. Schildkraut later worked with Stan Kenton, Pete Rugolo, Oscar Pettiford, George Handy, and Miles Davis in the fifties. He freelanced in the sixties and later fell into obscurity. He recorded with Davis, Kenton, and trombonist Eddie Bert.

Schroeder, Eugene "Gene" (1915–1975). Schroeder, a pianist, started his professional career in the late thirties with Joe Marsala and Wild Bill Davison. Around 1943, Schroeder began working with Eddie Condon at his New York City nightclub while appearing on television and touring. In the early sixties, Schroeder began freelancing and appearing with the Dukes of Dixieland. He recorded with Condon, Sidney Bechet, Jack Teagarden, Bobby Hackett, Bud Freeman, and the *Esquire* All-American Poll Winners.

Schuller, Gunther (b. 1925). Schuller is an author-composer-conductor-French hornist who studied privately with two top-ranking French horn players and began playing professionally in 1943 with the American Ballet Theatre. He played in the Cincinnati Symphony Orchestra between 1943 and 1945 and worked for the Metropolitan Opera from 1945 to 1959. On the jazz side, Schuller recorded with the Miles Davis Nonet in 1949 and 1950 and became associated with the "third stream" movement around 1957. Schuller wrote such compositions as "Concertino for Jazz Quintet and

Orchestra" and "Abstraction" in 1959, and "Variants on a Theme of Thelonious Monk" in 1960, which synthesized jazz and European music. He worked frequently with John Lewis after the late forties on such projects as co-founding the Lenox School of Jazz and preparing special performances with the Modern Jazz Quartet. Schuller wrote articles for *Jazz Review*, composed "Conversation" for the MJQ and Beaux Arts String Quartet along with "Variants" for jazz ballet, and directed jazz festivals in the early sixties. He also conducted the John Lewis Orchestra, lectured in Europe for the U.S. State Department, and produced the first jazz concert at Tanglewood in Lenox, Massachusetts. From 1967 to 1977, Schuller served as president of the New England Conservatory, where he formed the NEC Ragtime Ensemble and the NEC Jazz Repertory Orchestra. He is the author of *Early Jazz: Its Roots and Musical Development* and *The Swing Era: The Development of Jazz, 1930–1945*, published by Oxford University Press. He has recorded with Davis, Lewis, Charles Mingus, Gigi Gryce, and Dizzy Gillespie.

Schulman, Ira (b. 1926). A multi-reed instrumentalist, Schulman played professionally in Chicago during the fifties before working with Onzy Matthews, Don Ellis, and others on the West Coast in the sixties. During the seventies, Schulman gave numerous educational clinics on topics that ranged from Bach to Ellington. He formed a woodwind quartet in the eighties called the Four Winds that performed a wide variety of genres including jazz and European music. He has recorded with Don Ellis.

Scobey, Robert "Bob" (1916–1963). A trumpeter-bandleader who began playing professionally in the thirties around the San Francisco Bay area. He played in the forties with Lu Watters' band except for an interruption to serve in the military. Scobey formed the Frisco Jazz Band in 1950 and began recording for the Good Time Jazz label in the early fifties. His band performed at a number of colleges and universities, major Dixieland festivals, and nightclubs. Scobey was a solid trumpeter and highly effective bandleader. In fact, Scobey had one of the best Dixieland bands in the country. His recordings of tunes such as "Sobbin' Blues," "Indiana," and "Just a Closer Walk with Thee" display a tight and well-rehearsed ensemble with fine soloists. Scobey's contribution to the revival movement deserves wider recognition.

Scott, Anthony "Tony" (b. 1921). Scott, a clarinetist-saxophonist-composer-pianist, studied at Juilliard and led an army band from 1940 to 1945. After discharge, he played with Buddy Rich, Ben Webster, Sid Catlett, Trummy Young, Charlie Ventura, and Claude Thornhill in the late forties. He also worked off and on as a piano accompanist for vocalists. He wrote charts for Billie Holiday and Sarah Vaughn, played briefly with Duke

Ellington, freelanced as a clarinetist-pianist-arranger, led his own groups, and worked as Harry Belafonte's music director in the fifties. Since the early sixties, Scott has embraced Asian and Indian music as part of his stylistic approach. He traveled and performed internationally during the seventies. Scott has recorded with Holiday, Vaughn, Benny Carter, Dizzy Gillespie, Carmen McRae, and Coleman Hawkins.

Scott, Hazel (1920–1981). A pianist-vocalist, Hazel Scott studied at Juilliard as a child prodigy when she was only eight years old. She had her own radio show and sang on Broadway in her teens. From 1939 to 1945, she rose to prominence through her performances at the Café Society and appeared at the White House with Billie Holiday during World War II for President Franklin D. Roosevelt. She recorded "Relaxed Piano Moods" with Charles Mingus and Max Roach for Debut Records in 1955 and worked in clubs, concerts, and movies until 1957.

Scott, James "Little Jimmy" (b. 1925). Scott, a vocalist, toured the South and Midwest in the mid-forties with Estelle "Caledonia" Young. He joined Lionel Hampton in 1948 and recorded a hit, "Everybody's Somebody's Fool," in 1950. Scott began a solo career in the early fifties and recorded "The Masquerade Is Over." From that point on, he experienced a twenty-year absence from the music scene until making a comeback in the mid-eighties, when he performed many club dates and recorded into the early nineties. His small stature and youthful look caused the public to assume he was a child, which led to his nickname.

Severinsen, Carl "Doc" (b. 1927). Widely known as bandleader for Johnny Carson's *Tonight Show* for twenty-five years, Severinsen first played trumpet in the bands of Ted Fio Rito, Charlie Barnet, Sam Donahue, and Tommy Dorsey during the late forties. Severinsen joined NBC as a staff musician in 1949 and spent the fifties playing on the *Steve Allen Show* and with Billy Taylor's band for an NBC television series. In 1962, he joined the *Tonight Show* as an assistant conductor, became the bandleader five years later, and remained with the show until Carson retired in 1992. Severinsen has recorded with Lena Horne, Joe Morello, Stan Getz, Gerry Mulligan, Jimmy Smith, Gil Evans, and others.

Shank, Clifford "Bud" (b. 1926). An altoist, Shank studied music in college before working with Charlie Barnet and Alvino Rey on the West Coast in the late forties. He worked with Stan Kenton, George Redman, and The Lighthouse All-Stars in the early fifties and led his own group until the early sixties. Shank later freelanced in nightclubs around Los Angeles and in film and television studios through the mid-seventies before forming his own group, which worked off and on until the early eighties. He received awards from *Downbeat* and the National Academy of Recording Arts and Sciences. Shank performed at many jazz festivals in the United States and Europe, and he recorded with Chet Baker, Lorez Alexandria, Billy Eckstine, Ella Fitzgerald, Mel Tormé, Charlie Byrd, and Miles Davis. Shank is best known as a versatile musician who can excel in both jazz and commercial music.

Shavers, Charles "Charlie" (1917–1971). A trumpeter, Shavers began playing professionally as a teenager with Willie Gant, and he worked briefly with Frankie Fairfax, Tiny Bradshaw, and Lucky Millinder before earning a national reputation in John Kirby's sextet from 1937 to 1944. Shavers was Kirby's chief arranger-composer and contributed a great deal to the band's unique sound while playing on recording dates for Jimmie Noone, Johnny Dodds, and Sidney Bechet. Afterward, Shavers played in Tommy Dorsey's orchestra from 1945 to 1956, where he was featured prominently and became known as one of the most exciting trumpeters of the Swing Era. He later recorded with the Esquire All-Stars, toured with Jazz at the Philharmonic, and worked with Benny Goodman before leading his own quartet.

Shaw, Arvell (b. 1923). Shaw, a bassist, began playing professionally at age nineteen on a riverboat with Fate Marable. Shaw played in a navy band during the war, worked in Louis Armstrong's big band in the mid-forties, and served as a member of Armstrong's All-Stars from 1947 to 1950. After studying theory and harmony in Switzerland for a year, Shaw worked at various times with Armstrong throughout the fifties. He later played with such artists as Coleman Hawkins, Charlie Shavers, Teddy Wilson, Red Allen, Lionel Hampton, Cozy Cole, Rex Stewart, Benny Goodman, Vic Dickenson, and Roy Eldridge. Shaw rejoined Louis Armstrong's All-Stars in the sixties, led his own trio, worked with Dorothy Donegan, and performed in many educational concerts. He played with Barney Bigard and toured France with Earl Hines in the seventies. In the eighties, Shaw worked in Broadway pit orchestras before spending the nineties with Lionel Hampton's Golden Men of Jazz and the Louis Armstrong Legacy All-Stars. Shaw appeared in several films and on television and recorded with Armstrong, Goodman, Hampton, Hawkins, Sammy Price, Doc Cheatham, and others.

Shearing, George (b. 1919). A pianist-composer-bandleader, Shearing was born in London, England. He began playing professionally in the late thirties and established himself as the leading jazz pianist in the United Kingdom before moving to New York City in 1947. Shearing formed his first quintet in 1949 and developed the "Shearing sound," which consisted of Milt Buckner's "locked-hands" style and the chordal sound of Glenn Miller's saxophone section. After creating a sound that was accessible to the average listener, Shearing became a highly popular artist. Some of his most successful recordings include "September in the Rain" and his own composition, "Lullaby of Birdland." After his renowned quintet disbanded in 1967, he continued to perform in both trio and duo formats. Shearing currently performs, and he is still a highly popular artist.

Shepard, Ernest "Ernie" (1916–1965). A bassist, Shepard began playing professionally in Texas swing bands and worked later on the West Coast with Gerald Wilson, Phil Moore, and the Charlie Parker–Dizzy Gillespie quintet in the forties. Shepard recorded with Slim Gaillard, Sonny Stitt, Gene Ammons, and Johnny Hodges before touring with Duke Ellington and recording with Paul Gonsalves in the early sixties. Afterward, Shepard moved to Germany where he worked in studios, on television, and participated in a number of recording sessions.

Shepherd, Berisford "Shep" (b. 1917). Shepherd, a drummer, worked with Benny Carter, Artie Shaw, Cab Calloway, Earl Bostic, and Bill Doggett throughout most of the fifties. He wrote "Honky Tonk," which was one of Doggett's biggest hits. After leaving Doggett in 1959, Shepherd played in Broadway shows for a while and moved to San Francisco where he freelanced into the nineties.

Sherman, Ray (b. 1923). A pianist, Sherman played in the local California bands of Hal Grayson, Paul Neighbors, and Jimmy Walsh. Sherman later worked with Jan Savitt and Gus Arnheim and served in the military during the mid-forties, where he played with a band co-led by Ray Bauduc and Gil Rodin. In 1948, Sherman became a studio musician and spent thirty-five years performing in numerous shows and sessions, including Bob Crosby's live television show. He can be heard on the soundtrack of *Pete Kelly's Blues* and has worked with Stan Kenton, Benny Goodman, Jack Sheldon, Doc Cheatham, Bob Wilber, Pete Fountain, and others.

Sherock, Clarence "Shorty" (1915–1980). A trumpeter, Sherock gained national visibility in the thirties with the bands of Ben Pollack, Jimmy Dorsey, and Bob Crosby. Sherock later played with Gene Krupa, Tommy Dorsey, Horace Heidt, and Jazz at the Philharmonic, and led his own band during the forties. He then worked in Los Angeles as a studio musician and recorded with Frank Sinatra, Benny Carter, Ella Fitzgerald, and Muggsy Spanier. Sherock was a well-respected Swing Era–styled trumpeter.

Short, Robert "Bobby" (b. 1924). Short, a pianist-vocalist, became a featured artist at the Blue Angel in New York City, the Gala in Hollywood, and the Haig in Los Angeles during the forties. In the fifties and sixties, he performed at clubs in Paris and has worked at New York City's Café

Carlyle off and on since 1968. Over the past decade, Short has performed with large ensembles and toured occasionally. He is considered one of the best supper-club vocalists in the music industry. He has recorded as a leader and with Marian McPartland.

Shrine Auditorium. A landmark performance venue in Los Angeles that housed some of jazz history's most famous events. Gene Norman's "Just Jazz" concerts were presented in the late forties, along with the Norman–Frank Bull Dixieland Jubilee concerts from the late forties to the early sixties. Other events included Norman Granz's Jazz at the Philharmonic concerts in the late forties and the fifties. Some famous concerts recorded at the hall were *Stan Getz at the Shrine Auditorium* and *Edward "Kid" Ory and His Creole Band at the Dixieland Jubilee.*

Shu, Edward "Eddie" (1918–1986). Shu, a multi-instrumentalist, toured with a harmonica band at age seventeen before working with Major Bowes as a harmonica soloist and ventriloquist. Although Shu was proficient on clarinet, saxophones, and trumpet, he mostly played tenor. He performed with Tadd Dameron in 1947 following military service and worked later with George Shearing, Buddy Rich, and Lionel Hampton. During the fifties, Shu played with Charlie Barnet, Chubby Jackson, Gene Krupa, and others. Afterward, he toured with Louis Armstrong in the mid-sixties before performing and teaching in the U.S. Virgin Islands for a number of years. Shu's ability to fit comfortably into traditional jazz, swing, and bebop settings made him an ideal sideman for recordings with Armstrong, Roy Eldridge, and Anita O'Day.

Signature. A record company established by Bob Thiele in the early forties, the label recorded such artists as Eddie Heywood, Flip Phillips, Barney Bigard, Art Hodes, Earl Hines, and Anita O'Day. One of the label's best-known sessions is Coleman Hawkins' famous recording of *The Man I Love.*

Sims, John "Zoot" (1925–1985). A saxophonist-clarinetist, Sims began his professional career at age fifteen. He played in the bands of Ken Baker, Bobby Sherwood, Sonny Dunham, Bob Astor, Benny Goodman, and Sid Catlett in the early forties. After military service, Sims rejoined Goodman for a year and became a member of the famous Four Brothers saxophone section in Woody Herman's band in the late forties. After his tenure with Herman, Sims worked with Buddy Rich, Artie Shaw, Roy Eldridge, Chubby Jackson, Elliot Lawrence, and Stan Kenton while based in New York City between 1949 and 1953. Sims performed on both the East and West coasts in the fifties, including a period with Gerry Mulligan's sextet. He continued to work in small groups and big bands, recording with such artists as Al Cohn, Chet Baker, Charles Mingus, Miles Davis, Joe Williams, and

Bucky Pizzarelli. Sims' concept of swing and ballad playing rates him among the best in jazz.

Sinatra, Francis Albert "Frank" (1915–1998). A vocalist, Sinatra started singing professionally in the late thirties after winning a Major Bowes Amateur Hour radio contest. After more radio appearances, he joined Harry James' band in 1939 for a year and worked with Tommy Dorsey's band until 1942. Sinatra's recording of "All or Nothing at All" with James became a hit in 1943 and helped him gain worldwide attention after starting a solo career in 1942. Sinatra spent the forties and fifties as one of the most popular vocalists in the Later Swing Era with regular live performances, radio appearances, acting/singing roles in movies, and recording contracts with the Columbia and Capitol labels. His most successful recordings such as "Come Swing with Me" and "Come Fly with Me" were made in the fifties with Capitol. Sinatra recorded with big-band jazz arrangers such as Nelson Riddle, Billy May, Quincy Jones, Neal Hefti, and Johnny Mandel in the sixties and found the formula he needed to highlight his vocal style successfully. After a two-year retirement in the early seventies, Sinatra returned with international tours, more recordings, and television appearances. He also received numerous awards during his career that continued into the nineties.

Singer, Harold "Hal" (b. 1919). Singer, a tenorist, studied agriculture at Hampton University in Virginia and received a degree in 1937. After graduation, he chose the music profession and played in the bands of Ernie Fields, Nat Towles, Lloyd Hunter, Tommy Douglas, and Jay McShann from 1938 to 1943. Singer freelanced in New York City with Willie "The Lion" Smith, Chris Columbus, Earl Bostic, Roy Eldridge, Sid Catlett, Don Byas, Trummy Young, Red Allen, Hot Lips Page, Lucky Millinder, and Bullmoose Jackson between 1943 and 1948. Duke Ellington hired Singer in 1948, but he played in the band for only six months. He left Ellington after he made his hit record, "Cornbread," and formed his own band. Singer worked successfully as a bandleader for two decades.

Sky Bar. A Cleveland nightclub that opened in 1948 and featured Ohio-born musicians such as Tadd Dameron and Benny Bailey. The early fifties witnessed bookings of other artists, however, such as Billie Holiday, Stan Getz, Oscar Peterson, Johnny Hodges, and Erroll Garner.

Smalls, Clifton "Cliff" (b. 1918). A pianist-trombonist-arranger, Smalls traveled with the Carolina Cotton Pickers while studying at the Kansas City Conservatory. He worked with Earl Hines as a trombonist-arranger-second pianist from 1942 to 1946, and served as an arranger-conductor for Billy Eckstine, Brook Benton, Clyde McPhatter, and others from the late forties through the sixties. Smalls also accompanied Roy Hamilton and Ella Fitzgerald during that period. He later played with Sy Oliver and recorded with Buddy Tate, Bennie Green, Oliver Jackson, Paul Gonsalves, and Roy Eldridge.

Small's Paradise. A famous Harlem, New York, nightclub that operated at various times from the twenties to the mid-eighties. The club hosted numerous resident bandleaders in the forties and fifties such as Gus Aitken, Harry Dial, and the great drummer Chris Columbus.

Smith, Edna (b. 1924). Smith, a bassist, began performing professionally with the International Sweethearts of Rhythm in the forties. She later played in the Vi Burnside Orchestra and her own trio in the fifties. After establishing herself as a renowned jazz bassist, Smith earned two degrees in music from the Manhattan School of Music, as well as two degrees in education (including a doctorate) from Columbia University. She has taught in New York City's public schools and at the University of Nigeria in West Africa, New York's Queens College, and Medgar Evers College.

Smith, Maybel "Big Maybelle" (1924–1972). A vocalist, Smith won an amateur vocal contest in Memphis, Tennessee, at age nine and later sang professionally with Dave Clark's band. Smith gained national recognition with Tiny Bradshaw from 1947 to 1950 and spent the next two decades working as a soloist. She recorded for the Savoy and Okeh record labels.

Smith, William "Bill" (b. 1926). Smith, a clarinetist-composer, studied at Juilliard in New York City and Mills College in California before playing in an octet with Dave Brubeck in the late forties. After receiving a master's degree in 1952, Smith recorded with Shelly Manne and Red Norvo while teaching at the University of Southern California in the fifties. He later organized the American Jazz Ensemble, performed frequently with Brubeck, and toured the United States and Europe.

Spanier, Francis "Muggsy" (1906–1967). Spanier, a cornetist-bandleader, began his professional career in his teens and played with Ted Lewis and Ben Pollack in the mid-thirties. Spanier organized his Ragtime Band in the late thirties before working with Lewis, Miff Mole, and his own band again in the forties. In the fifties, Spanier freelanced on the West Coast and worked with Earl Hines. Afterward, Spanier performed regularly until the end of his life. He was noted for his ability to lead an ensemble effectively and solo efficiently with a growl mute. Spanier's warm sound was influenced by King Oliver, and his Chicago-style Dixieland playing is heard to great effect in his album, *Muggsy Spanier and His Ragtimers*, on the Commodore label.

Sproles, Victor (b. 1927). A bassist, Sproles played during military service and worked with such musicians as Ira Sullivan, Coleman Hawkins, and Vernel Fournier in the early fifties. Sproles later gained national recognition with Art Blakey's Jazz Messengers, the Al Cohn–Zoot Sims Quintet, and Carmen McRae. Sproles has a full sound and an elastic walking bass style that can be heard on albums by McRae, Blakey, and Buddy DeFranco.

Starr, Kay [Katherine Laverne Starks] (b. 1922). A vocalist, Starr began working professionally during her teens with hillbilly bands in Memphis, Tennessee, and was discovered by bandleader Joe Venuti. While touring with Venuti, Starr had the opportunity to appear with Bob Crosby, Johnny Mercer, and Glenn Miller. She made her recording debut with Miller and waxed two sides, "Baby Me" and "Lone With a Capital A." Starr later sang with Charlie Barnet's band from 1943 to 1945 and recorded with Wingy Manone and the Capitol Jazzmen. She began working as a single in 1946 and signed with the Capitol label, recording such hits as "Bonaparte's Retreat" and "So Tired" in the late forties. Starr was a versatile vocalist who could sing in a variety of genres such as rock and roll, country, and swing. She also appeared on radio shows with Bing Crosby and Spike Jones and hosted her own radio show on ABC. Starr was a popular Swing Era vocalist who performed into the nineties and influenced a generation of vocalists such as Liza Minnelli and Rosemary Clooney.

Stein, Louis "Lou" (b. 1922). Stein, a pianist, began playing in jam sessions with Bill Harris, Buddy DeFranco, and Charlie Ventura before joining Ray McKinley's band in 1942. Stein played in Glenn Miller's Army Air Force Band in Connecticut and rejoined McKinley after discharge during 1946 and 1947. Stein joined Ventura's group again in 1947, and his most famous composition "East of Suez" was recorded by that band. He freelanced with Kai Winding, Benny Goodman, Joe Newman, Louis Bellson, Sarah Vaughn, Red Allen, Coleman Hawkins, Lester Young, and others while spending many years as a studio musician. He also played with Joe Venuti, recorded several albums as a leader, and continued to perform into the late nineties.

Stewart, Leroy "Slam" (1914–1987). Stewart studied bass at the Boston Conservatory, and he developed his style of humming an octave above his arco bass solos after hearing violinist Ray Perry sing along with his violin playing. Stewart began playing professionally with Peanuts Holland in 1936 and 1937 and worked with Slim Gaillard as part of Slim and Slam from 1938 to 1942. The duo performed mostly as a quartet and recorded a hit, "Flat Foot Floogie," that boosted the group's popularity. After military service, Stewart worked as a member of the famous Art Tatum trio along with Tiny Grimes in 1943 and 1944. Stewart later worked in Grimes' band and was featured with Benny Goodman's bands in the mid-forties. Stewart rejoined Tatum in the late forties and later led his own trio with Billy Taylor or Beryl Booker on piano and John Collins on guitar. Stewart also played with Roy Eldridge and Rose Murphy and made return engagements with Tatum. Stewart later taught at the university level and performed with a variety of name artists.

Stitt, Edward "Sonny" (1924–1982). Stitt, a saxophonist, began his professional career on alto in Tiny Bradshaw's band during the early forties. He played later in the big bands of Billy Eckstine and Dizzy Gillespie. In 1949, he began playing tenor with a distinctive sound that combined the stylistic approaches of Charlie Parker and Lester Young. Stitt co-led a two-tenor group with Gene Ammons in the early fifties and led several of his own small bands. He recorded albums for Prestige, Argo, and Verve, rejoined Gillespie, and toured with Jazz at the Philharmonic in the late fifties. Stitt worked with Miles Davis in 1960 and 1961, played Parker tributes at Newport, and toured with the Giants of Jazz featuring Gillespie, Kai Winding, Thelonious Monk, Al McKibbon, and Art Blakey.

Stokes, Irvin (b. 1926). A trumpeter, Stokes first played with local bands in Greensboro, North Carolina, and worked with Cecil Payne, Duke Jordan, Leonard Gaskin, Ernie Henry, and Max Roach in New York City. He played with Mercer and Duke Ellington in the late forties. Stokes later worked with Erskine Hawkins and played in Buddy Johnson's orchestra in the late fifties. He worked with Andy Kirk's orchestra and freelanced during the sixties before playing in Broadway shows, with the Thad Jones–Mel Lewis Orchestra, and with the Savoy Sultans in the seventies. Stokes worked with Arnett Cobb, Oliver Jackson, and Illinois Jacquet in the eighties prior to joining the Count Basie Orchestra led by Frank Foster in 1990. Stokes has appeared in films and commercials and recorded with Panama Francis, Jackson, and Jacquet.

Storyville. A nightclub that was established in Boston during the early fifties and hosted Dixieland and swing musicians. Billie Holiday, George Shearing, Ruby Braff, Duke Ellington, Wild Bill Davison, Count Basie, Pee Wee Russell, and Jo Jones were among numerous artists who performed at the venue.

Storyville Records. A company established in Boston by George Wein in 1951 that made both studio and live (from the Storyville club) recordings in the fifties. The label recorded a number of major swing and traditional jazz musicians, including Vic Dickenson, Ellis Larkins, Sidney Bechet, Ruby Braff, Zoot Sims, Joe Newman, Serge Chaloff, and vocalists Jackie Cain and Roy Kral.

Strayhorn, William "Billy" (1915–1967). Strayhorn, a pianist-composer-arranger-lyricist, began writing songs as a teenager and by age twenty-one had written "Lush Life," which later became a jazz standard. Duke Ellington was impressed with Strayhorn's work and hired him in 1938 as a lyric writer. Over the years, Strayhorn became Ellington's chief arranger and associate composer. Strayhorn made noteworthy musical contributions with his independent writing as well as his collaborations with Ellington. The collaborations resulted in compositions such as "The Far East Suite," "Such Sweet Thunder," and "A Drum Is a Woman." Some of Strayhorn's own writing includes "Take the 'A' Train," "Chelsea Bridge," "Passion Flower," and "Something to Live For." Strayhorn mostly recorded with Ellington's sidemen but made two of his own albums entitled *The Peaceful Side* and *Lush Life*. He was recognized by *Esquire* with two Silver awards as an arranger in the mid-forties. The eighties witnessed such artists as Art Farmer, Toshiko Akiyoshi, Marian McPartland, and Joe Henderson dedicating full albums to Strayhorn by featuring his compositions. His work has made a major impact on American popular music.

Streets of Paris. A famous venue on Hollywood Boulevard in Los Angeles that presented mostly Dixieland and small swing groups from the thirties through the fifties. Some of the musicians who performed at the club include Zutty Singleton and Jimmy Noone.

Stuyvesant Casino. A ballroom in New York City that became popular when Bunk Johnson and his New Orleans band played at the venue in 1945. Other musicians such as Buck Clayton, Henry "Red" Allen, Sidney Bechet, and Zutty Singleton performed there during the forties and early fifties.

Sulieman, Idrees (b. 1923). Sulieman, a trumpeter, started playing professionally with the Carolina Cotton Pickers and worked in Earl Hines' band in 1943 and 1944. Sulieman later played with Cab Calloway, Mercer Ellington, Illinois Jacquet, Count Basie, Erskine Hawkins, Lionel Hampton, Dizzy Gillespie, and Gerry Mulligan. Sulieman also performed with Friedrich Gulda at Birdland and at the Newport Jazz Festival. Sulieman later moved overseas and eventually settled in Denmark. He has a unique sound and style that can be heard on recordings by Mal Waldron, Horace Parlan, the Clarke-Boland big band, and Joe Henderson.

Sunset Terrace. Located on famous Indiana Avenue in Indianapolis, the Terrace featured big-name musicians such as Ella Fitzgerald, Billy Eckstine, and Count Basie during the Swing Era.

Swanee Inn. A small restaurant and bar in Los Angeles that presented small groups from the late thirties to the early fifties. Nat "King" Cole, Art Tatum, Meade "Lux" Lewis, and Oscar Pettiford's trio performed at the venue.

Tate, George "Buddy" (1915–2001). Tate, a saxophonist-clarinetist-flutist, began playing professionally in 1927 and worked in the thirties with Terrance Holder, Count Basie, Andy Kirk, and Nat Towles. Tate played again with Basie's band from 1939 to 1949, and worked with Lucky Millinder, Hot Lips Page, and Jimmy Rushing between 1950 and 1952. In 1953, Tate formed his own band and worked at the Celebrity Club, the Savoy Ballroom, the Waldorf-Astoria, and Biltmore Hotel. He toured Europe and Japan until the mid-seventies, and, in the late seventies, toured with the Saints and Sinners, co-led a band with tenorist Paul Quinichette, and played with Jay McShann and Jim Galloway. In the eighties, Tate toured with Illinois Jacquet and the Texas Tenors before playing with the Countsmen and Lionel Hampton's Golden Men of Jazz in the early nineties. Tate recorded with Basie, Hampton, Rushing, Jacquet, Ruby Braff, Buck Clayton, Milt Buckner, Joe Turner, and many others.

Tatum, Arthur "Art" (1909–1956). Tatum, a pianist, began playing professionally at age seventeen and traveled to New York City as vocalist Adelaide Hall's accompanist in 1932, where he captured the attention of the jazz world. He performed frequently around the country in nightclubs and on radio and toured England during the thirties. Tatum formed his famous trio with bassist Slam Stewart and guitarist Tiny Grimes in 1943, which became one of the most popular small groups in the Later Swing Era. Tatum mostly performed and recorded as a soloist throughout his career, but his trio recordings from the forties highlight his consummate skills as a pianist and bandleader. Although Tatum's piano skill superceded that of most jazz and classical pianists, he actually achieved his greatest success with his trio.

Taylor, William "Billy" (b. 1921). A pianist-arranger-composer, Taylor began his professional performing career in 1944 with Ben Webster's band at the Three Deuces in New York City. From 1944 to 1946, Taylor worked with Stuff Smith, Billie Holiday, Dizzy Gillespie, Foots Thomas, Cozy Cole, and Slam Stewart, and toured with Don Redman in Europe before freelancing in Paris during 1946 and 1947. After playing in a duo with Bob Wyatt in 1948, Taylor led his own group in 1949 and 1950 and worked at Birdland as its house pianist in 1951. Since 1952, he has led his own trios, hosted numerous radio and television jazz programs, performed and lectured at numerous colleges and universities, served as music director of David Frost's television show, written several articles and books on jazz, founded Jazzmobile in New York City, written music extensively, and received a doctorate from the University of Massachusetts–Amherst.

Terry, Clark (b. 1920). Terry, a trumpeter-flugelhornist-vocalist, started playing professionally in the early forties. After playing in a navy band during World War II, he worked with George Hudson, Lionel Hampton, Charlie

Barnet, Eddie Vinson, and Charlie Ventura in the mid-forties. In 1948, Terry played with Count Basie's orchestra and small group until 1951, and he gained national recognition as a member of Duke Ellington's orchestra from 1951 to 1959. From 1960 to 1972, Terry was a staff musician for NBC in New York City and became a popular member of the *Tonight Show* orchestra. Terry has performed and recorded with numerous top-ranking artists such as J. J. Johnson, Oscar Peterson, Bob Brookmeyer, and Ella Fitzgerald. He has appeared as a soloist and/or bandleader at many jazz festivals, served as a clinician and teacher at numerous colleges and universities, and directed several summer big-band camps. Although Terry's playing evolved alongside bebop, he has retained a happy and swinging trumpet style along with his popular vocal scat-singing commonly referred to as "Mumbles." Terry is still an active performer and clinician.

Thompson, Eli "Lucky" (b. 1924). Thompson, a tenor and soprano saxophonist, first played in local Detroit groups that included Hank Jones before joining Lionel Hampton in 1943. After four months with Hampton, he worked with Hot Lips Page, Sid Catlett, and Billy Eckstine's band before joining Count Basie for a year. Thompson became one of the most prolific jazz recording artists in Los Angeles in the late forties, and he worked with such artists as Dizzy Gillespie, Louis Armstrong, Boyd Raeburn, Benny Carter, Johnny Richards, Buddy Baker, and Jimmy Mundy. Thompson's highly melodic style is featured on Basie's recordings of "I Didn't Know About You," "Avenue C," and "Taps Miller."

Thompson, Sir Charles (b. 1918). A solid swing-styled pianist, Thompson joined the Lloyd Hunter Orchestra at age fifteen. He went on to play with Nat Towles in the late thirties, Lionel Hampton in 1940, and Lester Young in 1941. Thompson worked with Don Byas, Roy Eldridge, and Hot Lips Page before playing with Coleman Hawkins and Howard McGhee in California in 1944 and 1945. After returning to New York City, Thompson led his own recording date in 1945 and played with Illinois Jacquet in 1947 and 1948. While playing with Jacquet, Thompson composed "Robbin's Nest," which became the saxophonist's big hit recording. He later worked with Charlie Barnet, rejoined Jacquet for a while in 1952, and led his own small groups in and around New York City. He performed off and on before moving to Japan.

Thornhill, Claude (1909–1965). Thornhill, a pianist-composer, began his professional career in the thirties as an arranger for Hal Kemp, Freddie Martin, Russ Morgan, Ray Noble, and Benny Goodman. Thornhill later arranged and conducted for Maxine Sullivan's recordings of "Loch Lomond" and "Gone with the Wind," and served as the music director for the *Bob Hope Show* during the summer of 1939. Thornhill organized his first band in 1940 and gained national recognition with recordings of traditional tunes such as "Auld Lang Syne" and "Londonderry Air." It was difficult to keep a big band together during the war, so he disbanded in 1942 and served in the navy as a bandleader until 1946. After discharge, he formed another big band with Gil Evans as its chief arranger. Evans arranged bebop tunes such as "Donna Lee" and "Anthropology," which paved the way for modern jazz arranging. Thornhill's band also appealed to dancers with charts such as "Polka Dots" and "Moonbeams" and his own "Snowfall." Although Thornhill developed one of the most original-sounding bands in the forties, he disbanded in 1948 because of the competition with commercial orchestras. Subsequently, he worked off and on with temporary big bands and small groups until the end of his life.

Tic Toc Club. A Boston establishment that began presenting jazz in the early forties. Many musicians including Joe Williams, Fats Waller, and Lionel Hampton appeared at the club.

Timer, Joseph "Joe" (1923–1955). Timer, a drummer, studied music during military service and began playing professionally in the late forties with Johnny Scat Davis. Timer played in Elliot Lawrence's orchestra, recorded an album under his own name, and performed on several television shows in the early fifties.

Tiny and Ruby's Gay Spot. Opened by trumpeter Ernestine "Tiny" Davis and Ruby Lucas in the mid-fifties, this Chicago nightclub featured Vi Burnside, Davis' all-female band, Paul Bascomb, and other swing musicians.

Tjader, Callen "Cal" (1925–1982). A vibist, Tjader received a bachelor's degree in music education from San Francisco State College and played with Dave Brubeck for two years. Tjader played in George Shearing's quintet in the early fifties before forming his own group and later gaining an international reputation. His album, *Several Shades of Jade*, recorded on the Verve label was highly successful with a musical style that encompassed Latin, jazz, and soul music. Tjader also recorded with Carmen McRae, Woody Herman, Anita O'Day, Stan Getz, and others.

Tormé, Melvin "Mel" (b. 1925–1999). Tormé, a vocalist-songwriter, sang with the Coon-Saunders Orchestra at age four, started playing drums at age seven, and acted in radio soap operas for six years. He published his first song at age fifteen and wrote "The Christmas Song" in 1944 when he was only nineteen. Nat "King" Cole's recording made the song famous two years later. Tormé also wrote "Born to Be Blue," which became a standard. He toured with the Chico Marx band during 1942 and 1943, made his movie debut in 1943, led his own vocal group, and served in the army in 1945 and 1946. He became a solo act in 1947 and was a major attraction throughout the fifties. After his 1962 hit, "Comin' Home Baby," Tormé's recording career reached a low point, but he made a comeback twenty years later when he signed with Concord Records in 1983. He reached his artistic peak in the mid-nineties at age seventy, just prior to a major illness that ended his singing career.

Touff, Cyril "Cy" (b. 1927). A bass trumpeter, Touff started out playing trombone in the army band in the mid-forties with Conte Condoli and Red Mitchell. After military service, Touff worked with Bill Russo, Charlie Ventura, Ray McKinley, Boyd Raeburn, and the New York Opera Company. After hearing Johnny Mandel play a bass trumpet in the late forties, Touff switched to that instrument. He toured with Woody Herman from 1953 to 1956. Touff, who has amazing facility and a dark sound on the seldom-heard instrument, is featured on Woody Herman's 1954 recording of Bill Holman's "The Third Herd."

Town Hall. A large, historic New York City establishment where Eddie Condon organized his Dixieland jam sessions in the early and mid-forties, along with appearances by Louis Armstrong, James P. Johnson, Muggsy Spanier, Bunk Johnson, and others.

Travis, Nicholas "Nick" (1925–1964). A trumpeter, Travis played with Vido Musso, Woody Herman, Ray McKinley, Benny Goodman, Gene Krupa, and others in the forties. He played in the bands of Tommy Dorsey, Tex Beneke, Bob Chester, Elliot Lawrence, and Jimmy Dorsey, as well as with the Sauter-Finegan Orchestra in the fifties. He later worked as a staff musician for NBC. Travis, who had a keen awareness of both swing and bop, could express himself equally well in big-band and small-group settings. He recorded with artists ranging from Coleman Hawkins to George Shearing.

Treadwell, George (1919–1967). A trumpeter, Treadwell began his career with the house band at New York City's Monroe's Uptown House during 1941 and 1942. From 1942 to 1947, he worked with Benny Carter, the Sunset Royals, Cootie Williams, and J. C. Heard. Treadwell became Sarah Vaughn's music director (and husband) in 1947—and later her manager. In the fifties and sixties, Treadwell worked full time as a manager for such artists as Ruth Brown and the Drifters, served as an A&R man, and wrote songs. In the mid-forties, he recorded with Williams, Heard, Vaughn, Ethel Waters, and Dicky Wells.

Trianon Ballroom. A major Chicago jazz venue that presented some of the top swing bands for whites-only dances from the mid-thirties until 1950.

The ballroom closed for a while and reopened in the mid-fifties as the New Trianon, which was desegregated. It later featured artists such as Louis Jordan, Count Basie, Dinah Washington, and Earl Bostic.

Trianon Ballroom. A Cleveland, Ohio, venue that featured big bands led by Count Basie, Benny Goodman, Duke Ellington, Andy Kirk, Bob Crosby, Benny Carter, and others between the mid-thirties and mid-fifties.

Trotman, Lloyd (b. 1923). Trotman, a bassist-composer, studied at the New England Conservatory before touring with Blanche Calloway in 1941. He moved to New York City in 1945 and worked with Eddie Heywood, Hazel Scott, Duke Ellington, Edmond Hall, Wilbur DeParis, and Boyd Raeburn in the late forties. Trotman worked with Johnny Hodges, Sonny Dunham, and Jerry Wald in the fifties while working as a studio musician. He recorded with Lucky Millinder, Ray Charles, Bud Powell, Joe Turner, Red Allen, Chuck Willis, and Ivory Joe Hunter. Trotman's versatility as a musician is compelling in that he played and recorded with many first-rate swing, bebop, and rhythm-and-blues artists.

Troup, Robert "Bobby" (1918–1999). A vocalist-pianist-songwriter, Troup taught himself to play the piano during his youth and wrote his first hit song "Daddy" at age twenty-three. He worked as Tommy Dorsey's staff writer before serving in the U.S. Marines and attaining the rank of captain between 1942 and 1946. After military duty, Troup moved to Los Angeles and wrote "Route 66," which became an even bigger hit than his first song. He recorded "Brand New Dolly" with Count Basie's band in the late forties while working with trios in bars until his recording debut as a leader in 1952. After the early fifties, Troup made numerous appearances on television and in movies. Some of his most popular songs include "You're Looking at Me," "Baby, Baby All the Time," "Girl Talk," and "Snooty Little Cutie."

Tucker, George (1927–1965). Tucker, a bassist, developed an interest in jazz by listening to Duke Ellington's recordings while serving in the army. He moved to New York City in the late forties and studied at the Conservatory of Modern Music. Tucker played with Earl Bostic and Sonny Stitt before working as the house bassist at Brooklyn's Continental Lounge in the fifties. He continued in the same capacity at Minton's Playhouse with Jerome Richardson, Horace Parlan, and Booker Ervin. Tucker also played with Junior Mance and Jaki Byard and toured with Lambert, Hendricks, and Bavan in the sixties. He recorded with Byard, Lucky Thompson, Earl Hines, Zoot Sims, Howard McGhee, Dexter Gordon, Clifford Jordan, Walt Dickerson, and others.

Tucker, Robert "Bobby" (b. 1923). A pianist, Bobby Tucker started working as a musician at age fourteen and studied at the New York Institute of

Music and Art. He played trombone during military service in the mid-forties and served as a pianist-arranger-leader for a dance band during that period. He accompanied Mildred Bailey and Billie Holiday between 1946 and 1949 and played in groups led by Stuff Smith, Babs Gonzales, and Lucky Thompson on 52nd Street. In 1949, Tucker became Billy Eckstine's music director and toured around the world with him until 1992. He also toured with Tony Bennett in the mid-nineties. Tucker is not only an excellent accompanist but also a first-rate soloist who can swing and play ballads with exquisite musical taste, as heard in recordings by Holiday, Eckstine, Gonzales, and Joe Wilder.

Turner, Joseph "Big Joe" (1911–1985). Turner, a vocalist, began his career as a singing bartender during his teens in his hometown of Kansas City, Missouri. John Hammond brought Turner and Pete Johnson to New York City to perform at Carnegie Hall in 1938, and Turner made a favorable impression on the audience. He recorded some major hits such as "Roll 'Em Pete" (with Johnson) and "Cherry Red." Throughout the forties, he made numerous recordings with Johnson and various groups that included such pianists as Art Tatum, Willie "The Lion" Smith, Joe Sullivan, Sammy Price, Albert Ammons, and Freddie Slack for several small labels. During the fifties, Turner recorded for Atlantic Records and topped the charts with such popular hits as "Chains of Love" and "Shake, Rattle, and Roll" that helped lay the foundation for rock and roll. Turner won *Esquire*'s Silver Award in 1945 for his intense and powerful style, which ranged from boogie-woogie to swing.

Turney, Norris (1921–2001). Turney, a saxophonist-clarinetist-flutist, first played professionally in A. B. Townsend's band from 1941 to 1943. Turney later played in the Jeter-Pillars Orchestra, Tiny Bradshaw's band, and Billy Eckstine's band in the mid-forties. For the next twenty years, he worked in Ohio in obscurity until touring Australia with Ray Charles in 1967. Turney joined Duke Ellington two years later and remained with him until 1973. After Ellington, Turney played in pit orchestras in New York City, worked with Panama Francis' Savoy Sultans, and performed with the Newport All-Stars. Turney recorded under his own name for the Master Jazz, Harlem, Black and Blue, and Mapleshade record labels.

Turrentine, Thomas "Tommy" (1928–1997). A trumpeter and brother of saxophonist Stanley Turrentine, Tommy began playing professionally at age seventeen with Snookum Russell's band and worked with Benny Carter, George Hudson, and Dizzy Gillespie's big band in the forties. After military service, Turrentine played with Count Basie, Earl Bostic, Charles Mingus, Lloyd Price, Max Roach, and local Pittsburgh bands from 1951 to 1960. Turrentine freelanced in New York City with such artists as Booker Ervin,

Lou Donaldson, Dexter Gordon, John Patton, Sonny Clark, and Paul Chambers until the mid-sixties. Afterward, he played off and on, mostly on New York City's Lower East Side, until the late eighties. Although he was somewhat overshadowed by his brother's stature, Tommy Turrentine was a musician's musician who brought the art of swing to bebop in recordings by Max Roach and Buddy Rich.

Ulano, Sam (b. 1920). Ulano, a drummer, played in Hawaii and Japan with an army band during World War II and returned to civilian life as a drum-shop owner in New York City from 1946 to 1970. In the meantime, he played with Bill Snyder, Tony Parrenti and Dick Wellstood, and Sol Yaged between 1956 and 1975. Ulano also taught at the New York College of Music and wrote for *International Musician* and *Big Bands* magazines. He has also led his own bands, worked with Max Kaminksy, appeared on many television shows, and published books and instructional videos for drummers. He has recorded with Sol Yaged.

Urso, Phil (b. 1925). A tenorist, Urso played saxophone before serving in the navy during World War II. After discharge in 1947, he moved to New York City and worked with Elliot Lawrence in the late forties. The next decade found Urso with Woody Herman, Terry Gibbs, Miles Davis, Oscar Pettiford, and Claude Thornhill. Afterward, Urso worked with Chet Baker off and on until the early seventies and continued to perform until the mid-nineties. His recordings with Baker, Pettiford, and Art Pepper display his immaculate tenor playing.

Valdes, Carlos "Patato" (b. 1926). Valdes, a percussionist, began playing the Cuban guitar and took up the bass before switching to the congas. He played in Cuba with Chano Pozo and others in the forties and moved to the United States in 1953, where he worked with Machito and Tito Puente in the fifties. From 1959 to 1972, Valdes played with Herbie Mann and later made a number of recordings to demonstrate Latin percussion techniques between 1974 and 1980. Valdes also freelanced and recorded with such jazz artists as Art Blakey, Cal Tjader, Quincy Jones, Max Roach, Kenny Dorham, Billy Taylor, Elvin Jones, and Dizzy Gillespie. Valdes has appeared in film and on television.

Valentine, Gerald "Jerry" (b. 1914). Valentine, a trombonist-arranger, worked with Earl Hines, Dallas Bartley, and King Kolax; wrote arrangements for shows at Chicago's Club DeLisa; and became well known as an arranger for Billy Eckstine's big band in the forties. Two of his most popular charts were "Blowin' the Blues Away" and Sarah Vaughn's recording of "I'll Wait and Pray" with Eckstine's band. Valentine worked as an A&R

man for National Records in the early fifties and later wrote charts for Coleman Hawkins, Pepper Adams, and Art Farmer.

Vaughn, Sarah (1924–1990). Like many Swing Era vocalists, Vaughn started out at a young age by winning amateur contests and moving on to a professional career. Vaughn's career began in 1943 as a member of Earl Hines' band, and she recorded a year later with Dizzy Gillespie's small group for Continental Records. Vaughn left Hines and joined John Kirby's Sextet during the winter of 1945–1946 before embarking on a solo career. She made her first hit record, "It's Magic," in 1947 and signed with Columbia Records in 1949. She toured internationally and reached into the commercial market during the fifties, which culminated in her biggest hit, "Broken-hearted Melody," in 1958. Vaughn also continued to record with major jazz artists such as Miles Davis, Clifford Brown, Cannonball Adderley, Count Basie, and Ernie Wilkins in the sixties for the Roulette, Mercury, and Columbia labels. After a break from recording, Vaughn resumed her career in 1971 with recordings and performances during the seventies and eighties. She received a Grammy Award in 1989.

Ventura, Charles "Charlie" (1916–1992). A tenorist who performed in his early years with Buddy DeFranco, Lou Stein, Bill Harris, and Teddy Waters, Ventura played in Gene Krupa's band between 1942 and 1946. Ventura led a small swing band in the late forties that played bop themes, with arrangements written for voices and wind instruments in unison. In the fifties, he led a big band, a quartet (with Marty Napoleon, Chubby Jackson, and Buddy Rich), returned to Krupa's band, and worked again with two of his former employees: Jackie Cain and Roy Kral. Ventura had a hard-swinging and robust saxophone style, and he made a notable contribution to the Later Swing Era with quality recordings of such tunes as "Euphoria" and "Sweet Georgia Brown" with his group. After the fifties, he worked off and on with Krupa and various small groups through the eighties until his health began to deteriorate.

Venus Club. A San Francisco nightclub that operated in the late forties and featured many resident bands including a group led by Kid Ory.

Village Vanguard. Established in New York City's Greenwich Village in the early thirties, the downstairs basement venue did not become known as a jazz club until the close of the Later Swing Era. Prior to that time, however, swing and Dixieland musicians such as Mary Lou Williams, Jimmy Hamilton, Sidney Bechet, Eddie Heywood, and Zutty Singleton performed at the club.

Vinnegar, Leroy (1928–1999). A bassist-composer, Vinnegar played with Shelly Manne in Los Angeles in the mid-fifties and recorded the popular

My Fair Lady album with Manne and Andre Previn. Shortly afterward, Vinnegar won the *Downbeat* New Star Award and went on to play/record with Gerald Wilson, Teddy Edwards, Art Tatum, Harold Land, Art Blakey, Carmen McRae, Helen Humes, Ben Webster, Max Roach, Earl Hines, Barney Kessel, and many others. Vinegar was considered a master jazz bassist who also freelanced as a studio musician for radio, movies, and television.

Vinson, Eddie "Cleanhead" (1917–1988). A vocalist-saxophonist, Vinson began performing professionally with Chester Boone's big band and toured with blues musicians before joining Cootie Williams' orchestra in 1942. Vinson spent three years with Williams and recorded such hits as "Somebody's Got to Go" and "Cherry Red Blues." After leaving Williams, Vinson formed his own big band and recorded some big hits such as "Kidney Stew Blues" and "Juice Head Baby." Vinson later changed over to a small group and toured regularly throughout the country while recording for the Mercury and King labels until 1954. From the mid-fifties to the mid-sixties, his career reached a low point, and he worked outside of the music profession. Noted producer Bob Thiele rejuvenated Vinson's career, however, with a Bluesway recording session in 1967. From that point on, he toured nationally and internationally, won France's Grand Prix Award, and continued to record into the eighties. Vinson was a versatile performer who excelled in jazz, rhythm-and-blues, and blues idioms. The jazz classics "Tune Up" and "Four" are connected with Miles Davis' name, but Vinson is generally considered the true composer.

Viola, Alfred "Al" (b. 1919). A self-taught guitarist, Viola first worked with the Page Cavanaugh Trio in the late forties. The fifties found him with Bobby Troup, Ray Anthony, Harry James, and Buddy Collette's quintet. He recorded with numerous vocalists including June Christy, Kay Starr, Mavis Rivers, Helen Humes, Julie London, Bobby Troup, and Frank Sinatra. Viola also recorded with instrumentalists such as Terry Gibbs, Pete Rugolo, and Shelly Manne.

Wald, Jerry (1919–1973). Wald, a clarinetist-saxophonist-leader, led a swing band in the forties that included such sidemen as Billy Bauer, Lee Konitz, and Al Cohn. From 1949 to 1951, Wald led another group and managed Hollywood's Studio Club. In 1952, he returned to New York City and led bands intermittently until the early seventies. He recorded for the Columbia, Decca, MGM, and Mercury labels.

Waldron, Malcolm "Mal" (1926–2002). A pianist-composer, Waldron started out as an altoist and switched to piano at Queens College, where he received a bachelor's degree in composition. From 1949 to 1953, he worked in New York City with Big Nick Nicholas and Ike Quebec before playing with a few rock-and-roll bands. Waldron spent the fifties with Charles Mingus, Lucky Thompson, Lucky Millinder, Billie Holiday, Abbey Lincoln, and his own quintet. He later played in the Booker Little–Eric Dolphy Quintet, wrote scores for three movies and a play, and toured Europe during the sixties. Afterward, Waldron toured Japan and performed frequently in the United States. He played at all of the major jazz festivals in Japan and Europe as well as the Newport Jazz Festival. He recorded with many major jazz artists, and his composition "Soul Eyes" has become a jazz standard.

Wally's Café. A popular Boston nightclub that opened in 1947 as Wally's Paradise and presented big bands as well as small jazz groups during the late forties and the fifties.

Ward, Helen (1916–1998). Ward, a vocalist, gained big-band singing experience in the thirties with Benny Goodman, Gene Krupa, and Bob Crosby. During the forties, she sang for Hal McIntyre and Harry James before working for a radio station as its music director. She worked with Peanuts Hucko and, occasionally, with Goodman in the fifties while in semi-retirement. She recorded with Goodman, Krupa, and Red Norvo.

Washington, Dinah [Ruth Lee Jones] (1924–1963). Washington, a vocalist, began performing professionally during her teens in Chicago nightclubs and toured with a gospel choir as a pianist for two years. After Washington returned to singing in nightclubs, Lionel Hampton hired her to sing with his band in 1943, where she remained until 1946. In the meantime, she recorded two of Leonard Feather's tunes, "Blow Top" and "Salty Papa Blues," on the Keynote label that became hits. She also recorded with Lucky Thompson, Milt Jackson, and Charles Mingus for the Apollo label in Los Angeles. Washington signed with Mercury Records in 1946 and recorded such standards as "The Man I Love" and "Embraceable You." She also recorded a variety of popular songs such as "Wheel of Fortune" and "I Don't Hurt Anymore" that made the Top 10 R&B charts prior to the mid-fifties. In 1959, Washington moved further into the pop arena by recording "What a Difference a Day Makes," which became her biggest hit and topped the pop charts. Washington's ability to fuse gospel and jazz styles made her one of the most influential vocalists in American music.

Watkins, Julius (1921–1977). A French hornist, Watkins played trumpet in the swing bands of Ernie Fields and Milt Buckner during the forties, and he studied at the Manhattan School of Music in New York City. During the fifties, he toured with Pete Rugolo's band, co-led Les Jazz Modes, and worked with Thelonious Monk, Sonny Rollins, and Oscar Pettiford, as well as George Shearing's big band. Afterward, Watkins worked in the studios and with Broadway show pit orchestras while recording with such artists as Gil Evans, Tadd Dameron, John Coltrane, Freddie Hubbard, and Curtis Fuller. Watkins was the first French hornist to evolve from the Later Swing Era and play bebop as an accomplished soloist. Although his instrument never achieved popularity in the jazz world, his skills as a section player and creative improviser were on a par with those of any other wind instrumentalist.

Wayne, Charles "Chuck" (1923–1997). Wayne, a guitarist-composer-arranger, played with local bands in New York City, served in the army for two years, and played with Bennie Harris, Joe Marsala, Dizzy Gillespie, Red Norvo, Woody Herman, Jack Teagarden, Coleman Hawkins, and Lester Young in the forties. After working with George Shearing from 1949 to 1952, Wayne played with Brew Moore, Zoot Sims, George Wallington, and Tony Bennett. He also played in Gil Evans' orchestra and worked as a staff musician for NBC in the fifties. Afterward, he worked for CBS, freelanced, played in many Broadway shows, accompanied a number of high-profile vocalists, and taught at several different colleges. He appeared in films, published three method books for guitar, and recorded with Gillespie, Herman, Hawkins, Wallington, Benny Goodman, and Wingy Manone.

Wayne, Frances (1919–1978). A vocalist, Frances Wayne started working professionally with Charlie Barnet in 1942 and gained prominence with Woody Herman in the mid-forties. Her big hit with Herman's band was "Happiness Is a Thing Called Joe." Wayne married Herman's trumpeter-arranger Neal Hefti, and they moved to the West Coast in 1946. After working as a single for a few years, she semi-retired and worked/recorded occasionally from the fifties through the seventies. She won *Esquire*'s New Star Award in 1946, recorded with Barnet and Herman, and led her own recording session for Atlantic Records in 1957.

Webster, Freddie (1917–1947). Webster, a trumpeter, formed a band with Tadd Dameron when he was only sixteen years old. He played with Erskine Tate and Earl Hines in the late thirties before working with Benny Carter at various times between 1939 and 1943. Webster played in the bands of Lucky Millinder, Jimmie Lunceford, Sabby Lewis, Cab Calloway, Dizzy Gillespie, and John Kirby in the mid-forties. Webster was well respected by both Dizzy Gillespie and Miles Davis. He recorded with Georgie Auld and Sarah Vaughn during his short life and career.

Wein, George (b. 1925). A pianist-bandleader-producer, Wein is best known for founding the Newport Jazz Festival in 1954. After several years of piano study, Wein spent the forties in military service and as a student at Boston

University. During that time he had the opportunity to play with Wild Bill Davison, Edmond Hall, and Max Kaminsky. Wein first opened the Storyville jazz club in Boston in 1950, where he played with Vic Dickenson, Jimmy McPartland, Pee Wee Russell, Bobby Hackett, and Jo Jones. Wein also started the Storyville record label and opened the Mahogany Hall Dixieland club in 1952. He recorded with the Mahogany All-Stars, including Doc Cheatham and Vic Dickenson, and with Ruby Braff in the mid-fifties. Wein also taught a course in jazz history at Boston University at that time. After the mid-fifties, he established other music festivals in the United States, toured Europe with the Newport Jazz Festival All-Stars, and served as a visiting artist at Harvard University. Wein has received numerous awards including entrance into the Rhode Island Hall of Fame, the Louisiana Governor's Award, the Hampton Institute's Centennial Medallion, the U.S. State Department Tribute of Appreciation, an honorary doctorate from Berklee College of Music, and *Downbeat*'s Lifetime Achievement Award.

Weiss, Sid (1914–1994). Weiss, a bassist, began playing professionally in the thirties with Wingy Manone, Charlie Barnet, Louis Prima, Joe Marsala, Artie Shaw, and Tommy Dorsey. He played in the bands of Benny Goodman and Hal McIntyre and worked a studio musician from 1945 to 1954. Weiss quit playing full time in 1970 and worked in the legal profession. He recorded with Dorsey, Goodman, Shaw, Marsala, Rex Stewart, Eddie Condon, Buck Clayton, and others during his twenty-year career as a professional musician.

Wellstood, Richard "Dick" (1927–1987). A pianist, Wellstood first played professionally with Bob Wilber from 1946 to 1950. Known for versatility in playing swing, boogie-woogie, and stride, Wellstood recorded with Sidney Bechet in 1947 and 1949. He worked with Jimmy Archer, Roy Eldridge, and Conrad Janis in the fifties. During the sixties, Wellstood played with many Dixieland revival bands and toured South America with Gene Krupa. In the seventies, he worked with the World's Greatest Jazz Band. He practiced law and played regularly with Kenny Davern in the eighties. Wellstood recorded with Eldridge, Wilber, Marian McPartland, Bunk Johnson, Wild Bill Davison, and Doc Cheatham.

Wess, Frank (b. 1922). A flutist-saxophonist, Wess played with local dance bands in Washington, D.C., from 1937 to 1941, and he served in the army band as a solo clarinetist and assistant bandleader overseas in the early forties. After returning to the United States, he played with Billy Eckstine, Eddie Heywood, Lucky Millinder, and Bullmoose Jackson in the late forties before studying at the Modern School of Music from 1949 to 1953. From 1953 to 1964, Wess played in Count Basie's orchestra and later freelanced in New York City as a studio musician and in Broadway shows. He also worked with numerous jazz artists and bands including Elliot Lawrence,

Bobby Rosengarden, the New York Repertory Orchestra, the New York Jazz Quartet, Benny Carter's big band, Dizzy Gillespie's Dream Band, and vocalists such as Dinah Washington, Frank Sinatra, Ella Fitzgerald, and Tony Bennett. Wess has made countless numbers of recordings as a sideman and leader, worked as a clinician at a number of colleges and universities, and appeared on radio and television.

West, Harold "Doc" (1915–1951). West, a drummer, began playing professionally with Tiny Parham in 1932 and worked with Erskine Tate, Roy Eldridge, and as a substitute for Chick Webb in Webb's band. In the forties, West played with Hot Lips Page, Count Basie, Tiny Grimes, Slam Stewart's trio, and Erroll Garner's trio. He later rejoined Eldridge and passed away while touring with him. During West's short life and career, he recorded with Eldridge, Garner, Stewart, Grimes, Charlie Parker, Don Byas, Jay McShann, Billie Holiday, Oscar Pettiford, and others.

Wetzel, Bonnie (1926–1965). A bassist, Wetzel started out on the violin and switched to the bass before joining Ada Leonard's all-female band in 1945. Wetzel played guitar in Marion Gange's trio from 1947 to 1948, and she played with Tommy Dorsey in 1951. She also worked with Roy Eldridge, Charlie Shavers, the Soft Winds Trio (with Herb Ellis and Lou Carter), and the Beryl Booker trio, and toured with the *Jazz USA* show in the mid-fifties. She recorded with Booker and Don Byas.

Wetzel, Ray (1924–1951). Ray, a trumpeter, became well-known with Woody Herman's mid-forties band, which recorded such classics as "Caldonia," "Apple Honey," and "Northwest Passage." Wetzel was featured as a lead and solo trumpeter on Stan Kenton's recordings of "Dynaflow" and "Intermission Riff" and on "Over the Rainbow" with Charlie Barnet's orchestra between 1945 and 1949. In 1950 and 1951, Wetzel played with Henry Jerome, Kenton (again), and Tommy Dorsey. Unfortunately, a fatal accident silenced Wetzel's life and brief career.

White City Ballroom. A Chicago venue that presented jazz for dancing and featured artists such as Muggsy Spanier up to the early forties. After 1942, the ballroom became an African-American establishment and showcased performances by Lionel Hampton, Nat "King" Cole, Louis Jordan, Duke Ellington, Benny Carter, the International Sweethearts of Rhythm, Count Basie, King Kolax, and others until the mid-forties.

White, Ellerton "Sonny" (1917–1971). White, a pianist, made his professional debut at age nineteen with Jesse Stone. White worked with Willie Bryant and Teddy Hill in the late thirties before accompanying Billie Holiday and working with Benny Carter in the early forties. After military service,

White worked with Hot Lips Page and Harvey Davis' band from 1944 to 1954. He later worked with Wilbur DeParis and Louis Metcalf and played with Jonah Jones' quartet from 1969 to 1971.

Wiggins, Gerald (b. 1922). Pianist-organist Wiggins worked professionally with Les Hite and Louis Armstrong in the early forties, and with Benny Carter off and on from 1942 to 1992. Wiggins toured with Lena Horne during 1950 through 1952, played for Kay Starr from 1953 to 1963, and toured with Helen Humes between 1974 and 1981. Wiggins played at numerous jazz festivals, appeared in many movies and television shows, and worked frequently with Scott Hamilton from the seventies through the nineties. Wiggins is a highly versatile pianist, and his skills as a jazz artist are also on recordings with instrumentalists such as Armstrong, Hamilton, Frank Wess, Zoot Sims, Ben Webster, Art Pepper, Joe Pass, Milt Jackson, Kenny Clarke, Mercer Ellington, and Buddy Colette.

Wilber, Robert "Bob" (b. 1928). Clarinetist-saxophonist Wilber studied privately with Paul Dahm and Sidney Bechet, and he attended the Eastman and Manhattan schools of music. Wilber organized a revival band called the Wildcats in 1947 that made its recording debut on the Commodore label, and he led bands at Boston's Savoy and Storyville nightclubs in the late forties and early fifties. After military service, he performed with Benny Goodman, Eddie Condon, Bobby Hackett, and Max Kaminsky in the fifties. Wilber led his own Jazz Repertory Orchestra and directed the Smithsonian Jazz Repertory Ensemble. He has also conducted performances for several tribute concerts in the United States and overseas, served as an artist-teacher at a number of colleges and universities, and worked as a music director for several notable films. His clarinet and saxophone work has been recorded on the Arbors, Laser, and Atlantic labels.

Wilder, Joseph "Joe" (b. 1922). A trumpeter-flugelhornist, Wilder studied at the Mastbaum School of Music in Philadelphia before playing with Les Hite and Lionel Hampton in the early forties. Wilder served in the U.S. Marines as an assistant bandmaster from 1943 to 1945 and rejoined Hampton from 1945 to 1946. In the late forties, he played with Jimmie Lunceford's orchestra and worked later with Lucky Millinder, Sam Donahue, Herbie Fields, and Noble Sissle. Wilder played in Broadway pit orchestras, toured Europe with Count Basie in the early fifties, and worked as a staff musician for ABC from 1957 to 1973. Wilder's versatility is evidenced by his work in pit bands for the television shows of Dick Cavett and Jack Parr, by his tour of the Soviet Union with Benny Goodman, and as principal trumpeter for the Symphony of the New World from 1965 to 1971. He has freelanced with Tony Bennett, Michel Legrand, Steve Allen, Lena Horne, and Terry Gibbs, as well as played in numerous studio sessions, jingles, and on movie soundtracks. Wilder also played in four concerts with the New York Philharmonic Orchestra.

Williams, Charles "Cootie" (1910–1985). A trumpeter-composer, Williams began working professionally during his teens and played with Lester Young, Chick Webb, Fletcher Henderson, Duke Ellington, and Benny Goodman before starting his own big band in 1942. Williams' band had high-quality personnel and featured vocalists Pearl Bailey and Eddie "Cleanhead" Vinson. In fact, Vinson's renditions of "Cherry Red" and "Outskirts of Town" made a big hit with audiences at New York City's Apollo Theater and Savoy Ballroom. Williams also recognized young talent and recorded Thelonious Monk's "Epistrophy" and "Round About Midnight." Williams' band had an eclectic sound, and it performed a diverse repertoire that appealed to jazz fans and dancers alike. Like many leaders of big bands in the forties, he disbanded and led a small group from 1950 until he rejoined Duke Ellington in the mid-sixties. Williams spent the next twenty years in the big bands of Duke and Mercer Ellington.

Williams, Joseph "Joe" (1918–1999). A vocalist, Williams made his professional debut with Chicago bandleader-clarinetist Jimmie Noone in 1937. Williams worked in the forties with Coleman Hawkins, Lionel Hampton, Andy Kirk's Clouds of Joy, Albert Ammons and Pete Johnson, and Red Saunders. In 1950, Williams performed with Count Basie's septet and Hot Lips Page before recording "Everyday I Have the Blues" with King Kolax in 1951. After struggling for more than a decade, Williams sang with Count Basie's orchestra in 1954 and, a year later, recorded "Everyday I Have the Blues" with Basie, which became a big hit. Williams worked with Basie until 1960 and began a solo career, with frequent appearances in nightclubs, on television, and at major jazz festivals around the world. He toured with his own trio and worked with major artists such as Cannonball Adderley and George Shearing. Williams also appeared on numerous television shows hosted by Johnny Carson, Art Linkletter, Merv Griffin, and others. Throughout a career that lasted for approximately four decades, *Downbeat* recognized Williams a number of times as the "Best Jazz Singer," and he received several awards including a Grammy.

Williams, Rudy (1919–1954). Williams, a saxophonist-clarinetist, started playing professionally with Al Cooper's Savoy Sultans from 1937 to 1943. In the mid-forties, Williams worked with Hot Lips Page, Chris Columbus, Henry Johnson, Dud Bascomb, and John Kirby and led his own group. Williams toured the Far East with USO shows and worked with Babs Gonzales, Tadd Dameron, Illinois Jacquet, and Gene Ammons in the late forties and early fifties. His style on alto resembled Don Byas' tenor work while foreshadowing Ornette Coleman. Williams freelanced and led his own bands before his accidental death. His free-styled saxophone playing is on recordings with Byas, Ammons, Dameron, Gonzales, Eddie "Lockjaw" Davis, and Johnny Hodges.

Wilson, Gerald (b. 1918). Wilson, a trumpeter-composer-arranger, began playing professionally in Detroit's Plantation Club Orchestra before touring with Jimmie Lunceford's band from 1939 to 1942. Wilson moved to Los Angeles and worked with Phil Moore, Les Hite, and Benny Carter before military service. After discharge, he organized his own big band in 1944, which made its debut at Shepp's Playhouse in Los Angeles. The band became successful after backing Joe Williams and Dinah Washington and recording for Excelsior Records in 1945. A year later, Wilson recorded charts such as "Warm Mood" and "Cruisin' with Cab" for the Black & White label. After the band had reached its peak of success in 1947, Wilson decided to disband because he wanted to study harmony and orchestration. He continued to perform and arrange for Duke Ellington, Count Basie, Dizzy Gillespie, and others. Wilson also wrote charts for vocalists Ella Fitzgerald, Al Hibbler, Sarah Vaughn, Carmen McRae, and Julie London. He organized another big band in the early sixties, wrote film scores, composed for symphony orchestras, and taught at three universities in the Los Angeles area. Wilson continues to conduct big bands and recorded recently with an all-star big band in New York City.

Wilson, Nelson "Cadillac" (1917–1973). A trumpeter-vocalist, Wilson specialized in using the "wah-wah" mute to express his Eldridge-Gillespie style of playing in addition to singing in a style influenced by Louis Armstrong. During the thirties, Wilson played and toured with territory bands before serving as music director for Birmingham's Dixie Rhythm Girls. His big break came when he joined Tiny Bradshaw in 1939 before his career was interrupted by three years of military service in an army band. After discharge, he played in Billy Eckstine's band and the John Kirby–Billy Kyle Quintet. Wilson gained prominence with Duke Ellington's orchestra from 1945 to 1951. After leaving Ellington, he worked in Europe and with Ellington intermittently between 1956 and 1970. He also recorded with Ellington.

Wilson, Rossiere "Shadow" (1919–1959). Wilson, a drummer, made his professional debut with Frankie Fairfax's band in 1938 and went on to play with Lucky Millinder, Jimmy Mundy, and Benny Carter in the late thirties. Wilson later worked in the bands of Tiny Bradshaw, Lionel Hampton, Earl Hines, Georgie Auld, Louis Jordan, Count Basie, and Illinois Jacquet in the forties. Wilson received the 1947 *Esquire* New Star Award for his accomplishments as an expert big-band and small-group drummer. He moved on to Woody Herman's orchestra in 1949, returned to Jacquet's band in 1950, and became a member of Erroll Garner's trio in 1951–1952. Wilson rejoined Jacquet in 1953–1954, played with Ella Fitzgerald in 1954–1955, and worked with Thelonious Monk at the famed Five Spot during 1957–1958. Wilson also performed with Joe Newman, Lee Konitz, and Sonny Stitt, and recorded with Stitt, Basie, Jacquet, Jordan, Stan Getz, Tadd Dameron, Gil Melle, Milt Jackson, Lester Young, J. J. Johnson, and Gerry Mulligan.

Wilson, Theodore "Teddy" (1912–1986). Wilson, a pianist-composer-arranger-bandleader, began his professional career with Speed Webb's band in Chicago from 1929 to 1931. Wilson subsequently worked with Milton Senior, Erskine Tate, and Louis Armstrong in the early thirties. Producer John Hammond discovered Wilson in 1933 and encouraged him to move to New York City, where he worked with Benny Carter and Willie Bryant until 1935. Wilson recorded with Benny Goodman and Red Norvo, and he began leading the famous small-group sessions for Billie Holiday between 1935 and 1942 for Columbia Records. During that period, Wilson played in Benny Goodman's trio/quartet, led his own big band, and formed a sextet. Wilson later rejoined Goodman, accepted a studio position with CBS radio in 1946, led his own trios, and taught at the Juilliard and Metropolitan music schools until 1952. He toured Europe during 1952 and 1953 and returned to CBS as a radio show host and leader of a trio until 1955. Wilson later toured around the world and appeared on television shows and in film. A 1945 Musicraft recording of *Teddy Wilson and His All-Stars* provides an excellent showcase of his skill as a pianist-bandleader.

Wilson, Violet "Vi" (b. 1925). Wilson, a bassist, played in the forties with the International Sweethearts of Rhythm and the Darlings of Rhythm. She later worked with pianist-organist Sarah McLawler in Chicago from 1948 to 1953. Afterward, she changed professions but sang in community and church choirs on the West Coast as an avocation.

Winding, Kai (1922–1983). As a trombonist, Winding developed his skill in the coast guard band during the early forties. In 1945, he worked briefly with Benny Goodman and became well known as a member of Stan Kenton's orchestra in the mid-forties. Winding played with Tadd Dameron in the late forties and participated in one of Miles Davis' famous Nonet recording sessions. Winding later worked with Charlie Ventura and Benny Goodman before co-leading a quintet with J. J. Johnson from 1954 to 1956. Winding performed and recorded both as a leader and a sideman during the rest of his career. His modern trombone style is featured prominently on his recording, "Always Grab Your Ax, Max," for the Savoy label.

Witherspoon, James "Jimmy" (1923–1997). Witherspoon became known as a major singer and was equally at home in both jazz and rhythm-and-blues styles. He began performing as a blues singer with pianist Teddy Weatherford's band while stationed in the Pacific as a merchant marine in the early forties. He gained national fame while touring with Jay McShann from 1944 to 1948. He made a hit recording of "Tain't Nobody's Business If I Do" on Supreme Records as a solo artist in 1947, as well as subsequent hits such as "Big Fine Girl" and "No Rollin' Blues." His career was dwarfed by rock and roll throughout part of the fifties, but he made a comeback in 1959 with an appearance at the Monterey Jazz Festival. He later recorded with Ben Webster, toured Europe with Buck Clayton's All-Stars, and performed in Japan with the Count Basie Orchestra. Witherspoon recorded with the Savoy Sultans and worked off and on until his death.

Woodman, Britt (1920–2000). Woodman, a trombonist, began performing with his brothers in a family band, worked with Phil Moore in 1938 and Les Hite from 1939 to 1942, and served in the army during the mid-forties. After discharge, he worked with Boyd Raeburn, Eddie Heywood, and Lionel Hampton before studying at Westlake College in Los Angeles in the late forties. He replaced Lawrence Brown in Duke Ellington's orchestra in 1951 and remained there until 1960. During the sixties, he worked with Charles Mingus, Johnny Richards, Quincy Jones, Chico Hamilton, Oliver Nelson, Ernie Wilkins, and Lionel Hampton, and played for a number of Broadway shows. During the seventies, he worked in California with Bill Berry, the Akiyoshi-Tabackin big band, Nelson Riddle, Benny Carter, and others. Woodman returned to New York City and worked as a studio musician in the eighties while recording with numerous first-rate jazz artists. Although Woodman was not usually featured as a soloist, he was a creative and versatile artist who could play in several different music styles.

Woods, Christopher "Chris" (1925–1985). An altoist, Woods studied clarinet, saxophone, theory, and harmony before working with Tommy Dean, George Hudson, and the Jeter-Pillars Orchestra from 1948 to 1951. He played with Ernie Fields and led his own group in the fifties. Woods later worked with Howard McGhee, Dizzy Gillespie, and Buddy Rich, toured Europe, and played at several major jazz festivals. He recorded with Wilkins, Gillespie, Clark Terry, Count Basie, and Sy Oliver.

Woodyard, Samuel "Sam" (1925–1988). Woodyard, a drummer, was self-taught and learned to play by sitting in with local groups in the Newark, New Jersey, area. He first worked with Paul Gayten's rhythm-and-blues band in 1950 and 1951 and played with Roy Eldridge in 1952. From 1953 to 1955, Woodyard played with Milt Buckner and spent eleven years (1955–1966) with Duke Ellington's orchestra. Afterward he worked periodically with such artists as Bill Berry, Claude Bolling, and Ella Fitzgerald. Woodyard spent his final years freelancing in Europe and made his last recording with Steve Lacy's sextet just before his death.

Wright, Charles "Specs" (1923–1963). A drummer, Wright was comfortable in both swing and bop styles, and he became a proficient musician in the army band in the mid-forties. After discharge, he worked with Howard McGhee in 1948 and Dizzy Gillespie from 1949 to 1951. During the fifties, Wright played in Earl Bostic's band, freelanced around Philadelphia, toured with Cannonball Adderley, played for Carmen McRae, and freelanced in New York City. Wright toured with Lambert, Hendricks, and Ross in 1960–1961, and he recorded with Red Garland, Adderley, Ray Bryant, Betty Carter, and John Coltrane.

Wright, Eugene "Gene" (b. 1923). Wright, mostly a self-taught bassist, led the Dukes of Swing in Chicago in the early forties before working with Gene Ammons and Count Basie in the late forties, and again with Ammons between 1949 and 1951. Wright played with Arnett Cobb and with Buddy DeFranco in the early fifties, and he became well known as the bassist for Dave Brubeck's famous quartet for ten years (1958–1968). He also led his own group for one year before playing in Monty Alexander's trio from 1970 to 1974. Wright later freelanced with Gene Harris, Jack Sheldon, Erroll Garner, and others on the West Coast. In addition to several reunions with Brubeck, Wright has toured with Herbie Mann and recorded with such artists as Sonny Stitt, Louis Armstrong, Cal Tjader, Buddy Collette, and Dorothy Ashby.

Wyble, Jimmy (b. 1922). A guitarist, Wyble started playing professionally with local bands in Houston and worked as a staff musician for a local radio station. After serving in the army during World War II, he worked as a studio musician on the West Coast in the forties and fifties, and he toured with Red Norvo, Benny Goodman, and Frank Sinatra in the early sixties. Wyble has appeared in films, recorded with Norvo and Goodman, taught guitar, and written several method books.

Yaged, Solomon "Sol" (b. 1922). Yaged, a clarinetist, played in two symphony orchestras before leading his own groups in New York City and playing with the Memphis Five in the forties. He later worked with Woody Herman, Dizzy Gillespie, Roy Eldridge, and Henry "Red" Allen from the mid-fifties to the early sixties. Yaged later led his own groups, performed as a featured artist in many jazz concerts, appeared in film and on television, and recorded with such artists as Coleman Hawkins, Chubby Jackson, and Jack Teagarden.

Young, Eugene "Snooky" (b. 1919). Young, a trumpeter, played with Eddie Heywood, Sr., Graham Jackson, The Wilberforce Collegians, and

Clarence "Chic" Carter while a teenager. Young played in Jimmie Lunceford's orchestra from 1939 to 1942 and worked briefly in the bands of Count Basie, Lionel Hampton, Les Hite, Benny Carter, and Gerald Wilson before rejoining Basie in the late forties. He led his own band in Dayton, Ohio, for a decade prior to rejoining Basie from 1957 to 1962. Young later became a full-time studio musician, played in the *Tonight Show* band, and worked in the big bands of Benny Goodman, Thad Jones and Mel Lewis, and again with Gerald Wilson. Young had an incredible range and could play exciting lead trumpet as well as impressive solos. He also had one of the longest and most successful careers in music.

Zanzibar. An important nightclub in New York City that featured some of the top African-American big bands in the mid-forties. Duke Ellington, Sabby Lewis, Don Redman, and Claude Hopkins led their bands in performances at the venue.

Zentner, Simon "Si" (1917–2000). A trombonist-bandleader, Zentner started playing professionally in the early forties with the bands of Les Brown, Harry James, and Jimmy Dorsey. He moved to the West Coast and worked with different bands and studio groups from 1944 to 1957. He later led his own band, which recorded a hit, "Lazy River," before he toured with other bands and worked in Las Vegas with vocalists such as Nancy Wilson and Johnny Mathis. Zentner recorded with Louis Armstrong and Jack Teagarden.

♪

Appendix: Selected Discography

Ray Anthony and His Orchestra: Young Man with a Horn, 1952–1954, Hindsight Records HCD-412 (CD).

Count Basie in Disco Order, vol. 14, Ajaz Records AJAZ-248 (LP).

The Essential Count Basie, Verve V6-8407 (LP).

Tex Beneke Directs the Glenn Miller Orchestra: On the Beam, Submarine DAWE 107 (CD).

The Great Composer: Tiny Bradshaw, Official Record Company SING-653 (LP).

Les Brown and His Orchestra 1949, vol. 2, Hindsight Records HCD-131 (CD).

George Brunis and His Jazz Band, LP, Commodore Jazz Classics CCL 7011 (LP).

Cab Calloway: Hi De Ho Man, Columbia Records CG-32593 (LP).

Big Band Bounce: Benny Carter & Cootie Williams, vol. 2, Capitol Jazz Classics M-11057 (LP).

Wild Bill Davison & His Commodores, Commodore Jazz Classics CCL 7011 (LP).

Wilber DeParis, Collectables Jazz Classics COL-CD-6816 (CD).

Billy Eckstine: Mr. B. and the Band—The Savoy Sessions, Savoy SJL 2214 (LP).

Ella: Ella & Friends, Decca Records GRD-663 (CD).

Les Elgart and His Orchestra: The Elgart Touch, Columbia Records CL 875 (LP).

Big Bands: Duke Ellington, Time-Life Music STBB 05 (LP).

Dizzy Gillespie & His Orchestra 1946/1948, Jazz Archives 150, EPM-159552 (CD).

Dizzy Gillespie Big Band: Things to Come, Laserlight Digital 17-107 (CD).

Woody Herman: Blowin' Up a Storm, Affinity AFS-1043 (LP).

Woody Herman: Early Autumn, Bluebird 61062-2 (CD).

Billie Holiday, 1944, Classics Records 806 (CD).

Jazz at the Philharmonic: The Ella Fitzgerald Set, Verve 815-147-1 (LP).

Jazz at the Philharmonic: Oscar Peterson—The Trio Set, Verve 825-099-1 (LP).

Jazz Women: A Feminist Retrospective, Stash ST-109 (LP).

Bunk Johnson and His Superior Jazz Band, Good Time Jazz M-12048 (LP).

Jonah Jones at the Embers, RCA Victor LPM-2004 (LP).

Louis Jordan's Greatest Hits, MCA Records MCA-274 (LP).

Stan Kenton and His Orchestra 1944–1945, vol. 4, Hindsight Records HSR-147 (LP).

Stan Kenton: Innovations in Modern Music, Creative World Records ST 1009 (LP).

Elliot Lawrence Plays Gerry Mulligan Arrangements, Fantasy F-3-206 (LP).

The Complete Peggy Lee & June Christy Capitol Transcription Sessions, Mosaic Records MD5-184 (CD).

George Lewis on Parade, Delmark 202 (LP).

Ray McKinley: One Band—Two Styles, RCA Camden CAL-295 (LP).

The Finest of Carmen McRae, Bethlehem Records BCP-6004 (LP).

Lucky Millinder and His Orchestra: Apollo Jump, Affinity AFS 1004 (LP).

Modern Jazz Quartet: Concorde, Prestige OJCCD-002-2 (CD).

Joe Mooney, Koch Jazz KOC-CD-7886 (CD).

Turk Murphy at the New Orleans Jazz Festival, Columbia Records CL 793 (LP).

The Complete Anita O'Day Verve/Clef Sessions, Mosaic Records MD9-188 (CD).

Edward "Kid" Ory and His Creole Band at the Dixieland Jubilee, GNP Crescendo DJ 519 (LP).

Boyd Raeburn and His Orchestra: Jubilee Performances 1946, HEP Records HEPCD 1 (CD).

Buddy Rich and His Legendary 1947–1948 Orchestra, HEP Records HEPCD 12 (CD).

Bob Scobey's Frisco Band: Direct from San Francisco, Good Time Jazz L-12023 (LP).

Sentimental Journey: Great Ladies of Song, Capitol Records CDP 7980142 (CD).

George Shearing: George Meets the Lion, Jasmine Records JASCD 363 (CD).

George Shearing: So Rare, Savoy SJL 1117 (LP).

Frank Sinatra: Sinatra Swings, Columbia 40228 (LP).

Muggsy Spanier and His Ragtimers: Nick's New York, April, 1944, Commodore XFL 15777 (LP).

Billy Strayhorn: Lush Life, Red Baron AK 52760 (CD).

Art Tatum: Masterpieces, MCA Records MCA2-4019 (LP).

Claude Thornhill and His Orchestra 1947, Hindsight Records HSR-108 (LP).

V Disc: Stomp, International Association of Record Collectors IAJRC 51 (LP).

Charlie Ventura: Euphoria, Savoy 2243 (LP).

The Complete Dinah Washington, Vol. 2 1946–1947, Official 3005 (LP).

Joe Williams: A Man Ain't Supposed to Cry, Emus Record Corporation ES 12002 (LP).

Gerald Wilson and His Orchestra 1945–1946, Classics Records 976 (CD).

Teddy Wilson and His All-Stars, Musicraft Records MVS 502 (LP).

♪

Selected Bibliography

BOOKS

Carr, Ian, et al., eds. *Jazz: The Rough Guide*. London: Penguin Books, 1995.

Chilton, John. *Who's Who of Jazz: Storyville to Swing Street*. Philadelphia: Chilton Book Co., 1978.

Collier, James L. *The Making of Jazz: A Comprehensive History*. New York: Dell Publishing Co., 1978.

Cook, Richard, and Brian Morton. *The Penguin Guide to Jazz on CD*. 3rd ed. New York: Penguin Books, 1996.

Dahl, Linda. *Stormy Weather: The Music and Lives of a Century of Jazzwomen*. New York: Limelight, 1989.

Dance, Stanley. *The World of Swing: An Oral History of Big Band Jazz*. New York: Da Capo Press, 1974.

Dexter, Dave. *The Jazz Story*. Englewood Cliffs, NJ: Prentice-Hall, Inc., 1964.

Driggs, Frank. *Women in Jazz: A Survey*. Brooklyn, NY: Stash Records, 1977.

Erenberg, Lewis A. *Swingin' the Dream: Big Band Jazz and the Rebirth of American Culture*. Chicago: The University of Chicago Press, 1998.

Feather, Leonard. *The Encyclopedia of Jazz*. New York: Bonanza Books, 1960.

Feather, Leonard, and Ira Gitler. *The Biographical Encyclopedia of Jazz*. New York: Oxford University Press, 1999.

Ferrett, Gene. *Swing Out: Great Negro Dance Bands*. New York: Da Capo Press, 1970.

Giddins, Gary. *Visions of Jazz: The First Century*. New York: Oxford University Press, 1998.

Handy, D. Antoinette. *Black Women in American Bands and Orchestras*. 2nd ed. Metuchen, NJ: Scarecrow Press, 1998.

———. *The International Sweethearts of Rhythm*. Metuchen, NJ: Scarecrow Press, 1983.

Hazell, Ed. *Berklee: The First Fifty Years*. Boston: Berklee Press, 1995.

Hitchcock, H. Wiley, and Stanley Sadie, eds. *The New Grove Dictionary of American Music*. Vol. 3. New York: MacMillan Press, 1986.

Jackson, Arthur. *The World of Big Bands*. New York: Arco Publishing Co., 1977.

Kernfeld, Barry, ed. *The New Grove Dictionary of Jazz*. 2 vols. New York: MacMillan Press, 1988.

———. *The New Grove Dictionary of Jazz*. 3 vols. New York: Macmillan Press, 2002.

Knopper, Steve, ed. *Music Hound Swing: The Essential Guide*. Farmington Hills, MI: Visible Ink Press, 1999.

Leder, Jan. *Women in Jazz: A Discography of Instrumentalists, 1913–1968*. Westport, CT: Greenwood Press, 1985.

McCarthy, Albert. *Big Band Jazz*. New York: Exeter Books, 1983.

McClellan, Lawrence Jr. "Edward 'Kid' Ory." In *Dictionary of American Biography: Supplement Nine, 1971–1975*, edited by Kenneth T. Jackson. New York: Charles Scribner's Sons, 1994.

McPartland, Marian. *All in Good Time*. New York: Oxford University Press, 1987.

Meadows, Eddie S. *Jazz Research and Performance Materials*. New York: Garland Publishing, Inc. 1995.

Oliphant, Dave. *The Early Swing Era, 1930–1941*. Westport, CT: Greenwood Press, 2002.

Pener, Degen. *The Swing Book*. Boston: Back Bay Books, 1999.

Placksin, Sally. *American Women in Jazz, 1900 to the Present: Their Words, Lives, and Music*. New York: Seaview Books, 1982.

Scanlan, Tom. *The Joy of Jazz: Swing Era, 1935–1947*. Golden, CO: Fulcrum Publishing, 1996.

Schuller, Gunther. *The Swing Era: The Development of Jazz, 1930–1945*. New York: Oxford University Press, 1989.

Shipton, Alyn. *A New History of Jazz*. London: Continuum, 2001.

Simon, George T. *The Big Bands*. New York: Schirmer Books, 1981.

Tucker, Sherrie. *Swing Shift: "All-Girl" Bands of the 1940s*. Durham, NC: Duke University Press, 2000.

Walker, Leo. *The Big Band Almanac*. New York: Da Capo Press, 1989.

———. *The Wonderful Era of the Great Dance Bands*. New York: Doubleday and Co., 1972.

Yanow, Scott. *Swing: The Essential Listening Companion*. San Francisco, CA: Miller-Freeman Books, 2000.

ARTICLES

Anthony, Ray. "The Anthony Statement." *Metronome* 68 (3) (1952): 11, 21.

Associated Press. Sarah Vaughn Obituary. *The Times-Picayune*, April 5, 1990.

Balliett, Whitney. "Jazz Records: Miss Holiday." *New Yorker*, March 26, 1960, 1–2.

Birnbaum, Larry. "Review of Dinah Washington—*A Slick Chick (On the Mellow Side): The Rhythm and Blues Years* (Emarcy 814 1841)." *Downbeat* 51 (5) (1984): 31.

———. "Eddie Cleanhead Vinson." *Downbeat* 49 (10) (1982): 28–30.

Brodacki, Krystian. "Carmen McRae." *Jazz Forum* 123 (February 1990): 16–19.

Coates, Claudia. Billy Eckstine Obituary. *The Times-Picayune*, March 9, 1993: A-2.

Coburn, Marcia Froelke. "Sweethearts of Swing: The Rise and Fall of an All-Girl Band." Institute of Jazz Studies–Rutgers University File Folder: 8–9+.

Coss, Bill. "Elliot Lawrence: In Person." *Metronome* 68 (8) (1952): 19.

———. "Ray Anthony." *Metronome* 68 (3) (1952): 11, 21.

Crowther, Bruce. "Carmen McRae." *Jazz Journal International* 48 (4) (1995): 19.

Dance, Helen. "The Immutable Cootie Williams." *Downbeat* 34 (9) (1967): 20–22.

Dance, Stanley. "An Interview with Billy Strayhorn." *Downbeat* 34 (4) (1967): 18–19.

Early, Gerald. "Passion Flower." *The New Republic*, September 30, 1996: 42–45.

Elie, Lolis Eric. "The Defining of Miss Ella." *The Times-Picayune*, June 24, 1996: B-1.

Feather, Leonard. "Dizzy Is Crazy Like A Fox." *Metronome* (July 1944): 16, 31.

———. "Dizzy—21st Century Gabriel." *Esquire* (October 1945): 91.

———. "Ella Today (And Yesterday Too)." *Downbeat* 32 (24) (1965): 20–23.

———. "Europe Goes Dizzy." *Metronome* 64 (5) (1948): 18–19.

———. "Fate Finally Smiles on Bandleader." *The Times-Picayune,* November 14, 1980: 11.

———. "Feather's Nest." *Downbeat* 34 (15) (1967): 12.

———. "Louis Jordan: The Good Times Still Roll." *Downbeat* 3 (2) (1969): 16–17.

Fonder, Mark. "Les Is More: A Sentimental Journey with Les Brown." *The Instrumentalist* 45 (2) (1990): 36–43.

Foster, Lorne. "They Call Him Mister Cleanhead." *CODA Magazine* 218 (1988): 7.

Friedwald, Will "Silent Partner." *New York Times*, July 14, 1996: 8.

"Band of the Year: Dizzy Gillespie." *Metronome* 64 (1) (1948): 17–18.

Garcia, Antonio, ed. "1997 NEA Jazz Masters." *Jazz Educators Journal* 29 (January 1997): 19.

Gardner, Barbara. "Is Joe Williams Really Joe Williams?" *Downbeat* 30 (32) (1964): 19–21.

———. "Sarah." *Downbeat* 28 (5) (1961): 18–21.

Gottlieb, Bill. "Review of Buddy Rich's performance at the Arcadia Ballroom." *Downbeat* 14 (11) (1947): 14.

Hill, Don. "George Lewis: New Orleans Jazzman." *Cadence* 13 (1) (1987): 17–20.

Hodgkins, Barbara. "Starr Bright." *Metronome* 65 (8) (1949): 13, 31.

———. "That's Rich!" *Metronome* 62 (10) (1946): 19, 42.

Hoefer, George. "The First Big Bop Band." *Downbeat* 32 (16) (1965): 23–26.

Jones, James T. "Cut The Crap." *Downbeat* 58 (6) (1991): 24–25.

Jurkowska, Maria. "The Divine Sarah." *Jazz Forum* 123 (1990): 14–15.

Korall, Burt. "Ray McKinley: Swing Pioneer." *Modern Drummer* 10 (4) (1986): 30–33.

Long, Doug. "George Shearing: An Interview." *CODA Magazine* 189 (1983): 4–6.

Matthews, Bunny. "Music Brings Her 'High Times' Today." *The Times-Picayune*, June 25, 1982: 6–7.

McDonough, John. "Teddy Wilson: History in the Flesh." *Downbeat* 4 (4) (1977): 17–18.

———. "What Becomes a Legend Most: Ella Fitzgerald." *Downbeat* 60 (6) (1993): 22–25.

McNamara, Helen. "The Odyssey of Jimmy Rushing." *Downbeat* 32 (8) (1965): 22–24.

Otto, A. S., ed. "Riding on A Meteor: Gerald Wilson." *Clef* 1 (2) (1946): 12–14.

Palmer, Richard. "Larry Elgart: Interview." *Cadence* 11 (9) (1985): 8–10.

———. "Les Elgart." *Cadence* 12 (11) (1986): 17–18.

Scott, Allen. "Rediscovering Boyd Raeburn." *Radio Free Jazz* (July 1979): 13–14.

Simon, George. "A Style Is Born." *Metronome* 64 (10) (1948): 17.

———. "Latest Prescription: More Dancing, Les Elgart." *Metronome* 70 (10) (1954): 14.

———. "Review of Hal MacIntyre's performance at the Glen Island Casino." *Metronome* 58 (3) (1942): 12, 22.

———. "Carmen McRae." *Metronome* 70 (12) (1954): 17, 36.

———. "June's in Tune!" *Metronome* 65 (7) (1949): 11, 20.

Simon, George, and Barry Ulanov, eds. "The Band that Came Back!" *Metronome* 68 (9) (1952): 16.

Southern, Eileen. "Conversation with William Clarence 'Billy' Eckstine." *The Black Perspective in Music* 7 (2) (1979): 182–198.

Stacy, Frank. "Herman's Is Finest Ofay Swing Band." *Downbeat* 12 (5) (1945): 9.

Stewart, Zan. "Orchestral Man: Gerald Wilson Excites with His Complex Sounds." *Downbeat* 69 (2) (2002): 40–43.

Surpin, Alan. "Dawn of a New O'Day." *Downbeat* 36 (23) (1969): 16, 38.

Swenson, John. R&B/Jazz. *Saturday Review* (January/February 1986): 94.

"Tatum Time." *Bandleader* 10 (May 1944): 34.

Tiegel, Eliot. "Riffs: Peggy Lee." *Downbeat* 57 (6) (1990): 13.

Tracy, Frank, ed. "The Elgart Brothers and How They Grew." *Downbeat* 21 (20) (1954): 2, 7.

———. "Swee'pea." *Downbeat* 23 (11) (1956): 15.

Tracy, Jack. "Is 'Kenton Era' End for Stan?" *Downbeat* 22 (5) (1955): 6–7.

Tynan, John. "Peggy Lee." *Downbeat* 24 (6) (1957): 13.

———. "That Misty Miss Christy." *Downbeat* 23 (22) (1956): 13.

Ulanov, Barry. "Dizzy Atomosphere." *Metronome* 64 (8) (1948): 13, 18.

———. "He's In and He's Out!" *Metronome* 65 (1) (1949): 15–16.

———. "Not Just a Singer's Singer—But Everbody's!," *Metronome* 64 (4) (1948): 19, 30.

———. "The Early Boyd." *Metronome* (September 1945): 17, 37.

———. "The Function of the Critic in Jazz." *Metronome* 65 (8) (1949): 16–17.

———. "What's Wrong with Stan Kenton?" *Metronome* 64 (2) (1948): 17.

———. "Review of Cootie Williams' performance at the Apollo Theatre on May 21, 1942." *Metronome* 58 (6) (1942): 20.

———. "Review of Cootie Williams' performance at the Savoy Ballroom." *Metronome* 58 (10) (1942): 11, 24.

Weaver, Gretchen. "Good Music...That's All!" *Bandleaders* 2 (2) (1944): 40–41.

Williams, Martin. "Billie Holiday: Triumphant Decline." *Saturday Review,* October 31, 1964: 68, 83.

Wilson, John S. "Billy Strayhorn: Alter Ego for the Duke." *New York Times,* June 6, 1965: 13X.

Winter, Margaret E. "Hi De Ho!" *Bandleaders* (8) (January 1944): 6, 46.

Wong, Hannah. "LC Collection Tells Ella Fitzgerald Story." *LC Information Bulletin* 56 (13) (1997): 276–278.

Woolley, Stan. "Elliot Lawrence—Forgotten Big Band Leader." *Jazz Journal International* 50 (5) (1997): 8–10.

———. "The Forgotten Ones: Boyd Raeburn." *Jazz Journal International* 37 (2) (1984): 18–19.

———. "The Misty Miss Christy." *Jazz Journal International* 40 (October 1987): 18–19.

Zych, David. "Joe Williams: Celebrating Every Day." *Jazz Times* (March 1994): 43–45.

ELECTRONIC SOURCES

Richard S. Ginell, "Frank Sinatra Biography." *All-Music Guide* (2000), http://www.sonicnet.com/artists.

Index

Note: Page numbers in **bold** type indicate main entries.

About the Author

LAWRENCE McCLELLAN, JR., is Dean of the Professional Education Division at Berklee College of Music in Boston, Massachusetts. Prior to joining the administration at Berklee, he was a public-school band director in Georgia and Tennessee and Director of Music Education at the University of the Virgin Islands. Lawrence has served as an adjudicator/clinician/presenter at numerous conferences, music festivals, and academic institutions, including MusicFest USA; MusicFest Canada; The International Association for Jazz Education; The Music Educators National Conference; The International Society for Music Education in Pretoria, South Africa; the European Music Educators Conference in Oberursel, Germany; University of Colorado at Boulder; Governors State University; The University of Missouri–Kansas City, University of the Virgin Islands; Jackson State University; American School of Modern Music in Paris, France; and Fundacio L'Aula de Musica in Barcelona, Spain. As an author, he has written for *Downbeat*, the *Jazz Education Journal*, and *The American Dictionary of Biography*. Lawrence has performed as a trombonist with major artists such as Patti Labelle, Terence Blanchard, Aretha Franklin, Donald Brown, Nancy Wilson, Bill Pierce, Glen Campbell, Kenny Burrell, Marvin Stamm, James Spaulding, Don Braden, Cecil Brooks III, and others. He has recorded with Larry Ridley's Jazz Legacy Ensemble, Jimmy McCracklin, and Walter Beasley. Lawrence's CD, *Movin' Up,* was released by IGMOD Records in 1998. He currently serves as a resource team member for The International Association for Jazz Education. He holds a bachelor's degree from Knoxville College, a master's degree from the University of Tennessee, and a doctorate from Michigan State University.